Ordnance Survey

CW00321617

STREET
Warwickshire

Contents

III	Key to map symbols
IV-V	Key to map pages
VI-VII	Route planning
VIII	Administrative and post code boundaries
1	Street maps
151	Extra-large-scale map of Coventry town centre
152	Town maps of Banbury and Tamworth
153	Index of hospitals, industrial estates, railway stations, schools, shopping centres, street names and universities

PHILIP'S

First edition published 1992
First colour edition published 1998 by

Ordnance Survey® and George Philip Ltd
Romsey Road   a division of Octopus Publishing Group Ltd
Maybush   Michelin House, 81 Fulham Road,
Southampton   London SW3 6RB
SO16 4GU

ISBN 0-540-07562-0 (pocket)

Digital Data

The exceptionally high-quality mapping
found in this book is available as digital
data in TIFF format, which is easily
convertible to other bit-mapped (raster)
image formats.

The index is also available in digital
form as a standard database table.
It contains all the details found in the
printed index together with the National
Grid reference for the map square in
which each entry is named and feature
codes for places of interest in eight
categories such as education and
health.

For further information and to discuss
your requirements, please contact the
Ordnance Survey Solutions Centre on
01703 792929.

Key to map symbols

III

	Motorway (with junction number)	Walsall	British Rail station
	Primary route (dual carriageway and single)		Midland Metro
	A road (dual carriageway and single)	(M)	Metrolink station
	B road (dual carriageway and single)		Underground station
	Minor road (dual carriageway and single)	D	Docklands Light Railway station
	Other minor road	M	Tyne and Wear Metro
	Road under construction		Private railway station
	Pedestrianised area		Bus, coach station
DY7	Post code boundaries		Ambulance station
	County and Unitary Authority boundaries		Coastguard station
	Railway		Fire station
	Tramway, miniature railway		Police station
	Rural track, private road or narrow road in urban area	+	Accident and Emergency entrance to hospital
	Gate or obstruction to traffic (restrictions may not apply at all times or to all vehicles)	H	Hospital
	Path, bridleway, byway open to all traffic, road used as a public path	+	Church, place of worship
	The representation in this atlas of a road, track or path is no evidence of the existence of a right of way	i	Information centre (open all year)
105	Adjoining page indicators (The colour of the arrow indicates the scale of the adjoining page – see scales below)	P P&R	Parking, Park and Ride
85		PO PO	Post Office
143 152	The map areas within the pink/blue bands are shown at a larger scale on the page, indicated by the red/blue blocks and arrows	Prim Sch	Important buildings, schools, colleges, universities and hospitals
		River Medway	Water name
			Stream
			River or canal (minor and major)
			Water
			Tidal water
			Woods
			Houses
		House	Non-Roman antiquity
		VILLA	Roman antiquity

Acad	Academy	Ct	Law Court
Crem	Crematorium	L Ctr	Leisure Centre
Cemy	Cemetery	LC	Level Crossing
C Ctr	Civic Centre	Liby	Library
CH	Club House	Mkt	Market
Coll	College	Meml	Memorial
Ent	Enterprise	Mon	Monument
Ex H	Exhibition Hall	Mus	Museum
Ind Est	Industrial Estate	Obsy	Observatory
Inst	Institute	Pal	Royal Palace

PH	Public House
Recn Gd	Recreation Ground
Resr	Reservoir
Ret Pk	Retail Park
Sch	School
Sh Ctr	Shopping Centre
TH	Town Hall/House
Trad Est	Trading Estate
Univ	University
YH	Youth Hostel

The dark grey border on the inside edge of some pages indicates that the mapping does not continue onto the adjacent page

The small numbers around the edges of the maps identify the 1 kilometre National Grid lines

The scale of the maps is 3.92 cm to 1 km (2¹/₂ inches to 1 mile)	0 ¹/₄ ¹/₂ ³/₄ 1 mile 0 250m 500m 750m 1 kilometre
The scale of the maps on pages numbered in red is 7.84 cm to 1 km (5 inches to 1 mile)	0 220 yards 440 yards 660 yards ¹/₂ mile 0 125m 250m 375m ¹/₂ kilometre
The scale of the maps on pages numbered in green is 1.96 cm to 1 km (1¹/₄ inches to 1 mile)	0 ¹/₄ ¹/₂ ³/₄ 1 mile 0 250m 500m 750m 1 kilometre

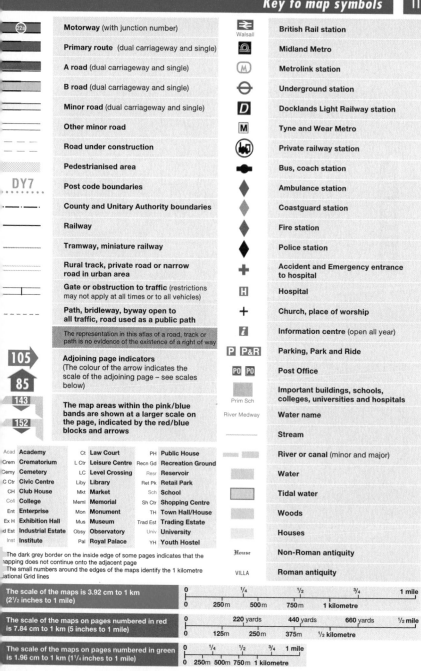

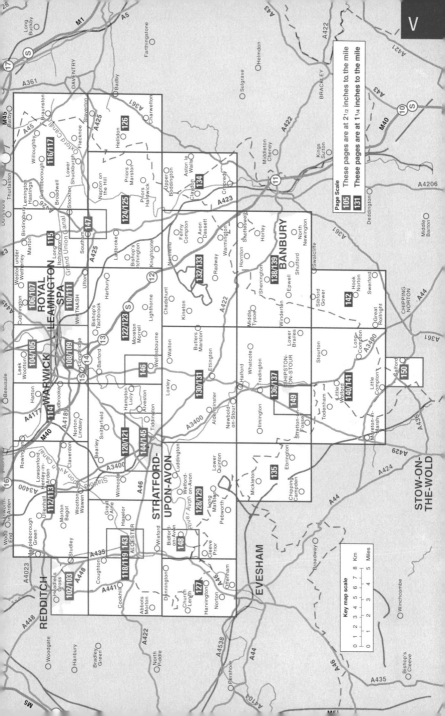

V

Page Scale

105   These pages are at 2½ inches to the mile

131   These pages are at 1¼ inches to the mile

Key map scale

Km   0 1 2 3 4 5 6 7 8

Miles   0 1 2 3 4 5

Route planning

Route map scale

| Km | 0 | 1 | 2 | 3 | 4 | 5 | 6 | 7 | 8 |
| Miles | 0 | 1 | 2 | 3 | 4 | 5 |

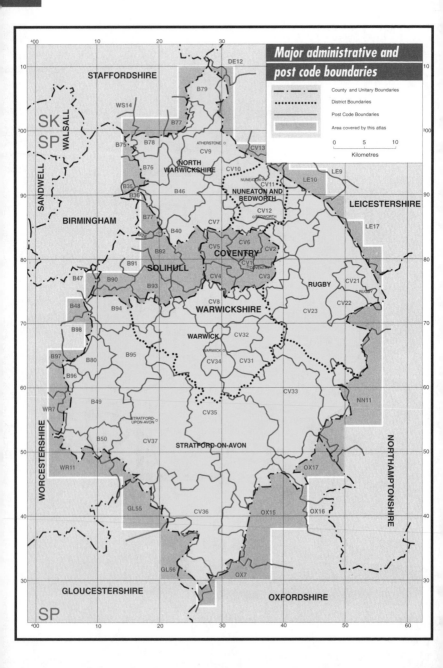

Major administrative and post code boundaries

County and Unitary Boundaries
District Boundaries
Post Code Boundaries
Area covered by this atlas

0   5   10
Kilometres

STAFFORDSHIRE

DE12

B79

WS14

SK

SP

WALSALL

B77

SANDWELL

B75   B78

B76

ATHERSTONE   CV13

CV9

NORTH
WARWICKSHIRE

CV10

LE9

LE10

NUNEATON

CV11

NUNEATON AND
BEDWORTH

LEICESTERSHIRE

B35

B36

B46

CV12

BEDWORTH

LE17

BIRMINGHAM

B77

B40

CV7

B92

CV5   CV6   CV2

COVENTRY

B91

SOLIHULL

CV1

COVENTRY

B47   B90

CV4   CV3

B93

RUGBY

CV21

RU36

B48   B94

CV8

CV23

CV22

B98

WARWICKSHIRE

WARWICK   CV32

B97   B80

B95

WARWICK

B96

CV34   CV31

B49

CV33

NN11

WR7

CV35

NORTHAMPTONSHIRE

WORCESTERSHIRE

B50

STRATFORD-
UPON-AVON

CV37

STRATFORD-ON-AVON

WR11

OX17

GL55

CV36

OX15   OX16

GL56   OX7

GLOUCESTERSHIRE

OXFORDSHIRE

SP

A
B
C

4

09

3

08

2

07

1

06

Clifton
Campville

Far Barn

Thorpe
Constantine

Home
Farm

Thorpe
Hall

The
Dale

Highfields

Brinstone
Barn

Palmer's
Spinney

Gorse
Farm

Clifton
Rough

B79

Old Gorse

Podmore
Cottages

Lonkhill
Farm

B5493

Statfold
Farm

The
Larches

Darlaston
Spinney

Thorpegorse
Cottages

GORSE LA

Statfold
Hall

Statfold
Cottages

The
Poplars

Hayter's
Spinney

Shuttington
House

Copnill
Farm

ELMS RD

Poplars
Cottages

Statfold
Barn
Farm

B5493

1

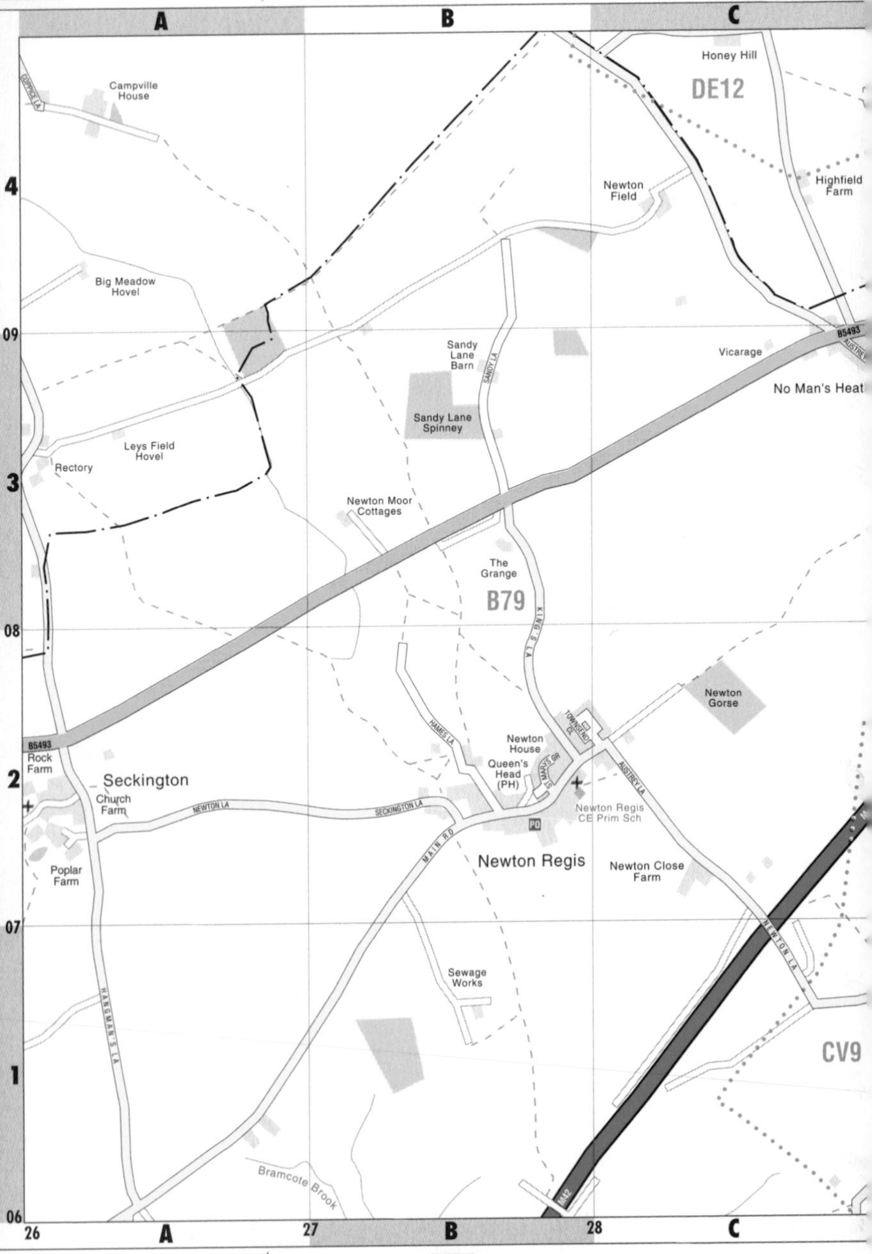

A
B
C
4
09
3
08
2
07
1
06
26
27
28
Campville House
COPPICE LA
Honey Hill
DE12
Highfield Farm
Newton Field
Big Meadow Hovel
Sandy Lane Barn
SANDY LA
B5493
AUSTREY
Vicarage
No Man's Heat
Sandy Lane Spinney
Leys Field Hovel
Rectory
Newton Moor Cottages
The Grange
B79
KING'S LA
Newton Gorse
TOWNSEND CL
HAMES LA
Newton House
Queen's Head (PH)
ST MARYS GR
AUSTREY LA
Rock Farm
Seckington
Church Farm
NEWTON LA
SECKINGTON LA
Newton Regis CE Prim Sch
PO
MAIN RD
Newton Regis
Newton Close Farm
Poplar Farm
NEWTON LA
Sewage Works
HANGMAN'S LA
CV9
Bramcote Brook
M42

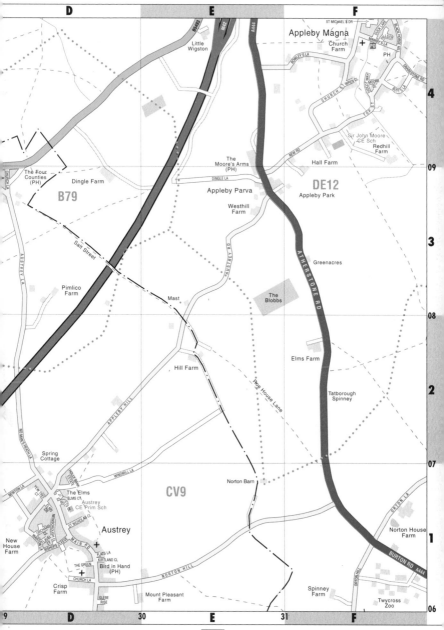

St Michael's Dr

Appleby Magna

Church Farm

PH

4

Little Wigston

B589

M42

A444

BURLEY'S LA

CHURCH ST, WIGM's

FOX

MOORE'S LA

BLACK HORSE RD

SHERSTONE RD

The Four Counties (PH)

Dingle Farm

B79

The Moore's Arms (PH)

DINGLE LA

Appleby Parva

Westhill Farm

Hall Farm

NEW RD

Sir John Moore CE Sch

Redhill Farm

DE12

Appleby Park

09

Salt Street

Pimlico Farm

Mast

AUSTREY RD

Greenacres

ATHERSTONE RD

The Blobbs

3

08

Hill Farm

Page House Lane

Elms Farm

Tatborough Spinney

2

Spring Cottage

APPLEBY HILL

WINDMILL LA

Norton Barn

07

NO MAN'S HEATH LA

The Elms

ELMS CT

Austrey CE Prim Sch

ST NICHOLAS DR

NEWTON LA

CV9

Norton House Farm

ORTON LA

New House Farm

Austrey

MAIN RD

Bird in Hand (PH)

FLATS LA

KIRTLAND CL

THE GREEN

CHURCH LA

Crisp Farm

GLEBE RISE

NORTON HILL

Mount Pleasant Farm

Spinney Farm

ORTON HILL

BURTON RD

A444

Twycross Zoo

1

06

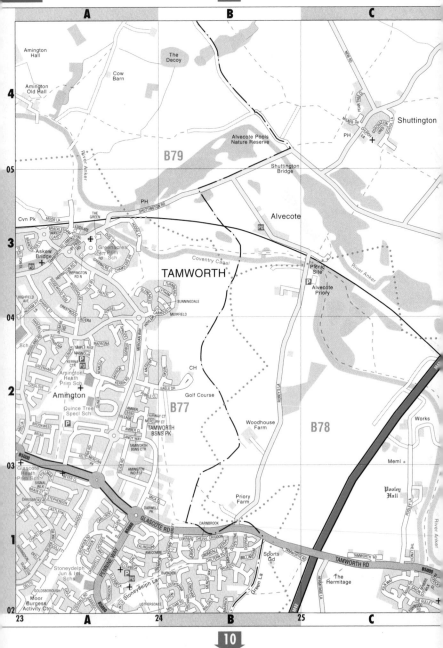

4

Amington
Hall

The
Decoy

Cow
Barn

Amington
Old Hall

Shuttington

4

PH

Alvecote Pools
Nature Reserve

B79

Shuttington
Bridge

05

Alvecote

PH

THE
GREEN

Cvn Pk

MOOR LA

BRACKLESHAM

Greenacres Prim
Sch

Askew
Bridge

Coventry Canal

Picnic
Site

River Anker

3

TAMWORTH

Alvecote
Priory

HIGHFIELD
AVE

Arpington
Heath Prim Sch

04

SUNNINGDALE

MUIRFIELD

CH

2

Golf Course

Amington

Quince Tree
Specl Sch

B77

Woodhouse
Farm

B78

Works

TAMWORTH
BSNS PK

TAMWORTH
BSNS CTR

Meml

Pooley
Hall

03

Glascote
Heath
Prim Sch

Priory
Farm

DARWELL
PK

1

GLASCOTE RD

DARNBROOK

Sports
Gd

TAMWORTH RD

The
Hermitage

Stoneydelph
Jun & Inf
Schs

Stoneydelph La

Green La

Moor
Burgess
Activity Ctr

02

23 A **24** B **25** C

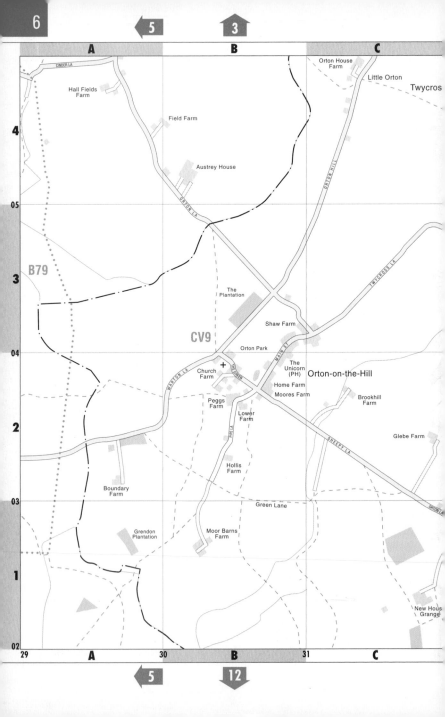

CINDER LA

Hall Fields
Farm

Field Farm

Austrey House

ORTON LA

Orton House
Farm

Little Orton

Twycros

ORTON HILL

4

05

B79

3

The
Plantation

Shaw Farm

ENTCROSS LA

CV9

Orton Park

04

Church
Farm

MAIN ST

The
Unicorn
(PH)

Orton-on-the-Hill

WARTON LA

THE GREEN

Home Farm

Moores Farm

Brookhill
Farm

Peggs
Farm

Lower
Farm

2

Hollis
Farm

SHEEPY LA

Glebe Farm

Boundary
Farm

03

Green Lane

ORTON LA

Grendon
Plantation

Moor Barns
Farm

1

New Hous
Grange

02

7

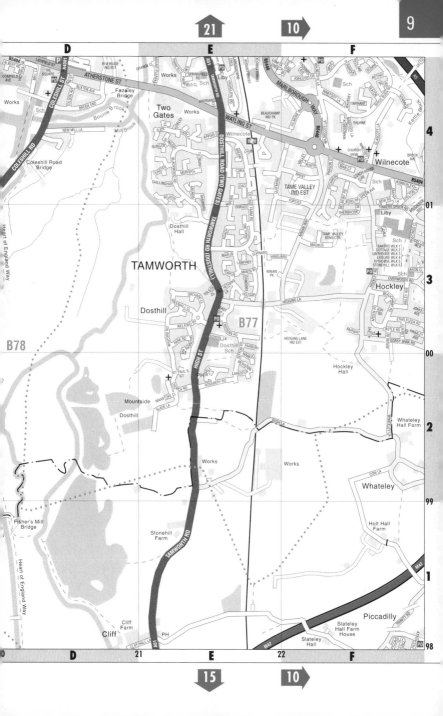

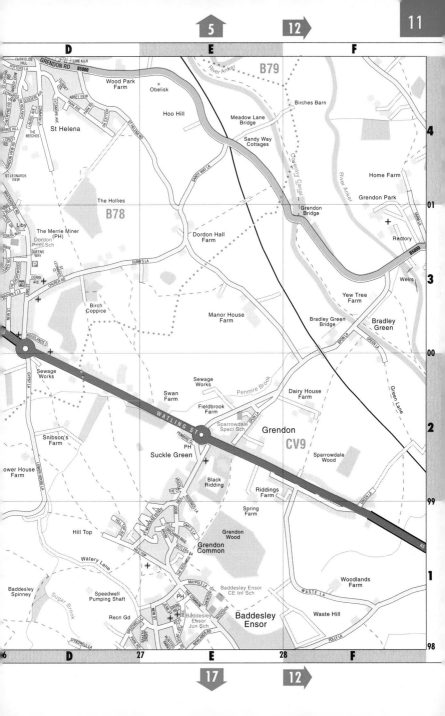

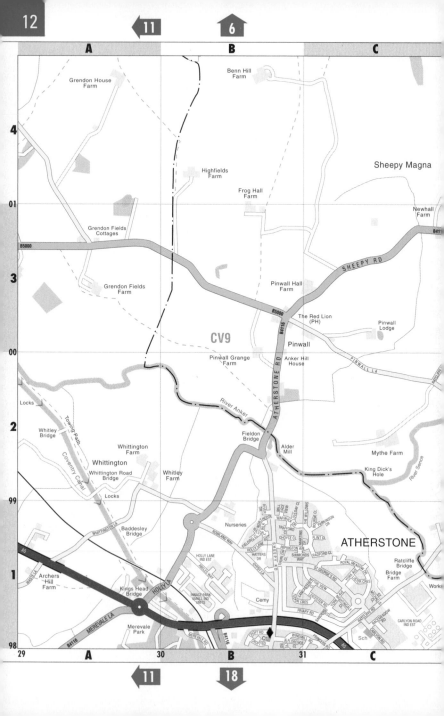

D E F

4

High Heath
Cottage

High Heath
Farm

New Park
Farm

New Park
Wood

Littleworth
End

Withy
Hill

WITHY HILL RD

Langley
Brook
Farm

Langley Brook

Aldermore
Spinney

Withy Hill
Farm

Langley Mill
Farm

LONDON RD

B78

Hill
Farm

Barn
Farm

Cock
Hill

Stoke
End

97

Lindridge
Pool

Osier
Bed

Langley
Pool

Allen End
Farm

Allen End

Lindridge
House

LINDRIDGE RD

The
Lindridge

B75

Masts

Langley
Sch

FALCON LODGE CRES

Lindridge
Jun Sch

Works

MIDDLETON LA

3

Falcon
Lodge

WOODINGTON RD

THE FALCONS

LANGLEY HALL RD

ARDEN RD

Liby

Woddington
Est Sch

CHURCHILL RD

STONE AVE

Brockhurst
Farm

Moxhull Wood
Cottage

LICHFIELD RD A446

Moxhull Hall
(Hotel)

REDDICAP HEATH RD

EALING GROVE CL

96

The
Knoll

HOLLY LA

STEPHENS RD

Holly Lane
Farm

SUTTON
COLDFIELD

Langley Park
House

Grounds
Farm

2

Collings
Farm

Springfield
Farm

OX LEYS RD

Ox Leys
Farm

The
Croft

PENNS LA

Grove
End

95

Ash
Farm

Langley
Gorse

FOX HOLLIES RD

B76

Fair View
Farm

Ramshurst
Farm

BULLS LA

Hermitage
Farm

1

Langley Heath
Farm

Fox
Covert

Linda Vista
Farm

Bricklyn
Farm

Over
Green

PH

Fox
Hollies

CHURCH LA

Thimble
End

BROAD
OAKS

THE
HAYBARN

WYCHBURY

A38

Grove
Farm

WISHAW LA

Pool
Hall

94

4 D 15 E 16 F

A   **B**   **C**

Langley Brook

Riding Stables

Stables

Roger's Coppice

Coneybury Farm

Ash End House Farm

Ash End Farm

Park Farm

Hunts Green

4

Coneybury Wood

97

Hunts-green Farm

Cross Green Farm

Stoke End Farm

B78

Pool House Farm

BRICK KILN LA

Sports Gd

Lower Farm

GREEN LA

WISHAW LA

Primrose Cottage

BODYMOOR HEATH RD

3

A446

Maple Leaf

Cheatle's Farm Bridge

PH

Tidy Cottage

Middleton House Farm

Boundary Plantation

96

Lea Farm

North Wood

Marston Farm Hotel

Noel Grange

Birmingham and Fazeley Canal

M42

2

Wishaw Hall Farm

Moxhull Pool

Fox Wood

The Belfry Golf Ctr.

CUTTLE MILL LA

CROFT LA

LICHFIELD RD

THE BELFRY

B76

Cuttle Mill Farm

Cockssparrow House Farm

95

The Belfry (Hotel)

Mill Pools

A4091

White Bridge

Church Farm

Grange Farm Cottages

THE CANAL

KINGSBURY RD

A4097

1

CHURCH LA

Wishaw

Rye Farm

School Farm

Church Pit

BLUNTS LA

DUNTON LA

Marston Lane Bridge

MARSTON LA

M42

BLACKGREAVES LA

Willday's Farm Bridge

Fox's Bridge

Mullensgrove Farm

Blackgreaves Farm

A446

94

17   **A**   **18**   **B**   **19**   **C**

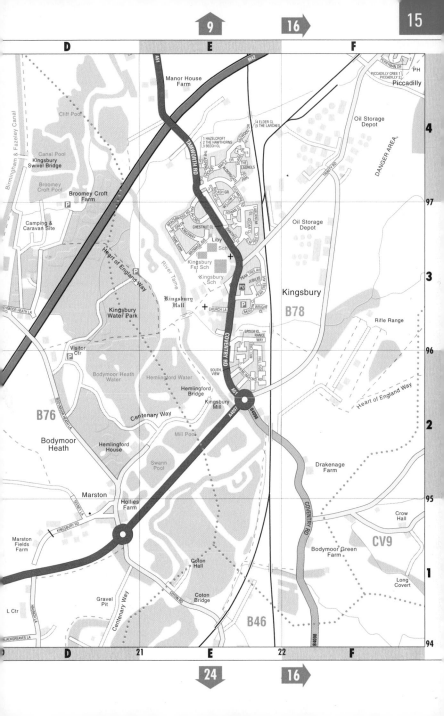

D
E
F

Birmingham & Fazeley Canal

Manor House Farm

Cliff Pool

FERRYMAN DR
1
2
PICCADILLY CRES 1
PICCADILLY 2
Piccadilly
PH

Oil Storage Depot

DANGER AREA

4

Canal Pool
Kingsbury Swivel Bridge

Broomey Croft Pool

Broomey Croft Farm

P

4 ELDER CL
5 THE LARCHES

1 HAZELCROFT
2 THE HAWTHORNS
3 BEECH CL

TAMWORTH RD

97

Camping & Caravan Site

Heart of England Way

P

Oil Storage Depot

ASH GR

ROWAN CL

CHESTNUT CL

Liby
Sch

LABURNUM

PEAR TREE AVE

JUBILEE

Kingsbury Fst Sch

Kingsbury Sch

PO

WRIGHT CL

Kingsbury

B78

3

River Tame

Kingsbury Hall

CHURCH LA

P

Rifle Range

Kingsbury Water Park

BROOK CL

RANGE WAY

COVENTRY RD

96

Visitor Ctr
P

Bodymoor Heath Water

Hemlingford Water

SOUTH VIEW

Heart of England Way

B76

BODYMOOR HEATH LA

Hemlingford Bridge

Centenary Way

Kingsbury Mill

A51

A4097

A4098

Kingsbury Mill

2

Bodymoor Heath

Hemlingford House

Mill Pool

Drakenage Farm

95

Swann Pool

Marston

Hollies Farm

KINGSBURY RD

DIGBY CT

COVENTRY RD

Crow Hall

CV9

Marston Fields Farm

Coton Hall

Bodymoor Green Farm

Long Covert

1

L Ctr

Gravel Pit

Centenary Way

Coton Bridge

COTON RD

B46

B4098

BLACKGREAVES LA

HAUNCH LA

94

D
21
E
22
F

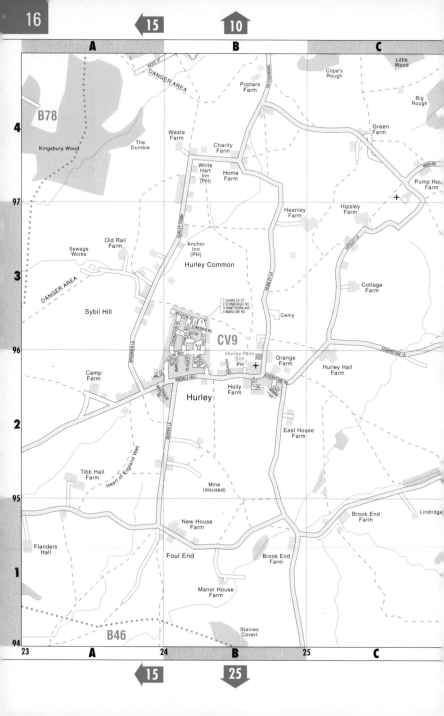

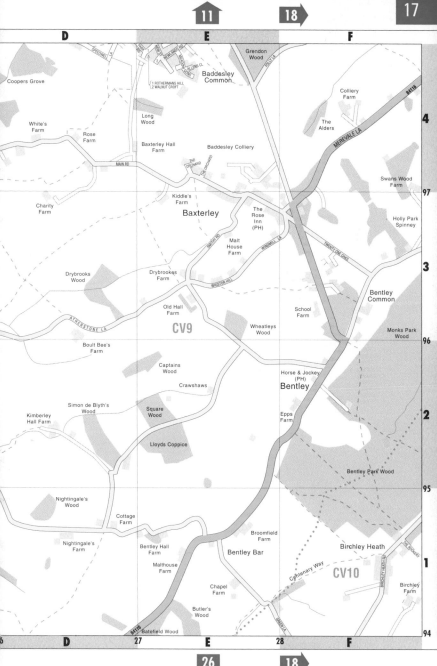

D
E
F

SPEEDWELL

NEWLANDS RD
MEADOW CLOSE
ALLENS CL.

1 ROTHERMANS HILL
2 WALNUT CROFT

Grendon
Wood

TOLL LA

B4116

Coopers Grove

Baddesley
Common

Colliery
Farm

MEREVALE LA

The Alders

4

White's
Farm

Rose
Farm

Long
Wood

Baxterley Hall
Farm

Baddesley Colliery

Swans Wood
Farm

MAIN RD

THE ORCHARD
THE ORCHARD

97

Charity
Farm

Kiddle's
Farm

Baxterley

The Rose
Inn
(PH)

Holly Park
Spinney

SMITH RD

Malt
House
Farm

WINDMILL LA

TWENTY ONE OAKS

3

Drybrooks
Wood

Drybrookes
Farm

WIGSTON HILL

Bentley
Common

ATHERSTONE LA

Old Hall
Farm

School
Farm

Monks Park
Wood

CV9

Wheatleys
Wood

96

Boult Bee's
Farm

Captains
Wood

Crawshaws

Horse & Jockey
(PH)

Bentley

Simon de Blyth's
Wood

Square
Wood

Epps
Farm

2

Kimberley
Hall Farm

Lloyds Coppice

Bentley Park Wood

95

Nightingale's
Wood

Cottage
Farm

Birchley Heath

THE BONGERY

Nightingale's
Farm

Bentley Hall
Farm

Broomfield
Farm

BIRCHLEY HEATH RD

1

Malthouse
Farm

Bentley Bar

Chapel
Farm

Centenary Way

CV10

Birchley
Farm

Butler's
Wood

B4116

Batefield Wood

GREEN LA

94

D
27
E
28
F

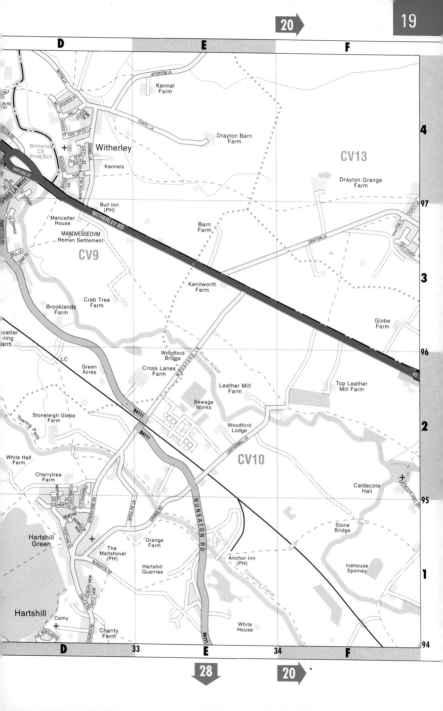

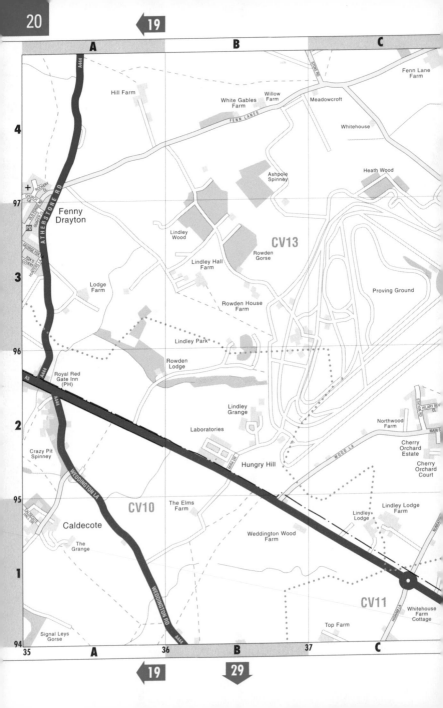

19

A444

Hill Farm

Fenn Lane Farm

White Gables Farm

Willow Farm

Meadowcroft

FENN LANES

Whitehouse

4

Ashpole Spinney

Heath Wood

RISK RD

CHURCH

ROOKERY CL

ATHERSTONE RD

OLD FORGE RD

GATED RD

97

Fenny Drayton

PO

GEORGE ELIOT

FOX'S COVERT

Lindley Wood

CV13

Rowden Gorse

Lindley Hall Farm

3

Lodge Farm

Rowden House Farm

Proving Ground

Lindley Park*

96

Rowden Lodge

A5

A444

Royal Red Gate Inn (PH)

Lindley Grange

Laboratories

Hungry Hill

MAIN DR

WOOD LA

STATION RD

HILARY BEV CL

MAIN S

Northwood Farm

2

Cherry Orchard Estate

Cherry Orchard Court

Crazy Pit Spinney

WEDDINGTON LA

95

CV10

The Elms Farm

Lindley Lodge

Lindley Lodge Farm

Weddington Wood Farm

Caldecote

TARCOTE

CALDECOTE

The Grange

1

CV11

Whitehouse Farm Cottage

WEDDINGTON RD

NUNEATON RD

94

Signal Leys Gorse

Top Farm

A444

35 **A** **36** **B** **37** **C**

D
E
F

STAPLETON LA

THE GREEN

STOKE LA

Grange
Farm

Fox
Covert
Farm

Ivy
House
Farm

Crown Hill

Crown Hill
Farm

WILLOW PARK
IND EST

Lodge
Farm

4

ROSEWAY

WHITEMOORS
CL

CHURCH
CL

BLACKSMITHS WY

PURLING CT

St Martin's
Convent

UPTON LA

SHERWOOD RD

HINCKLEY RD

St Martin's
Catholic
High Sch

Brook
Farm

STATION RD

CHURCH
WK
PO

St Margarets
CE Prim Sch

PINE CL

HALL DR

PH

Higham
Fields
Court

Stoke
Golding

BENNET

Stoke Fields
Farm

97

TITHE CL

POST OFFICE LA

AVE

NEW RD

STOKE RD

Willow
Farm

Brook House

Brook Farm

CV13

Millfield
Farm

Highfield
Farm

3

Cuckoos Nest
Farm

Compass Fields
Farm

Oaklands

Basin
Bridge
Farm

Basin
Bridge

Ashby de la Zouch Canal

Vale
Farm

Wykin
Fields

96

Higham on the Hill
CE Prim Sch

Church
Farm

Hall Farm

The
Hollows

Spring Hill
Farm

Manor
Farm

PH

PO

MAIN ST

Higham on the Hill

HINCKLEY LA

Towing Path

Wykin
House
Farm

HIGHAM LA

Wykin

2

Higham Hall

Wykin
Hall

LE10

95

BURBAGE LA

A47

Grange
Farm

Harper's Hill

Higham
Grange

Higham
Thorns

1

Range Brook

Higham
Gorse

CV11

Hollow
Farm

A5

1 BRASCOTE RD
2 LOVETTS CL

BRASCOTE

FOSTON DR

D
39
E
40
F
94

30

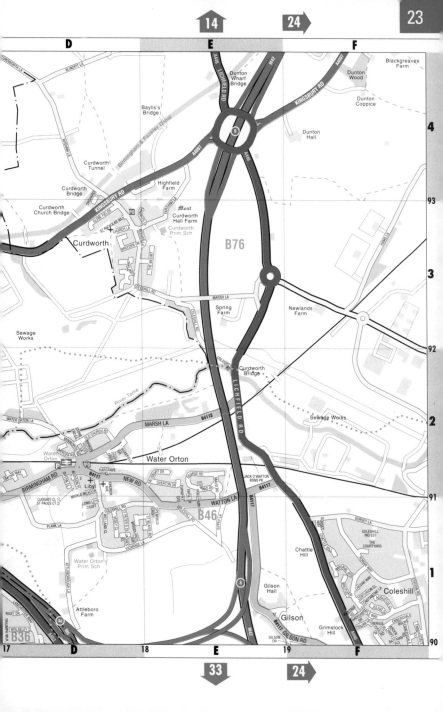

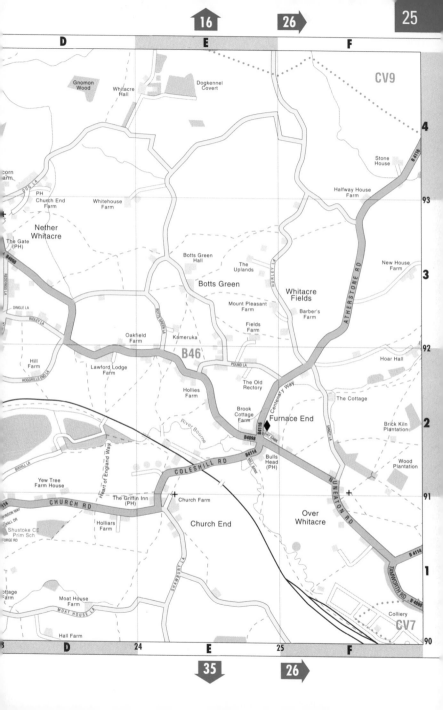

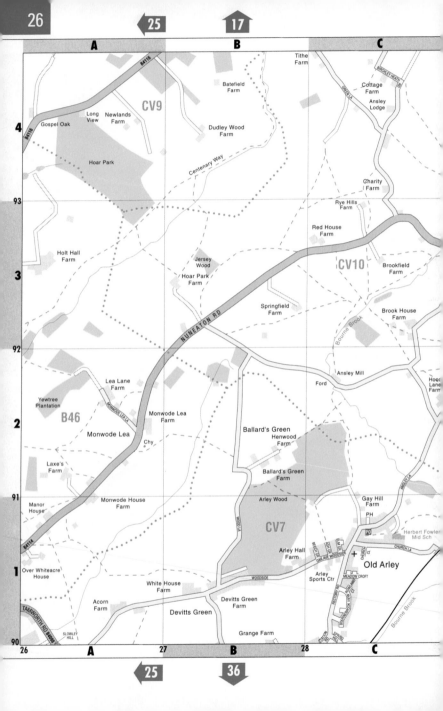

A   **B**   **C**

Tithe
Farm

B4116

Cottage
Farm

Ansley
Lodge

CV9

Batefield
Farm

Long
View

Newlands
Farm

Dudley Wood
Farm

4

Gospel Oak

B4116

Charity
Farm

Hoar Park

Centenary Way

Rye Hills
Farm

93

Red House
Farm

Holt Hall
Farm

Jersey
Wood

CV10

Brookfield
Farm

3

Hoar Park
Farm

NUNEATON RD

Springfield
Farm

Brook House
Farm

Bourne Brook

92

Ansley Mill

Lea Lane
Farm

Ford

Hoo
Lane
Farm

Yewtree
Plantation

MONWODE LEA LA

Monwode Lea
Farm

B46

2

Ballard's Green

Henwood
Farm

Monwode Lea

Chy

Laxe's
Farm

Ballard's Green
Farm

ANSLEY LA

91

Arley Wood

Gay Hill
Farm

Manor
House

Monwode House
Farm

WOOD LA

CV7

PH

PO

Herbert Fowler
Mid Sch

B4114

CHURCH LA

1

Over Whiteacre
House

Arley Hall
Farm

BEECH CL
ASH GR
OAK AVE WOODSIDE

Old Arley

Arley
Sports Ctr

MEADOW CROFT

WOODSIDE

White House
Farm

Acorn
Farm

Devitts Green
Farm

Devitts Green

Grange Farm

Bourne Brook

TAMWORTH RD B4098

SLOWLEY
HILL

90

18
28

D E F

Works
Slack's
Farm
Moor Wood

Common
Farm
Nursery Hill
Fst Sch
Ansley Common
MOORWOOD LA

Ox Hayes
Farm
COLESHILL RD
THORNCLIFFE
CORNISH CL
ST JOHN'S RD
4

Ansley Hall
B4114

BRETTS HALL
EST

Ansley Park
Bret's Hall
Wood
Bret's Hall
Farm
93

Manor Farm
NUNEATON RD
Wood Barn
Farm
Hockley

Manor House
Farm
Thornyfield
Wood
Centenary Way
Freesland
Farm
Galley
Common
Fst Sch
3

B4112
Church End
SCHOOL LA
PLOUGH HILL RD
MANLOVE CL

Little Brook
Farm
THE ROWERS
DRYDEN CL
ST CARLE

Barn Moor
Wood
Galley
Farm
ROBINS

New Park
Farm
Barn Moor
Farm
Galley Common
CHESTERTON DR
92

Village
Farm
BIRMINGHAM RD
ST PETER'S CH
VALLEY RD
WELLS CL

ANSLEY LA
ST LAWRENCE RD
CV10
PO

Hood Lane
Farm
PH
TUNNEL RD
Works
Sports
Gd
PARK LA
2

Malthouse
Farm
PO
NUTHURST CRES
Hill Farm
Centenary Way

Ansley
Arley Tunnel
Robinson's End

Golf Course
Mast
B4112
Robinson's End
Mid Sch

Woodlands Cottage
Farm
B4112

NUTHURST LA
PO
ANSLEY RD
91

CH
Nuthurst Heath
Farm
Robinson's End
Farm

Arley House
Farm
Lady
Wood
1

CV7
CHURCH LA

Hill Top
Church
Farm
Lodge
Farm
90

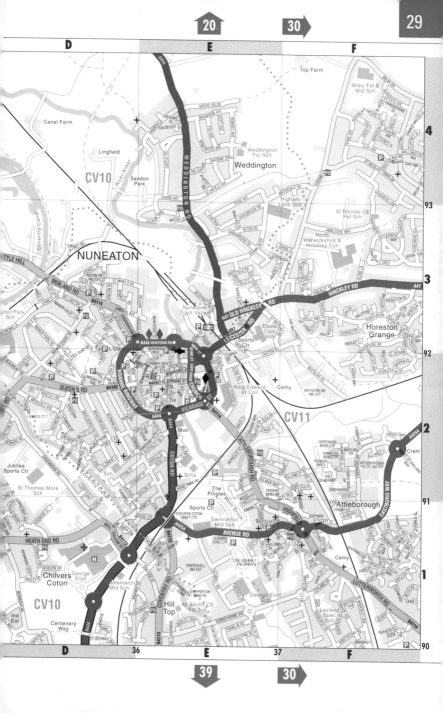

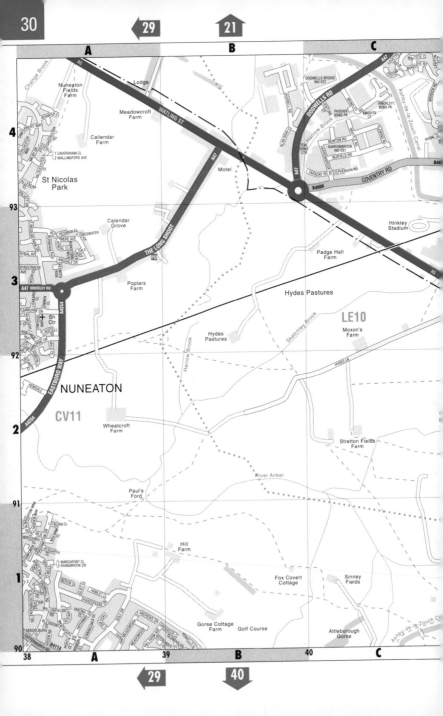

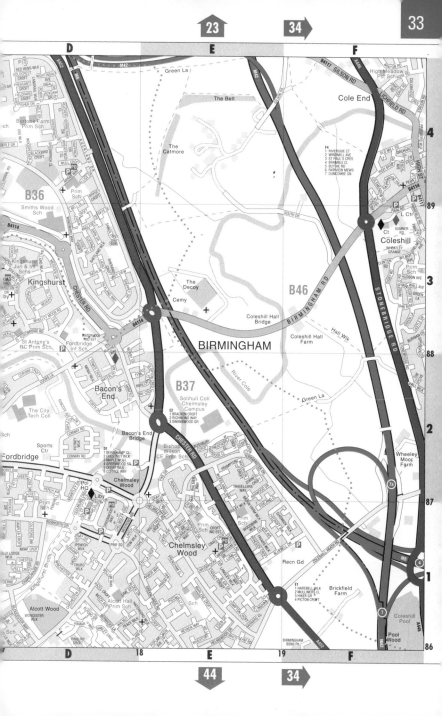

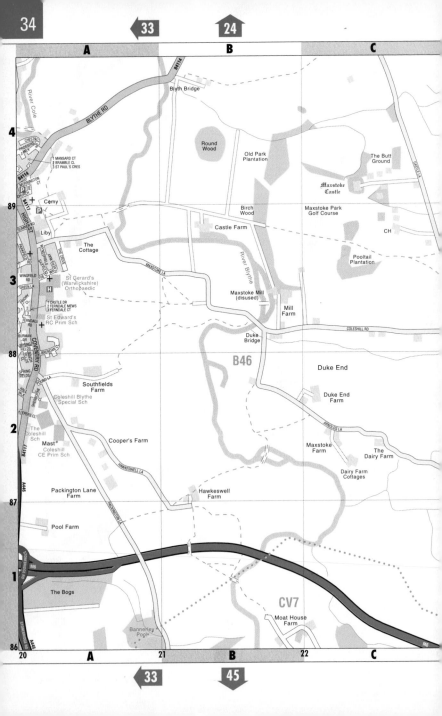

35
26

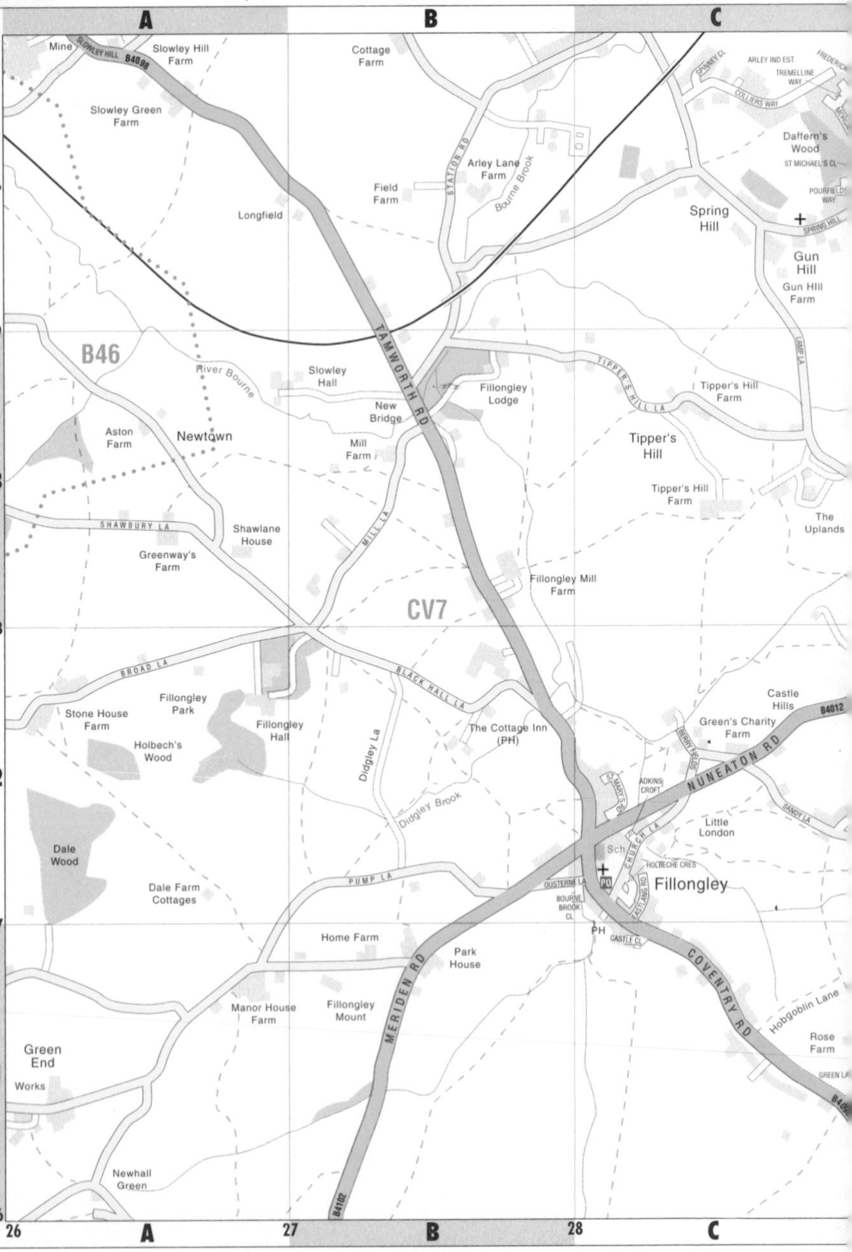
A
B
C
Mine
SLOWLEY HILL
B4098
Slowley Hill Farm
Cottage Farm
SPINNEY CL
ARLEY IND EST
FREDERICK
TREMELLINE WAY
COLLIERS WAY
Slowley Green Farm
Daffern's Wood
STATION RD
Arley Lane Farm
Bourne Brook
ST MICHAEL'S CL
Field Farm
POURFIELDS WAY
Longfield
Spring Hill
SPRING HILL
Gun Hill
Gun Hill Farm
TAMWORTH RD
LAMP LA
B46
River Bourne
Slowley Hall
Fillongley Lodge
TIPPER'S HILL LA
Tipper's Hill Farm
New Bridge
Aston Farm
Newtown
Mill Farm
Tipper's Hill
Tipper's Hill Farm
The Uplands
SHAWBURY LA
MILL LA
Shawlane House
Greenway's Farm
Fillongley Mill Farm
CV7
BROAD LA
BLACK HALL LA
Castle Hills
Fillongley Park
Stone House Farm
Fillongley Hall
The Cottage Inn (PH)
Green's Charity Farm
B4012
BERRY FIELDS
Holbech's Wood
Didgley La
NUNEATON RD
ST MARY'S RD
ADKINS CROFT
SANDY LA
Didgley Brook
Dale Wood
CHURCH LA
Little London
Sch
HOLBECHE CRES
PUMP LA
PO
Fillongley
Dale Farm Cottages
OUSTERNE LA
BOURNE BROOK CL
EASTLANG RD
PH
CASTLE CL
Home Farm
Park House
COVENTRY RD
MERIDEN RD
Hobgoblin Lane
Manor House Farm
Fillongley Mount
Rose Farm
Green End
Works
GREEN LA
Newhall Green
B4102
4
89
3
88
2
87
1
86
26
27
28

35
47

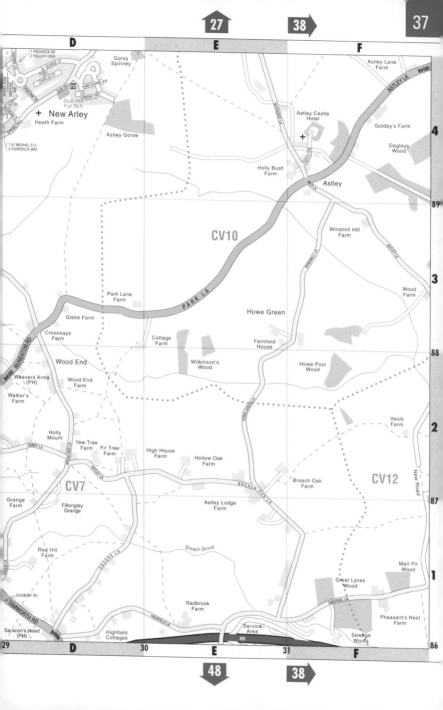

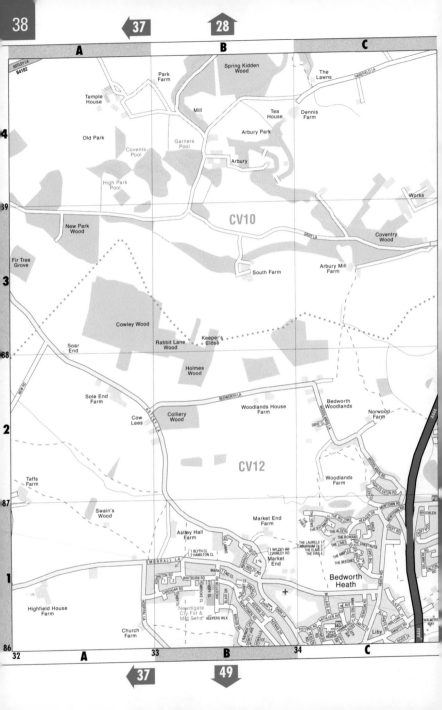

A
B
C

4

A5

Red Lion Farm

Watling Street Farm

B4114

Smockington

Pear Tree Farm

Smockington Farm

B4114

Wigston Parva

CHURCH LA

B4114

89

SMOCKINGTON LA

B4114

Copston Lodge Farm

Copston Spinney

High Cross Quarry

3

MILL LA

FENNIS BANK LA

Grange Farm

The Hollies Farm

Copston Magna

Copston Magna

GREEN LA

COPSTON LA

Orchard Farm

LE17

88

LE10

Copston Spinney

Wolvey Lodge Farm

Copston Fields Farm

2

MERE LA

Fosse Way Cottage

WOLDS LA

87

Grove Farm

1

FOSSE WAY

CV23

Wolvey Wolds

Cloudesley Bush

COAL PIT LA

B4455

MINNS CLOSE LA

Coal Pit Lane

CV7

Withybrook Spinney

86

44

A

45

B

46

C

The Bungalow

LE10

Bumble-Bee Farm

Frolesworth Hill

4

Lodge Farm

89

High Cross

Manor Farm

Inn

MANOR RD

Gables Farm

Claybrooke Magna Mill

Sewage Works

Victoria Farm

HIGH CROSS LA

Claybrooke Magna

FOSSE WAY

WOOD-LAND LA

BACK LA

THE VINEYARD

The Grange

Mount Pleasant Cottage

B577

B4455

High Cross Farm

The Leicestershire Round

The Leicestershire Round

BELL ST

STENBROOK LA

PO

HOLLY TREE WLK

Claybrooke Farm

3

The Leicestershire Round

WESTERN DR

Claybrooke Hall

88

LE17

Watling House

Claybrook Prim Sch

Avenue Villas

B577

Alma House

Cemy

Claybrooke Parva

Wibtoft

Woodway Cottage

WOODWAY LA

Laurel Bank

Glebe Farm

2

GREEN LA

PENN LA

Ullesthorpe Lodge

87

Whitehouse Fm (Kennels)

1

CV23

Tithe Platts Farm

86

B46
M6
M6

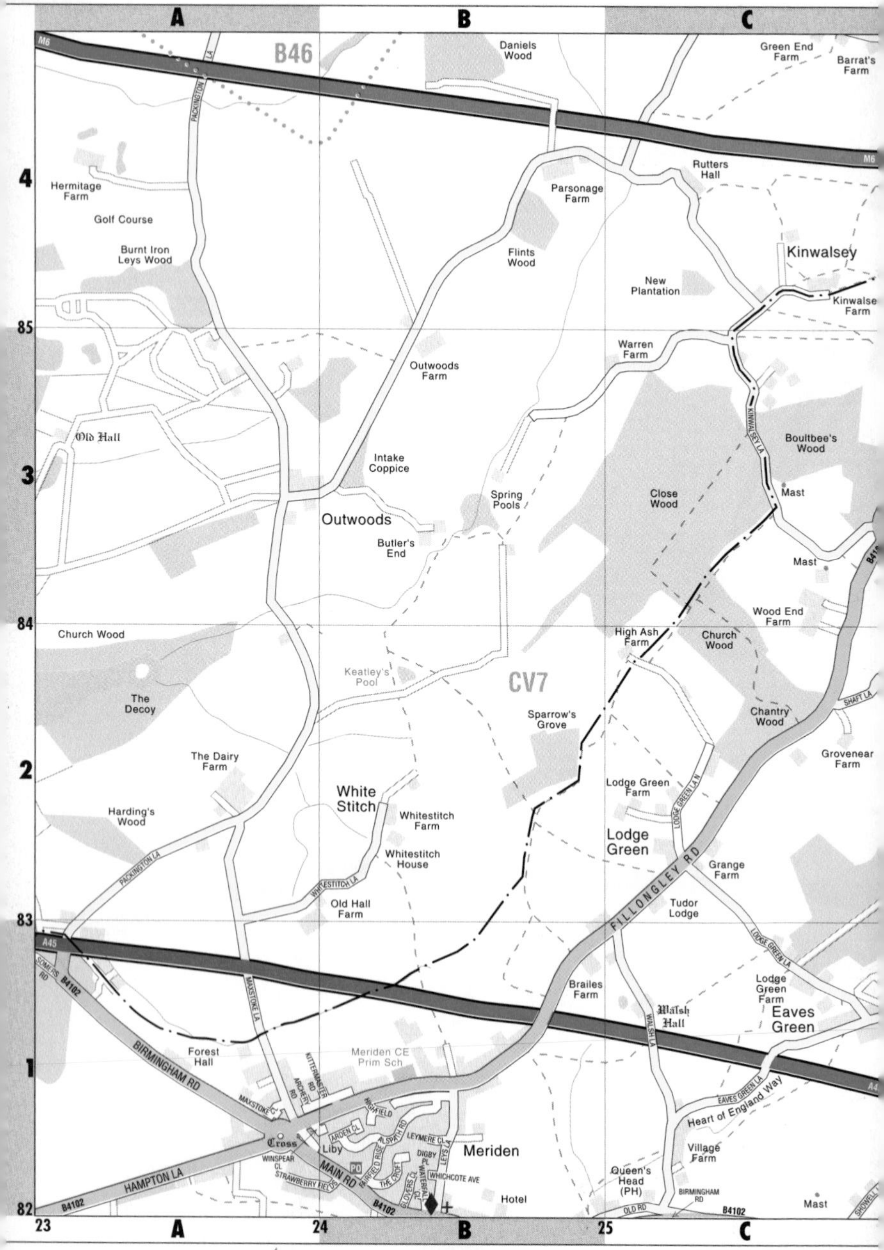

Daniels Wood
Green End Farm
Barrat's Farm

4
Hermitage Farm
Golf Course
Burnt Iron Leys Wood

Parsonage Farm
Rutters Hall

Flints Wood
New Plantation
Kinwalsey
Kinwalse Farm

85
Warren Farm

Outwoods Farm

Old Hall
Intake Coppice

Boultbee's Wood
Mast

3
Outwoods
Butler's End
Spring Pools
Close Wood
Mast

Mast

84
Church Wood
High Ash Farm
Church Wood
Wood End Farm

Keatley's Pool
CV7
Chantry Wood

The Decoy
Sparrow's Grove
Grovenear Farm

2
The Dairy Farm
Lodge Green Farm

Harding's Wood
White Stitch
Whitestitch Farm
Lodge Green

Whitestitch House
Grange Farm

WHITESTITCH LA
Old Hall Farm
FILLONGLEY RD
Tudor Lodge

83
A45
A45

BIRMINGHAM RD
B4102
Brailes Farm
Lodge Green Farm
Eaves Green

Welsh Hall

1
Forest Hall
Meriden CE Prim Sch
Heart of England Way

Village Farm

Cross
Liby
Meriden
Queen's Head (PH)
BIRMINGHAM RD

HAMPTON LA
B4102
MAIN RD
Hotel
B4102
Mast

82
23
A
24
B
25
C

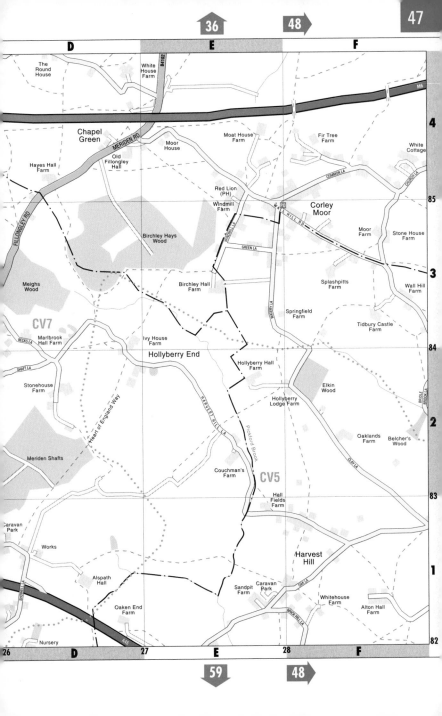

D   E   F

The Round House

White House Farm

B4102

4

Chapel Green

MERIDEN RD

Moor House

Moat House Farm

Fir Tree Farm

White Cottage

Old Fillongley Hall

Hayes Hall Farm

COMMON LA

CHURCH LA

Red Lion (PH)

85

FILLONGLEY RD

Windmill Farm

Corley Moor

WALL HILL RD

Moor Farm

Stone House Farm

Birchley Hays Wood

GREEN LA

WINDMILL LA

3

Meighs Wood

Birchley Hall Farm

Splashpitts Farm

Wall Hill Farm

CV7

WALL HILL LA

Springfield Farm

Tidbury Castle Farm

BECKS LA

Marlbrook Hall Farm

Ivy House Farm

84

Hollyberry End

Hollyberry Hall Farm

SHAFT LA

Elkin Wood

BRIDLE

BRIDLE LA

Stonehouse Farm

Hollyberry Lodge Farm

Heart of England Way

HARVEST HILL LA

2

Meriden Shafts

Pickford Brook

Oaklands Farm

Belcher's Wood

OLAF LA

Couchman's Farm

CV5

83

Hall Fields Farm

Caravan Park

Works

Harvest Hill

1

Alspath Hall

Sandpit Farm

Caravan Park

Whitehouse Farm

Alton Hall Farm

BRICK HILL LA

OLAF LA

BIRCHLEY LA

Oaken End Farm

A45

82

Nursery

26   D   27   E   28   F

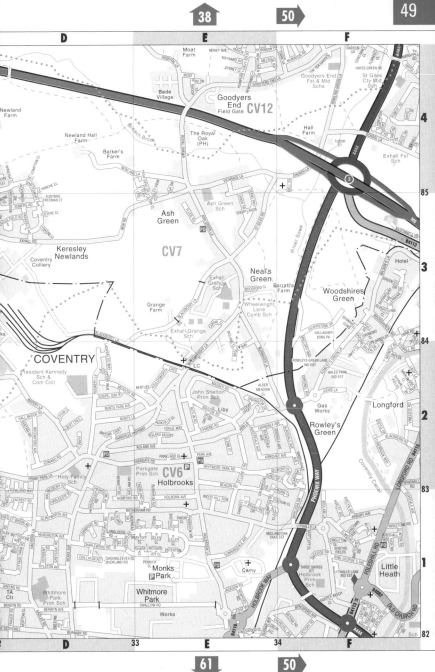

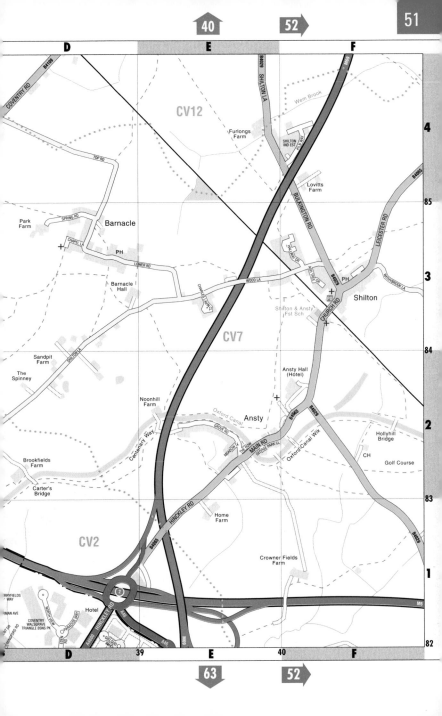

D E F

4

85

3

84

2

83

1

82

CV12

Wem Brook

SHILTON LA

B4029

M69

Furlongs Farm

SHILTON IND EST

Lovitts Farm

BULKINGTON RD

LEICESTER RD

B4065

COVENTRY RD

B4109

TOP RD

SPRING RD

Park Farm

Barnacle

CHAPEL LA

PH

LOWER RD

Barnacle Hall

CHARITY CROFT

WOOD LA

ASH TREE LA

HALL DR

B4029

PH

Shilton

CHURCH RD

PITTBROOK LA

Shilton & Ansty Fst Sch

CV7

SHILTON LA

Sandpit Farm

The Spinney

Noonhill Farm

CENTENARY WAY

Oxford Canal

Ansty

Ansty Hall (Hotel)

GROVE RD

THE TOW

MEADOW

MAIN RD

GROSE PARK GL

B4065

B4029

Oxford Canal Wlk

Hollyhill Bridge

CH

Golf Course

B4029

Brookfields Farm

Carter's Bridge

HINCKLEY RD

Home Farm

B4065

Crowner Fields Farm

CV2

M6

RRYFIELDS WAY

RMAN AVE

Hotel

HINCKLEY RD

A4600

COVENTRY WALSGRAVE TRIANGLE BSNS PK

PARADISE WAY

A46

M69

A46

D E F

E F

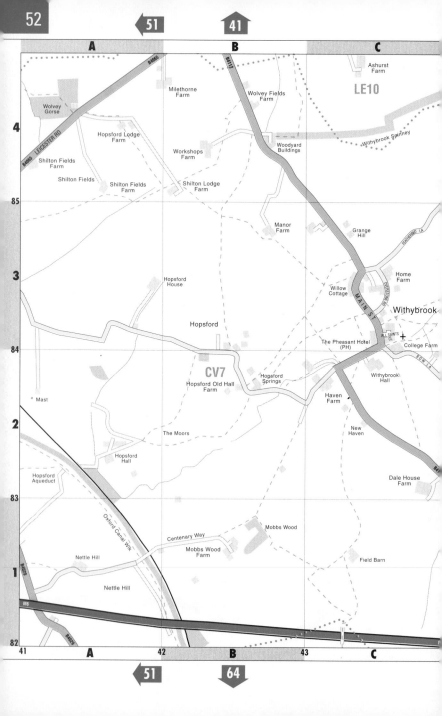

A   B   C

Ashurst Farm

LE10

B4065

B4112

Wolvey Gorse

Milethorne Farm

Wolvey Fields Farm

Withybrook Spinney

4

LEICESTER RD

Hopsford Lodge Farm

Workshops Farm

Woodyard Buildings

Shilton Fields Farm

Shilton Fields

Shilton Fields Farm

Shilton Lodge Farm

85

Manor Farm

Grange Hill

FEATHERBED LA

3

Hopsford House

Willow Cottage

Home Farm

DIRTSTONE RD

MAIN ST

Withybrook

Hopsford

ALL SAINTS

College Farm

84

The Pheasant Hotel (PH)

BOW LA

CV7

Hopsford Old Hall Farm

Hopsford Springs

Withybrook Hall

* Mast

Haven Farm

2

The Moors

New Haven

B4112

Hopsford Hall

Hopsford Aqueduct

Dale House Farm

83

Mobbs Wood

Oxford Canal Wlk

Centenary Way

Mobbs Wood Farm

B4029

Nettle Hill

Field Barn

1

Nettle Hill

M6

82

41   A   42   B   43   C

B4029

53
43

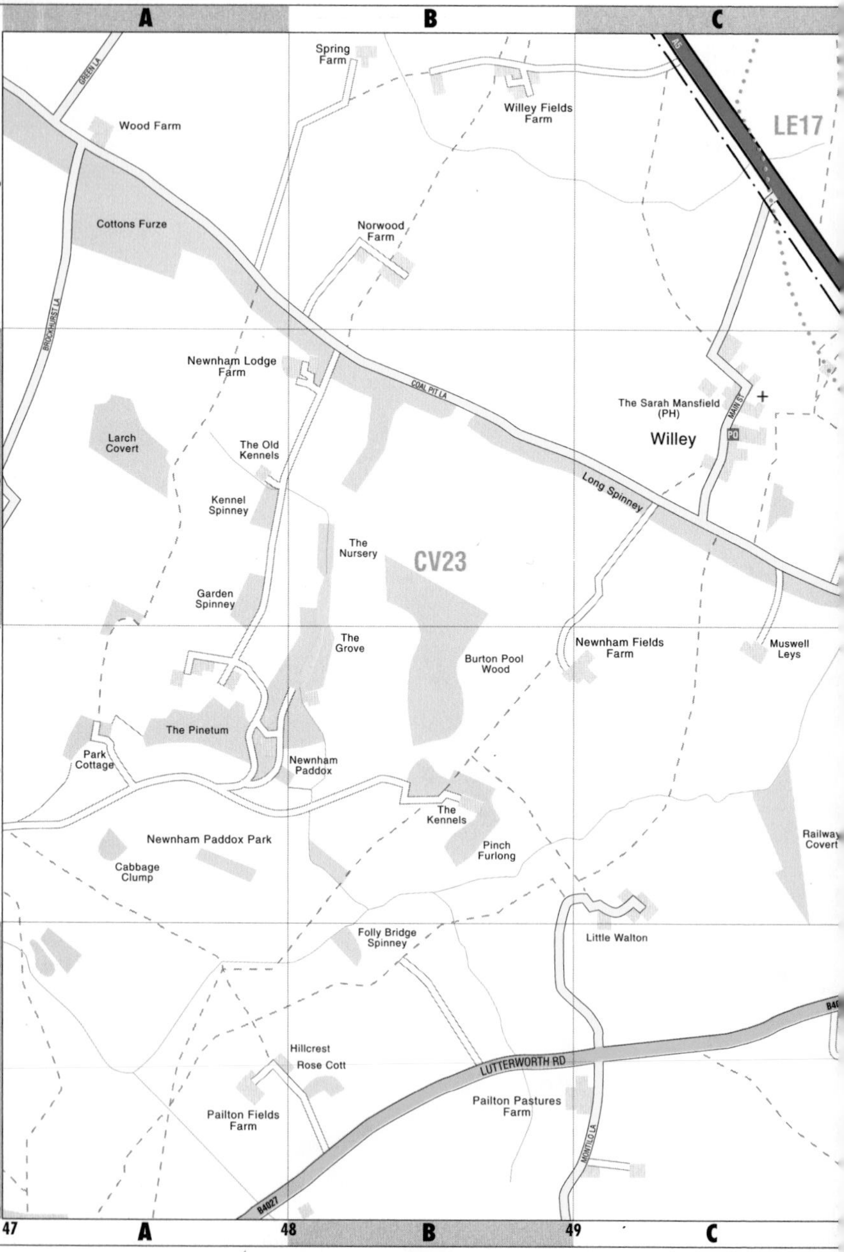
A
B
C
Spring Farm
GREEN LA
Wood Farm
Willey Fields Farm
LE17
A5
4
Cottons Furze
Norwood Farm
BROCKHURST LA
85
Newnham Lodge Farm
COAL PIT LA
The Sarah Mansfield (PH)
MAIN ST
Willey
PO
Larch Covert
The Old Kennels
3
Long Spinney
Kennel Spinney
The Nursery
CV23
Garden Spinney
84
The Grove
Newnham Fields Farm
Muswell Leys
Burton Pool Wood
The Pinetum
Park Cottage
Newnham Paddox
2
The Kennels
Newnham Paddox Park
Pinch Furlong
Railway Covert
Cabbage Clump
83
Folly Bridge Spinney
Little Walton
Hillcrest
1
Rose Cott
LUTTERWORTH RD
Pailton Pastures Farm
Pailton Fields Farm
MONTILO LA
B4027
82
47
48
49
A
B
C

53
66

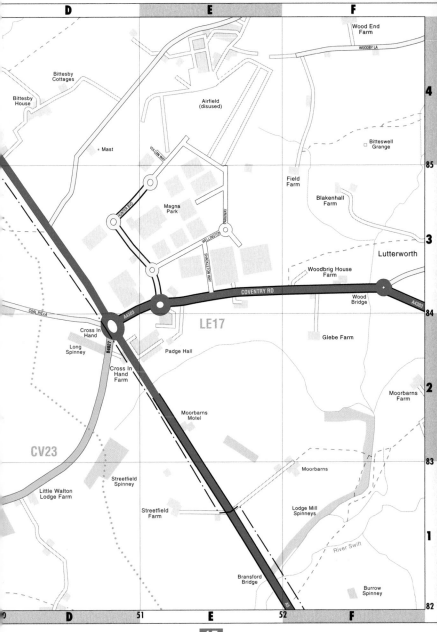

Hampton
Coppice

4

Heath
Farm

Home
Farm

Woodhouse
Farm

Four
Winds

SHADOW BROOK LA

81

Shadow Brook

Bunts
Wood

Catherine
de Barnes

Barber's
Coppice

Hampton Lane
Farm

SOLIHULL RD

B410

The
Limes

3

LUGTROUT LA

OAKFIELDS

APPLETREE CL

HAMPTON LA

Boat Inn
(PH)

Aspbury's
Copse

B92

Walford Hall
Farm

B4102

80

BERRY HALL LA

Bogay
Hall

Grand Union Canal

The
Woodlands

PRIORY LA

Sewage
Works

EASTCOTE LA

Berry
Hall

Brick Kiln Hole
Wood

B91

CATHERINE'S LA

HENWOOD LA

Henwood Mill
(dis)

BARSTON LA

Eastcote
House

WALSAL END LA

2

Ford

Ravenshaw
Hall

BARSTON LA

Eastcote
Hall

Eastcote

Wharley
Hall

Eastcote
Paddocks

79

RAVENSHAW WAY

Copt Heath
Wharf

Cow
Hayes

BARSTON LA

Wood Lane
Farm

NOBLE RD

BARSTON LA

PH

Th
Fw

A41

MA2

Henwood Hall
Farm

B37

River Blythe

Wood
Lane
Farm

WOOD LA

1

A4141

Sports
Gd

Grove
Farm

B93

WITCHFORD CL

River Blythe

HAMPTON RD

WARWICK RD A4141

Copt
Heath

78

17   A   18   B   19   C

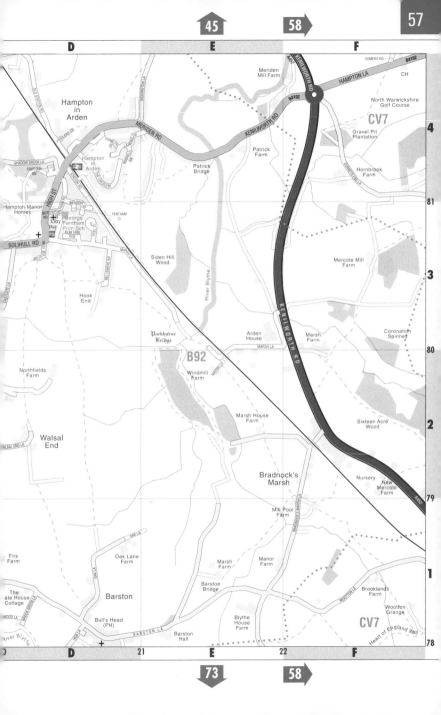

D
E
F

SOMERS RD
B4102
HAMPTON LA
CH

Meriden
Mill Farm

B4102

North Warwickshire
Golf Course

CV7

4

Hampton
in
Arden

MERIDEN RD
KENILWORTH RD

Patrick
Farm

Gravel Pit
Plantation

Hornbrook
Farm

SHADOW BROOK LA
FENTHAM

Patrick
Bridge

81

Hampton
in
Arden

HIGH ST

Hampton Manor
Homes

George
Fentham
Prim Sch
ELM TREE
RISE

Mercote Mill
Farm

3

SOLIHULL RD

Siden Hill
Wood

River Blythe

Hook
End

KENILWORTH RD

Packhorse
Bridge

B92

Arden
House

Marsh
Farm

Coronation
Spinney

MARSH LA

80

Northfields
Farm

Windmill
Farm

Marsh House
Farm

Sixteen Acre
Wood

2

Walsal
End

WALSAL END LA

Bradnock's
Marsh

Nursery

New
Mercote
Farm

79

Mill Pool
Farm

FILLONGLEY RD

A452

OAK LA

Firs
Farm

Oak Lane
Farm

Marsh
Farm

Manor
Farm

Brooklands
Farm

1

The
ate House
Cottage

BROOK END LA
WOOD LA

Barston

Bull's Head
(PH)

Barston
Bridge

Blythe
House
Farm

Barston
Hall

WOOTTON

Wootton
Grange

CV7

Heart of England Way

River Blythe

BARSTON LA

78

D
21
E
22
F

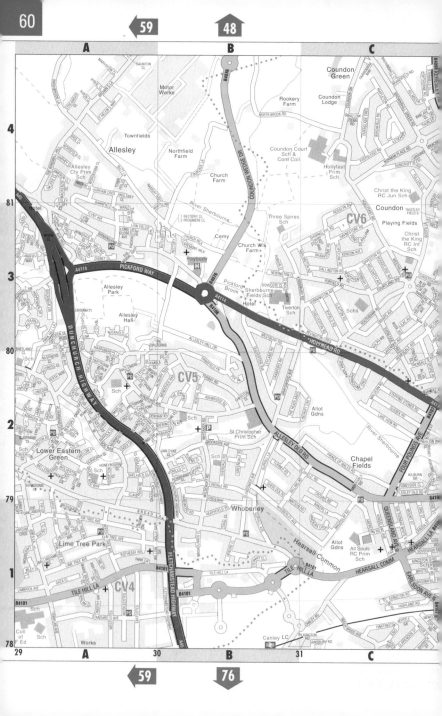

D2
1 BATEMAN'S ACRE S
2 CHILTERN LEYS
3 PRIORSFIELD RD N
4 PRIORSFIELD RD
5 RADFORD CIRC
6 HAWKSWORTH DR

7 COLLETT WLK
8 COMPASS CT
D3
1 NETHERMILL RD
2 PAKE'S CROFT
3 HUMBERSTONE RD

For full street detail of the
highlighted area see page
151.

77 62

F2
1 CANTHORNE CL
2 PENSILVA WAY
3 LEIGH ST
4 CLARENCE ST
5 NELSON ST
6 WATERLOO ST
7 GILBERT CL
8 VAUXHALL CL
9 VERNON CL

10 SPRING CL

A
B
C

COVENTRY RD
B4112
B4027 LUTTERWORTH RD
B4027
FOXFIELD
POST HOUSE GDNS
Yews Farm
RUGBY RD
Pailton

Pailton Pastures

Tithe Farm

4

Greenway Farm

COVE LA

Thwaite Farm

81

M6

Masts

Montilo Farm

Fieldgate Farm

3

MONTILO LA

Glebe Farm

80

Hospital Farm

CV23

Harborough Magna

2

BACK LA

PAILTON RD

Church Farm

PH

MAIN ST

Cosford

Grange Farm

Cosford Hall Farm

Spike Lane

Manor Farm

79

EASENHALL RD

Harborough Parva

Sandercock Farm

Lodge Farm

Cosford Grounds

CV21

Tuckey's Farm

Chestnut Farm

CATTHORPE LA

RUGBY RD

1

Oxford Canal

Tuckey's Bridge

Oxford Canal Wlk

High Oaks

CATTHORPE LA

B4112

78

47
A
48
B
49
C

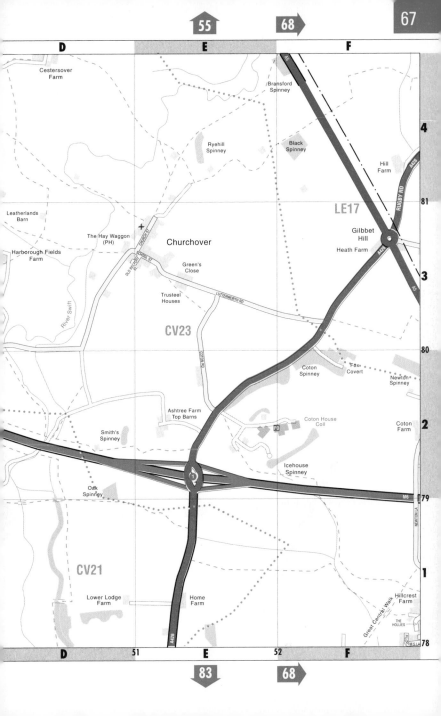

D

E

F

4

81

3

80

2

79

1

78

Cestersover
Farm

Bransford
Spinney

Ryehill
Spinney

Black
Spinney

Hill
Farm

LE17

Gilbbet
Hill

Leatherlands
Barn

The Hay Waggon
(PH)

Churchover

Heath Farm

Harborough Fields
Farm

Green's
Close

Trusteel
Houses

LUTERWORTH RD

River Swift

CV23

Fox
Covert

Coton
Spinney

Newton
Spinney

Ashtree Farm
Top Barns

Smith's
Spinney

Coton House
Coll

Coton
Farm

PO

Icehouse
Spinney

Oak
Spinney

M6

NEWTON LA

CV21

Lower Lodge
Farm

Home
Farm

Great Central Walk

Hillcrest
Farm

THE
HOLLIES

A426

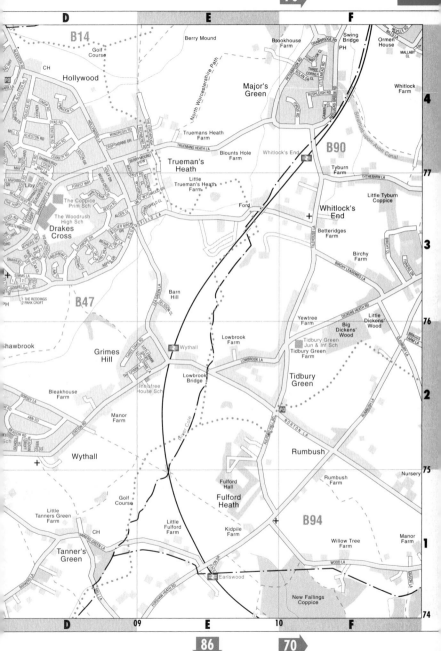

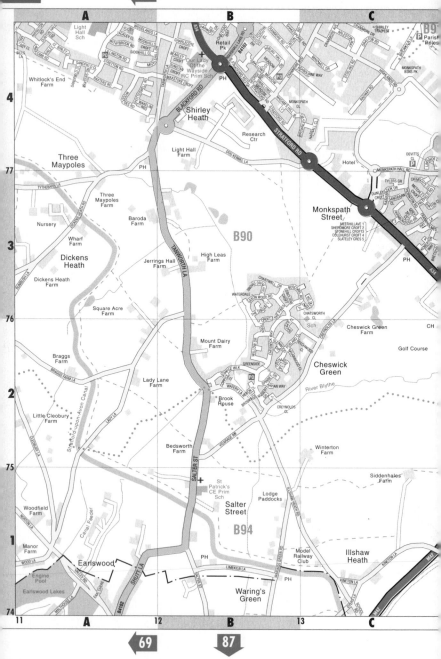

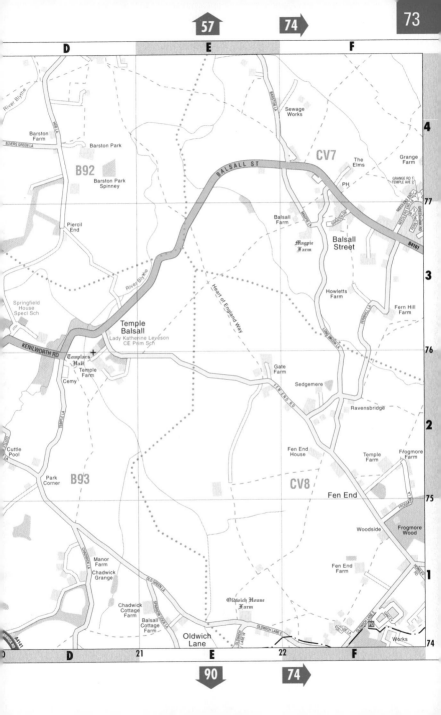

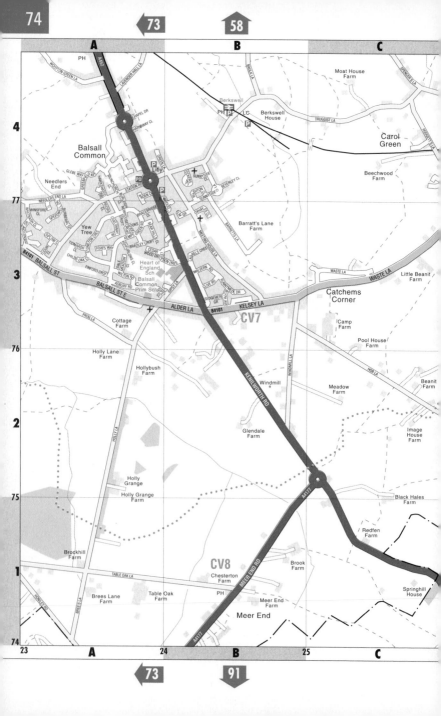

A B C

PH

WOOTTON GREEN LA

LAVENDER HALL LA

A452

BAILS LA

Moat House
Farm

PENNERLA

TRUGGIST LA

Berkswell
PH LC
Berkswell
House

Carol
Green

DOSTHILL FM LA

4

Balsall
Common

CHAPEL DR
HEATHWAY CL

Beechwood
Farm

TRUGGIST LA

Needlers
End

GLEBE WAY
GLA AV

NEEDLERS END LA

GREES WAY

Liby
P

SUNNYSIDE

CATON
STANFORD CL

BEVERLEY CL

STATION RD

HUNSFORD CL

77

WINSFORD
CL

BEICHWOOD LA
SPENCER HS

MACEBROOK

GOLT LA

Barratt's Lane
Farm

BARRETT'S LA

3

Yew
Tree

THUNDERGATE

CHILDE OAK

FOXES WAY

KEMPS

BRADLEY CROFT

CEDAR
WOOD DR
CRICKET CRES

Heart of
England
Sch
Balsall
Common
Prim School

ONION DR

MALVERN

CHELSEA CRES

WASTE LA

WASTE LA

Catchems
Corner

Little Beanit
Farm

B4101 BALSALL ST

BALSALL ST E

AGBURY RD

MILTON RD

ALDER LA

OLIVE RD

SEDGEMERE
GR

B4101

KELSEY LA

CV7

Camp
Farm

Pool House
Farm

HOB LA

Beanit
Farm

76

Holly Lane
Farm

Hollybush
Farm

KENILWORTH RD

Windmill

WINDMILL LA

Meadow
Farm

2

FROG LA

HOLLY LA

Glendale
Farm

Image
House
Farm

75

Holly
Grange

Holly Grange
Farm

A4177

Black Hales
Farm

Brockhill
Farm

CV8

TABLE OAK LA

Chesterton
Farm

MEER END RD

Brook
Farm

Redfen
Farm

1

BREES LA

DONE CL RD

Brees Lane
Farm

Table Oak
Farm

PH

Meer End
Farm

A4177

Springhill
House

Meer End

74

23 A 24 B 25 C

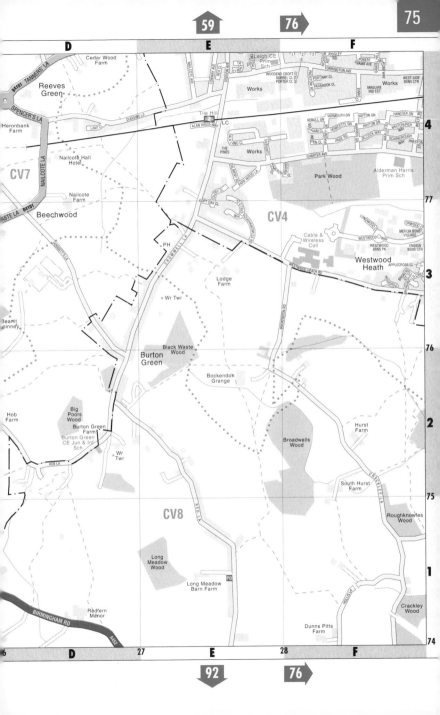

79
64

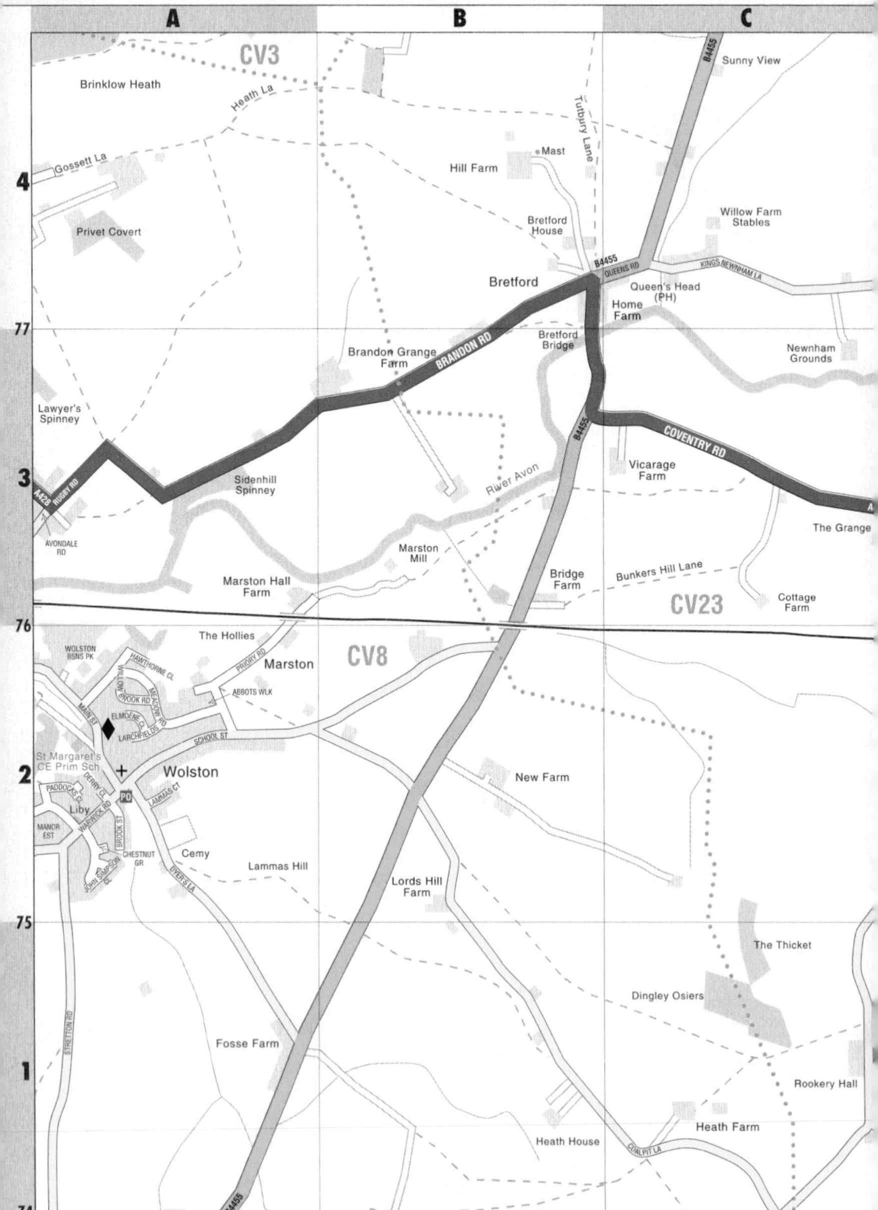
A
B
C
CV3
Brinklow Heath
Heath La
Gossett La
Privet Covert
Tutbury Lane
Hill Farm
Mast
Sunny View
B4455
Willow Farm
Stables
Bretford
House
Bretford
B4455
QUEENS RD
KINGS NEWNHAM LA
Queen's Head
(PH)
Home
Farm
Bretford
Bridge
Newnham
Grounds
Brandon Grange
Farm
BRANDON RD
Lawyer's
Spinney
COVENTRY RD
Vicarage
Farm
A428
RUGBY RD
Sidenhill
Spinney
River Avon
The Grange
AVONDALE
RD
Marston
Mill
Bridge
Farm
Bunkers Hill Lane
Marston Hall
Farm
Cottage
Farm
CV23
The Hollies
WOLSTON
BSNS PK
HAWTHORNE CL
WILLOW
BROOK RD
MEADOW RD
PRIORY RD
Marston
CV8
ABBOTS WLK
MAIN ST
ELMDENE CL
LARCHFIELDS
SCHOOL ST
St Margaret's
CE Prim Sch
Wolston
New Farm
PADDOCKS CL
DERRY CL
PO
LAMMAS CT
Liby
WARWICK RD
MANOR
EST
BROOK ST
CHESTNUT
GR
JOHN SIMPSON
CL
Cemy
Lammas Hill
DYER'S LA
Lords Hill
Farm
The Thicket
Dingley Osiers
STRETTON RD
Fosse Farm
Rookery Hall
Heath Farm
Heath House
COALPIT LA
B4455
4
77
3
76
2
75
1
74
41
42
43

79
97

Fennis
Fields

Rose's
Spinney

The
Lodge

Barnaby's
Spinney

Bath
Barn

Brown's
Spinney

4

Chapel
Wood

King's
Newnham

Hall
Farm

Fish
Ponds

Siloam

LITTLE LAWFORD LA

Little
Lawford

Newnham Hall

Ford

Manor
House

77

Avon
House

DALTON CL

FITZALAN CL

PO

THE SPINNEY

SAXON WAY

HOLLY DR

SCHOOL ST

GREEN LA

PH

Clayhill Farm

River Avon

3

Church Lawford
CE Fst Sch

Church
Lawford

CHURCH RD

Manor
House

CV23

COVENTRY RD

RUGBY RD

76

COVENTRY RD

Sunnyview
Farm

LIVINGSTONE AVE CL

SOUTH VIEW RD

A428

Hill
Farm

Mount
Pleasant

Long Lawford

2

LIMESTONE DELL LA

Limestone
Hall

Lodge Farm
Cotts

75

Lawford Heath

Fulham
Wood

LAWFORD HEATH LA

Fox Hill
Barn

Lawford
Grange

Lawford Hill
Farm

1

Lawford Lodge
Farm

74

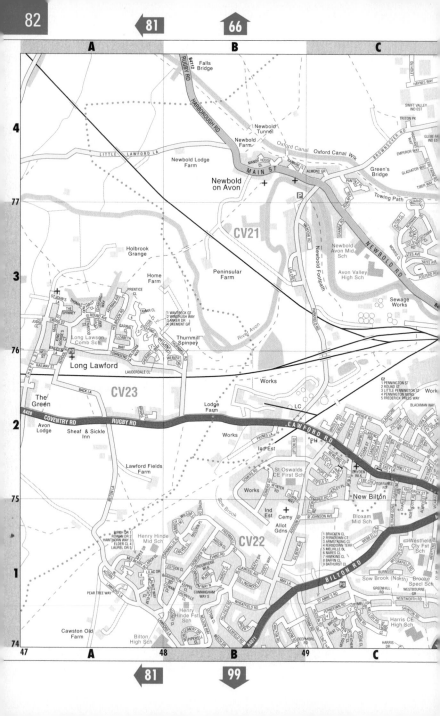

A   B   C

Mill Farm

Dow Bridge

River Avon

LE17

4

BS4114

NEWTON RD

STATION RD

Lilbourne Furze

Lilbourne Gorse

77

BUCKWELL LA

Dunsmore Farm

RUGBY RD

Lilbourne

Cemy

Manor Farm

Dunsmore

Magpie Lodge Farm

Almond Bank

NORTH RD

MANOR LA

3

HILL

LILBOURNE RD

Dunsmore House

MAIN

SOUTH RD

Clifton Hall Farm

Dunsmore Hall Farm

CV23

HILLMORTON LA

SHUTTLEWORTH RD

Clifton upon Dunsmore

Dunsmore Home Farm

Clifton Court Farm

76

Oakridge Farm

Clifton Hall

The Clifton Court Hotel

Masts

HILLMORTON LA

Masts

2

Grange Farm House

The Meadows

Home Farm

Masts

Clifton Brook

75

Double Bridge

Oxford Canal

Masts

Towing Path

Oxford Canal Wlk

CV21

1

Rugby Radio Station

Hillmorton Locks

Normandy Farm

Masts

1 LANDSEER CL
2 REYNOLDS CL

74

53   A   54   B   55   C

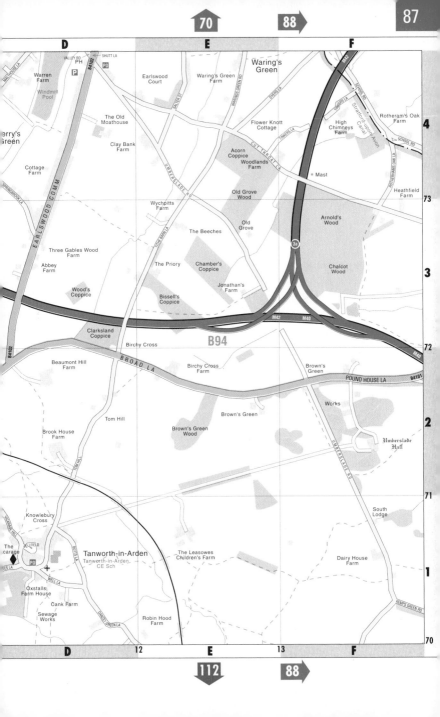

D **E** **F**

VALLEY RD
PH
SHUTT LA
B4102
P
P0
Warren
Farm
Windmill
Pool

Earlswood
Court

Waring's Green
Farm

Waring's
Green

erry's
reen

Cottage
Farm

The Old
Moathouse

Clay Bank
Farm

SALTER ST

WARINGS GREEN RD

DIVERS LA

Flower Knott
Cottage

TILMENS LA

High
Chimneys
Farm

Stratford-upon-Avon Canal

Rotheram's Oak
Farm

NORGES LA

SPOKE RD

SCHOOL RD

M42

4

Acorn
Coppice

Woodlands
Farm

Old Grove
Wood

Mast

Heathfield
Farm

ROTHERHAM OAK LA

73

SPRINGBROOK LA

EARLSWOOD COMM

B4102

Wychpitts
Farm

The Beeches

Old
Grove

Arnold's
Wood

Three Gables Wood
Farm

Abbey
Farm

The Priory

Chamber's
Coppice

Jonathan's
Farm

3a

Chalcot
Wood

3

Wood's
Coppice

Bissell's
Coppice

M42   M40

72

Clarksland
Coppice

B4102

Birchy Cross

B94

M40

Beaumont Hill
Farm

BROAD LA

Birchy Cross
Farm

Brown's
Green

POUND HOUSE LA   B4101

Tom Hill

Brown's Green

Works

Umberslade
Hall

Brook House
Farm

TOM HILL

Brown's Green
Wood

UMBERSLADE RD

2

71

Knowlebury
Cross

BALLFIELD

South
Lodge

The
arage

P0

BUTTS LA

Tanworth-in-Arden

Tanworth-in-Arden
CE Sch

The Leasowes
Children's Farm

Dairy House
Farm

TES LA

BELL LA

Oxstalls
Farm House

Cank Farm

Sewage
Works

CANKS GREEN LA

Robin Hood
Farm

KEMPS GREEN RD

1

70

D **E** **F**

12 **13**

CV8

Arbour Tree Farm

Rosemary Farm

Brookside Grange

Dadkin Farm

Sewage Works

OLDWICH LA E

Nunley Farm

Provi Grou

Chadwick End Farm

Hill Farm

Chadwick End

PO

Priests Park Wood

Heart of England Way

Works

WARWICK RD

CHADWICK LA

DUNGLE LA W

SPARROW COCK LA

NETHERWOOD LA

PH

WHELER CL

FERNHOUSE LA

Bedlam's End

B93

Baddesley Clinton

THISTLEWOOD BK

Priests Park Farm

CHADWICK MEWS

Nunley Pit

Breach Wood

Convent

Warren Farm

RISING LA

Manor Wood

Manor Park Farm

Haywood Farm

Nunnery Coppice

Brome's Park

SCHOOL LA

Cemy

Glendale

Abbey Farm

CV35

MANOR LA

Heart of England Way

Old Keeper's Lodge

HAY WOOD LA

Hay Wood

BIRMINGHAM RD

Wroxall

Wroxall CE Jun & Inf Sch

Wood Corner Farm

Picnic Area

Rowington Coppice

Wroxall Abbey (Sch)

The Park

Gilbert's Coppice

Rowington Green

Lyons Farm

BUSBY LA

Rowington Mill

Quarry Farm

Shrewley Lodge Farm

FIVE WAY

A4141

A4177

CASE LA

PH

ROWINGTON GN

BEECH CL

THE AVENUE

91
75

A   B   C

4

Chase Farm

Engadine House

BIRMINGHAM RD

Camp Farm

Spring Farm

Finham Brook

St Augustine's RC Comb Sch

BEEHIVE HILL

The Spring

Crackle Wood

Little Chase Farm

South Chase Farm

Priors Field Comb Sch

UPPER SPRING LA

73

CHASE LA

East Chase Farm

CLINTON LA

FIELDGATE LA

NEW ST

COVENTRY RD

Pleasance Farm

Castle Green

QUARRY RD

ROSE

AMHERST RD

BROMLEY

BERKELEY

MONMOUTH CL

BRIDGE ST

Sch

MANOR

3

The Pleasance

AVENUE RD
CLINTON AVE

HIGH ST

High House Farm

PURLIEU LA

CASTLE

Kenilworth Castle

Abbey Fields

Finham Brook

RICHARDS CL

CV8

CASTLE RD

72

Quail Cottage

BORROWELL LA

B4104

FORREST RD

ABBEY HILL RD

Liby

HIBBERD CT

Inchford Brook

Grounds Farm

KENILWORTH

BROOKSIDE AVE

MARGETTS CL

TALISMAN

2

Centenary Way

Clinton Comb Sch

Cemy

71

Oaks Farm

St John's Mid Sch

PERCY CRES

DUDLEY RD

Fernhill Farm

ESSEX RD

BEAUCHAMP

Bulkington

Ford

1

Kenilworth Sch Castle Sixth Form Ctr

SOVEREIGN

Roundshill Farm

HURST

70

26   A   27   B   28   C

91
104

A   B   C

Pypes Mill House

Works

CV3

The Rough

Manor Fields

A46

COVENTRY RD

Gospel Oak

Chantry Heath Wood

4

Stoneleigh Grange

River Sowe

73

Kings Wood

ABBEY CL

HALL CL

BIRMINGHAM RD

STONELEIGH CL

Stoneleigh

Stoneleigh Bridge

Chantry Heath Cottages

THE GREEN

WARWICK RD

VICARAGE RD

CHURCH LA

3

B4115

Sowe Mouth

Motslow Hill

Motslowhill Spinney

River Avon

Coach Bridge

CH

Cloud Bridge

Golf Course

72

Gilbert's Spinney

CV8

Centenary Way

Tantara Lodge

Sewage Works

Stoneleigh Deer Park

National Agricultural Ctr

Stoneleigh Park

Starr Bridge

STONELEIGH RD

2

Stareton

Waverle Farm

Park Farm

Ticknell Spinney

Home Farm

71

Hares Parlour

River Avon

A45

Brick Kiln Spinney

1

Decoy Spinney

CV32

LEICESTER LA

Stone House Farm

COVENTRY RD

Furzen Hill Farm

70

Bericote Wood

B4113

Leicester Lane Cotts

A45

32   A   33   B   34   C

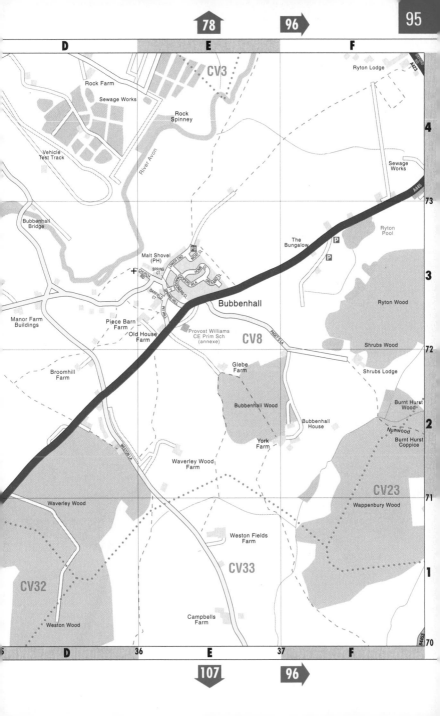

D
E
F

CV3

Ryton Lodge

Rock Farm

Sewage Works

Rock
Spinney

4

A445

Vehicle
Test Track

Sewage
Works

River Avon

73

Bubbenhall
Bridge

Ryton
Pool

The
Bungalow

P

3

Malt Shovel
(PH)

PO

MILL CT

LOWER END

SPRING
CT

HOME CL

CROFT FIELDS

CROCKERS WLK

P

Ryton Wood

CHURCH
RD

GROVE FIELDS CL

ORCHARD CL

DASGELL
CT

Bubbenhall

SPRING LA

Manor Farm
Buildings

Piece Barn
Farm

RYDER'S LA

Provost Williams
CE Prim Sch
(annexe)

CV8

Shrubs Wood

72

Old House
Farm

Glebe
Farm

Shrubs Lodge

Broomhill
Farm

Burnt Hurst
Wood

WESTON LA

Bubbenhall Wood

Bubbenhall
House

Nunwood

Burnt Hurst
Coppice

2

York
Farm

Waverley Wood
Farm

CV23

71

Waverley Wood

Wappenbury Wood

Weston Fields
Farm

1

CV32

CV33

Weston Wood

Campbells
Farm

FOSSE WAY

70

D
36
E
37
F

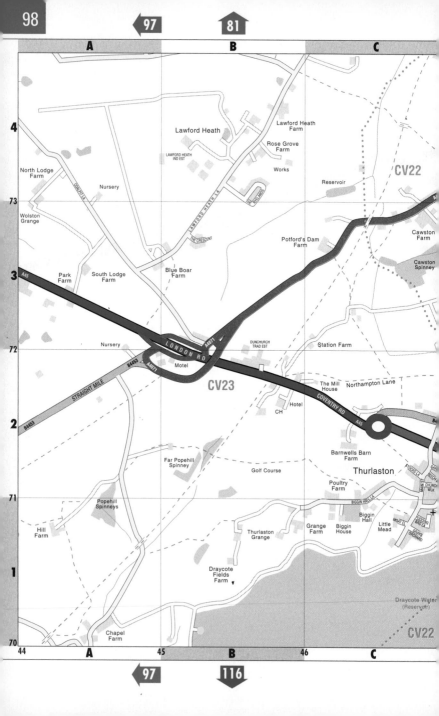

97

81

A

B

C

4

Lawford Heath

Lawford Heath Farm

Rose Grove Farm

LAWFORD HEATH IND EST

Works

CV22

North Lodge Farm

Nursery

Reservoir

73

Wolston Grange

THE VINEYARDS

Cawston Farm

THE CRESCENT

LAWFORD HEATH LA

Potford's Dam Farm

Cawston Spinney

3

A45

Park Farm

South Lodge Farm

Blue Boar Farm

72

Nursery

LONDON RD

A4071

DUNCHURCH TRAD EST

Station Farm

B4453

Motel

A4071

STRAIGHT MILE

CV23

The Mill House

Northampton Lane

COVENTRY RD

Hotel

A45

CH

2

B4453

Barnwells Barn Farm

Thurlaston

Far Popehill Spinney

HICKS LA

BEECH

Golf Course

Poultry Farm

CHURCH WLK

71

Popehill Spinneys

BIGGIN HALL LA

Biggin Hall

Little Mead

MOLE CL

Hill Farm

Thurlaston Grange

Grange Farm

Biggin House

THE ORCHARD

1

Draycote Fields Farm

Draycote Water (Reservoir)

Chapel Farm

CV22

70

44

A

45

B

46

C

97

116

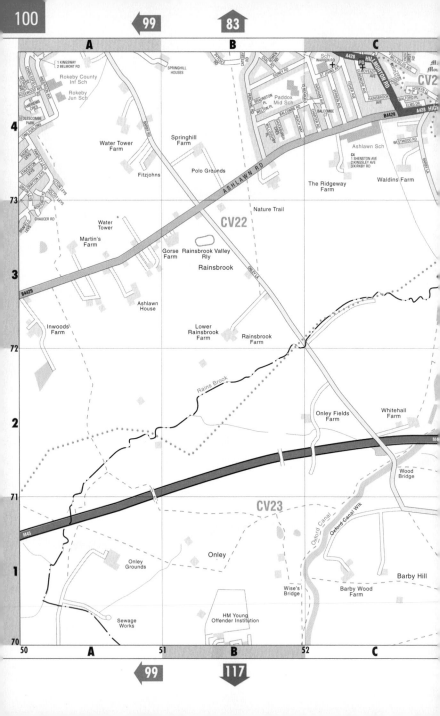

D   E   F

Masts

Dollman Farm

Mast

A428

4

HIGH ST

Hillmorton

CRICK RD

Wharf Bridge

The Old Royal Oak (PH)

Eastfield Farm

73

CV21

Marina

Wharf Farm

Tarry's Bridge

Nortoft Farm

Croft Farm

Barby Nortoft

Brook Farm

Oxford Canal Wlk

Oxford Canal

Nortoft Farm

3

Barby Lodge Farm

Norman's Bridge

RUGBY RD

72

Towing Path

BARBY LA

Rains Brook

CV23

Danetre Farm

Works

2

Kilsby

MAIN RD

Manor Works

ESSEN LA

BARBY RD

71

Ash Tree Farm

Home Farm

M45

CASTLE MOUND

The Arnold Arms (PH)

POSTLE CL 1
COWLEY WAY 2

RECTORY LA

Barby

THE RIDGEWAY

ELKINGTON LA

Hopthorne Farm

STAR CNR

1

D   54   E   55   F

70

114
92

A   B   C

Roundshill Farm

Abattoir

Camp Barn

Woodcote Lodge

Little Woodcote

Bannerhill Farm

Council Farm

ROUNCIL LA

4

Goodrest Cottages

Leek Wootton

CV8

WOODCOTE LA

DANGER AREA

Goodrest Farm

The Lunch

WALTER CL

Mast

Deer Park Farm

Woodcote (County Police HQ)

Stone Edge

WOODCOTE DR

PH

69

Terrace Hill Wood

Centenary Way

THE ELMS

HOME

WARWICK

3

Larch Covert

DANGER AREA

Golf Course

Wootton Court

DANGER AREA

DANGER AREA

CH

Blacklow Hill

68

Deer Park

Wedgnock Old Park

Prospect Farm

CV35

Gaveston's Cross

Wedgnock Rifle Range

Middle Woodloes

2

Blackbrake Plantation

Loes Farm

WOODLOES LA

67

Woodloes Farm

DWARRIS WLK

Woodloes Park

CV34

WARWICK

WARWICK BY-PASS

Nursery

PRIMROSE HILL

YARDLEY

1

Wedgnock Park Farm

WEDGNOCK IND EST

CHANDERS RD

Ind Est

Woodloes Fst & Mid Schs

PO

GIFFARD WAY

ROTHWELL RD

LINTON

Grand Union Canal Wlk

COVENTRY

A4177 BIRMINGHAM RD

A4177

66

Grand-Union-Canal

LADBROKE

26   A   **27**   B   **28**   C

114
108

C1
1 NEWSHOLME CL
2 ADDINGHAM CL
3 WATSON CL
4 RYLSTONE WAY
5 KILDWICK WAY
6 SHELDON GR
7 WEALE GR
8 HETTON CL
9 BUCKDEN CL
10 LEYBURN CL
11 ARNCLIFFE WAY
12 HUDDISDON CL
13 PHILLIPPES RD

CV8

Chesford Bridge

Bericote Wood

Field Barn Farm

Hotel

Cattle Brook

Hotel

New Farm

Blackdown Manor

BERICOTE RD

Tiger's Island

4

Wootton Spinnies

Works

69

Tower House

Leek Wootton

HILL WOOTTON

Hill Wootton

Meadow Cottage

Blackdown

Blackdown Hill

CV35

Sewage Works

Hill Wootton Farm

Hotel

3

New House Farm

KENILWORTH RD

STONELEIGH RD

eek Wootton CE Fst Sch

Woodland Grange

Cranford

The Warwickshire Nuffield

H

68

Gaveston Lodge

River Avon

B4115

A429

Sandy Lane Farm

North Leamington Sch

CV32

2

Church Farm

Old Milverton

SANDY LA

ROYAL LEAMINGTON SPA

Guy's Well

Manor Farm

RANGE ME

Allot Gdns

FARNHURST DR

COVENTRY RD

67

Guy's Cliffe

Guy's Cave

E1
1 LANDFORD RD
2 BIRCHWAY CL
3 EDWARD ST
4 WINSLOW CL
5 GUNNERY TERR
6 CROSS RD
7 PERCY TERR

The Trinity RC Sch

Milverton

1

Patten's Grove

CV34

Weir

THE SHOPPING PREC

MAPLE GR

GREVILLE RD

Cemy

Sch

RUGBY RD

A445

Sch

Sch

CLARENDON AVE

PARADE RD

WARWICK PL

B4099

WARWICK ST

B4087

66

F1
1 MILVERTON CRES
2 MILVERTON CRES W
3 UPPER GROVE ST
4 GROVE ST
5 WATERLOO PL
6 CLARENCE TERR
7 WINDSOR PL
8 BEDFORD ST
9 GUY PL W
10 GUY PL E
11 OXFORD ROW
12 KENILWORTH ST
13 RIPLINGHAM
14 ARLINGTON MEWS
15 BINSWOOD MANS

D | E | F

30 | 31

A · B · C

4

69

3

68

67

66

2

1

STONELEIGH RD
B4113
B4115

Bericote Fields
Farm

West
Hill

WESTHILL RD

Humber
Farm

Cubbington Heath
Farm

LEICESTER LA

West Hill
Farm

Cubbington

RUGBY RD

North
Cubbington
Wood

Tanner's
Barn

Oakdene

COVENTRY RD

THORN STILE CL
WILLOW SHEETS
MEADOW
SPINNEY
THREE
CORNERED
CL

B4453
LILLINGTON RD

PO

Schs

CV32

Our Lady &
St Teresa's
RC Comb Sch

PH
Cubbington CE
Comb Sch

QUEEN ST
PO
HIGH ST

Hill Farm
House

Works

New Manor
Farm

CHAMBERLAIN
CL

ALDWICK CL

CUBBINGTON RD

Sch
DENVILLE RD

Glebe
Farm

Tanner's
Farm

Lillington
Liby
Sch Schs

ROYAL
LEAMINGTON SPA

B4453
A445

Mast
Works

The
Runghills

Ford
Farm
CV33

River Leam

White
House

Campion
Hills
Mast

LEICESTER LA

St Paul's CE
Comb Sch

Golf
Course

Redhouse
Farm

Offchurch
Bury

CH

32 · A · 33 · B · 34 · C

A1
1 STOCKTON GR
2 WHITACRE RD
3 SHUCKBURGH GR
4 HELLIDON CL
5 BROWNLOW ST
6 CHESTNUT SQ
7 GRESHAM PL
8 MARSTON CL
9 LOWER VILLIERS ST
10 LANSDOWNE RD
11 KENNEDY SQ
12 ST PAUL'S SQ
13 LANSDOWNE CRES
14 WILLES RD

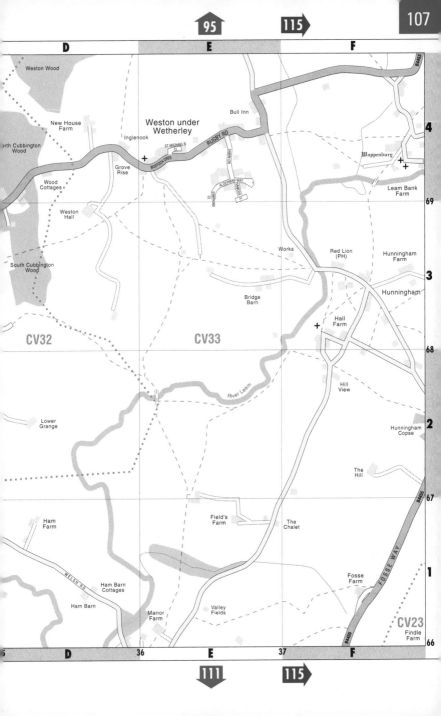

95
115

D E F

Weston Wood

New House Farm

North Cubbington Wood

Inglenook

Weston under Wetherley

Bull Inn

ST MICHAEL'S

RUGBY RD

BOSTOCK GDNS

AUBIN DR

ALDER DR

HARBUR'S CT

SHAWS CT

Wappenbury

Leam Bank Farm

4

Grove Rise

Wood Cottages

Weston Hall

69

South Cubbington Wood

Works

Red Lion (PH)

Hunningham Farm

3

Hunningham

CV32

CV33

Bridge Barn

Hall Farm

68

River Leam

Hill View

Lower Grange

Hunningham Copse

2

The Hill

67

Ham Farm

Field's Farm

The Chalet

B4455

Fosse Farm

1

WELSH RD

FOSSE WAY

Ham Barn Cottages

Ham Barn

Manor Farm

Valley Fields

CV23

Findle Farm

66

D 36 E 37 F

111
115

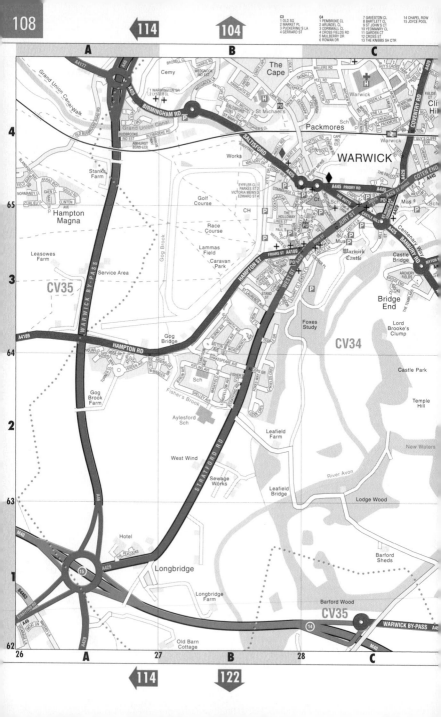

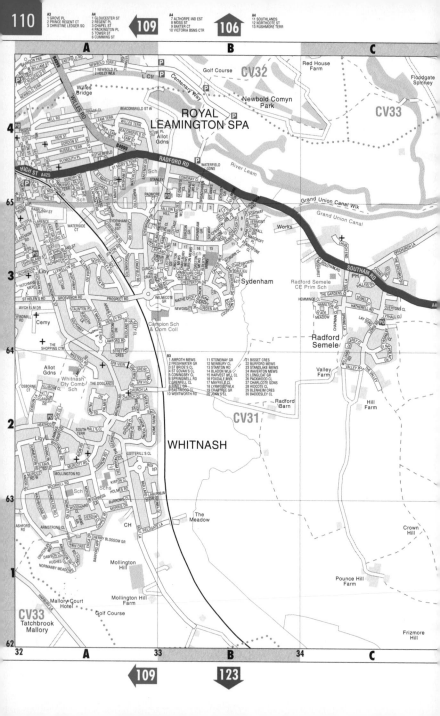

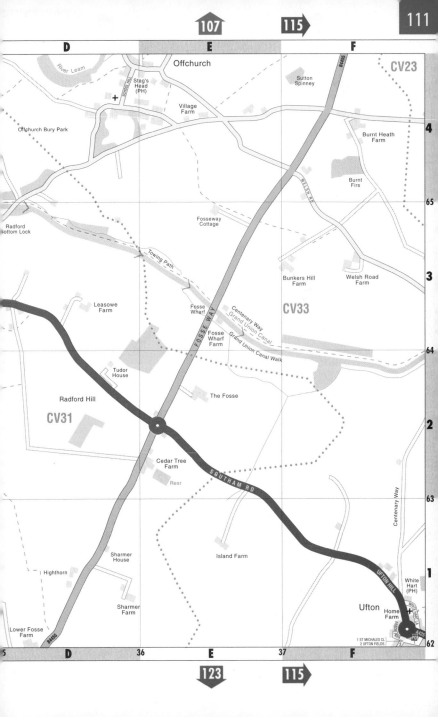

D
E
F

CV23

Offchurch

River Leam

Stag's Head (PH)

Sutton Spinney

Village Farm

Burnt Heath Farm

Offchurch Bury Park

4

Burnt Firs

65

Radford Bottom Lock

Fosseway Cottage

Towing Path

Bunkers Hill Farm

Welsh Road Farm

CV33

3

Leasowe Farm

Fosse Wharf

Centenary Way

Grand Union Canal

Grand Union Canal Walk

FOSSE WAY

Fosse Wharf Farm

64

Tudor House

Radford Hill

The Fosse

CV31

2

Cedar Tree Farm

Resr

SOUTHAM RD

63

Sharmer House

Island Farm

Highthorn

Centenary Way

UFTON HILL

1

White Hart (PH)

Sharmer Farm

Ufton

Home Farm

Lower Fosse Farm

B4455

1 ST MICHAELS CL
2 UFTON FIELDS

62

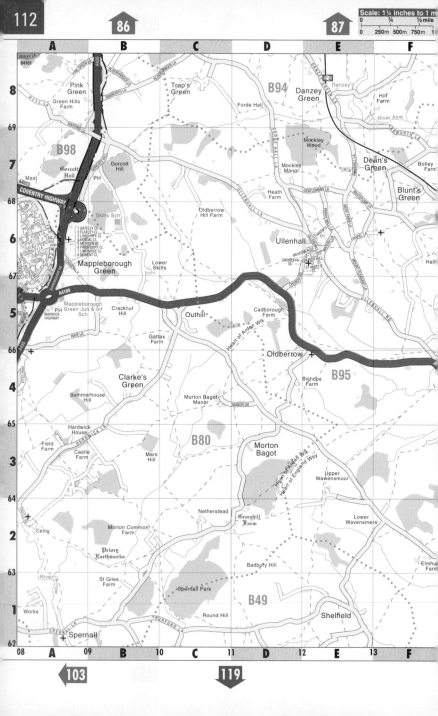

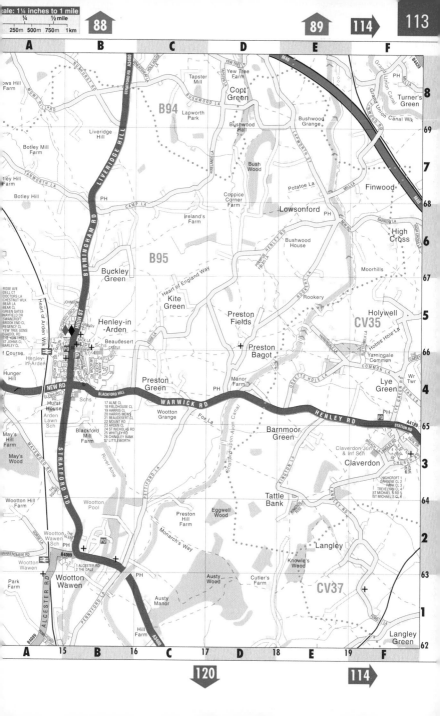

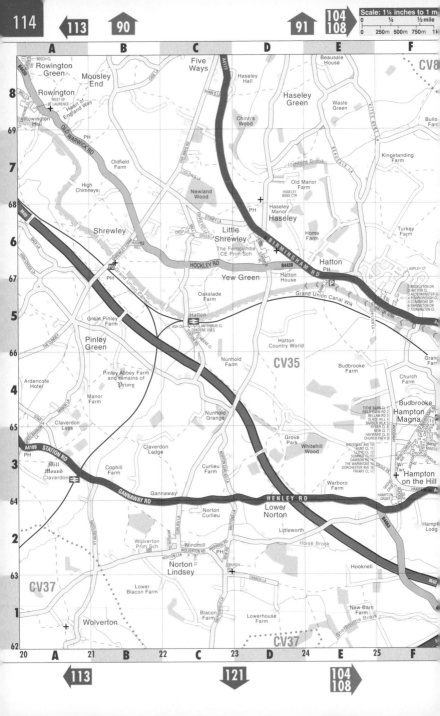

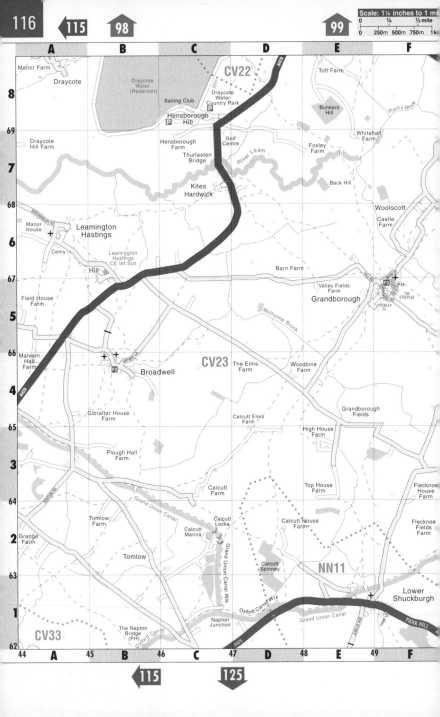

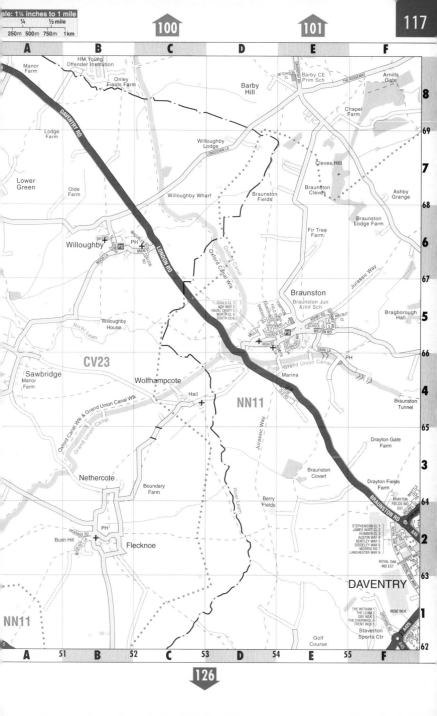

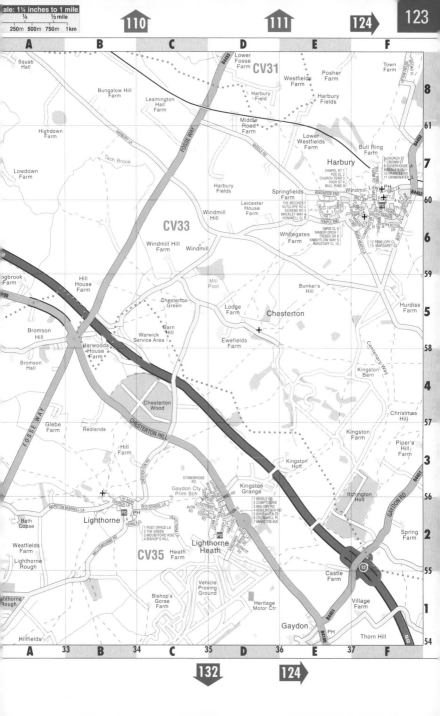

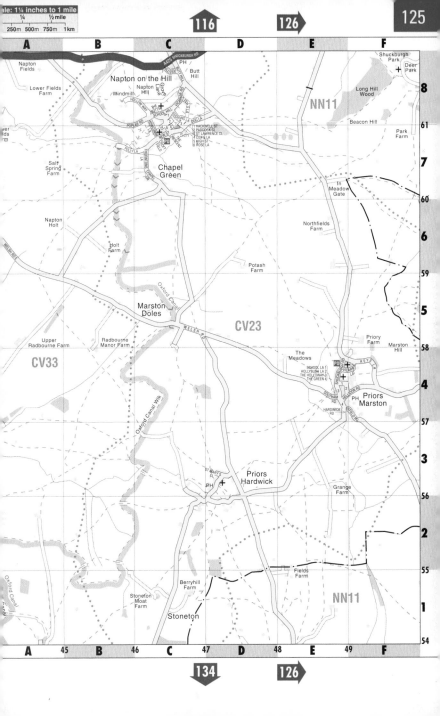

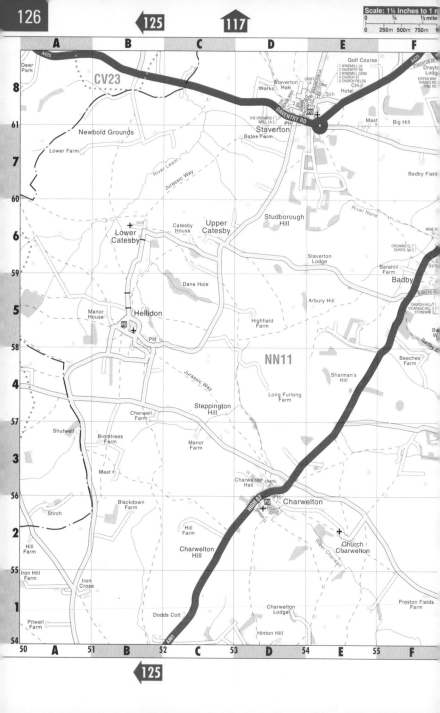

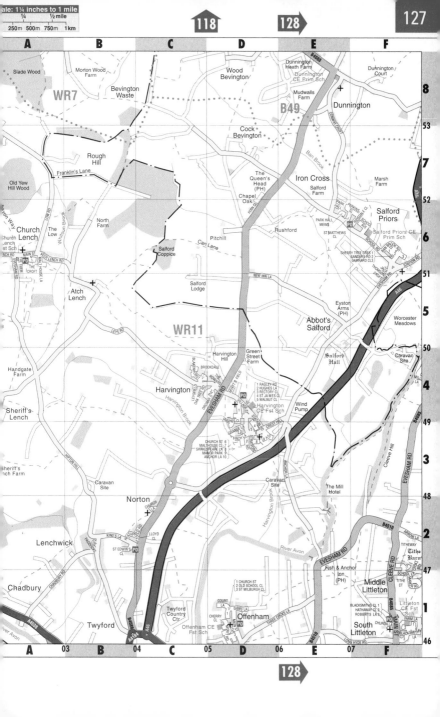

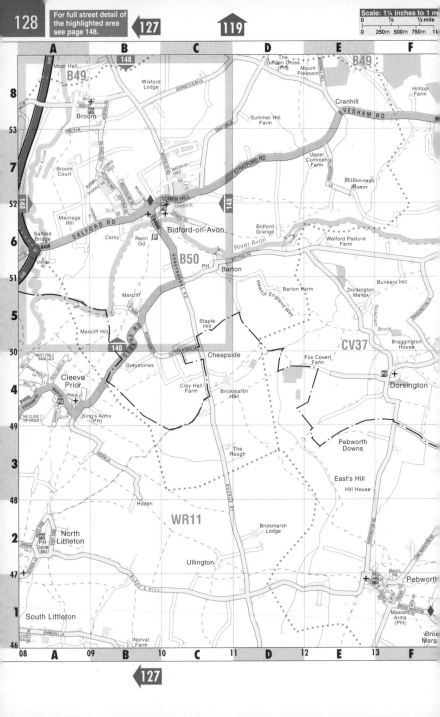

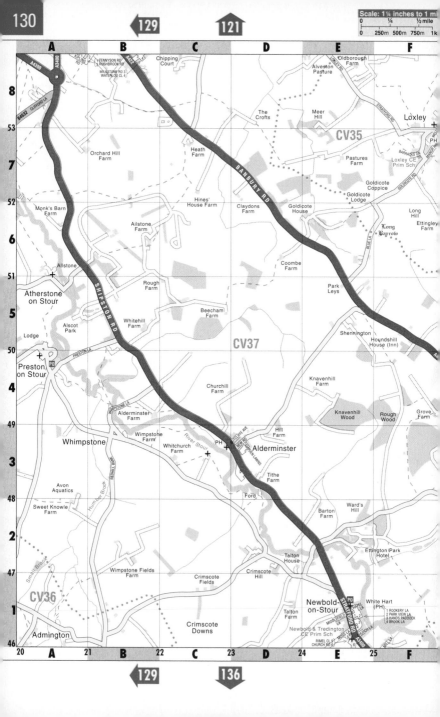

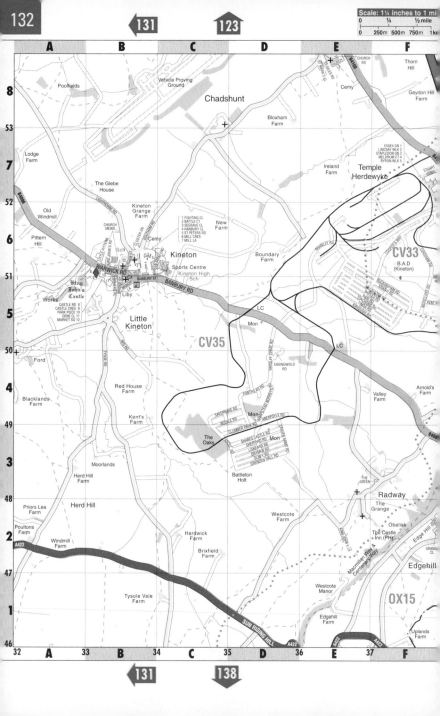

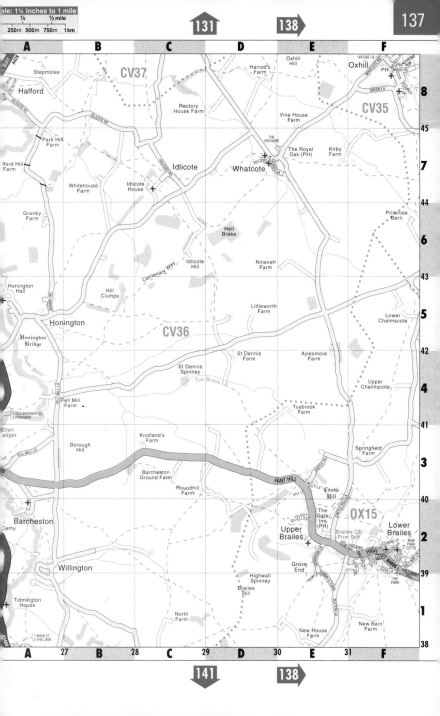

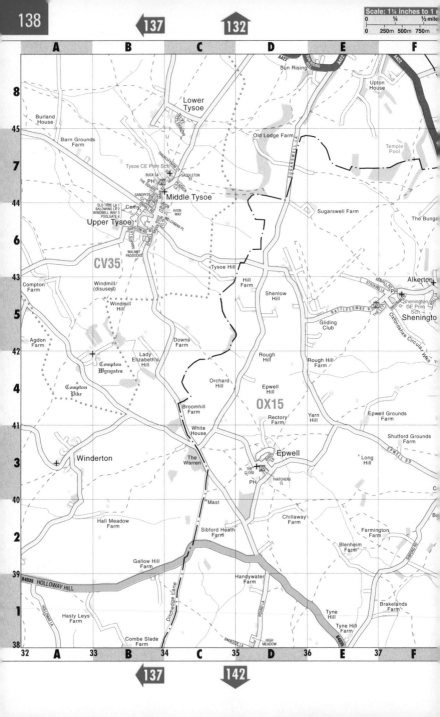

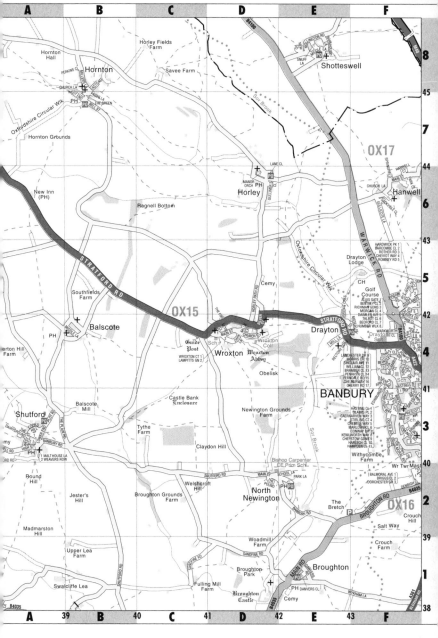

136

A | **B** | **C** | **D** | **E** | **F**

A429

Paddle Brook

High Furze

8

Middle
Ditchford

Ditchford
Frary

37

Neighbrook

Ditchford
Hill

Lower
Farm

7

Knee Brook

BECKET
CL

Farriers Arms
(PH)

STONE BRIDGE

36

CHURCH
VIEW

Todenham

WOLFORD RD

Aston Magna

CHURCH FARM LA

Oldborough
Farm

CV36

6

Aston Hale

35

Mount
Sorrell

Great
Wolford

5

Lower
Lemington

Woodhills
Farm

CARTERS
LEYS
PH

THE
GREEN

PO

Nethercote

GL56

Manor
Farm

Dorn

Lemington
Manor

34

Lemington
Grange

Rectory
Farm

NORTH CIRCULAR
RD

4

6TH AVE

Wolford Wood

Old
Covert

Shatford Brook

5TH AVE

1ST AVE

Moreton-
in-Marsh
District

33

3RD AVE

H

Moreton-
in-Marsh

2ND AVE

Gravels
Coppice

Barton-
on-the-Heath

PO

BOWLING
GREEN CL

P

STATION
RD

DAVIES
RD

ERRINGTON

PARKER WAY

MITCHELL WAY

3

SWAN CL

A44

LONDON RD

7TH AVE

4TH AVE

The Four Shires Stone

A44

EAST ST

SCH

COTSWOLD
BSNG VILLAGE

Musprott

BOURTON RD

STOW RD

HIGH ST

LIBY

EVENLODE
GDNS

WELLINGTON RD

Moreton-in-Marsh

32

BEDFORD

FOSSEWAY PL

1 GRAY'S LA
2 WARNSFORD PL
3 ST GEORGE'S CL

1 ST JAMES CT
2 BOWES LYON CL
3 FOSSEWAY CL
4 SARREY DR

Wells Folly

Kitebrook

Salter's Well/
Farm

2

Fosseway
Farm

Coldicote
Farm

31

Brookend
House

Frogmore Farm

POOL CLOSE COTTS 1
DEERHURST CL 2
BREWERY ROW 3

River Evenlode

Middle Brookend
Farm

1

Grove Farm

Inn

A429

Chastleton
Glebe

Little Compton

PILLE

30

20 | **A** | **21** | **B** | **22** | **C** | **23** | **D** | **24** | **E** | **25** | **F**

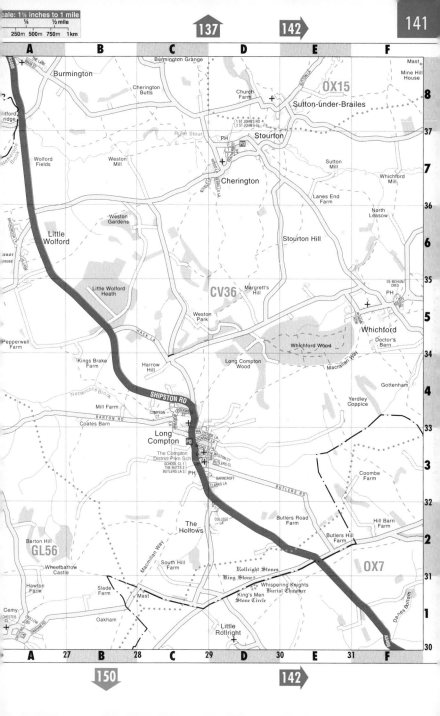

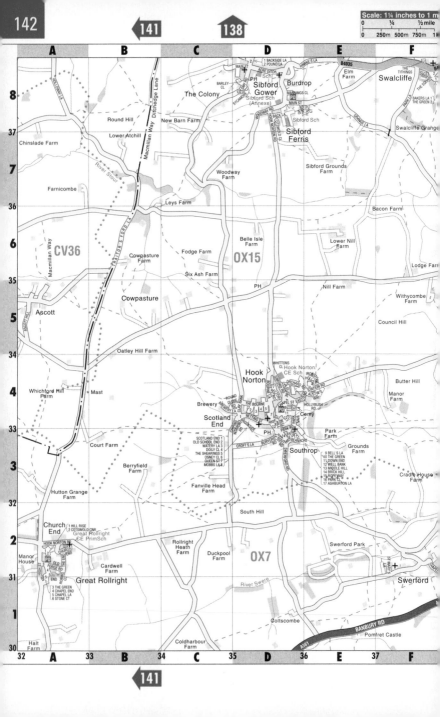

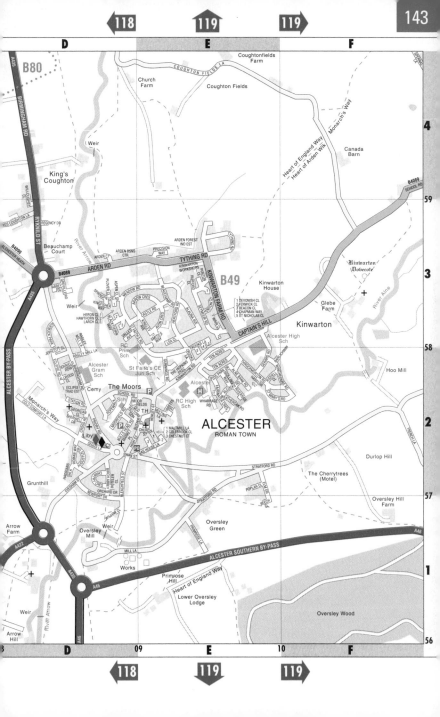

D   E   F

B80

BIRMINGHAM RD

Coughtonfields
Farm

COUGHTON FIELDS LA

Church
Farm

Coughton Fields

4

Weir

Monarch's Way

King's
Coughton

Heart of England Way
Heart of Arden Wlk

Canada
Barn

B4089
SCHOOL RD

59

WIGGS COUGHTON LA

RYKNILD ST

REGENCY DR

B4089

Beauchamp
Court

B4089
ALCESTER HEATH

River Arton

Weir

ARDEN RD

ARDEN RNSS
CTR

ARDEN CL

ARDEN FOREST
IND EST

PRECISION
WAY

TYTHING RD

KINWARTON
WORKSHOPS

B49

KINWARTON FARM RD

Kinwarton
House

Kinwarton
Dovecote

+

River Alne

Glebe
Farm

Kinwarton

3

ALCESTER BY-PASS

Weir

HERON CL
HAWTHORN CL
LARCH CL

MEADOW CRES

CASTLE RD

BEACONS...

1 DEVONISH CL
2 FENWICK CL
3 BEACON CL
4 CHAPMAN WAY
5 ST NICHOLAS CL

CAPTAIN'S HILL

Alcester High
Sch

Hoo Mill

58

RC
Prim
Sch

Alcester
Gram
Sch

St Faith's CE
Jun Sch

TEN ACRES

Alcester

S MARY'S RD

The Moors

P

RC High
Sch

H

WHARRAGE
RD

Monarch's Way

COLDCOMFORT LA

Cemy

MOOR
FIELDS

TH

1 MALTMILL LA
2 COLEBROOK CL
3 CHESTNUT CT

ALCESTER
ROMAN TOWN

2

Liby

CH

CHURCH
ST

SWAN ST

STRATFORD RD

Durlop Hill

Grunthill

EVESHAM ST

ORCHARD DR

NEWPORT DR

STRATFORD RD

POPLAR CL

The Cherrytrees
(Motel)

Oversley Hill
Farm

57

Arrow
Farm

A422

A435

Weir

Oversley
Mill

MILL LA

Works

Oversley
Green

Oversley Hill
Farm

A46

ALCESTER SOUTHERN BY-PASS

1

Weir

A46

Primrose
Hill

Heart of England Way

Lower Oversley
Lodge

Oversley Wood

Arrow
Hill

River Arrow

56

D   09   E   10   F

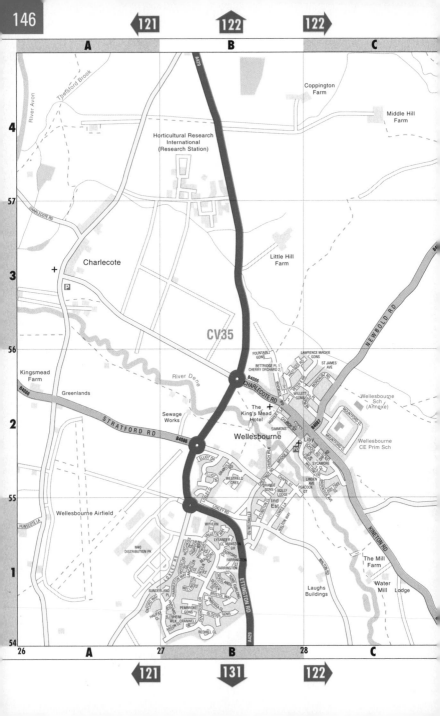

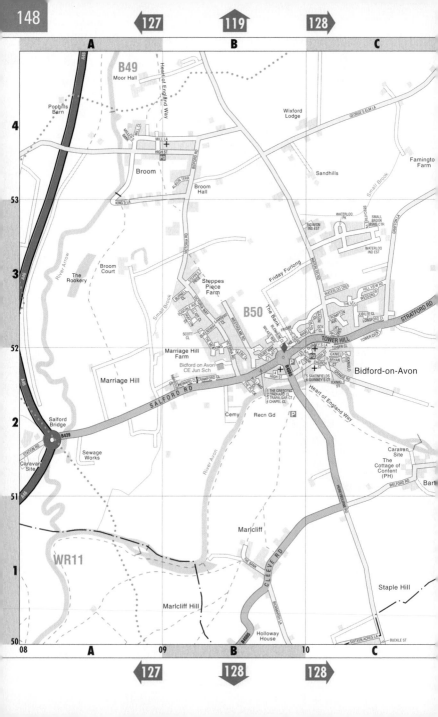

141

A **B** **C**

A44

Hillside

Pump House

Twin Brook Farm

Macmillan Way

4

Hirons Hill Farm

Quarry (dis)

29

Burnt Hill

Cross Hands (PH)

GREENDOWN LA

A436

Springhill Farm

Chastleton Hill

GL56

Hollis Hill Farm

3

Rushy Bottom

Salford

Fisher's Barn

Greathouse Barn

Manor Farm

THE LEYS

28

Fisher's Barn

CHAPEL LA

CROSS LA

RISES LA

LOWER END

A436

Cornwell Holt

OX7

Park Farm

2

Cornwell

Manor Farm

Glebe Farm

+ Cornwell Manor

27

Top Farm

Mill Copse

1

Whitequarry Hill

Swailsford Bridge

Kingham Hill Sch

Kingham Hill Farm

26

26 **A** 27 **B** 28 **C**

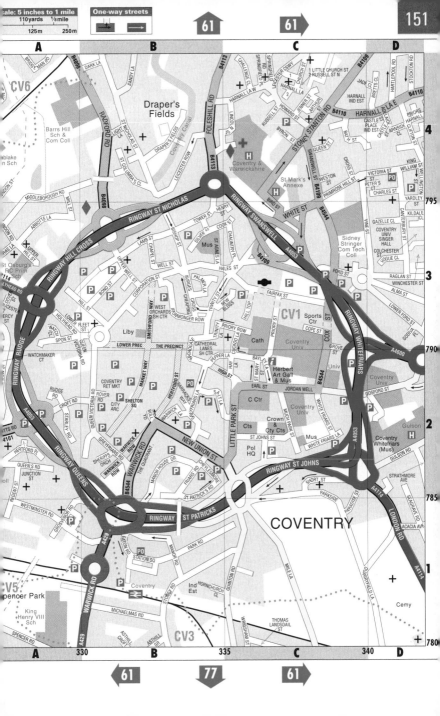

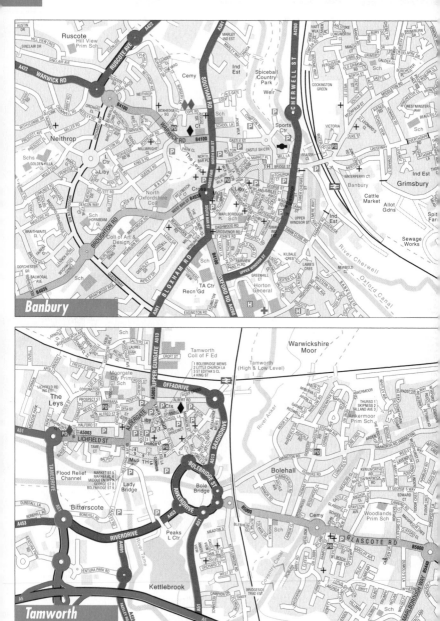

Banbury

Tamworth

eet names are listed alphabetically and show the locality, the Postcode District, the page number and
eference to the square in which the name falls on the map page

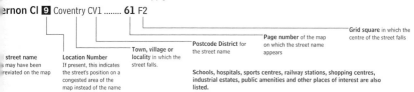

ernon Cl 🖪 Coventry CV1 .... 61 F2

Grid square in which the
centre of the street falls

Page number of the map
on which the street name
appears

Postcode District for
the street name

**Town, village or
locality** in which the
street falls.

Location Number
If present, this indicates
the street's position on a
congested area of the
map instead of the name

street name
may have been
reviated on the map

Schools, hospitals, sports centres, railway stations, shopping centres,
industrial estates, public amenities and other places of interest are also
listed.

Abbreviations used in the index

App Approach	Comm Common	Est Estate	N North	Sq Square
Arc Arcade	Cnr Corner	Gdns Gardens	Orch Orchard	Strs Stairs
Ave Avenue	Cotts Cottages	Gn Green	Par Parade	Stps Steps
Bvd Boulevard	Ct Court	Gr Grove	Pk Park	St Street, Saint
Bldgs Buildings	Ctyd Courtyard	Hts Heights	Pas Passage	Terr Terrace
Bsns Pk Business Park	Cres Crescent	Ho House	Pl Place	Trad Est Trading Estate
Bsns Ctr Business Centre	Dr Drive	Ind Est Industrial Estate	Prec Precinct	Wlk Walk
Bglws Bungalows	Dro Drove	Intc Interchange	Prom Promenade	W West
Cswy Causeway	E East	Junc Junction	Ret Pk Retail Park	Yd Yard
Ctr Centre	Emb Embankment	La Lane	Rd Road	
Cir Circus	Ent Enterprise	Mans Mansions	Rdbt Roundabout	
Cl Close	Espl Esplanade	Mdw Meadows	S South	

Town and village index

...ester 143 E2	Burton Green 75 E2	Grendon 11 E2	Middleton 8 A1	Stockton 147 F4
...erminster 130 D3	Burton Hastings 41 D4	Halford 137 A8	Mile Oak 8 A4	Stoke Golding 21 E3
...sley 60 A4	Butlers Marston 131 F5	Hampton in Arden 57 D4	Minworth 22 B3	Stoneleigh 94 A3
...cote 4 B3	Catherine de Barnes 56 A3	Hampton Lucy 121 F4	Mollington 134 A2	Stratford-upon-Avon 145 D2
...ston 121 D3	Catthorpe 68 B1	Hampton Magna 114 F4	Monks Kirby 53 F1	Stretton on Dunsmore 97 D3
...ey 27 D2	Chadwick End 90 A4	Hanwell 139 F6	Moreton Morrell 122 F2	Stretton on Fosse 136 B1
...ey 51 E2	Charwelton 126 D2	Harborough Magna 66 A2	Moreton-in-Marsh 140 C3	Stretton under Fosse 65 E4
...leby Magna 3 F4	Cherington 141 D7	Harbury 123 E7	Napton 125 C8	Studley 103 F2
...y 26 C1	Chesterton 123 D5	Hartshill 19 D1	Nether Whitacre 25 D3	Sutton Coldfield 13 D2
...Green 49 E3	Cheswick Green 70 C2	Harvington 127 C4	Newbold on Stour 130 E1	Swalcliffe 142 F8
...by 37 F4	Chipping Campden 135 B2	Hatton 114 E6	Newton 68 A1	Swerford 142 F1
...n Cantlow 119 F6	Chipping Warden 134 F3	Henley-in-Arden 113 B5	Newton Regis 2 B2	Tamworth 9 E3
...n Flamville 32 C3	Church Lawford 81 D3	Higham-on-the-Hill 21 D2	North Newington 139 D2	Tanworth-in-Arden 87 D1
...n le Walls 134 F5	Church Lench 127 A6	Hinckley 31 E4	Northend 133 B7	Temple Grafton 119 E2
...n Magna 140 A6	Churchover 67 E3	Hockley Heath 88 B3	Norton 127 C2	Temple Herdewyke 132 C6
...wood Bank 102 C1	Claverdon 113 F3	Hollywood 69 D4	Norton Lindsey 114 C2	Thorpe Constantine 1 C3
...erstone 18 C4	Claybrooke Magna 43 E3	Honiley 91 E3	Nuneaton 29 D3	Thurlaston 98 C2
...trey 3 D1	Claybrooke Parva 43 F2	Honington 137 A5	Offchurch 111 E4	Tidbury Green 69 F2
...n Dassett 133 C5	Claydon 134 B5	Hook Norton 142 D4	Offenham 127 D1	Tiddington 145 F2
...by 126 F5	Cleeve Prior 128 A4	Horley 139 D6	Orton-on-the-Hill 6 C2	Todenham 140 E7
...on 120 A1	Cliff 9 D1	Hornton 139 B8	Oxhill 137 F8	Tredington 136 F6
...inmoor 10 B4	Clifford Chambers 129 F6	Hurley 16 B2	Pailton 66 A4	Twycross 6 C4
...ingbury 115 F7	Clifton upon Dunsmore ... 84 A3	Ilmington 136 B6	Pebworth 128 F1	Tysoe 138 B6
...ingham 33 E3	Coleshill 33 F3	Kenilworth 92 C2	Piccadilly 9 F1	Ufton 111 F1
...ops Itchington 124 B4	Combrook 131 E6	Keresley 48 C2	Pilerton Hersey 131 E3	Ullenhall 112 D6
...ops Tachbrook 122 E7	Cookhill 118 D5	Kilsby 101 F2	Pillerton Priors 131 D2	Upper Boddington 134 D8
...kdown 105 F3	Corley 48 A4	Kineton 132 C6	Polesworth 5 D1	Upper Brailes 137 E2
...erton on Dunsmore 97 F1	Coughton 118 F7	Kingsbury 15 F3	Portway 86 A3	Upper Quinton 129 D1
...nock's Marsh 57 E2	Coventry 61 D2	Knightcote 124 B1	Preston Bagot 113 D5	Wardington 134 F1
...rcote 40 C3	Coventry 151 C3	Knowle 72 A3	Princethorpe 96 C1	Warmington 133 D2
...rdon 79 F3	Cropredy 134 C1	Ladbroke 124 D5	Ryton-on-Dunsmore 79 D1	Warton 5 F2
...anston 117 E5	Cubbington 106 B3	Lapworth 88 C2	Priors Hardwick 125 D3	Warwick 108 C4
...ford 80 B4	Curdworth 23 D3	Lawford Heath 98 B4	Priors Marston 125 F4	Water Orton 23 E2
...klow 64 C2	Darlingscott 136 D5	Lea Marston 24 A4	Radford Semele 110 C3	Welford on Avon 129 A6
...adwell 116 B4	Daventry 117 F1	Leamington Hastings 116 A6	Ratley 133 A2	Wellesbourne 146 B2
...om 148 A4	Dordon 10 C3	Leek Wootton 104 C4	Redditch 102 C4	Weston under Wetherley 107 E4
...ughton 139 E1	Dorridge 71 F2	Lighthorne 123 B2	Rowington 114 A8	Whatcote 137 D7
...kenhall 95 E3	Drayton 139 E4	Lighthorne Heath 123 D2	Rowington Green 90 A1	Whateley 9 F2
...ington 40 A1	Drayton Bassett 8 B3	Lilbourne 84 C3	Royal Leamington Spa 109 F4	Whichford 141 F5
...mington 141 A8	Dunchurch 99 E2	Little Compton 140 F1	Rugby 83 D1	White Stitch 46 B2
	Dunnington 127 E8	Little Packington 45 E3	Ryton-on-Dunsmore 79 D1	Whitnash 110 B2
	Earlswood 70 A1	Littleton 127 F1	Salford 150 C3	Wibtoft 43 D2
	Easenhall 65 F2	Long Compton 141 C3	Salford Priors 127 F6	Wigston Parva 42 C4
	Ebrington 135 E3	Long Itchington 115 F4	Sambourne 118 D8	Willey 54 C3
	Epwell 138 D3	Long Lawford 82 A2	Shawell 68 B3	Willoughby 117 B6
	Ettington 131 B3	Long Marston 129 B3	Sheepy Magna 12 C4	Wilmcote 120 C4
	Farnborough 133 E4	Lower Boddington 134 E7	Shenington 138 F5	Wishaw 14 A1
	Fazeley 8 C3	Lower Brailes 137 F2	Sherbourne 121 F8	Witherley 19 D4
	Fenny Compton 133 D7	Lower Quinton 129 D2	Shilton 51 F3	Withybrook 52 C3
	Fenny Drayton 20 A3	Lower Shuckburgh 116 F1	Shipston-on-Stour 149 E3	Wixford 80 A2
	Fillongley 36 C2	Lowsonford 113 E6	Shotteswell 139 E8	Wolvey 41 E2
	Flecknoe 117 B2	Loxley 130 F8	Shrewley 114 B6	Wood End 10 B1
	Frankton 97 E1	Luddington 129 C7	Shustoke 24 C1	Wootton Wawen 113 B1
	Furnace End 25 F2	Lutterworth 55 F3	Shutford 139 A3	Wroxall 90 C2
	G Wolford 140 F5	Mappleborough Green ... 112 B6	Shuttington 4 C4	Wroxton 139 D4
	Gaydon 123 E1	Marton 115 C7	Sibford Ferris 142 D7	Wythall 69 D2
	Grandborough 116 E5	Maxstoke 35 D3	Sibford Gower 142 D8	
	Great Alne 119 D6	Meriden 46 B1	Snitterfield 121 B6	
	Great Rollright 142 B1	Mickleton 135 C6	Southam 147 D2	
			Staverton 126 D7	

1st Ave GL56 140 B4
2nd Ave GL56 140 B4
3rd Ave GL56 140 B3
4th Ave GL56 140 C3
5th Ave GL56 140 C4
6th Ave GL56 140 B4
7th Ave GL56 140 B3
8th Ave GL56 140 B3
Ab Lench Rd WR11 127 A6
Abberley B77 4 B1
Abberton Gr B90 71 D4
Abberton Way CV4 76 C2
Abbey CE Fst Sch CV11 29 D3
Abbey Cl Alcester B49 143 D3
Southam CV33 147 D2
Abbey Croft B78 5 D1
Abbey End CV8 92 C2
Abbey Est CV2 62 C3
Abbey Gate CV11 29 E2
Abbey Gate Sh Ctr CV11 29 E2
Abbey Gn CV11 29 D3
Abbey Hill CV8 92 C3
Abbey La CV33 147 D2
Abbey Rd CV3 78 A3
Abbey St Nuneaton CV11 29 D3
Rugby CV21 83 E2
Abbey View B78 11 D4
Abbey Way CV3 77 F3
Abbeydale Cl CV3 62 C1
Abbeyfields Dr B80 103 F3
Abbots Cl B93 72 A4
Abbots Farm Jun & Inf Schs CV21 83 F1
Abbots Wlk CV8 80 A2
Abbots Wood Cl B98 112 A6
Abbotsbury Cl CV2 63 D2
Abbotsford Rd CV11 29 F1
Abbotsford Sch CV8 92 C3
Abbotts Gn LE10 31 F3
Abbotts La CV1 151 A3
Abbotts St 15 CV31 109 F4
Abbotts Way CV21 83 F1
Abbotts Wlk CV3 79 E4
Abeles Way CV9 12 B1
Abelia B77 4 A2
Abercorn Rd CV5 60 C1
Aberdeen Cl CV5 60 A3
Aberdeen Rd CV11 29 F1
Aberfoyle Rd CV35 132 D4
Abergavenny Wlk CV3 78 C3
Abingdon Way
Birmingham B35 22 A2
Nuneaton CV11 29 F4
Abu Sultan Rd CV35 132 F5
Acacia Ave CV1 61 F1
Acacia Gr CV21 83 D2
Acacia Rd Nuneaton CV10 28 C3
Royal Leamington Spa CV32 105 E1
Achal Cl CV6 49 F1
Achilles Rd CV6 62 A4
Acorn Cl Bedworth CV12 49 E4
Stoneleigh CV8 94 A4
Acorn Dr CV22 82 A1
Acorn St CV3 78 A4
Acre Cl CV31 110 A2
Acre Ditch OX15 142 D8
Adam Rd CV6 61 F4
Adams St CV21 82 C2
Adare Dr CV3 77 E4
Adcock Dr CV8 93 D3
Addenbrooke Rd CV7 49 D3
Adderley St CV1 61 F2
Addingham Cl 2 CV34 104 C1
Addison Cl CV10 28 A3
Addison Pl B46 23 D2
Addison Rd Coventry CV6 61 D4
Rugby CV22 82 B1
Adelaide Rd CV31 109 F4
Adelaide St CV1 151 D4
Adkins Croft CV7 36 C2
Adkinson Ave CV22 99 E2
Admington La CV36 135 E7
Admiral Gdns CV8 93 E3
Admirals Way CV11 40 C3
Agincourt Rd CV3 77 F4
Ainsbury Rd CV5 76 C4
Ainsdale Cl CV6 50 A2
Aintree Cl Bedworth CV12 39 D2
Coventry CV6 61 F3
Aintree Dr CV32 106 B2
Aintree Rd CV37 144 B1
Airport Way B26 44 B2
Akon Ho CV6 48 C1
Alan Bray Cl LE10 30 B4
Alan Higgs Way CV4 75 E4
Alandale Ave CV5 59 F2
Alauna Ave B49 143 E3
Albany Rd Coventry CV5 61 D1
Stratford-u-A CV37 144 C1
Albany Terr CV32 105 F1
Albert Cl B80 103 F2
Albert Cres CV6 49 D2
Albert Rd Allesley CV5 59 D4
Fazeley B78 9 D4
Albert Sq CV21 83 D2
Albert St Coventry CV1 61 F2
Nuneaton CV10 28 C1
Royal Leamington Spa CV32 105 E1
Rugby CV21 83 D2
Warwick CV34 108 B4
Albion Ind Est CV6 61 E4
Albion St CV8 93 D3
Albion Terr B50 148 B4
Albrighton Wlk CV11 30 A1
Albury Rd B80 103 F2
Alcester By-Pass B49 143 D2
Alcester Gram Sch B49 143 D2
Alcester Heath B49 118 E6
Alcester High Sch B49 143 E3
Alcester Highway B98 102 C4
Alcester Hospl B49 143 E2
Alcester Inf Sch B49 143 D2
Alcester Rd Hollywood B47 69 D4
Portway B48 85 F4
Stratford-u-A CV37 144 B2
Studley B80 103 F2
Wootton Wawen B95 113 A1
Wootton Wawen B95 113 B2
Alcester Southern By-Pass B49 143 E1
Alcocks Rd B49 143 E2
Alcott Cl B93 71 F1
Alcott Hall Prim Sch B37 33 D1
Aldbourne Rd CV1 61 E3
Aldbury Rise CV5 60 B2
Alder Cl B47 69 D3
Alder Dr B37 33 D1
Alder La CV7 74 B3
Alder Meadow Cl CV6 49 D4
Alder Rd CV6 50 A1
Alderbrooke Dr CV11 30 A1
Alderhanger La B98 112 B8
Alderman Callow Sch & Com Coll CV4 76 A3
Alderman Harris Prim Sch CV4 75 F4
Alderman Smith Sch CV10 28 B1
Alderman Way CV33 107 E4
Alderman's Green Ind Est CV2 50 B1
Alderman's Green Prim Sch CV2 50 B2
Alderman's Green Rd CV2 50 A2
Alderminster Gr CV35 114 F5
Alderminster Rd
Coventry CV5 60 A2
Solihull B90 71 E4
Aldermoor Farm Prim Sch CV3 78 A4
Aldermoor La CV3 62 A1
Alderney Cl Bramcote CV11 40 C3
Coventry CV6 49 D1
Alders Dr B98 112 A6
Alders Gr CV34 108 B2
Alders La CV10 28 A4
Alders The CV12 38 C1
Aldersgate B78 15 E4
Alderton Mews CV31 110 B3
Aldrich Ave CV4 59 F1
Aldridge Cl B78 10 C4
Aldridge Rd LE10 31 E3
Aldrin Way CV4 76 B3
Aldwick Cl CV32 106 A2
Alesworth Dr LE10 31 F2
Alex Grierson Cl CV3 78 C4
Alexander Rd CV12 39 E2
Alexandra Ct CV9 18 C4
Alexandra Hospl The B98 103 E3
Alexandra Rd Coventry CV1 61 F2
Royal Leamington Spa CV31 110 A3
Rugby CV21 83 D2
Alexandra St CV11 29 D2
Alfall Rd CV2 62 A3
Alfred Green Cl CV22 83 D1
Alfred Rd CV1 61 F2
Alfred St CV21 82 C1
Alfreda Ave B47 69 D4
Alfreton Cl LE10 31 F3
Alfriston Rd CV3 77 E2
Alice Cl CV12 38 C1
Alice Stevens Sch CV3 78 A3
Alison Sq CV6 50 A2
All Saints CE Fst Sch
Bedworth CV12 39 E1
Nuneaton CV10 29 E1
All Saints CE Mid Sch CV34 105 D1
All Saints CE Prim Sch CV1 61 F1
All Saints Cl CV7 52 C3
All Saints La CV1 61 F2
All Saints Rd Bedworth CV12 38 C1
Warwick CV34 109 D4
All Saints Sq CV12 39 D2
All Souls RC Prim Sch CV5 60 C1
Allan Rd CV6 60 C2
Allans Cl CV23 84 A3
Allans La CV23 84 A3
Allard Way CV3 78 B4
Allen Cl B80 103 F2
Allendale Ave B80 103 F2
Allendale Cres B80 103 F2
Allendale Ct B80 103 F2
Allens Cl CV9 17 E4
Allens Orch OX17 134 F3
Allerton Cl CV2 62 C1
Allesley Croft CV5 60 A4
Allesley Cty Prim Sch CV5 60 A4
Allesley Hall Dr CV5 60 B3
Allesley Hall Prim Sch CV5 60 A2
Allesley Old Rd CV5 60 B2
Allesley Rd CV21 82 C3
Alliance Cl CV11 29 F2
Alliance Way CV2 62 A3
Allibone Cl CV31 110 A2
Allied Cl CV6 49 E1
Allitt Gr CV8 93 D3
Allwood Cl B49 143 D2
Alma Ct CV11 40 C3
Alma St CV1 151 D3
Almond Ave Nuneaton CV10 28 B3
Royal Leamington Spa CV32 105 F2
Almond Cl CV23 101 E1
Almond Gr Rugby CV21 82 C4
Warwick CV34 105 D1
Almond Tree Ave CV2 50 B1
Almshouses B78 8 A1
Alne Bank Rd B49 143 E2
Alne Cl B95 113 B4
Alpha Bsns Pk CV2 50 B1
Alpine Ct CV8 93 D3
Alpine Rise CV3 77 D3
Alspath La CV5 59 F2
Alspath Rd CV7 46 B1
Althorpe Dr B93 71 F2
Althorpe Ind Est 7 CV31 110 A4
Althorpe St CV31 110 A4
Alton Cl CV2 50 B1
Alum Cl CV6 61 E4
Alvecote Pools Nature Reserve B79 4 B4
Alverstone Rd CV2 62 A2
Alveston CE Prim Sch CV37 145 F2
Alveston Gr B93 72 A4
Alveston La CV37 121 D3
Alveston Rd B47 69 D4
Alvin Cl CV3 62 C1
Alvis Gate OX16 139 F4
Alvis Ret Pk CV5 61 D2
Alvis Way NN11 117 F2
Alvis Wlk B36 22 C1
Alwyn B77 9 F4
Alwyn Rd CV22 99 E3
Alwynne Freeman Ct CV7 49 D3
Amber Bsns Village B77 4 A2
Amber Cl B77 4 A2
Amberley Ave CV12 40 B1
Ambien Rd CV9 18 B4
Ambler Gr CV2 62 B2
Ambleside Coventry CV2 50 C1
Rugby CV21 83 E4
Ambleside Way CV11 29 F3
Ambrose Cl CV21 83 E3
Amersham Cl CV5 60 A2
Amherst Rd CV8 92 C3
Amhurst Bsns Ctr CV34 108 A4
Amicombe B77 4 B1
Amington Heath Prim Sch B77 4 A2
Amington Ind Est B77 4 A1
Amington Rd B90 70 A4
Amos Ave CV10 29 D1
Amos Jacques Rd CV12 39 D2
Amroth Mews 1 CV31 110 B3
Amy Cl CV6 49 F2
Anchor La WR11 127 E3
Anchorway Rd CV3 77 D2
Anderson Ave CV22 100 A4
Anderson Dr CV31 110 A1
Anderton Rd Bedworth CV12 38 B1
Coventry CV6 50 A2
Andrew Cl CV13 21 E4
Angela Ave CV2 50 C1
Anglesey Ave B36 33 D3
Anglesey Cl CV5 60 A4
Angless Way CV8 92 C2
Angus Cl Coventry CV5 60 A2
Kenilworth CV8 93 E3
Anker Dr CV23 82 A3
Anker St CV11 29 E2
Anker View B78 11 D4
Ankerside B78 5 D2
Ann Rd B47 69 D2
Anne Cres CV3 78 B3
Annie Osborn Prim Sch CV2 62 B4
Ansell Rd CV34 108 B4
Ansley Comm CV10 28 A4
Ansley La CV7 26 C2
Ansley Rd CV10 27 F2
Anson Cl Rugby CV22 82 B1
Wellesbourne CV35 146 B1
Anson Way CV2 62 C4
Ansty Rd CV2 62 C3
Antelope Gdns CV34 108 B4
Anthony Way CV2 62 B1
Anton Dr B76 22 A3
Antrim Cl CV5 60 A4
Antrobus Cl CV35 114 C5
Apollo Way CV34 109 E3
Appian Cl B77 9 E4
Appian Way B90 70 B2
Apple Gr CV22 82 A1
Apple Pie La CV10 19 D1
Applebee Rd LE10 31 E3
Appleby Cl Banbury OX16 139 F4
Great Alne B49 119 D6
Appleby Gr 9 B90 71 D3
Appleby Hill CV9 3 D2
Applecross Cl CV4 75 F3
Appledore Dr CV5 59 F3
Appletree Cl B91 56 A3
Appletree La Cookhill WR7 118 A3
Cropredy NN11 134 F5
Appletree Rd OX17 134 F3
Approach The CV31 109 F3
Apsley Gr B93 71 F1
Aragon Dr CV34 109 E3
Arbor Way B37 33 E1
Arboretum The CV4 76 B2
Arbour Cl Kenilworth CV8 93 D2
Mickleton GL55 135 B6
Rugby CV22 99 E4
Arbour Tree La B93 89 F4
Arbury Ave Bedworth CV12 39 D2
Coventry CV6 49 F1
Arbury Banks OX17 134 F3
Arbury Cl CV32 106 A2
Arbury Ct B95 113 B5
Arbury Hall Rd B90 70 B4
Arbury Rd CV10 28 B1
Arbury Wlk B76 22 B3
Arch Rd CV2 62 C3
Archer Ave NN11 117 E5
Archer Cl B80 103 E2
Archer Rd CV8 92 C2
Archers Spinney CV21 101 D4
Archery Fields CV34 108 C3
Archery Rd Meriden CV7 46 A1
Royal Leamington Spa CV31 109 F4
Arches Bsns Ctr CV21 83 E3
Arches Ind Est CV21 83 E3
Arches Ind Est The CV5 61 D2
Arches La CV21 83 E3
Arden Ave CV9 18 C4
Arden Bsns Ctr B49 143 D3
Arden Cl Balsall Common CV7 74 A4
Henley-in-A B95 113 B4
Meriden CV7 46 B1
Royal Leamington Spa CV31 110 A3
Rugby CV22 99 E3
Warwick CV34 105 D1
Wilmcote CV37 120 C5
Arden Croft B46 23 F1
Arden Ct B49 143 D3
Arden Dr Dorridge B93 72 A1
Sutton Coldfield, Falcon Lodge B75 13 D3
Arden Forest Est CV10 18 A1
Arden Forest Ind Est B49 143 E3
Arden Forest Inf Sch CV12 40 A2
Arden Hill Inf Sch CV9 18 C4
Arden Lawn Sch B95 113 A4
Arden Leys B94 86 B1
Arden Meads B94 88 B3
Arden Rd Alcester B49 143 D3
Bulkington CV12 40 B1
Dorridge B93 71 F1
Henley-in-A B95 113 B4
Hollywood B47 69 D3
Kenilworth CV8 93 D2
Nuneaton CV11 30 A1
Tamworth B77 9 F3
Arden Sch B93 72 A3
Arden St Atherstone CV9 18 C4
Coventry CV5 76 C4
Stratford-u-A CV37 144 C2
Arden Vale Rd B93 72 A4
Ardens Cl B98 112 A5
Arderne Dr B37 33 D1
Argyle St CV21 83 E2
Argyle Way 5 CV33 122 F8
Argyll St CV2 62 A2
Ariel Way CV22 99 E3
Arkle B77 9 E2
Arkle Dr CV2 62 C4
Arleston Way B90 70 C4
Arley Ind Est CV7 36 C4
Arley La CV10 27 E2
Arley Mews CV32 105 F1
Arlidge Cres CV8 93 E3
Arlington Ave CV32 105 F1
Arlington Mews 14 CV32 105 F1
Arlington Way CV11 29 F1
Arlon Ave CV10 28 B4
Armarna Dr CV5 59 D4
Armfield St CV6 62 A4
Armorial Rd CV3 77 D4
Armour Cl LE10 31 E3
Armscote Rd
Ilmington CV36 136 B6
Tredington CV36 136 E6
Armscott Rd CV2 62 B3
Armson Rd CV7 39 D1
Armstrong Ave CV3 62 A1
Armstrong Cl Rugby CV22 82 C1
Whitnash CV31 110 A1
Armstrong Dr B36 22 C1
Arncliffe Cl CV11 30 A1
Arncliffe Way 11 CV34 104 C1
Arne Rd CV2 63 D3
Arnhem Cnr CV3 78 B3
Arnold Ave CV3 77 E3
Arnold Cl CV22 83 D1
Arnold Lodge Prep Sch CV32 105 F1
Arnold Rd CV13 21 E3
Arnold St CV21 83 D2
Arnolds La B46 34 C2
Arnside Cl CV1 151 D4
Arran Cl CV10 29 D2
Arran Way B36 33 D4
Arras Bvd CV35 108 A4
Arrow Cl B93 72 A3
Arrow Cres B49 143 E3
Arrow End WR11 128 A2
Arrow La WR11 127 F2
Arthingworth Cl CV3 62 C1
Arthur Rd CV37 145 D2
Arthur St Coventry CV1 151 C4
Kenilworth CV8 93 D3
Artillery Rd CV11 40 C3
Arun Way B76 13 D1
Arundel B77 9 E4
Arundel Cl 2 CV34 108 C4
Arundel Pl OX16 139 F3
Arundel Rd Bulkington CV12 40 B2
Coventry CV3 77 E3
Asbury Rd CV7 74 A3
Ascot Cl Bedworth CV12 39 D2
Coventry CV3 78 B3
Stratford-u-A CV37 144 B1
Ascot Rd CV35 132 D3
Ascot Ride CV32 106 B2
Ascote Way CV33 147 E2
Ascott Hill CV36 142 A5
Ascott Rd CV36 141 F5
Asfare Bsns Pk LE10 31 F1
Ash Cl CV35 114 C5
Ash Ct CV22 99 F4
Ash Dr Hartshill CV10 28 A4
Kenilworth CV8 93 D2
Ash Gr Arley CV7 26 C1
Ash Green CV7 49 E4
Kingsbury B78 15 E4
Southam CV33 147 D3
Stratford-u-A CV37 144 C3
Tamworth B77 9 F3
Ash Green La CV7 49 E3
Ash Green Sch CV7 49 E3
Ash La CV37 120 E7
Ash Priors Cl CV4 60 A1
Ash Tree Ave CV4 60 A1
Ash Tree Cl CV35 146 C2
Ash Tree Gr CV7 51 F3
Ash Way NN11 117 D5
Ashborough Dr B91 71 E4
Ashbourne Way B90 70 C4
Ashbridge Rd CV5 60 B2
Ashbrook Cres B91 71 E4
Ashbrook Rise CV10 19 D1
Ashburton Cl LE10 32 A3
Ashburton La OX15 142 D3
Ashburton Rd CV2 62 C4
Ashby Cl CV3 78 C4
Ashby Ct CV11 29 E2
Ashby Rd NN11 117 E5
Ashcombe Dr CV4 59 F2
Ashcroft Cl CV2 63 D4
Ashcroft Way CV2 63 D4
Ashdale Cl CV3 79 F4
Ashdene Gdns CV8 93 D2
Ashdown Cl CV3 78 B4
Ashdown Dr CV10 28 C1
Ashe Rd CV10 28 A2
Ashfield Ave CV4 59 E1
Ashfield Rd CV8 93 D2
Ashford Dr CV12 39 D2
Ashford Gdns CV31 109 F2
Ashford La B94 88 A4
Ashford Rd Hinckley LE10 31 D4
Whitnash CV31 109 F1
Ashfurlong Cl CV7 74 A3
Ashington Gr CV3 78 A3
Ashington Rd CV12 38 B1
Ashlawn Rd CV22 100 B4
Ashlawn Sch CV22 100 C4
Ashlea B78 10 C3
Ashleigh Cl CV23 101 E1
Ashleigh Dr Nuneaton CV11 29 F1
Tamworth B77 9 F4
Ashley Cres CV34 109 D3
Ashman Ave CV23 82 A3
Ashmore Rd CV6 61 D2
Ashmores Cl B97 102 B3
Ashorne Cl Coventry CV2 50 B1
Redditch B98 103 E4
Ashorne Hill Coll CV33 122 E5
Ashow Cl CV8 93 D2
Ashridge Cl CV11 39 F4
Ashstead Cl B76 22 A3
Ashwood Ave CV6 60 C3
Ashwood Dr B37 33 E2
Ashwood Rd CV10 28 C3
Aspbury Croft B36 22 B1
Aspen Cl Alcester B49 143 D3
Coventry CV4 59 E1
Aspen Dr B37 44 B4
Aspen Gr B47 69 D3
Aspens The B78 15 E4
Asplen Ct CV8 93 E2
Aspley Ct CV35 114 F6
Aspley Heath B94 86 B1
Aspley Heath La B94 86 B1
Asra Cl CV2 61 F2
Assheton Cl CV22 99 E4
Aster Cl Hinckley LE10 31 F3
Nuneaton CV11 30 A1
Aster Way LE10 31 E3
Asthill Croft CV3 77 E4
Asthill Gr CV3 77 E4
Astley Ave CV6 49 F1
Astley Cl Redditch B98 103 D4
Royal Leamington Spa CV32 105 E1
Astley La Bedworth CV12 38 B2
Fillongley CV7 37 D2
Nuneaton CV10 28 A1
Astley Wlk CV33 133 A7
Astley's Pl CV21 101 D4
Aston Cantlow Rd CV37 120 B5
Aston Flamville Rd LE10 32 B4
Aston Hill CV37 120 B5
Aston Ind Est CV12 39 E1
Aston La LE10 32 A3
Aston Pk Ind Est CV11 29 D3
Aston Rd
Chipping Campden GL55 135 B3
Coventry CV5 60 C1
Nuneaton CV11 29 D3
Astwood Bank Fst Sch B96 102 C1
Astwood La B96 102 B1
Atch Lench Rd WR11 127 A6
Atcheson Cl B80 103 F2
Athena Dr CV34 109 F3
Athena Gdns CV6 50 A1
Atherston Pl CV4 76 B3
Atherstone Coll CV9 18 C4
Atherstone La CV9 16 C3
Atherstone Rd
Appleby Magna DE12 3 F3
Fenny Drayton CV13 20 A3
Furnace End B46 25 F3
Hartshill CV10 19 D1
Hurley CV9 16 B2
Sheepy Magna CV9 12 B2
Twycross DE12 3 F3

Atherstone St B78 9 D4
Atherstone Sta CV9 18 B4
Athol Rd CV2 63 D3
Atholl Cres CV10 28 C1
Atkins Way LE10 31 F4
Atterton La CV9 19 E4
Attleborough Fields Ind Est CV11 29 F2
Attleborough Fst Sch CV11 29 F2
Attleborough La B46 23 D1
Attleborough Rd CV11 29 E2
Attoxhall Rd CV2 62 C2
Attwood Cres CV2 62 B4
Auckland Dr B36 33 D4
Auden Cl CV10 27 F2
Augusta Pl CV32 109 F4
Augustine Ave B80 103 E2
Augustus Cl B46 23 F1
Augustus Dr B49 143 D2
Augustus Rd CV1 61 F2
Austcliff Cl B97 102 B3
Austcliff Dr B91 71 E4
Austen Cl CV10 27 F3
Austen Ct CV32 106 C3
Austin Cl CV9 18 B4
Austin Croft B36 22 C1
Austin Dr Banbury OX16 139 F4
Coventry CV6 62 A4
Austin Edwards Dr 2 CV34 109 D4
Austin Way NN11 117 F2
Austin's Way OX15 142 E4
Austrey CE Prim Sch CV9 3 D1
Austrey Cl B93 72 A3
Austrey La Austrey B79 3 D3
Newton Regis B79 2 C2
Austrey Rd Appleby Magna CV9 3 E3
Warton B79 5 F3
Austwick Cl CV34 104 C1
Auxerre Ave B98 103 D4
Avebury Cl CV11 29 F1
Aventine Way CV21 82 C4
Avenue Cl B93 72 A2
Avenue Farm CV37 144 C3
Avenue Field Ind Est CV37 144 C2
Avenue Rd
Astwood Bank B96 102 C1
Dorridge B93 72 A2
Kenilworth CV8 92 B3
Nuneaton CV11 29 E1
Royal Leamington Spa CV31 109 F4
Rugby CV21 82 C2
Stratford-u-A CV37 145 D2
Avenue The Coventry CV3 78 A3
Rowington Green CV35 90 A1
Stratford-u-A CV37 144 B3
Aviemore Cl CV10 29 D1
Avill B77 10 A3
Avocet Cl CV2 50 A2
Avon B77 10 A3
Avon Aquatics CV37 130 A3
Avon Ave CV35 138 B6
Avon Carrow CV33 133 D4
Avon Cl Barford CV35 122 B8
Bulkington CV12 40 A3
Ettington CV37 131 B3
Avon Cres Alcester B49 143 E3
Stratford-u-A CV37 145 E1
Avon Ct CV8 92 C3
Avon Dassett Rd CV33 133 D6
Avon Ind Est Rugby CV21 83 E3
Stratford-u-A CV37 144 C2
Avon Rd Kenilworth CV8 92 C2
Lighthorne Heath CV35 123 D2
Whitnash CV31 110 A2
Avon St Clifton u D CV21 83 F2
Coventry CV2 62 A3
Rugby CV21 83 D2
Warwick CV34 109 D4
Avon Valley High Sch CV21 82 C3
Avon Way CV35 138 B6
Avonbank Cl B97 102 B3
Avonbank Dr CV37 129 E8
Avonbank Paddocks CV37 145 D1
Avonbrook Cl CV37 144 B2
Avondale Rd Brandon CV8 79 F3
Coventry CV5 77 D4
Royal Leamington Spa CV32 106 B2
Avonfields Cl CV37 121 D3
Avonlea Rise CV32 105 E1
Avonmeadow Cl CV37 144 C1
Avonmere CV21 82 C4
Avonside CV37 145 D1
Awson St CV6 61 F3
Axholme Rd CV2 62 C2
Axminster Cl CV11 29 F3
Aylesbury Cl B94 88 B3
Aylesbury Rd B94 88 B4
Aylesford Dr B37 44 A4
Aylesford Sch CV34 108 B2
Aylesford St Coventry CV1 61 F2
Royal Leamington Spa CV31 110 A3
Aylstone Cl CV37 129 D2
Aynho Cl CV5 60 A2
Aysgarth Cl CV11 30 A1
Azalea Cl LE10 31 F3
Azalea Dr LE10 31 F3
Azalea Wlk LE10 31 F3

Babbacombe Rd CV3 77 E3
Bablake Cl CV6 60 C4
Bablake Jun Sch CV1 151 A4
Bablake Sch CV1 61 D2
Bachelors Bench CV9 18 B4
Back Ends GL55 135 B2
Back La Birdingbury CV23 115 F7
Claverdon CV35 114 A6
Claybrooke Magna LE17 43 F3
Back La continued
Cleeve Prior WR11 128 A4
Harborough Magna CV23 66 A2
Henley-in-A B95 113 B5
Long Compton CV36 141 D3
Long Lawford CV23 82 A2
Lower Quinton CV37 129 E3
Meriden CV7 58 C3
Mickleton GL55 135 B6
Pebworth CV37 128 E1
Pillerton Priors CV35 131 D2
Shustoke B46 24 C1
Sibford Ferris OX15 142 D8
Warwick CV34 108 C3
Back St Ilmington CV36 136 B6
Nuneaton CV11 29 E3
Backside La OX15 142 D8
Badbury Cl B80 103 E2
Badby Cty Prim Sch NN11 126 F6
Badby Leys CV22 100 A4
Baddesley Cl 30 CV31 110 B3
Baddesley Clinton B93 89 F2
Baddesley Ensor CE Inf Sch CV9 11 E1
Baddesley Ensor Jun Sch CV9 11 E1
Badger Cl B90 70 B2
Badger Rd CV3 78 B4
Badgers Cres CV36 149 F4
Badgers Farm La CV35 138 C8
Badgers Field GL55 135 B2
Baffin Cl CV22 82 C1
Baginton Fields Sch CV3 78 A2
Baginton Rd Birmingham B35 22 A2
Coventry CV3 77 E3
Bagshaw Cl CV8 79 D1
Bailey Ave B77 9 F3
Bailey's La CV23 82 A2
Bakehouse La
Chadwick End B93 90 A3
Nether Whitacre B46 24 C3
Rugby CV21 82 C2
Shotteswell OX17 139 E8
Baker Ave
Royal Leamington Spa CV31 109 F3
Stratford-u-A CV37 144 B2
Baker St CV6 50 A3
Baker's Hill GL55 135 C5
Bakers Croft CV9 11 E1
Bakers Ct CV9 18 B4
Bakers La Coventry CV5 60 C1
Knowle B93 72 B1
Swalcliffe OX15 142 F8
Bakers Wlk B77 9 F3
Bakewell Cl CV3 78 C4
Balcombe Ct CV22 100 C4
Balcombe Rd CV22 100 B4
Baldwin Croft CV6 50 A1
Baldwins La CV35 138 B6
Balfour Cl LE10 31 F4
Ballantine Rd CV6 61 D3
Ballard Wlk B37 33 D3
Ballards Cl GL55 135 B6
Ballards La CV36 136 B6
Ballingham Cl CV4 60 A1
Balliol Rd Coventry CV2 62 B2
Hinckley LE10 31 F3
Balmoral Ave Banbury OX16 139 F3
Banbury, Crouch Hill OX16 139 F2
Balmoral Cl CV2 62 C3
Balmoral Rd B36 33 D4
Balmoral Way CV32 106 B3
Balsall Common Prim Sch CV7 74 A3
Balsall St B93, CV7 73 E4
Balsall St E CV7 74 A3
Bamburgh B77 9 E4
Bamburgh Gr CV32 105 F2
Ban Brook Rd WR11 127 F6
Banbury Rd
Bishops Tachbrook CV33 122 E7
Chipping Warden OX17 134 F3
Ettington CV37 131 B3
Kineton CV35 132 C5
Ladbroke CV33 124 D4
Lower Boddington NN11 134 E7
North Newington OX15 139 E2
Shutford OX15 139 A3
Southam CV33 147 D1
Southam CV33 147 D2
Stratford-u-A CV37 130 D7
Swerford OX7 142 E1
Warmington OX17 133 D1
Warwick CV34 109 D2
Banbury St CV35 132 B5
Bancroft Pl CV37 145 D2
Bangley La Drayton Bassett B78 7 F3
Mile Oak B78 8 A4
Banister Way CV36 149 F3
Bank Cl CV35 131 F5
Bank Croft CV31 110 B3
Bank Rd CV9 18 C4
Bank St CV21 83 D2
Bank The Bidford-on-A B50 148 B2
Bidford-on-A, Marlcliff B50 148 B1
Lighthorne CV35 123 B2
Bank View CV35 131 F5
Bankfield Dr CV32 105 E1
Banks Rd CV6 61 D3
Bankside Cl CV3 78 A3
Banky Mdw LE10 32 A4
Banner La CV4 59 E1
Banners La B97 102 C3
Bantam Gr CV6 49 D2
Bantock Rd CV4 59 F1
Barber Wlk CV35 114 F4
Barbers La B91 56 B3
Barbican Rise CV2 62 C1
Barbourne Cl B91 71 D4
Barbridge Cl CV12 40 B1
Barbridge Rd CV12 40 B2
Barby CE Prim Sch CV23 117 E8
Barby La CV22 101 D2
Barby Rd Kilsby CV23 101 F2
Rugby CV22 100 A4
Barcheston Rd B93 72 A2
Barcombe Cl OX16 139 F5
Bardon View Rd B78 11 D4
Barford App CV31 110 A1
Barford Cl CV3 78 B4
Barford Rd CV8 93 D2
Barham Cl 7 B90 71 D3
Bari Rd CV35 132 E5
Barker's Butts La CV6 61 D2
Barkers' Butts La CV1 61 D3
Barkers La B47 69 D1
Barkus Cl CV33 147 E2
Barle Gr B36 33 D4
Barley Cl Henley-In-A B95 113 B4
Rugby CV21 101 D4
Sibford Gower OX15 142 D8
Barley Lea The CV3 78 B4
Barlichway B49 143 E2
Barlow Rd CV2 50 B1
Barn Cl
Clifford Chambers CV37 129 F7
Dordon B78 10 C3
Whitnash CV31 110 A2
Barn End Rd B79 5 F2
Barn La CV23 96 B1
Barnack Ave CV3 77 D3
Barnack Dr CV34 104 C1
Barnacle La CV12 40 B1
Barnard Cl Birmingham B37 33 E1
Royal Leamington Spa CV32 106 B2
Barnbrook Rd B93 72 A4
Barncroft CV36 141 C3
Barne Cl CV11 40 A4
Barnfield Ave CV5 60 A3
Barnsley Cl CV9 18 B4
Barnstaple Cl CV5 59 F3
Barnwell Cl CV22 99 E2
Baron's Croft CV3 77 F4
Baron's Field Rd CV3 77 F4
Barons Croft CV10 28 B2
Barpool Rd CV10 28 C2
Barr La Brinklow CV23 64 C2
Higham-on-t-H CV13 21 D2
Barra Croft B35 22 A2
Barrack St CV34 108 C4
Barracks Gn CV35 130 F7
Barracks La CV35 91 E1
Barracks Way CV1 151 B2
Barras Gn CV2 62 A2
Barras La CV1 61 D2
Barretts La CV7 74 B3
Barrington Rd CV22 82 B1
Barrow Cl CV2 63 D3
Barrow Rd CV8 92 C2
Barrowfield La CV8 92 C2
Barrs Hill Sch & Com Coll CV1 151 A4
Barsby Cl CV9 18 B4
Barston Cl CV6 50 A1
Barston La
Balsall Common CV7 73 E4
Barston B92 57 E1
Catherine de B B91 56 A1
Hampton in A B92 56 B2
Bartleet Rd B98 103 F4
Bartlett Cl Coventry CV6 49 F1
8 Warwick CV34 108 C4
Barton Cres CV31 110 B3
Barton Dr B93 72 A2
Barton Fields CV37 129 A6
Barton Rd Bedworth CV12 39 D2
Coventry CV6 49 F1
Long Compton CV36 141 B4
Nuneaton CV10 29 E1
Rugby CV22 99 E4
Barton's Mdw CV2 62 A3
Barwell Cl Dorridge B93 71 F2
Royal Leamington Spa CV32 105 F2
Basant Cl CV34 109 D4
Bascote Rd CV33 115 C3
Bascote Rise CV33 147 D3
Basford Brook Dr CV6 49 F2
Basildon Wlk 3 CV2 63 D4
Basin Bridge La CV13 21 E2
Basley Way CV6 49 E2
Bassett Rd CV6 61 D3
Bastyan Ave CV37 129 D2
Bateman Rd B46 23 F1
Bateman's Acre S 1 CV6 61 D2
Bates Cl B76 22 A4
Bates La B94 86 C1
Bates Rd CV5 76 C4
Bath Pl 14 CV31 109 F4
Bath Rd Atherstone CV9 18 C4
Nuneaton CV11 29 E3
Bath St Coventry CV1 151 C4
Royal Leamington Spa CV31 109 F4
Rugby CV21 83 D2
Bathurst Rd CV6 61 D3
Bathway Rd CV3 77 D2
Batsford Cl B98 103 D3
Batsford Rd CV6 60 C2
Battle Ct CV35 132 B6
Baulk La CV7 58 B1
Bawnmore Ct CV22 99 E4
Bawnmore Cty Fst Sch CV22 99 F4
Bawnmore Pk CV22 99 F4
Bawnmore Rd CV22 99 E4
Baxter Cl CV4 60 A1
Baxter Ct 9 CV31 110 A4
Baxters Gn B90 70 A4
Baxters Rd B90 70 A4
Bay Tree Cl CV2 50 B1
Bayley La CV1 151 C2
Bayton Rd CV7 50 A4
Bayton Road Ind Est CV7 50 A4
Bayton Way CV7 50 B4
Baywell Cl 8 B90 71 D4
Bazzard La CV11 40 C3
Beacon Cl B49 143 E3
Beacon Rd CV6 49 E2
Beaconsfield Ave CV22 83 D1
Beaconsfield Ct CV11 29 E3
Beaconsfield Rd CV2 62 A1
Beaconsfield St CV31 110 A4
Beaconsfield St W CV31 110 A4
Beake Ave CV6 61 D4
Beale Cl B35 22 A1
Beamish Cl CV2 63 D3
Beanacre Rd OX15 142 D3
Beanfield Ave CV3 76 C2
Bear Cl B95 113 B5
Bear La B95 113 A5
Bear La Cl B78 5 D1
Bearcroft Gdns GL55 135 C6
Bearley Croft B90 70 B4
Bearley Cty Jun & Inf Sch CV37 120 D7
Bearley Gn CV37 120 E7
Bearley Halt B95 120 D7
Bearley Rd
Aston Cantlow B95 120 A7
Snitterfield CV37 121 A7
Beatty Dr CV22 82 B1
Beauchamp Ave CV32 105 F1
Beauchamp Cl
1 Birmingham B37 33 D1
Sutton Coldfield B76 22 A4
Beauchamp Gdns CV34 109 D3
Beauchamp Hill CV32 105 F1
Beauchamp Ind Pk B77 9 E4
Beauchamp Rd
Alcester B49 143 E3
Kenilworth CV8 92 C1
Royal Leamington Spa CV32 105 F1
Tamworth B77 9 F3
Warwick CV34 109 D4
Beaudesert Cl
Henley-in-A B95 113 B4
Hollywood B47 69 D3
Beaudesert La B95 113 B5
Beaudesert Rd Coventry CV5 61 D1
Hollywood B47 69 D3
Beaudesert St Mary's RC Prim Sch B95 113 B4
Beaufell Cl CV34 104 C1
Beaufort Ave CV32 106 B3
Beaufort Cl Hinckley LE10 31 F2
Wellesbourne CV35 146 B1
Beaufort Dr CV3 78 C4
Beaulieu Pk CV31 110 B3
Beaumaris Cl Banbury OX16 139 F4
Coventry CV5 59 F3
Beaumont Ave LE10 31 D4
Beaumont Cl CV33 133 A7
Beaumont Cres CV6 61 D2
Beaumont Pl CV11 29 D2
Beaumont Rd Keresley CV7 49 D3
Nuneaton CV11 29 D2
Beausale Croft CV5 60 A2
Beausale Dr B93 72 B4
Beausale La CV35 114 E7
Beck's Cl CV23 147 F4
Beck's La CV23 147 F4
Beckbury Rd CV2 62 C3
Becket Cl GL56 140 E7
Beckfoot Cl CV21 83 E4
Beckfoot Dr CV2 50 C1
Beckford Croft B93 71 F2
Becks La CV7 47 D3
Beconsfield Cl B93 71 F1
Bedale Rd CV35 132 D4
Bede Rd Bedworth CV12 39 D2
Coventry CV6 61 D3
Nuneaton CV10 28 B2
Bedford Cl OX16 139 F4
Bedford Pl CV32 109 F4
Bedford St Coventry CV1 61 D1
Royal Leamington Spa CV32 109 F4
Bedlam La CV6 49 F1
Bedworth Cl CV12 40 A1
Bedworth La CV12 38 B2
Bedworth Rd Bedworth CV12 39 F1
Bulkington CV12 40 A1
Coventry CV6 50 A3
Bedworth Sta CV12 39 E1
Beech Ave B37 33 D1
Beech Cl Alcester B49 143 E1
Hartshill CV10 28 A4
Hurley CV9 16 B3
Kingsbury B78 15 E4
Rowington CV35 114 A8
Southam CV33 147 D2
Stratford-u-A CV37 145 E1
Beech Cliffe CV34 108 C4
Beech Ct
Royal Leamington Spa CV34 109 F1
Rugby CV22 100 C4
Stratford-u-A CV37 145 D1
Beech Dr Kenilworth CV8 93 D3
Rugby CV22 99 E4
Thurlaston CV23 98 C2
Beech Gr Arley CV7 26 C1
Warwick CV34 105 D1
Beech Rd Coventry CV6 61 D3
Hollywood B47 69 D3
Oxhill CV35 137 F8
Beech Tree Ave CV4 60 A1
Beecham Wlk CV37 144 B2
Beechcroft Birmingham B36 22 B1
Long Itchington CV23 115 D4
Beecher's Keep CV8 79 F3
Beeches The Bedworth CV12 38 C1
Harbury CV33 123 E7
Polesworth B78 11 D4
Beeches Wlk CV37 145 F2
Beechtree Pk B50 148 C3
Beechwood Ave
Coventry CV5 76 C4
Hinckley LE10 31 E2
Beechwood Cl B90 70 B2
Beechwood Croft CV8 92 C1
Beechwood Rd
Bedworth CV12 39 E2
Nuneaton CV10 28 B3
Beehive Hill CV8 92 C4
Beehive La B76 23 E3
Beeston Cl CV3 78 C4
Begonia Cl LE10 31 F3
Begonia Dr LE10 31 F3
Belcony GL56 136 C1
Belgrave Dr CV21 83 E3
Belgrave Rd Coventry CV2 62 C2
Tamworth B77 9 F4
Belgrave Sq CV2 62 C2
Bell Brook CV37 121 B6
Bell Cl B36 33 D3
Bell Ct CV37 145 D1
Bell Dr CV7 49 F4
Bell Green Rd CV6 62 A4
Bell Hill OX15 142 D4
Bell La Monks Kirby CV23 53 F1
Snitterfield CV37 121 B6
Stratford-u-A CV37 144 B1
Studley B80 103 F2
Bell Mead B80 103 F2
Bell St Claybrooke Magna LE17 43 F3
Hornton OX15 139 B7
Bell Tower Mews CV32 105 F2
Bell Wlk CV21 101 D4
Bell's La OX15 142 D4
Bellairs Ave CV12 38 C1
Bellam Rd CV35 114 F4
Bellbrooke Cl CV6 50 A1
Belle Cotts B94 88 C3
Belle Vue CV10 28 C2
Belle Vue Terr B92 57 D3
Bellemere Rd B92 57 D3
Bellfield B94 87 D1
Bellingham B77 4 B1
Bellington Croft 5 B90 71 D3
Bells La OX15 137 E3
Bellview Way CV6 50 A1
Belmont Dr CV32 106 A2
Belmont Rd Coventry CV6 62 A4
Rugby CV22 83 D1
Tamworth B77 9 F4
Belton Cl B94 88 B3
Belvedere Rd CV5 77 D4
Belvoir B77 9 E4
Benedictine Rd CV3 77 E4
Bengrove Cl B98 103 D4
Benn Rd CV12 40 A1
Benn St CV22 83 E1
Bennet Cl CV13 21 E4
Bennett Ct CV8 79 F2
Bennett Dr CV34 109 E4
Bennett Pl CV36 136 B6
Bennett St CV21 82 C2
Bennett's Rd CV7 48 C2
Bennett's Rd N CV7 48 C4
Bennett's Rd S CV6 48 C1
Bennfield Rd CV21 83 D2
Benson Rd Coventry CV6 49 D1
Stratford-u-A CV37 145 D2
Benthall Rd CV6 49 F1
Bentley Cl Banbury OX16 139 F4
Royal Leamington Spa CV32 106 A2
Bentley Ct CV6 49 E2
Bentley Farm Cl B93 71 F2
Bentley Heath CE Jun & Inf Sch B93 71 F3
Bentley La B46 35 E2
Bentley Rd Bedworth CV7 39 D1
Nuneaton CV11 29 D2
Bentley Way NN11 117 F2
Benton Green La CV7 58 C1
Bentree The CV3 78 A4
Beoley La B98 86 A1
Berenska Dr CV32 106 A1
Beresford Ave CV6 49 F1
Bericote Rd CV32 105 F4
Berkeley Cl Banbury OX16 139 F4
Nuneaton CV11 29 D2
Redditch B98 112 A6
Berkeley Rd CV8 92 C3
Berkeley Rd N CV5 61 D1
Berkeley Rd S CV5 77 D4
Berkett Rd CV6 49 D1
Berkshire Cl CV10 28 C2
Berkswell CE Prim Sch CV7 58 B2
Berkswell Rd Coventry CV6 50 A1
Meriden CV7 58 B4
Berkswell Sta CV7 74 B4
Bermuda Bsns Pk CV10 39 D4
Bermuda Ind Est CV10 39 D4
Bermuda Rd CV10 29 D1
Berners Cl CV4 59 F1
Berrills La CV36 141 D7
Berrington Rd
Chipping Campden GL55 135 C2
Nuneaton CV10 28 B4
Royal Leamington Spa CV31 110 A3
Berry Ave CV36 149 F3

Berry Cl CV36 149 F3
Berry Hall La B91 56 A2
Berry Mdw CV33 133 E7
Berry St CV1 61 F2
Berryfields CV7 36 C2
Berryfields La CV37 136 C7
Berrymound View B47 69 E4
Bertie Rd CV8 93 D2
Berwick Cl Coventry CV5 60 A2
Warwick CV34 104 C1
Berwicks La B37 33 D1
Berwyn Ave CV6 49 D1
Berwyn Way CV10 28 B2
Besbury Cl B93 71 F1
Besford Gr B90 71 D3
Best Ave CV8 93 E4
Beswick Gdns CV22 99 E4
Bettina Cl CV10 28 A3
Bettman Cl CV3 77 F3
Bettridge Pl CV35 146 B2
Beverley Ave CV10 28 A2
Beverley Cl
Astwood Bank B96 102 C1
Balsall Common CV7 74 B4
Beverley Rd CV32 105 E1
Beverly Dr CV4 76 B1
Bevington Cres CV6 60 C3
Bexfield Cl CV5 60 A3
Beyer Cl B77 4 A1
Biart Pl CV21 83 E2
Bicester Sq B35 22 A2
Bickenhill La Birmingham B40 44 B2
Catherine de B B91 56 B3
Bickenhill Parkway B37 44 B3
Bickenhill Rd B37 44 A4
Bickmarsh La B50 148 B1
Bidavon Ind Est B50 148 C3
Biddles Hill B94 86 B3
Bideford Rd CV2 62 B4
Bidford on Avon CE
Jun Sch B50 148 B2
Bidford Rd B50 148 B4
Bigbury Cl CV3 77 F3
Biggin Cl B35 22 A2
Biggin Hall Cres CV3 62 A1
Biggin Hall La CV23 98 C1
Bignolds Cl OX17 134 B4
Bigwood Dr B75 13 D3
Bilberry Rd CV2 50 B1
Bilbury Cl B97 102 B3
Billesden Cl CV3 78 C4
Billesley La B48 85 F3
Billesley Rd CV37 120 C4
Billing Rd CV5 60 B2
Billingham Cl B91 71 D4
Billinton Cl CV2 62 C1
Bills La B90 69 F4
Bilton CE Mid Sch CV22 99 E3
Bilton Cty Fst Sch CV22 99 E4
Bilton Grange Sch CV22 99 F2
Bilton High Sch CV22 82 A1
Bilton Ind Est CV3 61 F1
Bilton La Dunchurch CV22 99 E2
Long Lawford CV23 82 A2
Bilton Rd CV22 82 C1
Binley Ave CV3 78 C4
Binley Cl B90 70 A4
Binley Gr CV3 78 C4
Binley Ind Est CV3 79 D4
Binley Rd CV2, CV3 62 B1
Binley Woods Cty Prim Sch
CV3 79 F4
Binns Cl CV4 75 F4
Binswood Ave CV32 105 F1
Binswood Cl CV2 50 B1
Binswood End CV33 123 E7
Binswood Mans 15
CV32 105 F1
Binswood St CV32 105 F1
Binton Rd Coventry CV2 50 B1
Welford on A CV37 129 A7
Bintonhill CV37 120 A1
Birch Abbey B49 143 D2
Birch Cl Bedworth CV12 39 E2
Coventry CV5 59 F3
Kingsbury B78 15 E4
Birch Croft B37 33 E1
Birch Ct CV34 109 F1
Birch Dr CV22 82 A1
Birch Gr Birchmoor B78 10 B4
Wellesbourne CV35 146 C2
Birches La CV8 93 D2
Birches The CV12 40 A2
Birchfield Cl CV9 10 B1
Birchfield Rd Coventry CV6 60 C4
Stratford-u-A CV37 145 D3
Birchgrave Cl CV6 62 A4
Birchley Heath Rd CV10 17 F1
Birchmoor Rd B78 10 C4
Birchtree Rd CV10 28 B3
Birchway Cl 2 CV32 105 E1
Birchwood Ave B78 10 C4
Birchwood Prim Sch
B78 10 C4
Birchwood Rd CV3 79 E4
Birchy Cl B90 69 F3
Birchy Leasowes La B90 69 F3
Bird Grove Ct CV1 61 E3
Bird Rd
Lighthorne Heath CV35 123 D2
Royal Leamington Spa CV34 109 E2
Bird St CV1 151 C3
Birdhaven Cl CV35 123 D2
Birdhope B77 4 B1
Birdingbury La CV23 115 E8
Birdingbury Rd
Birdingbury CV23 115 F8
Marton CV23 115 D7
Birds Bush Cty Prim Sch
B77 9 F4
Birds Bush Rd B77 9 F4
Birds La OX15 138 D3
Birkdale Cl CV11 30 A1
Birmingham Bsns Pk B37 44 C4
Birmingham Int Airport
B40 44 A2
Birmingham Int Sta B40 44 B2
Birmingham Rd
Alcester B49 143 D2
Allesley CV5 59 F4
Ansley CV10 27 D2
Burton Green CV8 75 D1
Coleshill B46 33 F3
Henley-In-A B95 113 B6
Kenilworth CV8 92 B4
Little Packington CV7 45 F2
Nether Whitacre B46 24 B4
Shrewley CV35 114 D6
Stoneleigh CV8 94 A3
Stratford-u-A CV37 144 C3
Studley B80 103 F4
Warwick CV34 108 B4
Water Orton B46 23 D2
Wilmcote CV37 120 D6
Wroxall B93, CV35 90 B2
Birstall Dr CV21 83 E3
Bishop Carpenter
CE Prim Sch Ox15 139 D2
Bishop St CV1 151 B3
Bishop Ullathorne
RC Sch CV3 76 C2
Bishop Wilson
CE Prim Sch B37 33 E2
Bishop Wulstan
RC High Sch CV22 83 D1
Bishop's Hill CV35 123 B2
Bishop's Itchington Sch
CV33 124 B4
Bishop's Tachbrook
CE Prim Sch CV35 122 F8
Bishopgate Bsns Pk CV1 61 E3
Bishopgate Ind Est CV1 61 E3
Bishops Bowl Lakes
Water Sports Ctr CV33 124 A5
Bishops Cl
16 Bishops Tachbrook CV33 122 F8
Stratford-u-A CV37 144 B2
Bishops Cleeve CV9 3 D1
Bishops Gate CV33 124 B5
Bishops Wlk CV5 77 D4
Bishopton Cl CV5 60 A2
Bishopton La CV37 144 B3
Bishopton Prim Sch CV37 144 B2
Bisset Cres 21 CV31 110 B3
Bitham Rd CV35 123 D3
Bixhill La B46 25 D2
Black Bank CV7 39 D1
Black Hall La CV7 36 B2
Black Horse Hill DE12 3 F4
Black Horse Rd CV6 50 A3
Black La CV32 106 B1
Black Prince Ave CV3 77 F3
Black-A-Tree Rd CV10 28 C2
Blackberry Ave B94 88 B3
Blackberry Cl CV23 83 E4
Blackberry La Ash Green CV7 49 E3
Coventry CV2 62 B3
Blackbird Croft B36 33 D4
Blackburn Rd CV6 49 F2
Blackcat Cl B37 33 D2
Blackdown B77 4 B1
Blackdown Rd B93 72 A3
Blackfirs La B37, B46 44 B4
Blackford Hill B95 113 B4
Blackford Rd B90 70 B4
Blackford Way CV35 137 F8
Blackgreaves La B76 14 C1
Blacklow Rd CV34 105 D1
Blackman Way CV21 82 C2
Blackshaw Dr CV2 62 C3
Blacksmith's La NN11 134 F5
Blacksmiths Cl WR11 127 F1
Blacksmiths La
Hockley Heath B94 88 B3
Littleton WR11 127 F1
Mollington OX17 134 A2
Blacksmiths Yd CV13 21 E4
Blackthorn Cl CV4 76 B3
Blackthorn Gr CV11 29 F1
Blackthorn Rd CV37 145 D3
Blackthorn Way B49 143 D3
Blackthorne Rd CV8 93 D2
Blackwatch Rd CV6 61 E4
Blackwell Rd Coventry CV6 61 F4
Tredington CV36 136 F6
Blackwood Ave CV22 82 B1
Blackwood Rd B77 9 E4
Blacon Way CV37 144 B2
Bladon Cl CV11 29 F4
Bladon Wlk 14 CV31 110 B3
Blair Dr CV12 38 B1
Blair Gr B37 33 E1
Blake Cl Nuneaton CV10 28 A3
Rugby CV22 82 B1
Blake's Hill WR11, CV37 128 B1
Blakelands Ave CV31 110 A3
Blakenhurst WR11 127 C4
Blandford Ave B36 22 C1
Blandford Dr CV2 62 C3
Blandford Rd 1 CV32 105 E1
Blandford Way CV35 108 A4
Blaze La B96, B97 102 A2
Bleaberry CV21 83 E4
Bleachfield St B49 143 D2
Blenheim Ave CV6 49 E1
Blenheim Cl
Bidford-on-A B50 148 B3
Nuneaton CV11 29 F1
Blenheim Cres 28 CV31 110 B3
Blenheim Wlk CV35 146 B1
Bletchley Dr CV5 60 A2
Blewgates OX15 137 F2
Blewitt Cl B36 22 B1
Blick Rd CV34 109 E2
Blind La Berkswell CV7 58 B2
Chipping Campden GL55 135 A1
Tanworth-In-A B94 86 B1
Blindpit La B76 23 D4
Bliss Cl CV4 59 F2
Blockley Rd CV12 39 E2
Blondvil St CV3 77 E4
Bloxam Gdns CV22 82 C1
Bloxam Mid Sch CV22 82 C1
Bloxam Pl CV21 83 D2
Bloxham Rd OX16 139 F1
Blue Cap Rd CV37 145 D3
Blue Coat CE Sch CV1 61 F1
Blue La CV35 130 E6
Blue Lake Rd B93 72 A1
Bluebell Cl CV23 83 E4
Bluebell Dr B37 33 F1
Bluebellwood Cl B76 13 D2
Blundells Croft CV37 129 A7
Blundells The CV8 93 D3
Blyth Ave CV7 74 B3
Blyth Cl CV12 38 B1
Blythe Cl B97 102 B4
Blythe Rd Coleshill B46 34 A4
Coventry CV1 61 F2
Boar Croft CV4 59 F1
Boat La CV37 129 A7
Bockendon Rd CV4 75 F3
Boddington Cl CV32 106 C3
Boddington Rd OX17 134 B5
Bodmin Rd CV2 62 C3
Bodnant Way CV8 93 E3
Bodymoor Heath La B76 15 D2
Bohun St CV4 59 F1
Boleyn Cl CV34 109 E3
Bolingbroke Rd CV3 62 A1
Bolton Cl CV3 77 F3
Bolyfant Cl CV31 110 A1
Bond Dr B35 22 A2
Bond End CV23 53 F2
Bond Gate CV11 29 E2
Bond St Coventry CV1 151 B3
Nuneaton CV11 29 E3
Rugby CV21 82 C2
Boningale Way B93 71 F2
Bonington Dr CV12 39 D2
Bonneville Cl CV5 59 D4
Bonniksen Cl CV31 109 F3
Bonnington Cl CV21 84 A1
Boot Hill CV9 11 E1
Booths Fields CV6 49 F1
Bordesley Ct CV32 106 A2
Bordon Hill CV37 144 B1
Bordon Pl CV37 144 C1
Borough The LE10 31 E4
Borrowdale CV21 83 E4
Borrowdale Cl CV6 61 D4
Borrowdale Dr CV32 105 E1
Borrowell La CV8 92 C2
Boscobel Rd B90 70 B3
Bosley Cl CV36 149 F2
Bostock Cres CV33 107 E4
Boston Pl CV6 61 E4
Boswell Dr CV2 63 D4
Boswell Gr CV34 104 B1
Boswell Rd CV22 99 F4
Bosworth Dr B37 33 D1
Bosworth Wood Jun &
Inf Sch B36 22 C1
Boteler Cl B49 143 D2
Botoner Rd CV1 61 F1
Bott Rd CV5 76 B4
Bott's La DE12 3 F4
Bottrill St CV11 29 D3
Botts Green La B46 25 E3
Boucher Cl CV37 144 B1
Boughton Leigh Cty Inf Sch
CV21 83 E4
Boughton Leigh Jun Sch
CV21 83 E4
Boughton Rd CV21 83 E3
Boulters La CV9 10 B1
Boultons La B97 102 B3
Boundary Rd CV21 83 E1
Bourne Brook Cl CV7 36 C2
Bourne Cl CV9 12 C1
Bourne End CV33 147 D2
Bourne La OX15 142 D4
Bourne Rd CV3 62 B1
Bourne The OX15 142 D4
Bournebrook View CV7 26 C1
Bourton Dr CV31 110 A3
Bourton La CV23 115 F8
Bourton Rd Frankton CV23 97 E1
Moreton-in-M GL56 140 A3
Bouts La WR7 118 B5
Bovey Croft B76 22 A4
Bovingdon Rd B35 22 A2
Bow Fell CV21 83 E4
Bow La CV7 53 D2
Bowbrook Ave B90 71 D3
Bowden Way CV3 62 C1
Bowen Rd CV22 83 E1
Bowers Croft CV32 106 A3
Bowes Lyon Cl GL56 140 A2
Bowfell Cl CV5 60 A2
Bowley's La DE12 3 F4
Bowling Green Ave B77 9 F4
Bowling Green Ct GL56 140 A3
Bowling Green La CV7, CV12 49 F4
Bowling Green St CV34 108 B3
Bowls Ct CV5 60 C2
Bowman Gn LE10 31 F3
Bowness Cl CV6 61 D4
Bowshot Cl B36 22 B1
Box Cl CV31 110 A2
Box Rd B37 44 B4
Box Trees Rd B93 71 E1
Boxhill The CV3 62 A1
Boyce Way CV23 82 A3
Boyd Cl CV2 63 D4
Boyslade Rd LE10 31 F3
Boyslade Rd E LE10 31 F3
Bracadale Cl CV3 63 D1
Bracebridge Cl CV7 74 A3
Bracebridge Rd
Atherstone CV9 18 B4
Kingsbury B78 15 E3
Bracebridge St CV11 29 D2
Bracken Cl CV22 82 C1
Bracken Croft 1 B37 33 E2
Bracken Dr Rugby CV22 82 C1
Sutton Coldfield B75 13 D3
Wolvey LE10 41 E2
Brackendale Dr Barby CV23 101 E1
Nuneaton CV10 28 C2
Brackenhurst Rd CV6 61 D4
Bracklesham Way B77 4 A3
Brackley Cl CV6 60 C4
Bracknell Wlk 1 CV2 63 D4
Braddock Cl CV3 63 D1
Brade Dr CV2 63 D4
Bradestone Rd CV11 29 E1
Bradewell Rd B36 22 B1
Bradford Rd 6 CV33 122 E8
Brading Rd CV10 29 E3
Bradley Croft CV7 74 A3
Bradney Gn CV4 75 F4
Bradnick Pl CV4 59 F1
Bradnock's Marsh La B92 57 F1
Braemar Cl CV2 62 C3
Braemar Rd CV32 106 A2
Braemar Way CV10 29 D1
Braeside Croft B37 33 E1
Brafield Leys CV22 100 A3
Braggington La CV37 128 F5
Braggs Farm La B90 70 A2
Brailes CE Prim Sch OX15 137 E2
Brain St B77 4 A1
Brakesmead CV31 109 F3
Bramber Cl OX16 139 F4
Bramble Cl 4 Coleshill B46 33 F4
Nuneaton CV11 29 F1
Bramble St CV1 61 F1
Brambles The B76 22 A4
Brambling B77 10 A4
Bramcote Cl CV12 40 B1
Bramcote Hospl CV11 40 C4
Bramdene Ave CV10 29 E4
Bramley Dr B47 69 D3
Bramley Rd CV35 132 E6
Brampton Way CV12 40 A2
Bramshall Dr B93 71 F2
Bramston Cres CV4 59 F1
Bramwell Gdns CV6 49 F3
Brancaster Cl B77 4 A3
Brandfield Rd CV6 60 C4
Brandon La CV3, CV8 79 E3
Brandon Marsh
Nature Reserve CV8 79 D2
Brandon Marsh
Visitor Ctr CV8 79 D2
Brandon Par CV32 110 A4
Brandon Rd Bretford CV23 80 B3
Coventry CV3 79 D4
Hinckley LE10 31 D4
Branksome Rd CV6 60 C3
Bransdale Ave CV6 49 E2
Bransford Ave CV4 76 B3
Bransford Rise B91 56 A3
Branstree Dr CV6 49 E1
Brascote Rd LE10 30 C4
Bratches The GL55 135 B3
Brathay Cl CV3 77 E3
Braunston Cl B76 13 D1
Braunston Jun & Inf Sch
NN11 117 E5
Braunston La NN11 126 E8
Braunston Pl CV22 100 B4
Braunston Rd NN11 117 F2
Bray Bank B46 25 E2
Bray's La CV2 62 A2
Brayford Ave CV3 77 E3
Brays Cl CV23 64 C2
Braytoft Cl CV6 49 E1
Brazil St CV4 59 F1
Breach La CV35 113 F3
Breach Oak La CV7 37 E2
Breaches La B98 103 E4
Bream B77 9 E4
Bream Cl B37 33 E1
Brechin Cl LE10 31 D4
Bredon Ave CV3 78 C4
Bredon View B97 102 B4
Bree Cl CV5 60 A4
Bree's La CV8 74 A1
Breeden Dr B76 23 D3
Brendan Cl B46 34 A3
Brendon B77 4 A1
Brendon Way CV10 28 A2
Brenfield Dr LE10 31 D4
Brent B77 9 F4
Brentwood Ave CV3 77 E2
Brese Ave CV34 104 C1
Bretch Hill OX16 139 F3
Bretford Rd CV2 50 B1
Bretshall Cl B90 70 C3
Brett Cl CV1 151 D4
Brewer Rd CV12 40 B1
Brewers Cl CV3 63 D1
Brewery La OX15 142 C4
Brewery Row GL56 140 F1
Brewery St CV37 144 C2
Brewster Cl CV2 62 C1
Briansway CV6 49 F2
Briar B77 4 A2
Briar Cl Hinckley LE10 31 F3
Royal Leamington Spa CV32 106 A1
Briar Hill Cty Fst Sch CV31 110 A2
Briardene Ave CV12 39 D1
Briarmead LE10 31 F2
Briars Cl Coventry CV2 62 B1
Long Lawford CV23 82 A2
Nuneaton CV11 29 F3
Briarwood Cl B90 70 B2
Brick Hill OX15 142 D3
Brick Hill La CV5 59 F4
Brick Kiln La Middleton B78 14 B3
Solihull B90 70 C4
Brick Kiln St LE10 31 E4
Brickhill Cl CV36 149 F3
Brickhill Dr B37 33 D1
Brickkiln La CV9 16 A2
Brickyard La B80 103 E2
Bridal Path The CV5 60 A3
Bridge End Southam CV33 147 D2
Warwick CV34 108 C3
Bridge Foot CV37 145 D1
Bridge La Ladbroke CV33 124 D5
Witherley CV9 19 D4
Bridge Meadow Dr B93 71 F3
Bridge Rd LE10 31 E4
Bridge St Barford CV35 122 A7
Coventry CV6 62 A4
Fenny Compton CV33 133 D7
Hampton Lucy CV35 121 F4
Hurley CV9 16 B2
Kenilworth CV8 92 C3
Kineton CV35 132 B5
Nuneaton CV11 29 E2
Nuneaton, Chilvers Coton
CV11 29 E1
Polesworth B78 5 D1
Rugby CV21 83 E2
Stratford-u-A CV37 145 D1
Warwick CV34 109 E4
Wellesbourne CV35 146 B2
Bridge Town Prim Sch
CV37 145 D1
Bridgeacre Gdns CV3 62 C1
Bridgecote CV3 78 C3
Bridgeman Rd CV6 61 D2
Bridget St CV22 82 C2
Bridgetown Rd CV37 145 D1
Bridgeway CV37 145 D2
Bridle Brook La CV5, CV7 48 A2
Bridle Rd
Lighthorne Heath CV35 123 D2
Rugby CV21 82 C2
Bridport Cl CV2 63 D2
Brierley Rd CV2 62 B4
Briggs Cl OX16 139 F2
Bright St CV6 61 F3
Brightmere Rd CV6 61 D2
Brighton St CV2 61 F2
Brightwalton Rd CV3 77 E4
Brightwell Cres B93 71 F2
Brill Cl CV4 76 B3
Brindle Ave CV3 62 B1
Brindley Rd Bedworth CV7 50 A4
Hinckley LE10 30 C4
Rugby CV21 84 A1
Brinklow CE Fst Sch CV23 64 C2
Brinklow Cl B98 103 E4
Brinklow Rd Coventry CV3 63 D1
Easenhall CV23 65 F2
Brisbane Cl CV3 77 F3
Briscoe Rd CV6 49 E2
Bristol Rd CV5 60 C1
Bristol Way CV35 146 B1
Britannia Rd LE10 32 A3
Britannia St CV2 61 F2
Briton Rd CV2 62 A2
Brittania Sh Ctr 2 LE10 31 E4
Britten Cl CV11 40 A4
Brittons La CV35 114 C2
Brixham Cl CV11 29 F3
Brixham Dr CV2 62 B4
Brixworth Cl CV3 78 C4
Broad Cl CV33 123 F8
Broad Heath Com
Prim Sch CV6 61 F4
Broad La Coventry CV5 59 E2
Fillongley CV7 35 F2
Tanworth-in-A B98 86 C2
Broad Marston Rd
Mickleton CV37,GL55 135 B7
Pebworth CV37 128 F1
Broad Oaks B76 13 D1
Broad Park Rd CV2 62 B4
Broad St Brinklow CV23 64 C2
Coventry CV6 61 F4
Long Compton CV36 141 C3
Stratford-u-A CV37 144 C1
Warwick CV34 108 C4
Broad Wlk CV37 144 C1
Broadfern Rd B93 72 A4
Broadgate CV1 151 B3
Broadhaven Cl CV31 110 B4
Broadlands Cl CV5 60 B1
Broadlee B77 4 B1
Broadmeadow La CV37 144 C3
Broadmere Rise CV5 60 A1

Broadmoor La CV36 141 A6
Broadsword Way LE10 31 E2
Broadwater CV5 77 D4
Broadway Coventry CV5 61 D1
Cubbington CV32 106 C3
Broadway Rd GL55 135 B6
Broadwell Ct CV4 75 F3
Broadwells Cres CV4 76 A3
Brockhill La B98 85 F1
Brockhurst Ave LE10 31 E2
Brockhurst Dr CV4 59 E1
Brockhurst La
Monks Kirby CV23 53 F2
Sutton Coldfield B75 7 D4
Brodick Cl LE10 31 D4
Brodick Rd LE10 30 C4
Brodick Way CV10 28 C2
Bromage Ave B78 15 E3
Brome Hall La B94 89 E1
Bromford Way CV37 144 B2
Bromleigh Dr CV2 62 B1
Bromley Cl CV8 92 C3
Bromsgrove Highway B98 102 C4
Bromsgrove Rd B80 103 E1
Bromwich Cl CV3 78 C4
Bromwich Rd CV21 83 F1
Bromyard Ave B76 22 A4
Bronte Cl Nuneaton CV10 27 F3
Rugby CV21 83 E2
Bronze Cl CV11 39 F4
Brook Ave B77 10 A4
Brook Cl Coventry CV1 61 F2
Kingsbury B78 15 E3
Shipston-on-S CV36 149 F3
Brook Croft B37 44 A4
Brook End B78 9 D4
Brook End Cl B95 113 A4
Brook End Dr B95 113 A4
Brook Farm Wlk B37 33 E1
Brook Green La B92 57 D1
Brook La
Moreton Morrell CV35 122 F3
Newbold-on-S CV37 130 E1
Nuneaton CV10 29 E3
Brook Piece Wlk B35 22 A2
Brook St Bedworth CV12 39 D3
Fenny Compton CV33 133 D7
Warwick CV34 108 C3
Wolston CV8 80 A2
Brook View CV22 99 E2
Brook Wlk CV9 18 C4
Brookdale Harvington WR11 127 C4
Hinckley LE10 31 D4
Brookdale Rd CV10 29 F4
Brooke Cl CV34 108 C3
Brooke Rd CV8 93 D2
Brooke Specl Sch CV22 82 C1
Brookfield Cl B97 102 B2
Brookfield Dr LE10 41 E2
Brookfield Rd
Cubbington CV32 106 C3
Hinckley LE10 31 E3
Brookford Ave CV6 49 D2
Brookhurst Ct CV32 105 E1
Brookhurst Cty Comb Sch
CV32 105 E1
Brookhus Farm Rd B76 22 A4
Brooklea CV12 38 C1
Brooklime Dr CV23 83 F4
Brooklyn Rd CV1 61 E3
Brooks Cl CV23 117 B6
Brooks Croft B35 22 A1
Brooksby Gr B93 72 A1
Brookshaw Way CV2 62 C4
Brookside
Cheswick Green B90 70 B2
Hinckley LE10 31 F4
Hook Norton OX15 142 D4
Snitterfield CV37 121 B7
Stretton on D CV23 96 C3
Brookside Ave Coventry CV5 60 B2
Kenilworth CV8 92 C2
Pailton CV23 66 A4
Wellesbourne CV35 146 C2
Brookside Cl Rugby CV22 83 D1
Stratford-u-A CV37 144 B2
Brookside Rd CV37 144 B2
Brookside Way B77 10 A3
Brookvale Ave CV3 62 C1
Brookvale Rd CV37 144 C1
Brookweed B77 4 A2
Broom Cl CV22 82 C1
Broome Croft CV6 49 D2
Broomey Croft Farm B76 15 D4
Broomfield Ave B78 9 D4
Broomfield Pl CV5 61 D1
Broomfield Rd CV5 61 D1
Broomfield Rise CV10 28 C1
Broomybank CV8 93 D3
Broughton Rd OX16 139 F2
Browett Rd CV6 61 D3
Brown's Bridge Rd CV33 147 D2
Brown's La Allesley CV5 48 B1
Dordon B78 11 D3
Browning Ave CV34 108 B3
Browning Cl CV10 28 A3
Browning Rd Coventry CV2 62 B2
Rugby CV21 101 D4
Brownley Rd B90 70 C4
Brownlow St 5 CV32 106 A1
Browns La B93 71 F3
Browns Rd NN11 117 F1
Brownshill Ct CV6 60 C4
Brownshill Green Rd CV6 48 C1
Brownsover Cl B36 22 A1
Brownsover Com Inf Sch
CV23 83 E4
Brownsover La CV21 83 D4
Brownsover Rd CV21 82 C4
Broxell Cl CV34 104 B1
Bruce Rd Bedworth CV7 49 F4
Coventry CV6 61 D4
Bruce Williams Way CV22 83 D1
Brunel Cl Coventry CV2 61 F2
Daventry NN11 117 F2
Whitnash CV31 110 A1
Brunel Rd LE10 31 E4
Brunel Wlk B78 5 D2
Brunswick Cl CV21 83 E3
Brunswick Rd CV1 61 D1
Brunswick St CV31 110 A3
Bruntingthorpe Way CV3 78 C4
Brunton Cl CV3 63 D1
Brutus Dr B46 23 F1
Bryan Ct B50 148 C2
Bryanston Cl CV2 63 D2
Bryant Rd CV7 50 A4
Brympton Rd CV3 62 B1
Bryn Jones Cl CV3 78 C4
Bryn Rd CV6 61 F4
Buccleuch Cl CV22 99 E2
Buchan Cl CV10 27 F2
Buchannan Rd CV22 82 C1
Buck La CV35 138 B7
Buckbury Croft B90 71 D3
Buckden B77 4 B1
Buckden Cl 9 CV34 104 C1
Buckfast Cl CV3 77 F3
Buckhold Dr CV5 60 A3
Buckingham Cl CV10 29 D1
Buckingham Rd CV33 132 F5
Buckingham Rise CV5 60 A2
Buckland Rd CV6 49 D1
Buckle St WR11,B50 128 C3
Buckley Rd CV32 106 B1
Buckminster Dr B93 71 F2
Bucks Hill CV10 28 B3
Buckwell La CV23 84 A3
Budbrooke Cl CV2 50 B1
Budbrooke Ind Est CV34 108 A4
Budbrooke Prim Sch CV35 114 F4
Budbrooke Rd CV34 108 A4
Bufferys Cl B91 71 D4
Bulkington Fst Sch CV12 40 B1
Bulkington La CV11 40 A4
Bulkington Rd
Bedworth CV12 39 E1
Shilton CV7 51 F3
Wolvey LE10 41 E2
Bull Ring Harbury CV33 123 F6
Nuneaton CV10 29 D1
Bull Ring Farm Rd CV33 123 F7
Bull St Nuneaton CV11 29 E1
Southam CV33 147 D2
Stratford-u-A CV37 144 C1
Bull Yd CV1 151 B2
Bull's Head La CV3 62 A1
Bull's La B76 13 F1
Bullaces La LE17 68 B2
Bullfield Ave CV4 59 F1
Bullfurlong La LE10 31 F2
Bullimore Gr CV8 93 D1
Bullivents Cl B93 71 F3
Bulls Head Yd B49 143 D2
Bulwer Rd CV6 61 D3
Bulwick Cl CV3 63 D1
Bunkers Hill NN11 126 F5
Burbage Ave CV37 144 C3
Burbage Cty Jun Sch LE10 31 F3
Burbage Rd
Aston Cantlow B95 119 F6
Hinckley LE10 32 A4
Burbages La CV6 49 E2
Burberry Gr CV7 74 A3
Burbury Cl Bedworth CV12 39 E2
Royal Leamington Spa CV32 106 B1
Burford La B49 112 C1
Burford Mews 22 CV31 110 B3
Burford Rd Hollywood B47 69 D3
Stratford-u-A CV37 145 E1
Burgage Pl CV11 29 E2
Burgage Wlk CV11 29 D3
Burges CV1 151 B3
Burges Gr CV34 104 C1
Burghley Cl CV11 29 F1
Burhill Way B37 33 D3
Burleigh Cl CV7 74 A4
Burlington Rd Coventry CV2 61 F2
Nuneaton CV10 39 D4
Burman Dr B46 34 A3
Burnaby Cl CV10 28 A3
Burnaby Rd CV6 49 D1
Burnaston Cres B90 71 E3
Burnell Cl B50 148 B3
Burnett Rd CV35 123 D2
Burnham Rd CV3 78 A3
Burnham Rise CV11 30 A3
Burns Ave CV34 108 B3
Burns Cl B97 102 B4
Burns Rd Coventry CV2 62 A2
Royal Leamington Spa CV32 106 A2
Burns Wlk CV12 39 E1
Burnsall Gr CV5 76 B4
Burnsall Rd CV5 76 B4
Burnside Coventry CV3 63 D1
Rugby CV22 82 C1
Burnthurst Cres B90 71 D4
Burrow Hill La CV7 48 B4
Burrows Cl CV31 110 A1
Burton Cl CV5 48 B1
Burton Dassett Hills
Ctry Pk CV33 133 B7
Burton Green CE
Jun & Inf Sch CV8 75 D2
Burton La CV11 40 C4
Burton Rd CV9 3 F1
Burtons Farm Prim Sch
B36 33 D4
Bury Rd CV31 109 F4
Burycroft Rd OX15 142 D3
Buryway La CV36 141 C4
Busby Cl CV3 78 C4
Bush Cl CV4 59 F2
Bush Heath La CV33 123 F6
Bush Hill La CV23 117 B2
Bush La B77 9 E2
Bushbery Ave CV4 59 F1
Bushbury Croft B37 33 E2
Bushley Cl B98 103 D4
Bushley Croft B91 71 D4
Bushwood Dr B93 72 A2
Bushwood La B94 113 C8
Butcher's Cl CV23 64 C2
Butcher's La CV5 60 B3
Butchers La OX15 137 F2
Butchers Rd B92 57 D3
Butler Cl CV8 93 E4
Butler St B96 102 C1
Butlers Cl Aston le W NN11 134 F5
Long Compton CV36 141 D3
Butlers Cres CV7 39 D1
Butlers End CV35 91 E1
Butlers La Grendon CV9 11 E1
Long Compton CV36 141 C3
Butlers Leap CV21 83 E3
Butlers Leap Ind Est CV21 83 E2
Butlers Rd CV36 141 E3
Butlin Rd Coventry CV6 49 E2
Rugby CV21 83 E2
Butt Hill CV23 125 C8
Butt La Allesley CV5 60 A4
Harbury CV33 123 F6
Butter St B49 143 E2
Buttermere Rugby CV21 83 E4
Tamworth B77 10 A4
Buttermere Ave CV11 30 A3
Buttermere Cl CV3 78 C4
Buttermilk La CV35 113 F5
Butterworth Dr CV4 76 A3
Butts CV1 61 D1
Butts Cl CV9 3 D1
Butts La B94 87 D1
Butts Rd CV1 61 D1
Butts The
Long Compton CV36 141 C3
Napton CV23 125 C8
Warwick CV34 108 C4
Buxton Ave B78 9 D4
By Pass Rd B77 4 A3
Byfield Rd
Chipping Warden OX17 134 F4
Coventry CV6 60 C3
Priors Marston CV23 125 F4
Byford St CV10 28 C2
Bygones Mus OX17 134 B4
Byron Ave Bedworth CV12 39 E1
Warwick CV34 108 B2
Byron Rd Redditch B97 102 B4
Stratford-u-A CV37 145 E1
Byron St CV1 151 C4
Byron Wlk CV33 132 F7
Bywater Cl CV3 77 D3

Cable & Wireless Coll CV4 75 F3
Cadbury Dr B35 22 A1
Cadden Dr CV4 60 A1
Cadman Cl CV12 39 E2
Cadogan Rd B77 9 E3
Caen Cl CV35 108 A4
Caernarfon Dr CV11 29 E2
Caernarvon Way OX16 139 F3
Caesar Rd CV8 92 C2
Caesar Way B46 23 F1
Caister B77 4 A3
Caistor Cl B78 8 A4
Caithness Cl CV5 60 A2
Calcutt Mdw CV33 147 E2
Caldecote Cl CV10 29 E4
Caldecote Hall Dr CV10 19 F2
Caldecote Rd CV6 61 E3
Caldecott Pl CV21 83 E1
Caldecott St CV21 83 E1
Caldeford Ave B90 71 D4
Calder B77 4 A1
Calder Cl Bulkington CV12 40 A1
Coventry CV3 77 F4
Calder Dr B76 22 A4
Calder Wlk CV31 110 B3
Caldon Cl LE10 31 D4
Caldwell Rd CV11 29 E1
Calf's La GL55 135 B2
Callaways Rd CV36 149 F2
Callendar Cl CV11 30 A4
Callow Hill La B97 102 A3
Calmere Cl CV2 62 C4
Caludon Castle Sch CV2 62 C2
Caludon Park Ave CV2 62 C3
Caludon Rd CV2 62 A2
Calvert Cl Coventry CV3 77 E3
Rugby CV21 83 F4
Camberwell Terr CV31 110 A4
Camborne Dr CV11 29 F3
Cambourne Rd LE10 32 A3
Cambria Cl B90 69 F4
Cambrian B77 4 A1
Cambridge Dr
Birmingham B37 33 D1
Nuneaton CV10 28 C2
Cambridge St Coventry CV1 61 F3
Rugby CV21 83 E2
Camden Cl GL56 140 F3
Camden St CV2 62 A2
Camellia Rd CV2 50 A1
Camelot Gr CV8 93 E3
Cameron Cl Allesley CV5 60 A4
Royal Leamington Spa CV32 106 A2
Camhouses B77 4 A1
Camp Hill Cty Jun Sch CV10 28 C3
Camp Hill Dr CV10 28 B4
Camp Hill Rd CV10 28 B4
Camp La Henley-in-A B95 113 B6
Warmington OX17 133 B2
Campbell St CV21 82 C2
Campden Cl B97 102 B3
Campden Lawns CV37 130 D3
Campden Pitch CV36 136 A6
Campden Rd
Ebrington GL55 135 D3
Lower Quinton CV37 129 D4
Mickleton GL55 135 B4
Shipston-on-S CV36 149 E3
Campden St CV36 136 A6
Campion Cl CV3 77 E3
Campion Gn CV32 106 A1
Campion Rd CV32 106 A1
Campion Sch & Com Coll
CV31 110 B3
Campion Terr CV32 106 A1
Campion Way CV23 83 E4
Camplea Croft B37 33 D1
Campling Cl CV12 40 A1
Campton Cl LE10 31 F4
Camville CV3 63 D1
Canada La CV35 114 D1
Canal La CV35 114 E5
Canal Rd CV6 61 F4
Canberra Cl CV35 146 B1
Canberra Rd CV2 50 B2
Canford Cl CV3 77 E2
Canley Ford CV5 76 C4
Canley Rd CV5 76 B4
Canley Sta CV5 60 B1
Cannocks La CV5 76 B3
Cannon Cl CV4 76 C3
Cannon Hill Rd CV4 76 B3
Cannon Park District Ctr
CV4 76 B3
Cannon Park Prim Sch CV4 76 B3
Cannon Park Rd CV4 76 C3
Canon Dr CV7 49 E3
Canon Evans CE Fst Sch
CV12 39 D1
Canon Hudson Cl CV3 78 B3
Canon Maggs CE Mid Sch
CV12 39 D1
Canon Young Rd CV31 110 A2
Canterbury Cl Kenilworth CV8 93 E2
Studley B80 103 E2
Canterbury Dr B37 44 A4
Canterbury St CV1 151 D3
Canterbury Way CV11 30 A4
Cantlow Cl CV5 60 A2
Canton La B76 24 A3
Canwell Dr B75 7 D3
Cape Ind Est CV34 108 C4
Cape Rd CV34 108 B4
Capmartin Rd CV6 61 E4
Captain's Hill B49 143 E3
Capulet Cl Coventry CV3 78 B3
Rugby CV22 99 F3
Caradoc B77 4 A1
Caradoc Cl CV2 62 B4
Cardale Croft 1 CV3 78 C4
Cardiff Cl CV3 78 B3
Cardigan Rd CV12 38 B1
Cardinal Newman RC Sch
CV6 48 C1
Cardinal Wiseman RC Sch
CV2 50 C1
Carding Cl CV5 59 F2
Carew Cl CV37 144 C3
Carey B77 10 A3
Carey St CV6 62 A4
Cargill Cl CV6 49 F3
Carhampton Rd B75 13 D3
Carisbroke B77 4 A1
Carisbrook Rd CV10 29 E3
Carisbrooke Ave B37 33 E1
Carlcroft B77 4 A1
Carlton Cl CV12 40 A2
Carlton Rd Coventry CV6 49 F1
Rugby CV22 82 B1
Carlyle Cl CV10 27 F3
Carlyon Rd CV9 18 C4
Carlyon Road Ind Est CV9 12 C1
Carmelite Rd CV1 61 F1
Carnbroe Ave CV3 78 C4
Carnegie Cl CV3 78 A3
Carnoustie B77 4 B3
Carnoustie Cl CV11 40 B4
Caroline Cl CV11 39 F4
Carpenters Cl LE10 31 F3
Carroway Head Hill B78 7 E2
Carsal Cl CV7 49 E3
Carson Cl GL56 136 C1
Cart's La CV9 11 E1
Carter Dr CV35 122 A7
Carter Rd CV3 78 A4
Carters La CV37 145 F2
Carters Leaze CV36 140 E5
Carthusian Rd CV3 77 E4
Cartmel Cl CV5 60 A2
Carver Cl CV2 62 C1
Cascade Cl CV3 77 F3
Case La CV35 114 B8
Cash's Bsns Ctr CV1 61 E3
Cash's La CV1 61 E3
Cashmore Ave CV31 109 F3
Cashmore Mid Sch CV31 109 F3
Cashmore Rd Bedworth CV12 38 C1
Kenilworth CV8 93 E2
Casia Gr CV8 93 E2
Caspian Way CV2 63 D4
Cassandra Cl CV4 76 B2
Cassandra Gr CV34 109 E2
Castello Dr B36 22 B1
Castle Bromwich Bsns Pk
B35 22 A1
Castle Cl Coventry CV3 77 E3
Fillongley CV7 36 C1
Henley-in-A B95 113 B4
Warwick CV34 108 C3
Castle Cres CV35 132 B5
Castle Ct LE10 31 E3
Castle Dr Astley CV10 37 F4
Coleshill B46 33 F3
Castle Gdns GL55 135 C2
Castle Gn CV8 92 B3
Castle Hill Kenilworth CV8 92 C3
Upper Brailes OX15 137 E3
Warwick CV34 108 C3
Castle Hill La OX15 137 E2
Castle La Maxstoke B46 34 C4
Warwick CV34 108 C3
Castle Mound CV23 101 E1
Castle Place Ind Est CV1 151 D4
Castle Rd Alcester B49 143 E3
Henley-in-A B95 113 B4
Kenilworth CV8 92 C3
Kineton CV35 132 B6
Nuneaton CV10 29 E4
Studley B80 103 F2
Tamworth B77 9 F3
Castle St Astwood Bank B96 102 C1
Coventry CV1 151 D4
Hinckley LE10 31 E4
Rugby CV21 83 D2
Warwick CV34 108 C3
Castle Vale Sec Sch B35 22 A2
Castle Vale Sports Ctr B35 22 A1
Castle View CV10 19 D1
Castleditch La B98 102 C4
Castlehall B77 4 A1
Caswell Rd CV31 110 A3
Catbrook Cl GL55 135 B1
Catesby La B94 89 D1
Catesby Rd Coventry CV6 61 D4
Rugby CV22 83 E1
Cathedral Lanes Sh Ctr
CV1 151 B3
Catherine de Barnes La
Bickenhill B92 44 B1
Catherine de B B92 56 B4
Catherine St CV2 61 F2
Catherines Cl B91 56 A2
Cathiron La CV23 65 E1
Cattell Dr B75 13 D3
Cattell Rd CV34 108 C4
Catthorpe Manor LE17 68 C1
Catthorpe Rd LE17 68 B2
Cavalier Cl CV11 29 F1
Cavans Way CV3 79 D4
Cavendish Rd CV4 59 F1
Caversham Cl CV11 30 A4
Cawdon Gr B93 71 F2
Cawnpore Rd CV6 49 D1
Cawston La CV22 99 D3
Cawston Way CV22 99 E4
Cawthorne Cl 1 CV1 61 F2
Cecil Leonard Knox Cres
CV11 40 C3
Cecily Rd CV3 77 F4
Cedar Cl Kingsbury B78 15 E3
Royal Leamington Spa CV32 106 A2
Stratford-u-A CV37 145 D2
Cedar Ct LE10 32 A3
Cedar Dr CV37 121 B7
Cedar Gr CV34 105 D1
Cedar Rd Mickleton GL55 135 C6
Nuneaton CV10 28 B3
Cedar Wlk 5 B37 33 D1
Cedar Wood Dr CV7 74 A3
Cedars Ave CV6 60 C3
Cedars Fst Sch CV7 50 A4
Cedars Rd CV7 39 D1
Cedric Cl CV3 78 B3
Celandine CV23 83 E4
Celandine Rd CV2 50 B1
Centaur Rd CV5 60 C1
Centenary Bsns Ctr CV11 29 F2
Centenary Rd CV4 76 B4
Central Ave Coventry CV2 62 A1
Nuneaton CV11 29 D3
Royal Leamington Spa CV31 109 F3
Central City Ind Est CV6 61 F3
Central Dr CV33 124 B4
Centrovell Ind Est CV11 29 E1
Centurion Cl B46 23 F1
Centurion Pk B77 10 A3
Centurion Way B77 10 A3
Ceolmund Cres B37 33 D1
Chace Ave CV3 78 B3
Chace Prim Sch CV3 78 B3
Chaceley Cl CV2 63 D4
Chadbury Croft 1 B91 71 D4
Chadbury Rd WR11 127 A1
Chadshunt Cl B36 22 B1
Chadstone Cl B90 71 D3
Chadwick Cl CV5 60 A2
Chadwick La
Chadwick End B93 90 A4
Knowle B93 73 D1
Chadwick Mews B93 90 A3
Chadworth Ave B93 71 F2
Chaffinch Dr B36 33 D4
Chalfont Cl Bedworth CV12 39 D2
Coventry CV5 60 A2

Challenge Bsns Pk CV1 61 E3
Challenge Cl CV1 151 C4
Chamberlain Cl CV32 106 C3
Chamberlain La B49 118 D5
Chamberlain Rd CV21 101 D4
Chamberlaine St CV12 39 D2
Chance Fields CV31 110 C3
Chancellors Cl CV4 76 B2
Chancery La CV10 28 A4
Chanders Rd CV34 104 B1
Chandlers Cl B97 102 B4
Chandlers Dr B77 4 A3
Chandlers Rd CV31 110 A1
Chandos St Coventry CV2 62 A2
  Nuneaton CV11 29 D2
  Royal Leamington Spa CV32 105 F1
Change Brook Cl CV11 29 F4
Chantries The CV1 61 F3
Chantry Cl B47 69 D4
Chantry Cres B49 143 D2
Chantry Heath Cres B93 72 B4
Chantry The CV34 105 D1
Chapel Cl B50 148 B2
Chapel Ct B96 102 C1
Chapel Dr
  Balsall Common CV7 74 A4
  Wythall B47 69 D2
Chapel End OX7 142 A2
Chapel Gdns GL56 136 C1
Chapel Gn CV23 125 C7
Chapel Hill OX7 142 F2
Chapel La Aston Cantlow B95 119 F7
  Barnacle CV7 51 D3
  Cropredy OX17 134 C1
  Great Rollright OX7 142 A2
  Lapworth B94 89 E4
  Mickleton GL55 135 B6
  Newbold-on-S CV37 130 E1
  Pillerton Priors CV35 131 D2
  Ratley OX15 133 A2
  Ryton-on-D CV8 79 D1
  Salford OX7 150 C3
  Stratford-u-A CV37 145 D1
  Ullenhall B95 112 E6
  Witherley CV9 19 E4
Chapel Rd B96 102 C1
Chapel Row 14 CV34 108 C4
Chapel St
  Astwood Bank B96 102 C1
  Bedworth CV12 39 E2
  Bishops Itchington CV33 124 A4
  Charwelton NN11 126 D2
  Coventry CV1 151 B3
  Harbury CV33 123 F6
  Hook Norton OX15 142 D4
  Long Lawford CV23 82 A2
  Nuneaton CV11 29 E2
  3 Royal Leamington Spa CV31 110 A4
  Rugby CV21 83 D2
  Stratford-u-A CV37 145 D1
  Warmington OX17 133 D2
  Warwick CV34 108 C4
  Welford on A CV37 129 B6
  Wellesbourne CV35 146 B2
Chapelhouse Rd B37 33 D1
Chapelon B77 4 A1
Chapman Cl CV31 110 C3
Chapman Way B49 143 E3
Chard Rd CV3 78 B4
Chariot Way CV21 83 D4
Charity Rd CV7 49 D4
Charlbury Mews CV31 110 B3
Charlecote Cl CV37 145 F2
Charlecote Croft B90 70 B4
Charlecote Gdns 27 CV31 110 B3
Charlecote Park CV35 121 F3
Charlecote Rd Coventry CV6 49 D1
  Wellesbourne CV35 146 B2
  Wellesbourne, Charlcote CV35 146 A3
Charlecote Wlk CV11 39 F4
Charles Eaton Rd CV12 38 C2
Charles Gardner Rd CV31 109 F3
Charles Lakin Cl CV7 51 E3
Charles Rd CV9 18 C4
Charles St Arley CV7 37 D4
  Coventry CV1 151 D4
  Hurley CV9 16 B3
  Nuneaton CV11 29 D3
  Rugby CV21 82 C2
  Warwick CV34 109 D4
Charles Warren Cl CV21 83 D2
Charlesfield Rd CV22 100 A4
Charlesworth Ave B90 71 D3
Charlewood Rd CV6 49 D1
Charlotte St
  Royal Leamington Spa CV31 109 F3
  Rugby CV21 83 D2
Charminster Dr CV3 77 E2
Charnwood Ave CV10 28 C1
Charnwood Dr CV10 19 D1
Charnwood Way CV32 106 B2
Charter App CV34 108 B3
Charter Ave CV4 76 A4
Charter Rd CV22 100 C4
Charterhouse Rd CV1 61 F1
Chartley Cl B93 71 F2
Chartwell Cl CV11 29 F1
Chartwell Dr B90 70 B3
Charwelton Dr CV21 83 F3
Chase Cl CV11 29 F3
Chase La CV8 92 A4
Chater Dr B76 13 D1
Chatham Cl CV3 78 B4
Chatsworth Cl
  Cheswick Green B90 70 C3
  Hinckley LE10 31 F3
Chatsworth Dr CV11 29 F1
Chatsworth Gr
  Kenilworth CV8 93 E3
  Royal Leamington Spa CV31 110 B3
Chatsworth Rise CV3 77 F3
Chattaway Dr CV7 74 A3
Chattle Hill B46 23 F1
Chaucer Dr CV10 28 A2
Chaucer Rd CV22 99 F3
Chauntry Pl CV1 151 C3
Chauson Gr B91 71 D4
Chaytor Rd B78 11 D4
Cheadle Cl CV2 50 A2
Cheam Cl CV6 50 A1
Cheedon Cl B93 71 F1
Chelmsley Ave B46 33 F3
Chelmsley Circ B37 33 D2
Chelmsley La B37 44 A4
Chelmsley Rd B37 33 E1
Chelney Wlk CV3 63 D1
Chelsea Cl CV11 29 F4
Chelsey Rd CV2 62 C4
Cheltenham Cl CV12 39 D2
Cheltenham Croft CV2 62 C4
Chelveston Rd CV6 60 C3
Chelwood Gr CV2 50 C1
Chenies Cl CV5 60 A2
Chepstow Cl Coventry CV3 78 B3
  Stratford-u-A CV37 144 C1
Chepstow Gdns OX16 139 F3
Chequer St CV12 40 B1
Cheriton Cl CV5 60 B2
Cherry Blossom Gr CV31 110 A1
Cherry Cl Coventry CV6 49 E1
  Ettington CV37 131 A3
  Hurley CV9 16 B2
  Offenham WR11 127 D1
Cherry Gr CV22 99 F4
Cherry La Bearley CV37 120 E7
  Hampton Magna CV35 114 F4
Cherry Orch
  Henley-in-A B95 113 B5
  Kenilworth CV8 93 D3
  Shipston-on-S CV36 149 F3
  Stratford-u-A CV37 144 C1
  Wellesbourne CV35 146 B2
Cherry Orchard Cl GL55 135 B1
Cherry Pit La B98 86 A1
Cherry Rd OX16 139 F4
Cherry St
  Stratford-u-A CV37 144 C1
  Warwick CV34 108 C4
Cherry Tree Ave CV10 28 C3
Cherry Tree Cres WR11 127 F6
Cherry Tree Wlk CV33 147 D3
Cherry Way CV8 93 D3
Cherry Wlk B47 69 D3
Cherrybrook Way CV2 50 B1
Cherryfield Cl CV10 19 D1
Cherrywood Cres 3 B91 71 E4
Cherrywood Gr CV5 59 F3
Cherwell Cl LE10 31 D4
Cherwell The NN11 117 F1
Cherwell Way CV23 82 A2
Chesford Cres Coventry CV6 50 A1
  Warwick CV34 105 D1
Chesford Gr CV37 144 B2
Chesham St CV31 110 A4
Cheshire Cl CV22 99 E4
Chesholme Rd CV6 49 D1
Chesils The CV3 77 E3
Chessetts Wood Rd B94 89 E4
Chester Cl B37 33 D1
Chester Rd Birmingham B36 33 D3
  Birmingham, Chelmsley Wood B37 44 C4
  Hampton in A B46, B92, CV7 45 D3
Chester St Coventry CV1 61 D2
  Rugby CV21 83 E2
Chester Way OX16 139 F3
Chesterton Cl B97 102 B2
Chesterton Dr
  Nuneaton CV10 28 A3
  Royal Leamington Spa CV31 110 B3
Chesterton Hill CV35 123 C3
Chesterton Rd Coventry CV6 61 D4
  Lighthorne CV35 123 B2
Chesterwood B47 69 D3
Chestnut Ave CV8 92 C2
Chestnut Cl Ettington CV37 131 B3
  Kingsbury B78 15 E3
Chestnut Cres CV10 28 C3
Chestnut Ct Alcester B49 143 E2
  Royal Leamington Spa CV34 109 F1
Chestnut Dr CV11 29 F2
Chestnut Field CV21 83 D2
Chestnut Gr Coleshill B46 34 A4
  Coventry CV4 60 A1
  Moreton Morrell CV35 122 E3
  Wolston CV8 80 A2
Chestnut Pl CV33 147 D3
Chestnut Rd
  Astwood Bank B96 102 C1
  Bedworth CV12 39 E2
  Mollington OX17 134 A2
Chestnut Sq
  6 Royal Leamington Spa CV32 106 A1
  Wellesbourne CV35 146 B2
Chestnut Tree Ave CV4 60 A1
Chestnut Wlk
  2 Birmingham B37 33 D1
  Henley-in-A B95 113 A5
  Stratford-u-A CV37 144 C1
Chestnuts The CV12 38 C1
Cheswick Cl Coventry CV6 62 A4
  Redditch B98 112 A6
Cheswick Green Jun & Inf Sch B94 70 C2
Cheswick Way B90 70 B2
Cheswood Dr B76 22 A3
Chetwode Cl CV5 60 A2
Chetwynd Dr CV11 40 A4
Chetwynd Mid Sch CV11 40 A4
Chetwynd Rd B78 11 D4
Cheveral Ave CV6 61 D3
Cheveral Rd CV12 39 D2
Cheverel Pl CV11 29 D1
Cheverel St CV11 29 D2
Cheviot B77 4 B1
Cheviot Cl CV10 28 A2
Cheviot Rise CV32 106 B2
Cheviot Way OX16 139 F5
Cheylesmore CV1 151 B2
Chichester Cl CV11 30 A4
Chichester Gr B37 33 D1
Chichester La CV35 114 F3
Chicory Dr CV23 83 E4
Chideock Hill CV3 77 D3
Chiel Cl CV5 59 F2
Chigwell Cl B35 22 A2
Childs Cl CV37 144 C3
Childs Oak Cl CV7 74 A3
Chilham Dr B37 33 E1
Chillaton Rd CV6 49 D1
Chillingham B77 9 E4
Chiltern Leys 2 CV6 61 D2
Chiltern Rd B77 4 B1
Chilterns The CV5 60 A2
Chilvers Coton Craft Ctr CV11 29 E1
Chilvers Coton Fst Sch CV11 29 D2
Chilworth Cl CV11 39 F4
Chingford Rd CV6 50 A2
Chingley Bank B95 113 B4
Chipping Campden Sch GL55 135 B2
Chipping Norton Rd OX15 142 D4
Chipstone Cl 1 B91 71 E4
Chiswick Wlk B37 33 F1
Chivenor Prim Sch B35 22 A1
Chivington Cl B90 71 D3
Choyce Cl CV9 12 B1
Christ the King RC Inf Sch CV6 60 C3
Christ the King RC Jun Sch CV6 60 C4
Christchurch Rd CV6 61 D3
Christine Ledger Sq 3 CV31 110 A3
Chub B77 9 E4
Chudleigh Rd CV2 62 C4
Church Ave B46 23 D2
Church Bank Binton CV37 129 A8
  Temple Grafton B49 119 E1
Church Cl Arley CV10 26 C1
  Birmingham B37 33 D3
  Bishops Itchington CV33 124 A4
  Drayton Bassett B78 8 C3
  Hartshill CV10 28 A4
  Hinckley LE10 32 A3
  Luddington CV37 129 C7
  Stoke Golding CV13 21 E4
  Wardington OX17 134 F1
  Whitnash CV31 110 A2
  Wolvey LE10 41 F2
  Wood End CV9 10 B1
Church Down Cl B97 102 B3
Church Dr B49 118 D5
Church End
  Great Rollright OX7 142 A2
  Radford Semele CV31 110 C3
Church Farm Ct CV35 138 C7
Church Farm La GL56 140 A6
Church Fields NN11 126 E8
Church Hill Badby NN11 126 F5
  15 Bishops Tachbrook CV33 122 F8
  Coleshill B46 34 A4
  Combrook CV35 131 E6
  Cubbington CV32 106 C3
  Royal Leamington Spa CV32 109 F4
  Stretton on D CV23 96 C3
  Ullenhall B95 112 E6
  Warmington OX17 133 D2
  Wolvey LE10 41 F2
Church La Alveston CV37 121 D3
  Ansley CV10 27 E1
  Arley CV7 26 C1
  Ash Green CV7 49 F4
  Aston Cantlow B95 119 F6
  Austrey CV9 3 D1
  Austrey, No Man's Heath CV9 3 D3
  Barford CV35 122 B7
  Bearley CV37 120 E7
  Berkswell CV7 58 B2
  Bickenhill B92 44 C1
  Cookhill B49 118 D5
  Corley CV7 48 A4
  Coventry, Middle Stoke CV2 62 A2
  Coventry, Upper Eastern Green CV5 59 E3
  Cropredy OX17 134 C1
  Cubbington CV32 106 C3
  Curdworth B76 23 D3
  Ettington CV37 131 A3
  Fenny Drayton CV13 19 F3
  Fillongley CV7 36 C2
  Gaydon CV35 132 E8
  Hanwell OX17 139 F6
  Hornton OX15 139 B7
  Kingsbury B78 15 E3
  Lapworth B94 88 C2
Church La continued
  Lea Marston B76 24 A4
  Lighthorne CV35 123 B2
  Littleton WR11 127 F1
  Meriden CV7 58 C4
  Middleton B78 8 B1
  Mollington OX17 134 A2
  Newbold-on-S CV37 130 E1
  Norton WR11 127 C2
  Nuneaton CV10 29 E4
  Oxhill CV35 137 F8
  Royal Leamington Spa CV32 106 A2
  Shawell LE17 68 B3
  Shuttington B79 4 C4
  Snitterfield CV37 121 B7
  Stoneleigh CV8 94 B3
  Stratford-u-A CV37 144 B2
  Thurlaston CV23 98 C1
  Welford on A CV37 129 A7
  Whatcote CV36 137 D7
  Whitnash CV31 110 A2
  Wigston Parva LE10 42 C4
  Wishaw B76 14 A1
Church Lees 7 CV33 122 F8
Church Lench Fst Sch WR11 127 A6
Church Mews CV35 132 B6
Church Park Cl CV6 48 C1
Church Path CV35 114 F3
Church Rd
  Astwood Bank B96 102 C1
  Baginton CV8 77 F1
  Braunston NN11 117 D5
  Bubbenhall CV8 95 E3
  Church Lawford CV23 81 E3
  Claverdon CV35 113 F3
  Dordon B78 11 D3
  Gaydon CV35 132 E8
  Grandborough CV23 116 F5
  Hartshill CV10 28 A4
  Ladbroke CV33 124 D5
  Long Itchington CV23 115 D4
  Newbold-on-S CV37 130 E1
  Norton Lindsey CV35 114 C2
  Nuneaton CV10 28 B2
  Pebworth CV37 128 F1
  Ryton-on-D CV8 79 D1
  Shilton CV7 51 F3
  Shustoke B46 25 D1
  Snitterfield CV37 121 B6
  Tamworth B77 9 E2
  Ullenhall B95 112 D5
  Upper Boddington NN11 134 E8
  Warton B79 5 E2
  Wilmcote CV37 120 C4
  Witherley CV9 19 D4
Church St Alcester B49 143 E2
  Appleby Magna DE12 3 F4
  Atherstone CV9 18 B4
  Barford CV35 122 B7
  Bidford-on-A B50 148 C2
  Bulkington CV12 40 B1
  Charwelton NN11 126 D2
  Chipping Campden GL55 135 B2
  Churchover CV23 67 E3
  Clifton u D CV23 84 A3
  Coventry CV1 151 C4
  Fenny Compton CV33 133 D7
  Hampton Lucy CV35 121 F4
  Harbury CV33 123 F6
  Harvington WR11 127 D3
  Hinckley LE10 32 A3
  Marton CV23 115 C7
  Moreton-in-M GL56 140 A3
  Nuneaton CV11 29 E2
  Offenham WR11 127 D1
  Royal Leamington Spa CV31 110 A4
  Rugby CV21 83 D2
  Shipston-on-S CV36 149 F3
  Staverton NN11 126 D8
  Stockton CV23 147 F4
  Stratford-u-A CV37 144 C1
  Studley B80 103 F2
  Warwick CV34 108 C3
  Welford on A CV37 129 A7
  Wellesbourne CV35 146 B2
  Wroxton OX15 139 D4
Church Terr Harbury CV33 123 F7
  Royal Leamington Spa CV31 110 A4
Church View
  Aston Magna GL56 140 A6
  Tamworth B77 9 F4
  Warton B79 5 F2
Church Way CV12 39 D1
Church Wlk Allesley CV5 60 B3
  Atherstone CV9 18 C4
  Barby CV23 101 E1
  Hinckley LE10 31 E4
  12 Royal Leamington Spa CV31 109 F4
  Rugby CV22 83 D1
  Rugby, Bilton CV22 99 E4
  Thurlaston CV23 98 C2
  Wellesbourne CV35 146 B2
Church Wlks CV13 21 E4
Churchdale Cl CV10 28 B2
Churchfield CV37 129 A7
Churchill Ave Coventry CV6 61 F4
  Kenilworth CV8 93 D3
Churchill Cl CV37 131 A4
Churchill Rd Rugby CV22 83 D1
  Sutton Coldfield B75 13 D3
Churchlea OX17 134 A2
Chylds Ct CV5 60 A3
Cicey La CV11 41 D4
Cinder La CV9 6 A4
Cinderhill La GL55 135 B2
Circle The CV10 28 C2
Circuit The CV37 129 C8
Circus Ave B37 33 E1
City Arc CV1 151 B2
City Tech Coll The B37 33 D2
Cladswell Cl B49 118 D5
Cladswell La B49 118 C6
Clapham Sq CV31 110 A4
Clapham St CV31 110 A3
Clapham Terr CV31 110 A4
Clapham Terrace Com Prim Sch CV31 110 A4
Clara St CV2 62 A1
Clare Cl CV32 106 B1
Clare Ct CV21 82 C2
Claremont Cl CV12 40 A2
Claremont Rd
  Royal Leamington Spa CV31 109 F3
  Rugby CV21 83 E2
Claremont Wlk CV5 60 B3
Clarence Rd Hinckley LE10 31 F4
  Rugby CV21 82 C2
  Stratford-u-A CV37 144 B2
Clarence St 4 Coventry CV1 61 F2
  Nuneaton CV11 29 D2
  Royal Leamington Spa CV31 110 A3
Clarence Terr 6 CV32 105 F1
Clarendon Ave CV32 105 F1
Clarendon Cres CV32 105 F1
Clarendon Pl CV32 105 F1
Clarendon Rd Hinckley LE10 31 E4
  Kenilworth CV8 93 D2
Clarendon Sq CV32 105 F1
Clarendon St Coventry CV5 60 C1
  Royal Leamington Spa CV32 106 A1
Clarewell Ave B91 71 D4
Clark Cl CV36 149 F3
Clark St CV6 50 A1
Clarke Ave GL56 140 C3
Clarke's Ave CV8 93 D2
Clarks La CV36 141 D3
Clarkson Dr CV31 110 A2
Claverdon Cl B97 102 B2
Claverdon Jun & Inf Sch CV35 113 F3
Claverdon Rd CV5 60 A2
Claverdon Sta CV35 114 A3
Clay Ave CV11 29 F4
Clay Bank OX15 142 D4
Clay La Allesley CV5 47 F2
  Coventry CV2 62 A2
Claybrook Dr B98 103 F4
Claybrook Prim Sch LE17 43 F2
Claydon Rd OX17 134 C2
Claymore B77 9 E4
Clayton Rd CV6 60 C3
Clayton Wlk B35 22 A1
Cleasby B77 4 B1
Cleaver Gdns CV10 29 E3
Cleeve Prior CE Fst Sch WR11 128 A4
Cleeve Rd Bidford-on-A B50 148 B1
  Littleton WR11 127 F2
Cleeves Ave CV34 109 E3
Clemens St CV31 110 A4
Clement St CV11 29 D2
Clements St CV2 62 A2
Clennon Rise CV2 62 B4
Clent Ave B97 102 B4
Clent Dr CV10 28 A2
Cleobury La B94 70 A2
Clevedon Gn WR11 128 A1
Cleveland Rd
  Bulkington CV12 40 A2
  Coventry CV2 62 A2
  Hinckley LE10 31 E4
Cleveley Dr CV10 28 B4
Clews Rd B98 102 C4
Clifden Gr CV8 93 E3
Cliff Hall La B78 9 E1
Cliffe Ct CV32 105 E1
Cliffe Rd CV32 105 E1
Cliffe Way CV34 109 D4
Clifford Bridge Prim Sch CV3 63 D2
Clifford Bridge Rd CV3 62 C2
Clifford La CV37 130 A8
Clifford Rd B93 71 F2
Clifton Cl B98 103 F4
Clifton La B79 1 A2
Clifton Rd Nuneaton CV10 28 C2
  Rugby CV21 83 E2
Clifton St CV1 151 D4
Clifton-on-Dunsmore CE Prim Sch CV23 83 F3
Clinic Dr CV11 29 E2
Clinton Ave Kenilworth CV8 92 B3
  Warwick CV35 108 A4
Clinton Comb Sch CV8 92 C2
Clinton La CV8 92 B3
Clinton Rd Coleshill B46 33 F3
  Coventry CV6 49 F1
  Solihull B90 70 B4
Clinton St CV31 110 A4
Clipstone Rd CV6 60 C3
Clive Rd CV7 74 B3
Cliveden Wlk CV11 39 F4
Clock La B92 44 B1
Cloister Croft CV2 62 C3
Cloister Crofts CV32 105 F2
Cloister Way CV32 105 F2
Cloisters The Atherstone CV9 18 C4
  Studley B80 103 E2
Clopton Cres B37 33 E2
Clopton Ct CV37 144 C2
Clopton Rd CV37 144 C2
Close The Brandon CV8 79 F3
  Chipping Warden OX17 134 F3
  Cleeve Prior WR11 128 A4

Close The continued
Epwell OX15 138 D3
Halford CV36 137 A8
Hampton Lucy CV35 121 F4
Hollywood B47 69 D3
Kenilworth CV8 93 D3
Lower Quinton CV37 129 E2
Royal Leamington Spa CV31 110 A3
Closers Bsns Ctr CV11 29 E1
Closter Gn CV35 132 B6
Cloud Gn CV4 76 B3
Cloudsley Bush La LE10 42 A3
Clovelly Gdns CV2 62 B3
Clovelly Rd CV2 62 A3
Clovelly Way CV11 29 F3
Clover Ave B37 33 E1
Clover Cl Rugby CV23 83 E4
Stratford-u-A CV37 144 C3
Cloweswood La B94 86 C4
Clumber Park Rd CV35 132 D3
Clunes Ave CV11 29 F3
Clyde Rd Bulkington CV12 40 A1
Dorridge B93 72 A1
Co-operative St CV2 50 A2
Coach House Rise B77 9 F4
Coal Pit La Willey CV23 54 B3
Wolvey LE10 41 E1
Coalpit Fields Rd CV12 39 E1
Coalpit La CV8 80 C1
Coat Of Arms Bridge Rd
CV3 77 D3
Cobbs Rd CV8 92 B3
Cobden Ave CV31 110 B3
Cobden St CV6 61 F3
Cobia B77 9 E4
Cockerills Mdw CV21 101 D4
Cockermouth Cl CV32 105 E1
Cocksfoot Cl CV37 144 C3
Cocksparrow St CV34 108 B4
Cockspur St B78 10 C4
Coffee Pot La CV35 114 C6
Colbourne Grove Dr
CV32 105 E1
Cold Comfort La B49 143 D2
Coldfield Dr B98 102 C4
Coldicotts Cl GL55 135 B2
Cole Ct B37 33 D1
Colebridge Cres B46 33 F4
Colebrook Cl Alcester B49 143 E2
Coventry CV3 62 C1
Coleby Cl CV4 75 E4
Coleford Dr B37 33 D1
Colehurst Croft B90 70 C3
Coleman St CV4 59 F2
Colemeadow Rd B46 33 F4
Coleridge Cl B97 102 B4
Coleridge Rd CV2 62 B2
Coleshill Blythe Specl Sch
B46 34 A2
Coleshill CE Prim Sch
Coleshill B46 33 F3
Coleshill B46 34 A2
Coleshill Cl B97 102 B3
Coleshill Heath Rd
Birmingham B37 44 B4
Coleshill B37, B46 33 F1
Coleshill Heath Sch B37 33 E1
Coleshill Ind Est B46 23 F1
Coleshill Rd Ansley CV10 27 E4
Atherstone CV9 18 B3
Birmingham, Marston Green
B37 44 A4
Curdworth B76 23 E3
Fazeley B78 9 D4
Furnace End B46 25 E2
Maxstoke B46 34 C3
Shustoke B46 24 C1
Water Orton B46 23 D1
Coleshill Sch The B46 34 A2
Coleshill St B78 9 D4
Colesleys The B46 34 A3
Coleville Rd B76 22 A3
Coley Cl LE10 31 E4
Colina Cl CV3 78 B3
Colledge Cl CV23 64 C2
Colledge Rd CV6 49 E1
College Dr CV32 105 F1
College La
Balsall Common CV8 73 F1
Long Compton CV36 141 D2
Stratford-u-A CV37 144 C1
College Mews CV37 144 C1
College Rd CV23 117 C6
College St Nuneaton CV10 29 E1
Stratford-u-A CV37 144 C1
Collets Brook B75 7 D1
Collett B77 4 A1
Collett Wlk 7 CV1 61 D2
Colliers Way CV7 36 C4
Colliery La CV7 39 D1
Colliery La N CV7 39 D1
Colling Wlk B37 33 D3
Collingham La CV23 115 E4
Collingwood Ave CV22 82 B1
Collingwood Rd CV5 61 D1
Collins Gr CV4 76 B3
Collins Rd CV34 109 E3
Collins Way B49 143 E2
Colmore Dr B75 13 D3
Colony Rd OX15 142 D8
Colts Cl LE10 31 E2
Columbia Gdns CV12 39 F1
Colyere Cl CV7 49 D3
Combe Fields Rd CV3 63 F2
Combroke Gr CV35 114 F5
Commaigne Cl CV34 108 B4
Commander Cl 11 CV33 122 F8
Commissary Rd B26 44 A2
Common La Claverdon CV35 113 F4
Corley CV7 47 F4
Kenilworth CV8 93 D4
Mappleborough Green B80 112 A6
Polesworth B78 11 D4
Common The CV9 11 E1
Common Way CV2 62 A3
Compass Ct 8 CV1 61 D2
Compton Cl CV32 106 B1
Compton Croft B37 33 E1
Compton Ct CV36 141 C4
Compton District
Prim Sch The CV36 141 C3
Compton Hill CV35 131 E7
Compton Rd Coventry CV6 49 E1
Lighthorne Heath CV35 123 D2
Compton Verney House
CV35 131 F7
Comrie Cl CV2 62 C3
Comyn St CV32 106 A1
Conduit Hill GL55 135 A1
Coneybury Wlk B76 22 B3
Congleton Cl CV6 49 F1
Congrave Wlk CV12 39 D1
Congreve Cl CV34 104 C1
Conifer Cl CV12 39 E2
Conifer Gr CV31 109 F3
Conifer Paddock CV3 62 C1
Coningsby Cl 5 CV31 110 B3
Coniston B77 10 A4
Coniston Cl Bulkington CV12 40 B2
Rugby CV21 83 E3
Coniston Dr CV5 59 E2
Coniston Rd Coventry CV5 60 C1
Royal Leamington Spa CV32 105 E1
Coniston Way CV11 29 F4
Conrad Cl CV22 99 F3
Conrad Rd CV6 61 D4
Constable Cl CV12 39 D3
Constable Rd CV21 84 A1
Constance Cl CV12 49 F4
Constance Dr CV33 123 F6
Constantine La B46 23 F1
Consul Rd CV21 83 D3
Convent Cl Atherstone CV9 18 C4
Kenilworth CV8 93 D4
Convent La CV9 18 C4
Conway Ave CV4 75 E4
Conway Croft B49 127 E8
Conway Dr OX16 139 F3
Conway Rd
Birmingham, Fordbridge B37 33 D2
Royal Leamington Spa CV32 109 E4
Conwy Cl CV11 29 E2
Cook Cl Knowle B93 72 B3
Rugby CV21 83 E4
Cook St CV1 151 C3
Cook's Hill OX15 139 A3
Cooke Cl CV34 104 C1
Cooks Cl CV9 18 B4
Cooks La Birmingham B37 33 D2
Frankton CV23 97 E1
Salford OX7 150 C3
Coombe Abbey
Ctry Pk CV3 63 F2
Coombe Ave CV3 78 C4
Coombe Ct CV3 63 D1
Coombe Dr CV3 79 F4
Coombe Park Rd CV3 62 C1
Coombe St CV3 62 A1
Cooper St CV11 29 E2
Cooper's Way CV33 132 F6
Coopers Wlk CV8 95 E3
Cope Arnolds Cl CV6 49 F2
Cope St CV1 151 C3
Copeland CV21 83 E4
Copeland Cl B79 5 F2
Copland Pl CV4 59 F1
Coplow Cl CV7 74 A3
Copper Beech Cl CV6 49 F1
Copperas St CV2 50 A1
Copperfield Rd CV2 62 A2
Coppice Cl
Cheswick Green B90 70 B2
Stratford-u-A CV37 145 D3
Coppice Dr B78 11 D3
Coppice La Middleton B78 7 E1
Thorpe Constantine B79 1 C4
Coppice Prim Sch The B47 69 D3
Coppice Rd CV31 110 A1
Coppice The Atherstone CV9 19 D3
Coventry CV3 78 A4
Hinckley LE10 31 F4
Nuneaton CV10 29 E4
Coppice Way 6 B37 33 D1
Coppice Wlk B90 70 B2
Copps Rd CV32 109 E4
Copse Cl CV5 59 D4
Copse The CV7 50 A4
Copsewood Ave CV11 40 A4
Copsewood Terr CV3 62 B1
Copston La LE10 42 A3
Copstone Dr B93 71 F2
Copt Heath Croft B93 72 A4
Copt Heath Dr B93 72 A4
Copt Oak Cl CV4 75 E3
Copthorne Rd CV6 60 C4
Coral Cl Coventry CV5 60 B1
Hinckley LE10 31 F2
Coralin Cl B37 33 E1
Corbett Rd B47 69 D4
Corbett St CV21 83 E2
Corbetts Cl B92 57 D4
Corbin Rd B78 11 D3
Corbison Cl CV34 104 B1
Corbizum Ave B80 103 E2
Cord La CV23 65 F2
Cordelia Gn CV34 109 F2
Cordelia Way CV22 99 F3
Corfe Cl CV2 62 C3
Corinne Croft B37 33 D2
Corley Sch CV7 48 A3
Corley View CV7 49 E3
Corncrake Dr B36 33 D4
Cornel Cl B37 44 B4
Cornelius St CV3 77 E4
Cornet's End La CV7 58 A3
Cornets End La CV7 57 F4
Cornfield Croft B37 33 E2
Cornfield The CV3 62 B1
Cornflower Dr CV23 83 E4
Cornhill Gr CV8 93 E3
Cornish Cl CV10 27 F4
Cornish Cres CV10 29 D1
Cornwall Cl 3 CV34 108 C4
Cornwall Pl CV32 105 E1
Cornwall Rd CV1 61 F1
Cornwallis Rd CV22 82 B1
Cornwell Cl B98 103 D3
Coronation Ave B78 5 D1
Coronation Cl GL55 135 A2
Coronation Cres B79 4 C4
Coronation Rd
Church Lawford CV23 81 D3
Coventry CV1 61 F2
Hurley CV9 16 B3
Coronel Ave CV6 49 F2
Corporation St
Coventry CV1 151 B3
Nuneaton CV11 29 D3
Rugby CV21 83 D2
Corpus Christi RC Prim Sch
CV3 78 B4
Correen B77 4 B1
Corsham Rd CV33 132 F6
Corston Mews CV31 110 B3
Cosford Cl CV32 106 A2
Cosford Cres B35 22 A2
Cosford La CV21 82 C4
Costard Ave CV36 149 F3
Coten End CV34 108 C4
Coten End Cty Fst Sch
CV34 109 D4
Coten End Prim Sch CV34 108 C4
Cotes Rd LE10 31 F3
Cotheridge Cl B90 71 E3
Cotman Cl CV12 39 D2
Coton House Coll CV23 67 F2
Coton Rd Churchover CV23 67 E2
Nether Whitacre B46 15 E1
Nuneaton CV11 29 E2
Rugby CV21 84 A1
Cotsmore Cl GL56 140 B3
Cotswold Bsns Village
GL56 140 B3
Cotswold Cl
Sibford Ferris OX15 142 D8
Tredington CV36 136 F6
Cotswold Cnr OX7 142 A2
Cotswold Cres CV10 28 A2
Cotswold Dr CV3 77 E2
Cotswold Edge GL55 135 B6
Cottage Cl CV31 110 B3
Cottage Farm Ct GL56 136 C1
Cottage Farm Rd
Coventry CV6 49 D1
Tamworth B77 9 E4
Cottage La Minworth B76 22 B3
Nether Whitacre B46 24 B3
Stratford-u-A CV37 144 B1
Cottage Leap CV21 83 E3
Cottage Wlk B77 9 F3
Cotterell Rd CV21 82 C3
Cotterill's Cl CV31 110 A2
Cotters Croft CV33 133 D7
Cottesbrook Cl CV3 62 C1
Cotton Dr CV8 93 E3
Cotton Mill Spinney CV32 106 C3
Coughton CE Jun &
Inf Schs B49 118 F7
Coughton Court B49 119 A7
Coughton Dr CV31 110 B3
Coughton Fields La B49 143 E4
Coughton La B49 118 F7
Coundon Court Sch &
Com Coll CV6 60 C4
Coundon Gn CV6 60 C4
Coundon Prim Sch CV6 60 C3
Coundon Rd CV1 61 D2
Coundon St CV1 151 A4
Coundon Wedge Dr CV5 60 B4
Countess Rd CV11 29 D2
Countess's Croft The CV3 77 E4
Countryside NN11 117 D5
Court Cl
7 Bishops Tachbrook CV33 122 E8
Warmington OX17 133 D2
Court La WR11 127 D1
Court Leet CV3 79 E4
Court Leet Rd CV3 77 F4
Court St CV31 110 A4
Court Way B50 148 B2
Courtaulds Way CV6 61 E3
Courthouse Croft CV8 93 E2
Courthouse Green Prim Sch
CV6 62 A4
Courtland Ave CV6 60 C3
Courtney Cl CV11 29 F4
Courtyard The B46 23 F1
Cove Pl CV2 62 B4
Coventry Airport CV8 78 A1
Coventry Cath Church
of St Michael CV1 151 C3
Coventry City FC CV1 61 F2
Coventry Golf Course CV8 77 E1
Coventry Highway B98 112 A7
Coventry Prep Sch CV3 77 D4
Coventry Rd Baginton CV8 77 F1
Barnacle CV12 51 D4
Bedworth, Hawkesbury
CV2, CV7 50 C3
Bedworth, Springfield CV12 39 D1
Berkswell CV7 58 C2
Brinklow CV23 64 B2
Bulkington CV12 40 A1
Church Lawford CV23 80 C3
Coleshill B46 34 A3
Cubbington CV32 106 C4
Dunchurch CV23 99 D2
Hampton in A B92 45 D2
Hinckley LE10 31 D4
Hinckley, Sketchley LE10 31 F3
Kenilworth CV8 93 D4
Kingsbury B78 15 F2
Long Lawford CV23 81 D3
Lutterworth LE17 55 E3
Marton CV23 115 C8
Nuneaton CV10 39 E4
Pailton CV23 66 A4
Solihull B26, B92 44 B1
Southam CV33 147 D3
Stoneleigh CV8 94 B4
Warwick CV34 108 C4
Wigston Parva LE10 32 C1
Coventry Ret Mkt CV1 151 B2
Coventry Road Exhall CV7 50 A4
Coventry St Coventry CV2 62 A2
Nuneaton CV11 29 E2
Southam CV33 147 D3
Coventry Sta CV1 151 B1
Coventry Tech Coll CV1 61 D1
Coventry Univ CV1 151 C3
Coventry Univ Singer Hall
CV1 151 D3
Coventry Walsgrave
Triangle Bsns Pk CV2 51 D1
Coventry & Warwickshire
Hospl CV1 151 C4
Coventry Whitefriars
(Mus) CV1 151 D2
Coverley Pl CV22 82 C2
Covers The B80 103 F3
Cow La Lower Brailes OX15 137 F2
Whateley B78 9 F2
Cowan Cl CV22 82 B1
Cowdray Cl CV31 110 B4
Cowley Cl B36 22 C1
Cowley Rd CV2 62 B2
Cowley Way CV23 101 F1
Cowper Cl CV34 104 C1
Cowper Rd LE10 31 E3
Cox Cl B50 148 C3
Cox Cres CV22 99 E2
Cox St CV1 151 C3
Cox's Cl CV10 29 D2
Cox's La CV23 125 C7
Cozens Cl CV12 39 D2
Crabbs Cross La B97 102 C3
Crabmill Cl B93 72 B4
Crabmill La CV6 61 F4
Crabtree Gr 19 CV31 110 B3
Crackley La Coventry CV4 75 F2
Kenilworth CV8 93 D4
Craddock Dr CV10 28 B4
Craig Cl CV31 110 A3
Craig Croft B37 33 E1
Craigends Ave CV3 78 C3
Crakston Cl CV2 62 C1
Crammond Cl LE10 31 D4
Cramper's Field CV6 61 D3
Cranborne Chase CV2 63 D3
Crane Cl Stratford-u-A CV37 144 B3
Warwick CV34 104 B1
Cranebrook Hill B78 7 F3
Craner's Rd CV1 61 F2
Cranford Rd CV5 60 B2
Cranham Cl B97 102 A4
Cranmore Ave B90 70 C4
Cranmore Bvd B90 70 B4
Cranmore Rd
Birmingham B36 22 C1
Solihull B90 70 B4
Crantock Way CV11 29 F2
Cranwell Dr CV35 146 B1
Cranwell Rise B78 8 A4
Cranwell Way B35 22 A2
Crathie Cl CV2 62 C3
Craven B77 4 A1
Craven Arms Rd CV35 132 D3
Craven Ave CV3 79 E4
Craven La CV33 147 D2
Craven Rd CV21 83 E2
Craven St CV5 60 C1
Crawford Cl
Bidford-on-A B50 148 B2
Royal Leamington Spa CV32 106 A3
Crawshaws Rd B36 22 B1
Creampot Cl OX17 134 C1
Creampot Cres OX17 134 C1
Creampot La OX17 134 C1
Crecy Rd CV3 77 F4
Crediton Cl CV11 29 F3
Crendon Cl B80 103 F3
Crescent Ave CV3 62 B1
Crescent Sch CV22 99 E4
Crescent The
Baddesley Ensor CV9 11 E2
Bidford-on-A B50 148 B2
Birmingham, Coleshill Heath
B37 44 C4
Brinklow CV23 64 C2
Hampton in A B92 57 D4
Keresley CV7 48 C3
Lawford Heath CV23 98 B3
Crescent The continued
Napton CV23 125 C7
Wootton Wawen B95 120 C7
Cressage Rd CV2 63 D3
Cresswell Cl CV10 29 E4
Crest Hill WR11 127 D3
Crest The CV32 106 B2
Crestwood B77 4 A3
Crew La CV8 93 F3
Creynolds Cl B90 70 B2
Creynolds La B90 70 C2
Crick Rd CV21 101 E4
Cricket Cl CV5 60 C2
Crigdon B77 4 B1
Crimscote Cl B90 70 C3
Cringlebrook B77 9 E4
Critchley Dr CV22 99 E2
Crockwell St CV36 141 C4
Croft Cl
6 Bishops Tachbrook CV33 122 F8
Stretton on D CV23 96 C3
Warwick CV34 109 E4
Wolvey LE10 41 F2
Croft Field CV23 125 C7
Croft Fields CV12 39 D1
Croft Holm GL56 140 B3
Croft Ind Est B37 33 E1
Croft La Shrewley CV35 114 C6
Staverton NN11 126 D8
Temple Grafton B49 119 E2
Croft Mead CV10 27 E2
Croft Mid Sch CV10 28 C2
Croft Pool CV12 38 C1
Croft Rd Atherstone CV9 12 B1
Bedworth CV12 38 C1
Coventry CV1 151 A2
Leek Wootton CV35 105 D4
Littleton WR11 127 F2
Nuneaton CV10 28 C2
Croft Sch The CV37 144 C1
Croft The Bulkington CV12 40 A1
Church Lench WR11 127 A6
Coventry CV6 49 F2
Meriden CV7 46 B1
Warton B79 5 F2
Croft's La OX15 142 D3
Crofts La B96 102 A1
Crofts The B76 22 A4
Cromarty Cl CV5 60 A3
Cromdale B77 4 B1
Cromdale Cl CV10 28 A2
Cromer Rd CV32 106 A1
Cromes Wood CV4 59 E1
Crompton Ave B50 148 C3
Crompton St CV34 108 B3
Cromwell La CV4 75 E3
Cromwell Pl CV35 123 D2
Cromwell Rd CV22 83 E1
Cromwell St CV6 61 F3
Crondal Rd CV7 50 A4
Crook House Yd CV23 64 C2
Crooks La Alcester B49 143 E3
Studley B80 103 E2
Croome Cl CV6 60 C2
Cropredy CE Prim Sch
OX17 134 C1
Cropthorne Cl B98 103 D4
Cropthorne Dr B47 69 D4
Crosbie Rd CV5 60 C2
Cross Cheaping CV1 151 B3
Cross Fields Rd 4 CV34 108 C4
Cross La Braunston NN11 117 E5
Cubbington CV32 106 C2
Cross Leys CV36 136 B6
Cross Rd Alcester B49 143 D2
Coventry CV6 61 F4
Keresley CV7 48 C3
6 Royal Leamington Spa
CV32 105 E1
Cross Road Ind Est CV6 61 F4
Cross St Coventry CV1 151 C4
Long Lawford CV23 82 A3
Nuneaton CV10 28 B2
Royal Leamington Spa CV32 106 A1
Rugby CV21 83 E2
12 Warwick CV34 108 C4
Cross Wlk B78 11 D3
Crossfell B77 4 A1
Crossgate Rd B98 103 E4
Crossland Row LE10 32 A3
Crosslands CV35 146 B1
Crossley Ct CV6 61 F4
Crossway Rd CV3 77 D2
Crossways LE10 31 F3
Crow Hill CV9 11 E1
Crow Thorns CV21 83 E3
Crowberry La B78 14 B4
Crowden Rd B77 4 A1
Crowhill Rd CV11 30 A1
Crowleys Cl B95 112 E6
Crowmere Rd CV2 62 C4
Crown St CV33 123 F7
Crown Terr CV31 109 F4
Crown Way CV32 106 A2
Crownhill Rd LE10 31 E2
Croxall Dr B46 25 D1
Croxhall St CV12 39 E2
Croy Dr B35 22 A2
Croydon Cl CV3 77 F3
Crummock Cl CV6 49 E2
Crutchley Way CV31 110 A1
Cryersoak Cl 7 B90 71 D4
Cryfield Grange Rd CV4 76 B1
Cubbington CE Comb Sch
CV32 106 C3

Cubbington Rd
Coventry CV6 50 A1
Royal Leamington Spa CV32 106 A2
Cuckoo La CV1 151 C3
Culey Wlk B37 33 E1
Culpepper Cl CV10 28 C2
Culverley Cres B93 71 F3
Culworth Cl
Royal Leamington Spa CV31 . 109 F3
Rugby CV21 83 F4
Culworth Ct CV6 61 F4
Culworth Row CV6 61 F4
Cumberland Cres CV32 106 B2
Cumberland Dr CV10 28 C2
Cumberland Wlk B75 13 D3
Cumbernauld Wlk 7 CV2 63 D4
Cumbria Cl CV1 61 D2
Cumming St 6 CV31 110 A4
Cumsey The CV35 114 A5
Cundall Cl CV31 110 A3
Cunningham Way N CV22 82 B1
Cunningham Way S CV22 82 B1
Cup & Saucer OX17 134 C1
Curdworth La B76 23 D4
Curdworth Prim Sch B76 23 E3
Curie Cl CV21 83 E2
Curlew B77 10 A4
Curlew Cl
Stratford-u-A CV37 144 B2
Warton B79 5 F2
Curlieu Cl CV35 108 A4
Curlieu La CV35 114 C2
Curran Cl CV31 110 A2
Curriers Cl CV4 75 E4
Curtis Rd CV2 62 B3
Curzon Ave CV6 61 F4
Curzon Cl LE10 31 F4
Curzon Gr CV31 110 B3
Cut Throat La B94 87 E4
Cuttle Mill La B76 14 B2
Cuttle Pool La B93 72 C2
Cutworth Cl B76 13 D2
Cymbeline Way CV22 99 E3
Cypress Croft CV3 78 C4
Cypress La CV31 110 A1
Cyprus Ave B96 102 B1

D'Aubeny Rd CV4 76 B4
Dace B77 9 E4
Dadglow Rd CV33 124 B4
Daffern Ave CV7 37 D4
Daffern Rd CV7 39 D1
Dagtail La B97 102 B2
Dahlia Cl LE10 31 F3
Daimler Ave OX16 139 F4
Daimler Cl B36 22 C1
Daimler Rd CV6 61 E3
Daintree Croft CV3 77 E4
Dairyground The OX15 139 A3
Dalby Cl CV3 78 C4
Dale Ave CV37 145 E1
Dale Cl
10 Bishops Tachbrook CV33 . 122 F8
Long Itchington CV23 115 C4
Warwick CV34 109 D4
Dale End CV10 28 C3
Dale End Cl LE10 31 D4
Dale Meadow Cl CV7 74 A3
Dale St
Royal Leamington Spa CV32 . 109 F4
Rugby CV21 83 D2
Dale The B95 113 B2
Dalehouse La CV8 93 E4
Dales Cty Jun &
Inf Schs The B77 10 A4
Daleway Rd CV3 77 D2
Dalkeith Ave CV22 99 E4
Dallington Rd CV6 60 C3
Dalmahoy Cl CV11 40 B4
Dalmeny Rd CV4 75 E4
Dalton Cl CV23 81 D3
Dalton Gdns CV2 62 C2
Dalton Rd Bedworth CV12 39 D1
Coventry CV5 61 D1
Dalwood Way CV6 50 A2
Daly Ave CV35 114 F3
Dama Rd B78 8 C4
Dame Agnes Gr CV6 62 A4
Damson Cl B97 102 B3
Damson Ct LE10 31 D4
Damson Rd CV35 114 F3
Danbury Cl B76 13 D1
Dane Rd CV2 62 A2
Danesbury Cres CV31 110 B3
Daneswood Rd CV3 79 F4
Daniel Ave CV10 28 B2
Daniel Rd CV9 18 C4
Danvers Cl OX15 139 E1
Danvers Rd OX15 139 E1
Danzey Cl B98 103 D3
Danzey Green La B94 112 E8
Danzey Green Rd B36 22 A1
Danzey Sta B94 112 E8
Daphne Cl CV2 50 B2
Darfield Ct CV8 95 E3
Dark La Astwood Bank B96 102 B1
Bedworth CV12 38 B1
Birchmoor B78 10 C4
Braunston NN11 117 E5
Coventry CV1 151 B4
Hollywood B47 69 D4
Tiddington CV37 145 F2
Wroxton OX15 139 D4
Darley Green Rd B93 72 A1
Darley Rd LE10 31 F3
Darlingscott Rd CV36 149 E2
Darnbrook B77 4 B1
Darnford Cl CV2 62 C4
Darrach Cl CV2 50 C1
Dart B77 10 A3
Dart Cl LE10 31 D4
Dartmouth Rd CV2 62 B3
Dartmouth Sch CV2 62 B3
Darwell Pk B77 4 A1
Darwin Cl CV2 63 D3
Dassett CE Prim Sch The
CV33 133 D7
Dassett Rd B93 71 F2
Datchet Cl CV5 60 B2
Davenport Dr B35 22 B2
Davenport Rd CV5 77 D4
Davenport Terr LE10 31 F4
Daventry Rd Barby CV23 101 E1
Coventry CV3 77 E4
Rugby CV22, CV23 99 F1
Southam CV33 147 E2
Staverton NN11 126 D8
Staverton NN11 126 E8
Daventry St CV33 147 D2
David Rd Bedworth CV7 49 F4
Coventry CV1 61 F1
Rugby CV22 99 E4
Davidson Ave CV31 110 A4
Davies Rd Bedworth CV7 49 F4
Moreton-in-M GL56 140 B3
Davis Cl CV32 105 E1
Dawes Cl CV2 62 A2
Dawley Cres B37 33 D1
Dawley Wlk 9 CV2 63 D4
Dawlish Cl CV11 29 F3
Dawlish Dr CV3 77 E3
Dawson Cl Redditch B97 102 B3
Whitnash CV31 110 A1
Dawson Rd CV3 62 A1
Day's La CV2 61 F2
Days Cl CV1 61 F2
Daytona Dr CV5 59 D4
De Mohun Cres CV36 141 F5
De Montfort Rd CV8 92 C3
De Montfort Way CV4 76 B3
De-Compton Cl CV7 49 D4
De-La-Bere Cres LE10 32 A3
Deacon Cl CV22 83 E1
Deacon St CV11 29 E2
Dean St CV2 62 A2
Deanbrook Cl B90 71 D3
Deane Par CV21 101 D4
Deane Rd CV21 101 D4
Deans Way CV7 49 E3
Deanston Croft CV2 50 C1
Deansway CV34 104 C1
Debden Cl Dorridge B93 71 F1
Wellesbourne CV35 146 B1
Dee Wlk Birmingham B36 33 D4
Daventry NN11 117 F1
Deedmore Rd CV2 50 B1
Deedmore Sch CV2 62 B4
Deegan Cl CV2 62 A3
Deeley B77 4 A1
Deep La B46 24 C3
Deepdale B77 4 B1
Deepmore Rd CV22 99 E4
Deer Leap The CV8 93 D3
Deerdale Way CV3 78 C4
Deerhill B77 4 B1
Deerhurst Cl GL56 140 F1
Deerhurst Mews CV22 99 E2
Deerhurst Rd CV6 49 D1
Deerings Rd CV21 101 D4
Deerpark Dr CV34 108 C4
Delage Cl CV6 50 A2
Delamere Cl B36 22 B1
Delamere Rd CV12 38 C1
Delamere Way CV32 106 B2
Delancey Keep B75 13 D3
Delaware Rd CV3 77 E3
Delhi Ave CV6 49 E1
Delius St CV4 59 F2
Dell Cl CV3 78 B3
Dell Ct B95 113 B5
Dell Farm Cl B93 72 A3
Delmore Way B76 22 A3
Delphi Cl CV34 109 F2
Deltic B77 4 A1
Delves Cres CV9 10 B1
Dempster Rd CV12 39 D2
Denbigh Cl OX16 139 F2
Denbigh Cnr B46 45 D3
Denbigh Rd CV6 60 C3
Denby Cl CV32 106 B2
Denby Croft B90 71 D3
Dencer Dr CV8 93 E2
Dene Cl CV35 132 B5
Denegate Cl B76 22 A3
Denehurst Way CV10 28 C2
Denewood Way CV8 93 E3
Denham Ave CV5 60 B2
Denham Ct CV9 18 C4
Denis Rd LE10 31 E3
Denne Cl CV37 145 D3
Dennett Cl CV34 104 C1
Dennis Rd CV2 62 A3
Denshaw Croft CV2 63 D4
Denton Cl CV8 92 B3
Denton Croft B93 71 E2
Denville Rd CV32 106 A2
Deppers Bridge CV33 124 B6
Derby Dr B37 33 D1
Derby La CV9 18 B4
Dereham Ct CV32 106 A1
Derek Ave B78 11 D3
Dering Cl CV2 62 B4
Deronda Cl CV12 39 D2
Derry Cl CV8 80 A2
Dersingham Dr CV6 50 A1
Derwent Cl Coventry CV5 59 F2
Royal Leamington Spa CV32 . 105 E1
Rugby CV21 83 E3
Derwent Rd Bedworth CV12 .. 39 D1
Coventry CV6 49 D1
Derwent Way CV11 29 F3
Despard Rd CV5 59 E2
Devereux Cl CV4 59 E1
Devitts Cl B90 70 C4
Devon Cl CV10 28 C3
Devon Gr CV2 62 A3
Devon Ox Rd CV23 101 F1
Devonish Cl B49 143 E3
Devoran Cl CV7 50 A4
Dew Cl CV22 99 E2
Dewar Gr CV21 83 F1
Dewsbury Ave CV3 77 D3
Dexter La CV9 16 B2
Dexter Way B78 10 C4
Dial House La CV5 59 F2
Diana Dr CV2 50 C1
Dickens Cl CV10 28 A2
Dickens Heath Rd B90 70 A3
Dickens Rd Coventry CV6 61 D4
Harbury CV33 123 E6
Rugby CV22 99 F3
Dickins Rd CV34 105 D1
Dickinson Ct CV22 83 D1
Didcot Cl B97 102 B3
Didcot Way DE12 3 F4
Diddington La B92, CV7 45 E1
Didgley Gr B37 33 D3
Didsbury Rd CV7 39 D1
Digbey Cl CV5 60 A3
Digby Cres B46 23 D2
Digby Dr B37 44 A3
Digby Pl CV7 46 B1
Digby Rd B46 33 F3
Dighton Cl CV37 129 F7
Dilcock Way CV4 75 F4
Dillam Cl CV6 50 A2
Dillotford Ave CV3 77 E3
Dingle Cl CV6 61 D3
Dingle La Appleby Magna CV9 ... 3 E3
Nether Whitacre B46 24 C3
Dingle The
Cheswick Green B90 70 B3
Nuneaton CV10 28 C3
Dingles Way CV37 145 D3
Dingleside Mid Sch B98 103 D4
Dingley Rd CV12 40 A1
Discovery Way CV3 79 D4
Ditchford Cl B97 102 B2
Ditton Cl CV22 82 B1
Dixon Cl B35 22 A1
Dobbie Rd CV37 129 D1
Dobson La CV31 110 A2
Dockers Cl CV7 74 B4
Doctors La B95 113 B5
Dodd Ave CV34 109 E4
Dodwells Bridge Ind Est
LE10 30 C4
Dodwells Rd LE10 30 C4
Doe Bank La CV1 61 D2
Dog Kennel La B90 70 B4
Dog La Fenny Compton CV33 133 D7
Napton CV23 125 C8
Nether Whitacre B46 25 D4
Tamworth B77 4 A3
Dogberry Cl CV3 78 B3
Doglands The CV31 110 A2
Doily Cl OX15 142 D4
Doll Mus CV34 108 C3
Doncaster Cl CV2 62 B4
Done Cerce Cl CV22 99 E2
Donegal Cl CV4 76 A4
Dongan Rd CV34 108 C4
Donibristle Croft B35 22 A2
Donnington Ave CV6 60 C3
Donnington Rd CV36 149 F4
Donnithorne Ave CV10, CV11 29 E1
Doone Cl CV2 62 C3
Dorado B77 9 E3
Dorcas Cl CV11 40 B4
Dorchester Ave CV35 114 F3
Dorchester Gr OX16 139 F2
Dorchester Rd LE10 32 A4
Dorchester Way
Coventry CV2 63 D2
Nuneaton CV11 30 A4
Dordon Prim Sch B78 11 D3
Dordon Rd B78 10 C4
Doris Rd B46 33 F4
Dorlecote Pl CV10 39 E4
Dorlecote Rd CV10 39 E4
Dormer Harris Ave CV4 59 F1
Dormer Pl CV32 109 F4
Dormston Cl B91 71 E4
Dorney Cl CV5 76 C4
Dorothy Powell Way CV2 50 C1
Dorridge Croft B93 71 F1
Dorridge Jun & Inf Schs
B93 72 A2
Dorridge Rd B93 72 A1
Dorridge Sta B93 71 F1
Dorset Cl CV10 28 C2
Dorset Rd CV1 61 E3
Dorsington Rd CV37 128 E2
Dosthill Rd
(Two Gates) B77 9 E4
Dosthill Sch B77 9 E3
Douglas Rd Hollywood B47 69 D4
Rugby CV21 83 E3
Doulton Cl CV2 50 C1
Dove Cl Bedworth CV12 38 C2
Hinckley LE10 31 D4
Dovecote Cl CV6 60 B3
Dovedale CV21 83 E4
Dovedale Ave CV6 49 F1
Dovehouse Dr CV35 146 B1
Dover Ave OX16 139 F3
Dover Farm Cl B77 10 A4
Dover St CV1 151 A3
Doverdale Cl B98 103 D4
Doverhouse La CV33 123 F7
Dovestone B77 4 B1
Dovey Dr B76 22 A4
Dowler's Hill Cres B98 103 D4
Dowley Croft CV3 63 D1
Down End OX15 142 D4
Downderry Way CV6 62 A3
Downing Cl B93 72 A2
Downing Cres CV12 39 E2
Downton Cl CV2 63 D4
Dowty Ave CV12 38 B1
Doyle Dr CV6 49 F2
Dr Phillips Sh Ctr The CV2 . 50 B1
Drake St CV6 61 E4
Drakes Cl B97 102 B3
Drakes Cross B47 69 D3
Draper Cl CV8 93 E2
Draper's Fields CV1 151 B4
Drawbridge Rd B90 69 F4
Draycote Water Ctry Pk
CV23 116 C8
Draycott Rd CV2 62 B4
Drayton Ave CV37 144 B2
Drayton Cl Bidford-on-A B50 148 B3
Fenny Drayton CV13 19 F3
Hartshill CV10 28 A4
Redditch B98 103 E4
Stratford-u-A CV37 144 B2
Drayton Cres CV5 59 E3
Drayton Ct CV34 104 C1
Drayton Fields Ind Est
NN11 117 F2
Drayton La Drayton Bassett
B78 8 B3
Fenny Drayton CV13 19 F3
Drayton Leys CV22 100 A4
Drayton Manor Dr
Fazeley B78 8 C4
Stratford-u-A CV37 120 C2
Drayton Manor Pk B78 8 C4
Drayton Rd Bedworth CV12 39 E1
Solihull B90 70 C4
Drayton Sch OX16 139 F4
Drayton Way Daventry NN11 117 F2
Nuneaton CV10 28 B4
Drem Croft B35 22 A1
Drew Cres CV8 93 D2
Dreyer Cl CV22 82 B1
Driftway The CV36 149 F3
Drinkwater Cl CV33 123 F6
Drive The Coleshill B46 34 A3
Coventry CV2 62 C2
Dunchurch CV22 99 F2
Drivers La GL56 141 A1
Dronfield Rd CV2 62 A2
Drovers Way CV33 147 E2
Droylsdon Park Rd CV3 77 D2
Druid Rd CV2 62 A2
Drummond Cl CV6 60 C4
Drummond Way B37 33 E1
Drury La CV21 83 D2
Drybrooks Cl CV7 74 A3
Dryden Cl Kenilworth CV8 92 C2
Nuneaton CV10 27 F3
Dryden Pl CV22 82 C2
Dryden Wlk CV22 82 C2
Drymen Rd CV35 132 D3
Duck La CV37 129 B7
Duck Lake DE12 3 F4
Dudley Gn CV32 106 A1
Dudley Rd CV8 92 C1
Dudley Rise LE10 31 E3
Dudley St Atherstone CV9 18 B4
Coventry CV6 50 A1
Duffy Pl CV21 101 D4
Dugard Pl CV35 122 B7
Dugdale Ave
Bidford-on-A B50 148 B3
Stratford-u-A CV37 145 D3
Dugdale Rd CV6 61 D3
Dugdale St CV11 29 E2
Duggins La CV4, CV7 75 D4
Duke Barn Field CV2 62 A3
Duke St Coventry CV5 60 C1
Nuneaton CV11 29 D2
Royal Leamington Spa CV32 106 A1
Rugby CV21 83 D2
Dukes Jetty CV21 83 D2
Dukes Rd B78 11 D3
Dulverton Ave CV5 60 B2
Dulverton Pl GL56 140 B3
Dumble Pit La B48 85 F4
Dumphouse La B48 85 E2
Dunblane Dr CV32 106 B3
Duncan Dr CV22 99 E3
Dunchurch Boughton
CE Mid Sch CV22 99 E2
Dunchurch Cl CV7 74 A4
Dunchurch Cty Fst Sch
CV22 99 E2
Dunchurch Hall CV22 99 E2
Dunchurch Highway CV5 60 A2
Dunchurch Rd CV22 99 F3
Dunchurch Trad Est CV23 98 B2
Duncombe Gn 7 B46 33 F4
Duncroft Ave CV6 60 C4
Duncumb Rd B75 13 D3
Dunedin B77 4 A1
Dunhill Ave CV4 59 F2
Dunley Croft B90 70 C3
Dunlop Rd B97 102 B3
Dunn's La B78 11 D3
Dunnerdale CV21 83 E4
Dunnington CE Prim Sch
B49 127 E8
Dunnose Cl CV6 61 F4
Dunrose Cl CV2 62 C1
Dunsmore Ave Coventry CV3 78 B3
Rugby CV22 100 C4
Dunsmore Heath CV22 99 E2
Dunstall Cres 2 CV33 122 E8
Dunstan Croft B90 70 B4
Dunster B77 9 E4
Dunster Pl CV6 49 E2
Dunster Rd B37 33 E1
Dunsville Dr CV2 62 C4
Dunton Hall Rd B90 70 A4
Dunton La B76 14 B1
Dunvegan Cl Coventry CV3 63 D1
Kenilworth CV8 93 E2
Duport Rd LE10 31 F4
Durbar Ave CV6 61 E4
Durham Cl CV7 48 C2
Durham Cres CV5 60 A4
Durham Croft B37 33 D1
Durlston Cl B77 4 A3
Dursley La B98 112 A6
Dutton Rd CV2 50 B2
Duttons Cl CV37 121 B7
Duxford Cl Redditch B97 102 A4
Wellesbourne CV35 146 B1
Dwarris Wlk CV34 104 C1
Dyas Rd B47 69 D4
Dyce Cl B35 22 A2
Dyer's La
Chipping Campden GL55 135 A2
Wolston CV8 80 A2
Dyers La B94 87 E4
Dyers Rd CV11 40 C3
Dymond Rd CV6 49 E2
Dysart Cl CV1 61 F2
Dyson Cl CV21 83 F1
Dyson St CV4 59 F2

Eacott Cl CV6 49 D2
Eadie St CV10 28 B2
Eagle Cl CV11 40 A4
Eagle Dr B77 4 B2
Eagle Gr B36 33 D4
Eagle Ho CV1 61 E3
Eagle La CV8 92 C2
Eagle St Coventry CV1 61 E3
Royal Leamington Spa CV31 110 A3
Eagle St E CV1 61 E3
Ealingham B77 4 A1
Earl St Bedworth CV12 39 E1
Coventry CV1 151 C2
Royal Leamington Spa CV32 106 A1
Rugby CV21 83 D2
Earl's Croft The CV3 77 E4
Earl's Wlk CV3 79 E4
Earles Cl CV23 147 F4
Earls Rd CV11 29 D3
Earlsdon Ave N CV5 60 C1
Earlsdon Ave S CV5 77 D4
Earlsdon Bsns Ctr CV5 76 C4
Earlsdon Prim Sch CV5 61 D1
Earlsdon St CV5 76 C4
Earlsmere B94 70 A1
Earlswood Comm B94 87 D3
Earlswood Rd B93 71 E1
Earlswood Sta B94 69 E1
Earlswood Trad Est B94 86 B3
Easedale Cl Coventry CV3 77 D3
Nuneaton CV11 30 A3
Easenhall Cl B93 72 A2
Easenhall Rd CV23 66 A1
Easingwold Rd CV35 132 D4
East Ave Bedworth CV12 39 E1
Coventry CV2 62 A1
East Car Park Rd B40 44 C2
East Cl LE10 31 E4
East Dene CV32 106 A1
East End OX15 142 D4
East Gr CV31 110 A3
East Green Dr CV37 144 B2
East House Dr CV9 16 B2
East Side WR11 128 A2
East St Coventry CV1 61 F2
Long Compton CV36 141 C3
Moreton-in-M GL56 140 A3
Rugby CV21 83 E2
Tamworth B77 9 E3
East Union St CV22 83 D1
East Way B92 45 D2
Eastboro Way CV11 29 F1
Eastbourne Cl CV6 60 C3
Eastcote La B92 56 C2
Eastcotes CV4 60 A1
Eastern Green Jun Sch
CV5 59 E3
Eastern Green Rd CV5 59 F2
Eastern Hill B96 102 C1
Eastfield Cl CV37 144 C3
Eastfield Pl CV21 83 D2
Eastfield Rd Nuneaton CV10 .. 29 E3
Royal Leamington Spa CV32 110 A4
Eastgate OX15 139 B8
Eastlands Cty Prim Sch
CV21 83 E1
Eastlands Gr CV5 60 C2
Eastlands Pl CV21 83 E2
Eastlands Rd CV21 83 E2
Eastlang Rd CV7 36 C2
Eastleigh Ave CV5 76 C4
Eastleigh Croft B76 22 A4
Eastley Cres CV34 108 A4
Eastnor Gr CV31 110 A4

Easton Gr B47 69 D4
Eastway B40 44 C2
Eastwood Cl 9 CV31 110 B3
Eastwood Gr CV21 101 E4
Easy La CV21 82 C2
Eathorpe Cl Coventry CV2 50 B1
Redditch B98 103 F4
Eaton Cl CV32 105 E1
Eaton Rd CV1 151 B1
Eaves Green La CV7 46 C1
Ebbw Vale Terr CV3 77 E4
Eborall Cl CV34 104 C1
Ebourne Cl CV8 93 D2
Ebrington Dr CV35 114 F5
Ebrington & St James
CE Prim Sch GL55 135 B1
Ebro Cres CV3 62 C1
Eburne Prim Sch CV2 50 B1
Eburne Rd CV2 50 B2
Eccles Cl CV2 62 B4
Eckington Cl B98 103 D4
Eclipse Rd B49 143 D2
Eclipse Trad Est B49 143 D2
Ecton Leys CV22 100 A4
Edale B77 4 A1
Edale Gn LE10 31 F3
Edale Way CV6 62 A4
Eddenswood Cl B78 8 C3
Eden Cl B80 103 E2
Eden Croft CV8 93 D2
Eden Gr B37 33 E1
Eden Rd Coventry CV2 63 D4
Rugby CV21 83 F1
Eden St CV6 61 F4
Edge Hill CV9 10 A1
Edge La B95 113 C5
Edgecote Cl CV21 83 F1
Edgefield Rd CV2 63 D4
Edgehill Ctry Pk OX17 133 B3
Edgehill Pl CV4 59 E1
Edgehill Rd CV35 123 C2
Edgewick Com Prim Sch
CV6 61 F4
Edgioake La B96 118 C7
Edgwick Park Ind Est CV6 61 F4
Edgwick Rd CV6 61 F4
Edinburgh Cl OX16 139 F4
Edinburgh Cres CV31 109 F3
Edinburgh Rd Hurley CV9 16 B3
Nuneaton CV10 28 B3
Edinburgh Way
Banbury OX16 139 F3
Long Lawford CV23 82 A3
Edingale Rd CV2 62 C4
Edison Rd B76 24 A2
Edmondes Cl CV34 104 C1
Edmonds Cl CV37 129 D1
Edmondscote Rd CV32 109 E4
Edmondson Cl CV22 99 E2
Edmund Rd CV1 61 E3
Edmunds Rd
Banbury OX16 139 F3
Wroxton OX15 139 D4
Edstone Cl B93 71 F2
Edward Bailey Cl CV3 78 C4
Edward Rd Bedworth CV12 39 E2
Coventry CV6 49 D2
Water Orton B46 23 E2
Edward St Coventry CV6 61 F3
Nuneaton CV11 29 E2
3 Royal Leamington Spa
CV32 105 E1
Rugby CV21 82 C2
Warwick CV34 108 B4
Edward Tyler Rd CV7 39 D1
Edwards Gr CV8 93 E3
Edyth Rd CV2 62 C2
Edyvean Cl CV22 99 F3
Egerton Cl CV21 82 C3
Eileen Gdns B37 33 D2
Elan Cl CV32 106 B2
Elborow St CV21 83 D2
Elbury Croft B93 71 F3
Eld Rd CV6 61 F4
Elder Cl Kingsbury B78 15 E4
Rugby CV22 82 A1
Elderberry Way CV2 62 A3
Eldersfield Gr B91 71 D4
Eldorado Cl B80 103 E2
Elford Gr B37 33 D1
Elgar Cl CV11 40 A4
Elgar Rd CV6 62 A4
Eliot Cl CV34 104 C1
Eliot Ct CV22 82 C2
Elizabeth Ave B78 5 D1
Elizabeth Ct CV34 109 D3
Elizabeth Rd CV31 109 F3
Elizabeth Way
Kenilworth CV8 92 C3
Long Lawford CV23 82 A3
Elkington Croft 8 B90 71 D3
Elkington La CV23 101 D1
Elkington St CV6 61 F4
Ell La CV23 64 C2
Ellacombe Rd CV2 62 B4
Ellen Badger Com Hospl
CV36 137 A4
Ellerbeck B77 4 A1
Ellerdene Cl B98 102 B4
Ellesmere Rd CV12 39 D1
Ellice Dr B36 33 D4
Elliot Cl B50 148 B3
Elliot Dr CV35 146 B2
Elliot's Field Ret Pk CV21 83 D3
Elliotts Orch CV35 122 A7
Elliston Gr CV31 110 B3
Ellys Rd CV1 61 E3
Elm Bank Cl CV32 106 A2
Elm Cl Binley Woods CV3 79 E4
Ilmington CV36 136 B6
Pebworth CV37 128 F1
Southam CV33 147 D2
Elm Dr B49 143 E2
Elm Gr Arley CV7 26 C1
Balsall Common CV7 74 B3
Ebrington GL55 135 F3
Hurley CV9 16 B2
Elm Rd
Royal Leamington Spa CV32 106 A2
Stratford-u-A CV37 144 C3
Elm Row CV23 115 F3
Elm Tree Ave CV4 60 A1
Elm Tree Cl B78 15 E3
Elm Tree Dr LE10 31 F4
Elm Tree Rd CV12 40 B1
Elm Tree Rise B92 57 D3
Elmbank CV33 147 D2
Elmbank Rd CV8 92 C3
Elmbridge Dr B90 71 D3
Elmdene Cl Hatton CV35 114 C5
Wolston CV8 80 A2
Elmdene Rd CV8 93 D2
Elmdon Ct B37 44 A4
Elmdon La Birmingham B37 44 A3
Solihull B26 44 A2
Elmdon Rd B37 44 A4
Elmdon Trad Est B37 44 B3
Elmfield Rd CV10 29 E4
Elmhurst Cl B97 102 B2
Elmhurst Rd CV6 50 A2
Elmore Cl CV3 78 B4
Elmore Rd CV22 82 C1
Elms Ct CV9 3 D1
Elms Dr Austrey CV9 3 D1
Rugby CV22 100 C4
Elms Paddock The CV23 83 F3
Elms The Bedworth CV12 38 C1
Leek Wootton CV35 104 C3
Stratford-u-A CV37 145 D2
Elmsdale Ave CV6 49 F1
Elmstone Cl B97 102 B3
Elmwood Ave CV6 60 C3
Elmwood Cl CV7 74 A3
Elmwood Gr B47 69 D3
Elphin Cl CV6 49 D2
Elsee Rd CV21 83 D2
Elter Cl CV21 83 E4
Eltham Rd CV3 77 F4
Elton Cl CV32 106 B1
Elton Croft B93 71 F2
Elva Croft B36 22 C1
Elvers Green La B93 72 C4
Elwy Circ CV7 49 E3
Ely Cl Birmingham B37 33 D1
Coventry CV2 63 D3
Ely St CV37 145 D1
Embassy Wlk CV2 62 B4
Emerald Way CV31 109 F3
Emerson Rd CV2 62 B2
Emery Cl CV2 62 C4
Emmott Dr CV31 110 A3
Emperor Way CV21 82 C4
Empire Rd CV4 59 F1
Emscote Cty Fst Sch CV34 109 D4
Emscote Lawn Prep Sch
CV34 109 D4
Emscote Rd Coventry CV3 62 B1
Warwick CV34 109 D4
Ena Rd CV1 61 E3
End The OX7 142 A2
Endemere Rd CV6 61 E4
Endsleigh Gdns CV31 110 A3
Enfield Rd Coventry CV2 62 A2
Redditch B97 102 B3
Engine La B77 4 A1
England Cres CV31 109 F4
Engleton Rd CV6 61 D3
English Martyrs
RC Prim Sch CV21 101 D4
Ennerdale CV21 83 E4
Ennerdale Cl CV32 105 E1
Ennerdale Cres CV11 29 F3
Ennerdale La CV2 62 C2
Ennersdale Bglws B46 23 F1
Ennersdale Cl B46 23 F1
Ennersdale Rd B46 23 F1
Enright Cl CV32 105 F1
Ensign Bsns Ctr CV4 75 F3
Ensign Cl CV4 59 E1
Ensor Cl CV11 30 A3
Ensor Dr B78 4 C1
Epping Way CV32 106 B2
Epsom Cl Bedworth CV12 39 D2
Redditch B97 102 B4
Epsom Rd
Royal Leamington Spa CV32 106 B2
Rugby CV22 82 B1
Epwell Rd Shutford OX15 138 F3
Upper Tysoe CV35 138 B6
Erdington Rd CV9 18 B4
Eric Grey Cl CV2 62 A3
Erica Ave CV12 38 C1
Erica Dr CV31 110 A1
Eringden B77 4 A1
Erithway Rd CV3 77 D2
Ernesford Grange Prim Sch
CV3 62 C1
Ernesford Grange Sch &
Com Coll CV3 78 B4
Ernest Richards Rd CV12 39 D2
Ernsford Ave CV3 62 A1
Ernsford Cl B93 71 F1
Errington GL56 140 B3
Esher Dr CV3 77 F4
Eskdale CV21 83 E4
Eskdale Rd LE10 31 D4
Eskdale Wlk CV3 78 B4
Essen La CV23 101 F2
Essex Cl Coventry CV5 60 A2
Kenilworth CV8 92 C1
Essex Gn CV33 132 F7
Essex St CV21 83 D2
Esterton Cl CV6 49 E1
Ethelfield Rd CV2 62 A2
Ethelfleda Rd B77 9 F3
Eton Rd CV37 145 E1
Etone Com Sch CV11 29 E3
Ettingley Cl B98 103 D3
Ettington CE Prim Sch
CV37 131 B3
Ettington Cl Dorridge B93 71 E1
Wellesbourne CV35 146 B1
Ettington Rd Coventry CV5 60 A2
Wellesbourne CV35 146 B1
Eunal Ct B97 102 C3
Europa Way
Birmingham B26 44 B2
Royal Leamington Spa CV34 109 E3
Eustace Rd CV12 40 B1
Euston Cres CV3 78 B3
Euston Pl CV32 109 F4
Evans Cl Bedworth CV12 39 E2
Stratford-u-A CV37 144 B1
Evans Gr CV31 110 A1
Evans Rd CV22 82 B1
Evelyn Ave CV6 49 F1
Evenlode Cl CV37 145 E1
Evenlode Cres CV6 60 C3
Evenlode Gdns GL56 140 B3
Evenlode Rd GL56 140 B3
Everard Cl CV23 84 A3
Everard Ct CV11 29 F1
Everdon Cl CV22 100 C4
Everdon Rd CV6 49 D1
Everest Rd CV22 99 F4
Everglade Rd CV9 10 B1
Everitt Dr B93 72 A3
Eversleigh Rd CV6 60 C4
Evesham Pl CV37 144 C1
Evesham Rd
Bidford-on-A B50 128 E8
Church Lench WR11 127 A6
Cookhill B49 118 D5
Harvington WR11 127 D4
Littleton WR11 127 F3
Offenham WR11 127 F3
Redditch,Dagtail End
B96, B97 102 C2
Redditch,Headless Cross
B97 102 B4
Salford Priors WR11 127 F5
Stratford-u-A CV37 144 B1
Evesham St B49 143 D2
Evesham Wlk CV4 76 B3
Evreux Way CV21 83 D2
Exbury Way CV11 39 F4
Exeter Cl CV3 78 B4
Exhall Cl CV37 145 E1
Exhall Fst Sch CV7 49 F4
Exhall Gn CV7 49 F4
Exhall Grange Sch CV7 49 E3
Exhall Rd CV7 49 D3
Exham Cl CV34 104 C1
Exhibition Way B40 44 B2
Exis Ct CV11 29 F1
Exminster Rd CV3 77 F3
Exmoor Dr CV32 106 B2
Exmouth Cl CV2 62 B4
Exton Cl CV7 49 E3
Eydon Cl CV21 83 F3
Eyffler Cl CV34 108 B4

Fabian Cl CV3 78 B4
Fair Cl CV23 97 E1
Fair Isle Dr CV10 28 C1
Fairbanks Cl CV2 63 D4
Fairbourne Way CV6 60 C4
Faircroft CV8 92 C2
Faircroft Rd B36 22 B1
Fairfax Cl CV35 122 A7
Fairfax St CV1 151 C3
Fairfield Ct CV3 78 A4
Fairfield Rise CV7 46 B1
Fairfields Hill B78 10 C4
Fairfields Wlk CV37 144 B2
Fairhurst Dr CV32 105 F2
Fairlands Pk CV4 76 C3
Fairlawn Cl CV32 105 E1
Fairlawns B76 22 A4
Fairmile Cl CV3 78 B4
Fairview Mews 6 B46 33 F4
Fairwater Cres B49 143 E2
Fairway Nuneaton CV11 40 A4
Tamworth B77 9 F3
Fairway Ct B77 4 A2
Fairway Rise CV8 93 E3
Fairway The Banbury OX16 139 F4
Hinckley LE10 31 F4
Fairways Cl CV5 60 A3
Fairways The CV32 105 E1
Falcon B77 10 A3
Falcon Ave CV3 78 C4
Falcon Cl CV11 40 A4
Falcon Cres B50 148 C3
Falcon Lodge Cres B75 13 D3
Falconers Gn LE10 31 F3
Falcons The B75 13 D3
Falkland Cl CV4 75 E4
Falkland Pl CV33 133 A7
Falkland Way B36 33 D3
Falkwood Gr B93 71 F3
Fallow Hill CV31 110 B3
Falmouth Cl CV11 30 A3
Falstaff Ave B47 69 D3
Falstaff Cl Nuneaton CV11 30 A1
Sutton Coldfield B76 22 A4
Falstaff Dr CV22 99 E3
Falstaff Rd CV4 59 F1
Fancott Dr CV8 92 C3
Fant Hill OX15 137 E3
Far Gosford St CV1 61 F1
Far Lash LE10 31 F4
Far Moor La B98 112 A6
Faraday Ave B76 24 A2
Faraday Rd Hinckley LE10 30 C4
Rugby CV22 83 E1
Farber Rd CV2 63 D3
Farcroft Ave CV5 59 E2
Fareham Ave CV22 100 C4
Farley Ave CV33 123 E6
Farley St CV31 110 A4
Farlow Cl CV6 62 A3
Farm Cl Coventry CV6 49 D2
Harbury CV33 123 E6
Shipston-on-S CV36 149 F3
Farm Gr CV22 83 E1
Farm La Easenhall CV23 65 F2
Grendon CV9 11 F3
Littleton WR11 127 F1
Farm Rd Hinckley LE10 31 F3
Kenilworth CV8 92 C1
Royal Leamington Spa CV32 106 A2
Farm St CV33 123 E6
Farm Stile NN11 134 E8
Farm Wlk 2 CV33 122 F8
Farman Rd CV5 61 D1
Farmcote Cl B97 102 B2
Farmcote Rd CV2 50 A2
Farmer Ward Rd CV8 93 D2
Farmhouse Way B90 71 D4
Farmside CV3 78 B3
Farmstead The CV3 78 A4
Farnborough CE Jun &
Inf Sch OX17 133 F4
Farnborough Dr B90 70 C3
Farnborough Hall OX17 133 F4
Farnborough Rd B35 22 A2
Farndale Ave CV6 49 E2
Farndon Ave B37 44 A4
Farndon Cl CV12 40 A2
Farnworth Gr B36 22 C1
Farr Dr CV4 60 A1
Farren Rd CV2 62 C3
Farriers Ct CV23 65 E4
Farriers Way Hinckley LE10 31 F3
Nuneaton CV11 29 F1
Farrington Cl CV35 146 B1
Farrington Ct CV35 146 B1
Farther Sand Cl CV35 121 F4
Farthing La B76 23 E3
Farvale Rd B76 22 B3
Faseman Ave CV4 59 F2
Faulconbridge Ave CV5 59 F2
Faultlands Cl CV11 39 F4
Fawley Cl CV3 78 B3
Fawsley Leys CV22 100 A4
Faygate Cl CV3 62 C2
Featherbed La
Bascote CV33 115 B1
Cherington CV36 141 D7
Coventry CV4 76 A3
Redditch B97 102 B3
Rugby CV21 84 A1
Wilmcote CV37 120 D5
Withybrook CV7 52 C3
Featherston Rd LE10 31 F3
Featherstone Cl CV10 29 E1
Feckenham Rd
Astwood Bank B96 102 C1
Redditch, Headless Cross
B97 102 B4
Redditch, Hunt End B97 102 B2
Feilding Cl CV2 63 D3
Feilding Way CV10 28 A3
Feldon Mid Sch CV23 115 E3
Felgate Cl B90 71 D3
Fell Gr CV32 106 B2
Fell Mill La CV36 137 A3
Fell's La CV23 125 C8
Fellmore Gr CV31 110 B4
Fellows Way CV21 100 C4
Felspar Rd B77 4 A2
Felton Cl CV2 50 C1
Fen End Rd CV8 73 F2
Fencote Ave B37 33 D2
Fenn Lanes CV13 20 B4
Fennis Cl B93 71 F2
Fenny Compton Rd OX17 134 B5
Fenside Ave CV3 77 E2
Fentham Cl B92 57 D3
Fentham Gn B92 57 D4
Fentham Rd B92 57 D3
Fenton Rd B47 69 D4
Fenwick Cl B49 143 E3
Fenwick Dr CV21 101 D4
Fern Cl Coventry CV2 50 B1
Salford Priors WR11 127 D6
Fern Dale Rd CV7 73 F3
Fern Hill Way LE10 41 E2
Ferncumbe CE Prim
Sch The CV35 114 D6
Ferndale Cl CV11 29 F3
Ferndale Ct B46 34 A3
Ferndale Dr CV8 93 D1
Ferndale Mews B46 34 A3
Ferndale Rd Banbury OX16 139 F4
Binley Woods CV3 79 E4
Ferndown Cl CV4 60 A2
Ferndown Ct CV22 82 C1
Ferndown Rd CV22 82 C1
Ferndown Terr CV22 82 C1
Fernhill Cl CV8 92 C3
Fernhill Dr CV32 106 A1
Fernhill La CV7 73 F3
Fernwood Cl B98 103 D3
Ferrers Cl CV4 59 F1
Ferrieres Cl CV22 99 E2
Ferry La CV37 121 D3
Fetherston Cres CV8 79 D1
Fiddlers Gn B92 57 D4
Field Barn Rd
Hampton Magna CV35 114 F4
Warwick CV35 108 A4
Field Cl Kenilworth CV8 93 D3
Warwick CV34 109 D4
Field Gate La CV33 133 E7
Field Head La CV34 109 D3
Field La B91 56 A3
Field March CV3 78 C3
Field View Braunston NN11 117 E5
Ryton-on-D CV8 79 D1
Field View Cl CV7 50 A4
Field Way B94 88 B3
Fieldfare Croft B36 33 D4
Fieldgate La Kenilworth CV8 92 C3
Whitnash CV31 110 A1
Fieldhouse Cl B95 113 B4
Fielding Cl CV9 12 B1
Fields Ct CV34 108 C4
Fields Park Dr B49 143 E2
Fieldside La CV3 62 C2
Fieldways Cl B47 69 D4
Fife Rd CV5 60 C1
Fife St CV11 29 D2
Fifield Cl CV11 29 E1
Fighting Cl CV35 132 B6
Fillingham Cl B37 33 E1
Fillongley CE Fst Sch CV7 36 C2
Fillongley Rd Maxstoke B46 35 E2
Meriden CV7 46 C2
Filton Croft B35 22 A2
Finch Cl CV6 49 E1
Finch La WR11 127 D3
Findon Cl CV12 40 B2
Fineacre La CV8,CV23 96 B3
Finford Croft CV7 74 A3
Fingal Cl CV3 78 B3
Fingest Cl CV5 60 A2
Finham Cres CV8 93 D3
Finham Gr CV3 77 E2
Finham Green Rd CV3 77 D2
Finham Park Comp Sch
CV3 77 D2
Finham Prim Sch CV3 77 D2
Finham Rd CV8 93 D3
Finmere CV21 83 E3
Finnemore Cl CV3 77 D3
Finwood Rd CV35 113 F8
Fir Gr CV4 60 A1
Fir Tree Ave CV4 60 A1
Fir Tree Gr CV11 39 E4
Fircroft B78 15 E4
Fire Service Tech Coll
GL56 140 C3
Fire Station Rd B26 44 B3
Firethorn Cres CV31 110 A1
Firleigh Dr CV12 40 B1
Firs Dr CV22 82 C1
Firs The Bedworth CV12 38 C1
Coventry CV5 77 D4
Kingsbury B78 15 E4
Lower Quinton CV37 129 E2
Wroxton OX15 139 D4
First Ave
Birmingham, Tyburn B76 22 A3
Coventry CV3 62 B1
First Exhibition Ave B40 44 B2
Firth Ave GL56 140 C3
Firtree Cl OX16 139 F5
Firtree La CV7 37 D4
Fisher Ave CV22 100 C4
Fisher Rd
Bishops Itchington CV33 124 A4
Coventry CV6 61 F4
Fisher's Ct CV34 108 B2
Fishers Cl CV23 101 F1
Fishers Dr B90 69 F3
Fishponds Rd CV8 92 C2
Fishpool La CV7 45 D3
Fitton St CV11 29 D2
Fitzalan Cl CV23 81 D3
Fitzroy Cl CV2 63 D3
Five Ways CV35 90 C1
Five Ways Rd CV35 114 C7
Fivefield Rd CV7 48 C3
Fladbury Cl B98 103 D4
Flamboro' Cl CV3 78 C4
Flamville Rd LE10 32 A3
Flats La CV9 3 D1
Flaunden Cl CV5 60 A2
Flavel Cres CV31 109 F4
Flavel Ct CV9 3 D1
Flax Cl B47 69 D3
Flaxley Cl B98 112 A6
Flecknoe Cl B36 22 B1
Flecknose St CV3 78 B3
Fleet Cres CV21 83 F1
Fleet St CV1 151 B3
Fleming Rd LE10 30 C4
Fletchamstead Highway
CV5 76 B4
Fletcher Gr B93 72 A2
Fletcher Rd LE10 31 F4
Fletchworth Gate CV5 76 B4
Flint Cl CV9 12 C1
Florence Cl Atherstone CV9 12 B1
Bedworth CV12 49 F4

Flower Rd CV37 144 C3
Flowerdale Dr CV2 62 A3
Flude Rd CV7 49 E3
Flying Fields Rd CV33 147 E2
Flynt Ave CV5 60 A3
Foldyard Cl B76 22 A4
Foleshill CE Prim Sch CV6 50 A1
Foleshill Rd CV1, CV6 61 E3
Folkland Gn CV6 61 D4
Folly Ct OX15 142 E8
Folly La Baddesley Ensor CV9 17 E4
Napton CV23 125 B7
Fontmell Cl CV2 63 D2
Ford Cotts CV33 106 C1
Ford La CV37 113 F1
Ford St Coventry CV1 151 C3
Nuneaton CV10 28 C2
Fordbridge Inf Sch B37 33 D3
Fordbridge Rd B37 33 D3
Forde Hall La B94,B95 112 D7
Fordham Ave CV37 145 D2
Fordrift The B37 44 A3
Fordrough The B90 69 E4
Fords Rd B90 69 F4
Fordwell Cl CV5 60 C2
Foredraught B80 103 F2
Foregate St B96 102 C1
Foreland Way CV6 49 D2
Forest Oak Specl Sch B36 22 C1
Forest Rd Dorridge B93 71 F2
Hinckley LE10 31 F4
Forest View B97 102 C3
Forest Way Hollywood B47 69 D3
Nuneaton CV10 28 C1
Forester's Rd CV3 77 F3
Foresters Pl CV21 101 D4
Forfield Pl CV31 110 A4
Forfield Rd CV6 60 C3
Forge Croft B76 22 A3
Forge La B76 22 A3
Forge Rd Kenilworth CV8 93 D3
Shustoke B46 25 D1
Forge Way CV6 49 E2
Forknell Ave CV2 62 B3
Fornside Cl CV21 83 E4
Forrest Rd CV8 92 C2
Forresters Cl LE10 31 F3
Forresters Rd LE10 31 F3
Forryan Rd LE10 31 F4
Forshaw Heath La B94 86 A4
Forshaw Heath Rd B94 69 E1
Forth Dr B37 33 D2
Forties B77 9 F4
Forum Dr CV21 83 E3
Forum Rd B40 44 C2
Forward Rd B26 44 A2
Fosberry Cl CV34 109 D4
Fossdale Rd B77 10 A4
Fosse Cres CV23 96 C2
Fosse Way Chesterton CV33 123 C6
Ettington CV35, CV37 131 C5
Moreton Morrell CV35 123 A3
Shipston-on-S CV36 149 D3
Stretton u F CV23 65 D4
Tredington CV36 136 F6
Ufton CV31,CV33 111 E3
Wolvey CV23 42 C1
Fosseway Ave GL56 140 A2
Fosseway Cl GL56 140 A2
Fosseway Cres CV36 136 F6
Fosseway Dr GL56 140 A2
Fosseway Gdns LE17 43 F3
Fosseway Rd CV3 77 D2
Foster Ave B80 103 F2
Foster Rd CV6 61 D4
Fosterd Rd CV21 82 C3
Founder Cl CV4 76 A4
Fountain Gdns CV35 146 B2
Fountain Way CV37 145 D1
Four Ashes Rd B93 71 F2
Four Oaks Cl B98 102 B4
Four Pounds Ave CV5 60 C2
Fourfields Way CV7 37 D4
Fourways CV9 18 C4
Fowey Cl B76 22 A4
Fowler Rd Coventry CV6 61 D2
Sutton Coldfield B75 13 E3
Fox Ave CV10 29 E4
Fox Cl Harbury CV33 123 F6
Rugby CV21 84 A1
Fox Hill Rd B75 7 D1
Fox Hollies Rd B76 13 D1
Fox's Covert CV13 19 F3
Foxbury Dr B93 72 A2
Foxcote Cl B90 70 B4
Foxcote Dr B90 70 B4
Foxcote Hill CV36 136 B6
Foxcovert La CV13 21 D4
Foxdale Wlk 16 CV31 110 B3
Foxes La CV37 120 C5
Foxes Mdw B76 22 A4
Foxes Way
Balsall Common CV7 74 A3
Warwick CV34 108 B2
Foxfield CV23 66 A4
Foxford Cl B36 22 B1
Foxford Cres CV2 50 A2
Foxford Sch CV6 50 A3
Foxglove B77 4 A2
Foxglove Cl Coventry CV6 49 E1
Rugby CV23 83 F4
Foxhills Cl CV11 30 B1
Foxholes La B97 102 A3
Foxland Cl Birmingham B37 33 E1
Cheswick Green B90 70 B2
Foxon's Barn Rd CV21 83 E3
Foxtail Cl CV37 144 B3
Foxton Rd CV3 62 C1
Foxwood Rd
Birchmoor B78 10 C4
Polesworth B78 4 C1
Framlingham Gr CV8 93 E3
Frampton Cl B37 33 E2
Frampton Wlk CV2 62 C2
Frances Ave CV34 109 D4
Frances Cres CV12 39 D2
Frances Rd Baginton CV8 77 F2
Harbury CV33 123 F6
Francis Cl B78 5 D1
Francis St CV6 61 F4
Franciscan Rd CV3 77 E4
Frank St CV11 29 D2
Frank Whittle Prim Sch
CV2 62 C4
Frankholmes Dr B90 71 D3
Frankland Rd CV6 50 A1
Franklin Gr CV4 59 F1
Franklin Rd Nuneaton CV11 29 E1
Whitnash CV31 110 A2
Frankpledge Rd CV3 77 F4
Frankton Ave CV3 77 E3
Frankton Cl B98 103 F4
Frankton La CV23 97 D3
Frankton Rd CV23 97 F1
Frankwell Dr CV2 50 C1
Fraser Cl CV10 28 A3
Fraser Rd CV6 49 D1
Frasers Way CV37 129 B6
Fred Lee Gr CV3 77 E2
Frederick Bird Prim Sch
CV1 61 F3
Frederick Neal Ave CV5 59 E2
Frederick Press Way 5
CV21 82 C2
Frederick Rd CV7 37 D4
Frederick St CV21 82 C2
Freeboard La CV23 96 C4
Freeburn Cswy CV4 76 B4
Freehold St CV1 61 F2
Freeman Cl CV10 28 B2
Freeman St CV6 61 F3
Freeman's La LE10 32 A3
Freemans Cl CV32 105 F1
Freemantle Rd CV22 82 B1
Freer St CV11 29 F1
Freesland Rise CV10 28 A3
Frensham Cl B37 33 E1
Frensham Dr CV10 28 A3
Freshfield Cl CV5 48 B1
Freshwater Gr 2 CV31 110 B3
Fretton Cl CV6 61 F4
Frevill Rd CV6 62 A4
Friar's Gate CV9 18 B4
Friars Cl CV3 79 F4
Friars La OX15 137 F2
Friars' Rd CV1 151 B2
Friars St CV34 108 B3
Friars Wlk B37 33 E1
Friary Ave B90 71 D3
Friary Cl CV35 114 F3
Friary Rd CV9 12 B1
Friary St CV11 29 D3
Friday Cl B50 148 B3
Friday La B92 56 B2
Friday St
Lower Quinton CV37 129 E2
Pebworth CV37 128 F1
Frilsham Way CV5 60 A2
Frisby Ct CV11 29 F1
Frisby Rd CV4 59 F1
Friswell Dr CV6 61 F4
Friz Hill CV35 131 D8
Frobisher Rd Coventry CV3 77 E3
Rugby CV22 82 B1
Frog La
Balsall Common CV7 74 A3
Ilmington CV36 136 A6
Upper Boddington NN11 134 E8
Welford on A CV37 129 B6
Froglands La WR11 128 A4
Frogmere Cl CV5 60 B3
Frogmore La CV8 73 F1
Frogmore Rd CV37 121 B6
Frolesworth La LE17 43 F4
Front St Ilmington CV36 136 B6
Pebworth CV37 128 E1
Froxmere Cl B91 71 E4
Fryer Ave CV32 105 F2
Frythe Cl CV8 93 E3
Fulbrook La CV35 121 F8
Fulbrook Rd CV2 50 B1
Fulford Dr B76 22 A3
Fulford Hall Rd B94 69 E2
Fullbrook Cl B90 71 D3
Fuller Pl CV35 122 F3
Fullers Cl CV6 60 C4
Fullwood Cl CV2 50 C1
Furlong Mdw CV36 149 F2
Furnace Rd CV12 39 E2
Furndale Rd B46 34 A3
Furness Cl CV21 83 E4
Furrows The CV33 147 E3
Furze Hill Rd CV36 149 F2
Furze La
Chipping Campden GL55 135 C4
Redditch B98 112 A6
Fynford Rd CV6 61 D3

Gables Cl CV22 99 E4
Gables The B78 5 D1
Gadsby St CV11 29 F2
Gadshill CV31 109 F2
Gainford Rise CV3 63 D2
Gainsborough Cres
Knowle B93 72 A3
Rugby CV21 84 A1
Gainsborough Dr
Bedworth CV12 39 D2
Mile Oak B78 8 A4
Royal Leamington Spa CV31 110 B3
Gainsborough Rd CV37 144 B1
Gainsborough Trad Est
CV33 147 D2
Galey's Rd CV3 77 E4
Gallagher Bsns Pk CV6 49 F3
Gallagher Rd CV12 39 D1
Galley Common Fst Sch
CV10 27 F3
Galliards The CV4 76 B2
Gallows Hill CV34 109 D2
Galmington Dr CV3 77 D3
Gannaway Rd CV35 114 B3
Garden Cl Hinckley LE10 31 E3
Knowle B93 71 F3
Mickleton GL55 135 B6
Garden Ct 11 CV34 108 C4
Garden Gr CV12 49 F4
Gardenia Dr CV5 60 A3
Gardens The Kenilworth CV8 93 D2
Radford Semele CV31 110 C3
Rugby CV22 99 E4
Thurlaston CV23 98 C2
Garlick Dr CV8 93 E3
Garnette Cl CV10 28 A3
Garrard Cl WR11 127 F6
Garratt Cl CV23 82 A3
Garrett St CV11 29 F1
Garrick Cl CV5 59 E2
Garrick Way CV37 144 C1
Garrigill B77 4 A1
Garth Cres CV3 78 B4
Garway Cl CV32 105 F2
Garyth Williams Cl CV22 99 F4
Gas House La B49 143 E2
Gas St
Royal Leamington Spa CV31 109 F4
Rugby CV21 83 D2
Gate Farm Dr CV23 53 F2
Gate La Dorridge B93 71 E2
Nether Whitacre B46 24 C3
Gatehouse Cl CV21 101 D4
Gatehouse La CV12 39 D1
Gateley Cl B98 112 A6
Gateside Rd CV6 49 F1
Gatwick Rd B35 22 A2
Gaulby Wlk CV3 63 D1
Gaveston Cl 7 CV34 108 C4
Gaveston Rd Coventry CV6 60 C3
Royal Leamington Spa CV32 105 F1
Gaydon Cl CV6 62 A4
Gaydon Cty Prim Sch
CV35 123 D2
Gaydon Rd CV33 124 A3
Gayer St CV6 50 A1
Gayhurst Cl CV3 78 C4
Gayle B77 4 A1
Gaza Cl CV4 60 A1
Gazelle Cl CV1 151 D3
Geeson Cl B35 22 A2
Gentian Way CV23 83 F4
Gentlemans La B94 112 E7
Geoffery Cl CV2 62 A3
Geoffrey Cl B76 22 A4
George Bach Cl CV23 64 C2
George Eliot Ave CV12 39 E1
George Eliot Hospl CV10 29 D1
George Eliot Rd CV1 61 E3
George Eliot Sch
Nuneaton CV11 29 E1
Nuneaton CV11 39 E4
George Eliot St CV11 29 E1
George Fentham Prim Sch
B92 57 D3
George Fox La CV13 20 A3
George Hodgkinson Cl CV4 59 F2
George La GL55 135 B1
George Marston Rd CV3 62 C1
George Park Cl Ansty CV7 51 E2
Coventry CV2 50 B1
George Rd Warwick CV34 109 D4
Water Orton B46 23 E2
George Robertson Cl CV3 78 C4
George St Arley CV7 37 D4
Coventry CV1 61 F3
Hinckley LE10 31 E4
Nuneaton CV11 29 F1
Royal Leamington Spa CV31 110 A4
Rugby CV21 82 C2
Stockton CV23 115 F3
George Street Ringway
CV12 39 D2
George's Elm La B50 148 C4
Georgian Cl B49 143 D2
Gerard Ave CV4 76 A4
Gerard Rd B49 143 E2
Gerrard St 4 CV34 108 C3
Gerrards Rd CV36 149 F3
Gibbet Hill Rd CV4 76 A2
Gibbet La LE17 68 A3
Gibbons Cl CV4 59 F1
Gibbs Cl CV2 63 D3
Gibbs La WR11 127 D1
Gibson Cres CV12 39 D1
Gibson Dr CV21 84 A1
Gielgud Way CV2 63 D4
Giffard Way CV34 104 C1
Gifford Rd CV35 123 D3
Gifford Wlk CV37 144 B2
Gigg La B76 14 A2
Gilberry Cl B93 72 A2
Gilbert Ave CV22 82 B1
Gilbert Cl 7 Coventry CV1 61 F2
Stratford-u-A CV37 144 C3
Gilberts Rugby Football
Mus CV21 83 D2
Giles Cl CV6 49 E1
Gilfil Rd CV10 29 D1
Gilkes La CV35 137 F8
Gillet Cl CV11 29 D2
Gillett's La OX15 137 E2
Gillians Wlk CV2 63 D4
Gillows Croft B90 71 D4
Gilson Dr B46 33 E4
Gilson Rd B46 33 F4
Gilson Way B37 33 D3
Gingko Wlk CV31 109 F3
Gipsy Cl CV7 74 A3
Gipsy La Balsall Common CV7 74 B3
Nuneaton CV10, CV11 39 E4
Girdlers Cl CV3 77 D3
Girtin Cl CV12 39 D2
Girvan Gr CV32 106 B3
Gisburn Cl CV34 104 C1
Glade The CV5 59 F2
Gladiator Way CV21 82 C4
Gladstone Rd B93 72 A1
Gladstone St CV21 82 C2
Gladstone Terr LE10 31 F4
Glaisdale Ave CV6 49 F2
Glamis Pl OX16 139 F3
Glamorgan Cl CV3 78 B3
Glamara Cl CV21 83 E4
Glascote Heath Prim Sch
B77 4 A1
Glascote La B77 9 F4
Glascote Rd B77 4 A1
Glasshouse La
Kenilworth CV8 93 E2
Lapworth B94 88 C3
Gleave Rd CV31 110 A2
Glebe Ave CV12 38 C1
Glebe Cl Bidford-on-A B50 148 B2
Coventry CV4 76 A4
Stockton CV23 147 F4
Glebe Cres Kenilworth CV8 93 D2
Rugby CV21 82 C2
Glebe Est CV37 120 B5
Glebe Farm Ind Est CV21 82 C4
Glebe Farm (Mus) CV37 120 C5
Glebe Farm Rd CV21 82 C4
Glebe Fields B76 23 D3
Glebe La Nuneaton CV11 29 F3
Staverton NN11 126 E8
Glebe Pl CV31 110 A4
Glebe Rd Claverdon CV35 113 F3
Hinckley LE10 31 F4
Nuneaton CV11 29 E2
Southam CV33 147 D3
Stratford-u-A CV37 144 B2
Glebe Rise CV9 3 D1
Glebe The Corley CV7 48 B4
Hook Norton OX15 142 D4
Wootton Wawen B95 113 B2
Glebe Way CV7 74 A4
Glebefarm Gr CV3 62 C2
Gleeson Dr CV34 104 C1
Glen Cl CV36 149 F3
Glenbarr Cl LE10 31 D4
Glenbarr Dr LE10 31 D4
Glencoe Rd CV3 62 A1
Glendale Ave CV8 93 D3
Glendale Fst Sch CV10 28 C1
Glendon Gdns CV12 40 B2
Glendon Way B93 71 F2
Glendower Ave CV5 60 B2
Gleneagles B77 4 A3
Gleneagles Cl CV11 30 B1
Gleneagles Rd CV2 62 C3
Glenfield Ave CV10 29 E4
Glenfield Cl Redditch B97 102 B3
2 Solihull B91 71 E4
Glenhurst Rd B95 113 A4
Glenmore Dr CV6 49 F3
Glenmount Ave CV6 49 F3
Glenn St CV6 49 E2
Glenridding Cl CV6 49 F3
Glenrosa Wlk CV4 76 A4
Glenroy Cl CV2 62 C3
Glentworth Ave CV6 49 D1
Glentworth Dr B76 13 D1
Glenville Ave CV9 10 B1
Glenwood Dr B90 70 B2
Glenwood Gdns CV12 39 D3
Gloster Dr CV8 92 C3
Gloster Gdns CV35 146 A4
Gloucester Cl CV11 30 A4
Gloucester La GL55 135 B6
Gloucester St
Coventry CV1 61 D2
1 Royal Leamington Spa
CV31 110 A4
Gloucester Way B37 33 D1
Glover Cl CV34 108 A2
Glover Rd B75 13 D3
Glover St CV3 77 E4
Glover's Cl CV9 18 C4
Glovers Cl CV7 46 B1
Godfrey Cl CV31 110 C3
Godiva Pl CV1 151 D3
Godiva Trad Est CV6 61 F4
Godsons La CV23 125 C8
Gofton B77 10 A4
Gold Cl CV11 39 F4
Goldcrest B77 10 A3
Goldcrest Croft B36 33 D4
Golden Acres La CV3 78 C4
Golden End Dr B93 72 B3
Goldicote Rd CV35 130 F7
Goldsborough B77 4 A1
Goldsmith Ave Rugby CV22 99 F3
Warwick CV34 108 B3
Goldthorn Cl CV5 59 E2
Golf Dr CV11 30 A1
Golf La CV31 110 A1
Good Shepherd Prim Sch
CV6 49 F1
Goodacre Cl CV23 84 A3
Goode Croft CV4 59 F1
Goodere Ave B78 11 D4
Goodere Dr B78 5 D1
Goodeve Wlk B75 13 D3
Goodfellow St CV32 105 E1
Goodman Way CV4 59 E1
Goodyers End Fst &
Mid Schs CV12 49 F4
Goodyers End La CV12 49 E4
Goose La CV37 129 D1
Goosehills Rd LE10 31 F3
Gorcott Hill B98 112 B7
Gordon Cl CV12 39 E2
Gordon St Coventry CV1 61 D1
Royal Leamington Spa CV31 110 A4
Goring Rd CV2 62 A2
Gorse Cl CV22 82 C1
Gorse Farm Rd CV11 40 A4
Gorse La B95 113 A2
Gorse Lea CV33 147 D3
Gorseway CV5 60 B2
Gorsey Cl B96 118 C8
Gorsey La Coleshill B46 23 F1
Wythall B47 69 D2
Gorsey Way B46 23 F1
Gorsy Bank Rd B77 9 F3
Gorsy Way CV10 28 B3
Gosford Ind Est CV1 61 F1
Gosford Park Prim Sch
CV1 61 F1
Gosford St CV1 151 D2
Gospel Oak La CV37 120 F5
Gospel Oak Rd CV6 49 D2
Gosport Rd CV6 61 F4
Gould Cl NN11 117 D5
Gould Rd CV35 108 A4
Grace Rd CV5 59 D4
Grafton Cl B98 103 D4
Grafton La B50 148 C3
Grafton Rd B50 128 C8
Grafton St CV1 61 F1
Graham Cl CV6 50 A1
Graham Rd CV21 83 E2
Graham St CV11 29 E3
Granborough Cl CV3 78 C4
Granbrook La GL55 135 C7
Granby Cl LE10 31 E4
Granby Rd Hinckley LE10 31 E4
Honington CV36 137 A5
Nuneaton CV10 28 C2
Grand Depot Rd CV11 40 C3
Grange Ave
Coventry, Binley CV3 78 C4
Coventry, Finham CV3 77 E2
Kenilworth CV8 92 C4
Grange Cl Nuneaton CV10 28 B4
Ratley OX15 132 F2
Southam CV33 147 D3
Tamworth B77 9 E4
Warwick CV34 109 E4
Grange Dr LE10 31 F3
Grange Farm Prim Sch
CV3 77 D3
Grange Gdns CV35 146 B2
Grange La Harvington WR11 127 D3
Sibford Ferris OX15 142 E8
Grange Pk CV37 145 D2
Grange Rd
Balsall Common CV7 73 F4
Bearley CV37 120 E7
Bidford-on-A B50 148 C2
Coventry CV6 50 A3
Dorridge B93 71 F1
Hartshill CV10 19 E1
Lapworth B94 88 C4
Royal Leamington Spa CV32 106 A2
Rugby CV21 82 C3
Grange The
Cubbington CV32 106 C3
Royal Leamington Spa CV32 106 A1
Grangehurst Prim Sch
CV6 50 A2
Grangemouth Rd CV6 61 D4
Grangers La B98 102 C3
Granhill Cl B98 103 D4
Granoe Cl CV3 78 C4
Grant Rd Bedworth CV7 39 D1
Coventry CV3 62 A1
Grantham St CV2 61 F2
Grantley Dr B37 33 D2
Grants Cl CV33 133 D7
Granvile Rd CV35 146 B2
Granville Gdns LE10 31 E4
Granville Rd Dorridge B93 72 A1
Hinckley LE10 31 E4
Granville St CV32 106 A1
Grapes Cl CV6 61 D3
Grasmere Ave CV3 76 C3
Grasmere Cl CV21 83 E3
Grasmere Cres CV11 29 F4
Grasmere Rd CV12 39 D1
Grasscroft Dr CV3 77 F3
Grassholme B77 10 A4
Grassington Ave CV34 104 C1
Grassington Dr CV11 30 A1
Gratton Ct CV3 76 C3
Gravel Hill CV4 59 F1
Gravel The B76 14 A1
Gray's La GL56 140 A3
Graylands The CV3 77 E2

Grayling B77 .... 9 E3
Grayling Wlk B37 .... 33 E2
Grays Orch CV23 .... 98 C1
Grayswood Ave CV5 .... 60 B2
Great Alne Sch B49 .... 119 D6
Great Balance CV23 .... 64 C2
Great Borne CV21 .... 83 E4
Great Central Way CV21 .... 83 E3
Great Rollright CE
Prim Sch OX7 .... 142 A2
Great William St CV37 .... 145 D2
Greatheed Rd CV32 .... 105 F1
Greaves Cl CV34 .... 109 E4
Greaves Way The CV33 .... 124 B4
Green Cl Long Lawford CV23 .. 81 F2
Studley B80 .... 103 F2
Whitnash CV31 .... 110 A2
Wythall B47 .... 69 D2
Green End CV23 .... 115 D4
Green Farm End CV35 .... 132 B6
Green Field The CV3 .... 78 A4
Green Gables B47 .... 69 D4
Green Gates B95 .... 113 B5
Green La Arley CV10 .... 26 C4
Balsall Common CV7 .... 74 A4
Brinklow CV23 .... 64 B2
Church Lawford CV23 .... 81 E3
Corley CV7 .... 47 E3
Coventry CV3 .... 77 D2
Grendon CV9 .... 11 F2
Middleton B78 .... 14 A3
Nuneaton CV10 .... 28 B4
Oxhill CV35 .... 137 F8
Redditch B97 .... 102 A4
Shipston-on-S CV36 .... 149 F3
Shrewley CV35 .... 114 C6
Shutford OX15 .... 139 A1
Studley B80 .... 103 D3
Swalcliffe OX15 .... 139 A1
Tamworth B78 .... 10 B4
Warwick CV34 .... 108 C4
Wibtoft CV23,LE17 .... 43 D2
Wolvey LE10 .... 42 B3
Green Lane Cl CV36 .... 149 F3
Green Lanes Prim Sch B36 33 D4
Green Lea B77 .... 10 A4
Green The Austrey CV9 .... 3 D1
Barby CV23 .... 101 E1
Chipping Campden GL55 .... 135 B1
Cleeve Prior WR11 .... 128 A4
G Wolford CV36 .... 140 E5
Great Rollright OX7 .... 142 A2
Hook Norton OX15 .... 142 D4
Hornton OX15 .... 139 B7
Kineton CV35 .... 132 F3
Kingsbury B78 .... 15 E3
Lighthorne CV35 .... 123 B2
Long Itchington CV23 .... 115 D4
Nuneaton CV11 .... 29 F1
Orton-on-t-H CV9 .... 6 B2
Priors Marston CV23 .... 125 E4
Rugby CV22 .... 99 E4
Shawell LE17 .... 68 B3
Shrewley CV35 .... 114 D6
Shustoke B46 .... 24 C1
Stoke Golding CV13 .... 21 F4
Stoneleigh CV8 .... 94 B3
Swalcliffe OX15 .... 142 F8
Tamworth B77 .... 4 A3
Wood End B78 .... 10 B2
Greenacre Cl B77 .... 4 A3
Greenacres B76 .... 22 A4
Greenacres Prim Sch B77 .... 4 A3
Greenbank Rd CV7 .... 73 F3
Greendale Cl CV9 .... 18 C4
Greendale Rd Atherstone CV9 18 C4
Coventry CV5 .... 60 B2
Greenfield Ave CV7 .... 74 A4
Greenfields Cl CV36 .... 149 F3
Greenfinch Cl B36 .... 33 D4
Greenfinch Rd B36 .... 33 D4
Greenhart B77 .... 4 A2
Greenhill Cl B77 .... 9 E3
Greenhill Rd Rugby CV22 .... 82 C1
Stoke Golding CV13 .... 21 E4
Whitnash CV31 .... 110 A2
Greenhill St CV37 .... 144 C2
Greenland Ave CV5 .... 59 F3
Greenland Ct CV5 .... 59 F3
Greenlands Dr B98 .... 102 C4
Greenlands Rd B37 .... 33 E1
Greenleaf Cl CV5 .... 60 A2
Greenmoor Rd Hinckley LE10 31 E3
Nuneaton CV10 .... 29 D2
Greenodd Dr CV6 .... 49 F3
Greens Rd CV6 .... 49 D1
Greenside B90 .... 70 B2
Greenside Cl CV11 .... 30 B1
Greensleeves Cl CV6 .... 49 D1
Greensward Cl CV8 .... 93 D3
Greensward The
Coventry CV3 .... 63 D1
Wardington OX17 .... 134 F1
Greenswood CV37 .... 120 E7
Greenway Braunston NN11 .. 117 D5
Nuneaton CV11 .... 40 A4
Polesworth B78 .... 5 D2
Warwick CV34 .... 104 C1
Greenway Cl CV36 .... 149 F3
Greenway Nature Trail The
CV37 .... 129 C5
Greenway Rd CV36 .... 149 F3
Greenway The B37 .... 44 A3
Greenways The CV32 .... 106 A2
Greenwood Cl CV23 .... 82 A3
Greenwood Ct CV11 .... 29 F2
Greenwood Rd CV13 .... 21 F4
Greenwood Sq 4 B37 .... 33 D1
Greenwood Way B37 .... 33 D1
Gregory Ave CV3 .... 77 D3
Gregory Hood Rd CV3 .... 77 F2
Grenden Hall Rd CV35 .... 132 D3
Grendon Cl CV4 .... 59 E1
Grendon Dr CV21 .... 83 F4
Grendon Rd B78 .... 11 D4
Grenfell Cl 7 CV31 .... 110 B3
Grenville Ave CV2 .... 62 A2
Grenville Cl CV22 .... 82 B1
Gresham Ave CV32 .... 106 A1
Gresham Pl 7 CV32 .... 106 A1
Gresham Rd CV10 .... 39 D4
Gresham St CV2 .... 62 A1
Gresley Rd CV2 .... 62 B4
Greswold Cl CV4 .... 59 F1
Greswoldes The CV31 .... 110 C3
Gretna Rd CV3 .... 76 C2
Grevel La GL55 .... 135 B2
Greville Rd Alcester B49 .... 143 D3
Kenilworth CV8 .... 92 C2
Warwick CV34 .... 105 D1
Greville Smith Ave CV31 .... 110 A2
Grewcock Cl LE17 .... 43 F3
Grey Mill Cl B90 .... 70 C3
Grey Tree Cres B93 .... 71 F2
Grey's Rd B80 .... 103 F2
Greycoat Rd CV6 .... 49 D1
Greyfriars La CV1 .... 151 B2
Greyfriars Rd CV1 .... 151 B2
Greygoose La GL56 .... 150 A3
Greyhurst Croft 5 B91 .... 71 D4
Greyrick Ct GL55 .... 135 B6
Greys Cl OX16 .... 139 F3
Griff La CV10 .... 38 C3
Griffin Rd CV34 .... 109 E4
Griggs Cl GL55 .... 135 B2
Grimston Cl CV3 .... 63 D1
Grindle Rd CV6 .... 49 F2
Grindsbrook B77 .... 10 A4
Grizebeck Dr CV5 .... 60 A3
Grizedale CV21 .... 83 E4
Grosvenor Cres LE10 .... 32 A3
Grosvenor Rd Coventry CV1 151 A1
Royal Leamington Spa CV31 110 A3
Rugby CV21 .... 83 E2
Grouse Cl CV37 .... 144 B3
Grove Croft CV35 .... 114 F3
Grove Fields CV10 .... 29 E4
Grove La Keresley CV7 .... 48 C4
Lapworth B94 .... 88 C2
Wishaw B76 .... 13 F1
Grove Pk
Hampton Magna CV35 .... 114 F3
Hinckley LE10 .... 32 A3
Grove Pl Nuneaton CV10 .... 28 B2
1 Royal Leamington Spa
CV31 .... 110 A3
Grove Rd Ansty CV7 .... 51 E2
Atherstone CV9 .... 18 B4
Dorridge B93 .... 72 A2
Hinckley LE10 .... 32 A3
Nuneaton CV10 .... 28 B2
Stratford-u-A CV37 .... 144 C1
Grove St Coventry CV1 .... 151 C3
Royal Leamington Spa CV32 . 109 F4
Grove The Bedworth CV12 .... 39 E2
Coleshill B46 .... 33 F2
Hampton in A B92 .... 45 D1
Hinckley LE10 .... 31 E4
Studley B80 .... 103 E2
Grovelands Ind Est CV7 .... 50 A3
Grump St CV36 .... 136 B6
Guardhouse Rd CV6 .... 61 D4
Guernsey Dr B36 .... 33 D3
Guild Rd Aston Cantlow B95 . 119 F6
Coventry CV6 .... 61 E4
Guild St CV37 .... 145 D2
Guilsborough Rd CV3 .... 78 C4
Guinness Cl B98 .... 102 B4
Gulistan Rd CV32 .... 105 F1
Gullet The B78 .... 4 C1
Gullicote La OX17 .... 139 F6
Gulliver's Cl OX15 .... 139 D6
Gulson Hospl CV1 .... 151 D2
Gulson Rd CV1 .... 61 F1
Gun Hill CV7 .... 37 D4
Gun Hill Fst Sch CV7 .... 37 D4
Gun La CV2 .... 62 A3
Gundry Cl CV31 .... 110 A4
Gunn Ct B49 .... 119 E6
Gunn End CV36 .... 149 F4
Gunners La B80 .... 103 F2
Gunnery Terr 5 CV32 .... 105 E1
Gunnings Rd B49 .... 143 E2
Gunton Ave CV3 .... 78 B3
Guphill Ave CV5 .... 60 B1
Guphill La CV5 .... 60 B2
Gurnard B77 .... 9 E3
Gurney Cl CV4 .... 59 F2
Gutteridge Ave CV6 .... 49 D1
Guy Pl E 10 CV32 .... 105 F1
Guy Pl W 9 CV32 .... 105 F1
Guy Rd CV8 .... 92 C1
Guy St
Royal Leamington Spa CV32 . 105 F1
Warwick CV34 .... 108 C4
Guy's Cl CV34 .... 109 D4
Guy's Cliffe Ave CV32 .... 105 E1
Guy's Cliffe Rd CV32 .... 109 F4
Guy's Cliffe Terr CV34 .... 108 C4
Guy's Cross Park Rd CV34 108 C4
Gypsy La Atherstone CV9 .... 12 B1
Dordon B78 .... 11 D2
Kenilworth CV8 .... 92 C1
Water Orton B46 .... 23 E1
Hack La CV36 .... 141 C5
Hackwell St CV23 .... 125 C8
Haddon End CV3 .... 77 F3
Haddon Rd CV32 .... 106 A1
Haddon St CV6 .... 62 A4
Hadfield Cl CV23 .... 84 A3
Hadleigh Croft B76 .... 22 A3
Hadleigh Rd CV3 .... 77 E2
Hadley Cl B47 .... 69 D3
Hadrian Cl CV32 .... 106 A2
Hadrian Dr B46 .... 23 F1
Hadrians Cl B77 .... 9 E4
Hadrians Way CV21 .... 82 C4
Hadrians Wlk B49 .... 143 D2
Halberd Cl LE10 .... 31 E3
Hales Cl CV37 .... 121 B7
Hales Park Ind Est CV6 .... 49 F2
Hales St CV1 .... 151 C3
Halford La CV6 .... 49 D1
Halford Rd Ettington CV37 .. 131 A3
Stratford-u-A CV37 .... 144 C1
Whatcote CV36 .... 137 C7
Halfpenny Field Wlk B35 .... 22 A2
Halfway La CV22 .... 99 D2
Halifax Cl Allesley CV5 .... 60 A4
Wellesbourne CV35 .... 146 A1
Hall Brook Rd CV6 .... 49 D2
Hall Cl CV8 .... 94 A3
Hall Cl The CV22 .... 99 E1
Hall Dr Baginton CV8 .... 77 F2
Birmingham B37 .... 44 A4
Stoke Golding CV13 .... 21 F4
Hall End CV11 .... 29 E1
Hall End Pl CV11 .... 29 E1
Hall Gr CV23 .... 64 C2
Hall Green Rd CV6 .... 50 A1
Hall La Coventry CV2 .... 62 C3
Harbury CV33 .... 123 F7
Witherley CV9 .... 19 D4
Wolvey LE10 .... 41 E2
Hall Rd Hinckley LE10 .... 31 E3
Royal Leamington Spa CV32 . 105 F1
Wolvey LE10 .... 41 E2
Hall Wlk B46 .... 33 F2
Hall's Cl CV31 .... 110 A2
Hallam Rd CV6 .... 49 D1
Hallcroft Way B93 .... 72 A3
Hallfields CV31 .... 110 C3
Hallway Dr CV7 .... 51 F3
Halstead Gr B91 .... 71 D4
Halston Green Rd B90 .... 69 F4
Haltonlea B77 .... 10 A4
Hamar Way B37 .... 33 D1
Hambridge Rd CV33 .... 124 C3
Hames La B79 .... 2 B2
Hamilton Cl CV12 .... 38 B1
Hamilton Ct CV10 .... 28 B2
Hamilton Dr B80 .... 103 E2
Hamilton Rd Coventry CV2 .... 62 A2
Radford Semele CV31 .... 110 C3
Redditch B97 .... 102 B4
Tiddington CV37 .... 145 F2
Hamilton Terr CV32 .... 109 F4
Hamlet Cl Nuneaton CV11 .... 30 A1
Rugby CV22 .... 99 E3
Hamlet The CV35 .... 105 D4
Hammersley St CV12 .... 38 C1
Hammerton Way CV35 .... 146 B1
Hammond Bsns Ctr CV11 .... 29 F2
Hammond Cl CV11 .... 29 F2
Hammond Rd CV2 .... 61 F2
Hampden Cl OX16 .... 139 F3
Hampden Ct CV33 .... 133 A7
Hampden Way CV22 .... 99 E4
Hampdon Way CV35 .... 146 B1
Hampshire Cl CV3 .... 78 C4
Hampstead Norreys Rd
CV35 .... 132 D4
Hampton Ave CV10 .... 28 A2
Hampton Cl Coventry CV6 .... 61 F3
Redditch B98 .... 103 D4
Hampton Croft CV35 .... 114 F2
Hampton in Arden Sta B92 . 57 D4
Hampton La Meriden CV7 .... 57 F4
Solihull B91 .... 56 A3
Hampton Lucy CE Prim Sch
CV35 .... 121 F4
Hampton Rd Coventry CV6 .... 61 F3
Knowle B93 .... 72 B4
Warwick CV34 .... 108 A3
Hampton St CV34 .... 108 B3
Hams La Curdworth B76 .... 23 F3
Lea Marston B76 .... 24 A4
Hanbury Cl CV35 .... 132 B6
Hanbury Rd Bedworth CV12 .... 39 E2
Dorridge B93 .... 71 F2
Hancock Gn CV4 .... 75 F4
Hancox Cl CV33 .... 107 E4
Handcross Gr CV3 .... 77 D3
Handley Gr CV34 .... 104 B1
Handley's Cl CV8 .... 79 D1
Hands Paddock CV37 .... 130 E1
Handsworth Cres CV5 .... 59 F2
Hanford Cl CV6 .... 61 F3
Hanger Rd B26 .... 44 A2
Hangmans La B79 .... 2 A1
Hanlith B77 .... 10 A4
Hanover Ct Hinckley LE10 .... 31 F3
Redditch B98 .... 102 B4
Hans Cl CV2 .... 61 F2
Hansell Dr B93 .... 71 F1
Hanson Ave CV36 .... 149 F3
Hanwell Cl B76 .... 22 A4
Hanwell Ct OX17 .... 139 F6
Hanwood Cl CV5 .... 59 E2
Hanworth Cl CV32 .... 106 B1
Hanworth Rd CV34 .... 108 B4
Harbet Dr B40 .... 44 C2
Harborough Dr B36 .... 22 B1
Harborough Rd
Coventry CV6 .... 49 D1
Long Lawford CV21 .... 82 B4
Harbour Cl B50 .... 148 B2
Harbury CE Sch CV33 .... 123 F6
Harbury Cl B76 .... 22 A3
Harbury La
Bishops Tachbrook CV33 .... 123 B7
Royal Leamington Spa
CV33, CV34 .... 109 F1
Harbury Rd CV33 .... 124 C6
Harcourt CV3 .... 78 C3
Harcourt Gdns CV11 .... 29 E2
Hardwick Cl CV5 .... 60 A2
Hardwick La B80 .... 112 B3
Hardwick Pk OX16 .... 139 F5
Hardwick Rd CV23 .... 125 E4
Hardwyn Cl CV3 .... 63 D1
Hardy Cl Nuneaton CV10 .... 28 A2
Rugby CV22 .... 82 B1
Hardy Rd CV6 .... 61 D4
Hare & Hounds La CV10 .... 29 D1
Harebell B77 .... 4 A2
Harebell Way CV23 .... 83 E4
Harebell Wlk 1 B37 .... 33 E1
Harefield La CV12 .... 38 C4
Harefield Rd Coventry CV2 .... 62 A2
Nuneaton CV11 .... 29 E2
Hareway La CV35 .... 122 C7
Harewood Rd CV5 .... 60 B1
Harger Ct CV8 .... 92 C2
Hargrave Cl Coventry CV3 .... 63 D1
Water Orton B46 .... 23 D2
Harington Rd CV6 .... 61 D3
Harlech Cl Banbury OX16 .... 139 F3
Kenilworth CV8 .... 93 E3
Harley St CV2 .... 62 A2
Harlow Wlk 8 CV2 .... 63 D4
Harmar Cl CV34 .... 104 B1
Harmer Cl CV2 .... 63 D4
Harnall Cl B90 .... 70 C4
Harnall Ind Est CV1 .... 151 C4
Harnall La CV1 .... 151 C4
Harnall La E CV1 .... 61 F2
Harnall La W CV1 .... 151 C4
Harnall Row Coventry CV1 .... 61 F1
Coventry CV1 .... 61 F2
Harold Cox Pl CV22 .... 99 F3
Harold Rd CV2 .... 62 B1
Harold St CV11 .... 29 E2
Harpenden Dr CV5 .... 60 A3
Harper Rd CV1 .... 61 F1
Harpers La CV9 .... 19 D4
Harriott Dr CV34 .... 109 E2
Harris CE High Sch CV22 .... 82 C1
Harris Cl B95 .... 113 B4
Harris Dr CV22 .... 99 F4
Harris Mews B95 .... 113 B4
Harris Rd Coventry CV3 .... 62 A1
Warwick CV34 .... 108 B4
Harrison Cl CV21 .... 101 D4
Harrison Cres CV12 .... 39 D1
Harrison Rd B97 .... 102 B4
Harrow La CV37 .... 144 C1
Harrow Rd CV31 .... 110 A2
Harrowbrook Ind Est LE10 .. 30 C4
Harrowbrook Rd LE10 .... 30 C4
Harry Rose Rd CV2 .... 62 C2
Harry Taylor Fst Sch B97 . 102 C3
Harry Truslove Cl CV6 .... 61 D4
Harry Weston Rd CV3 .... 63 D1
Hart Cl CV21 .... 83 E1
Hartington Cl B93 .... 71 F2
Hartington Cres CV5 .... 60 C1
Hartington Gn LE10 .... 31 F3
Hartland Ave CV2 .... 62 A3
Hartlebury Cl B93 .... 71 F2
Hartlepool Rd CV1 .... 151 D4
Hartleyburn B77 .... 10 A4
Hartridge Wlk CV5 .... 60 A2
Hartshill Hayes Ctry Pk
CV10 .... 18 C1
Hartshill Hayes Visitors Ctr
CV10 .... 18 C1
Hartshill Sch CV10 .... 28 A4
Harvard Cl CV35 .... 146 B1
Harvest Hill Cl 15 CV31 .... 110 B3
Harvest Hill La CV5, CV7 .... 47 E2
Harvesters Cl CV3 .... 63 D1
Harvey Cl CV5 .... 60 A4
Harvington CE Fst Sch
WR11 .... 127 D4
Harvington Dr B90 .... 71 D3
Harvington Way B76 .... 22 A4
Harwood Gr B90 .... 70 B4
Haselbech Rd CV3 .... 62 C1
Haseley Bsns Ctr CV35 .... 114 D7
Haseley Cl CV31 .... 110 A3
Haseley Rd CV2 .... 50 B1
Haselor Cl B49 .... 143 E2
Haselor Jun & Inf Sch
B49 .... 119 D4
Hasilwood Sq CV3 .... 62 A1
Haslucks Green Rd B90 .... 69 F4
Hassall Cl 9 CV33 .... 122 F8
Hastings Cl Banbury OX16 .... 139 F3
Tamworth B77 .... 9 F3
Hastings High Sch LE10 .... 31 F4
Hastings Rd Banbury OX16 .. 139 F4
Coventry CV2 .... 62 A2
Wellesbourne CV35 .... 146 B2
Haswell Cl CV22 .... 83 E1
Hatchford Wlk B37 .... 33 D1
Hathaway Cl
Balsall Common CV7 .... 74 A4
Littleton WR11 .... 127 F1
Hathaway Dr Nuneaton CV11 30 A1
Warwick CV34 .... 104 C1
Hathaway Green La CV37 . 144 C3
Hathaway Hamlet CV37 .... 144 B1
Hathaway La CV37 .... 144 B1
Hathaway Rd CV4 .... 59 E1
Hatherden Dr B76 .... 13 D1
Hatherell Rd CV31 .... 110 C3
Hatters Dr CV9 .... 12 B1
Hatton Bank La CV37 .... 121 D5
Hatton Cl CV35 .... 114 F5
Hatton Ctry World
CV35 .... 114 D5
Hatton Sta CV35 .... 114 C5
Hatton Terr CV35 .... 114 F5
Haunch La B76 .... 24 A4
Haunchwood Rd CV10 .... 28 B2
Havendale Cl CV6 .... 61 D3
Hawbridge Cl B90 .... 71 D3
Hawfinch B77 .... 10 A3
Hawk Cl CV11 .... 40 A4
Hawke's La OX15 .... 142 E8
Hawkes Dr CV34 .... 109 E2
Hawkes Mill La CV5 .... 48 A1
Hawkesbury Fields Sch
CV2 .... 50 B2
Hawkesbury La CV2 .... 50 B3
Hawkeshead CV21 .... 83 E4
Hawkeswell La B46 .... 34 A2
Hawkesworth Dr CV8 .... 93 D3
Hawkinge Dr B35 .... 22 A2
Hawkins Cl CV22 .... 82 C1
Hawkins Rd CV5 .... 61 D1
Hawkshead Dr B93 .... 71 F3
Hawkside B77 .... 10 A4
Hawkswood Dr CV7 .... 74 A4
Hawksworth Dr 6 CV1 .... 61 D2
Hawlands CV21 .... 83 E3
Hawley Rd LE10 .... 31 E4
Hawnby Gr B76 .... 13 D1
Hawthorn Ave CV9 .... 16 B3
Hawthorn Cl B49 .... 143 D3
Hawthorn Cres LE10 .... 31 F2
Hawthorn La CV4 .... 59 F1
Hawthorn Rd CV31 .... 109 F3
Hawthorn Way
Hartshill CV10 .... 28 A4
Rugby CV22 .... 82 A1
Hawthorne Ave CV7 .... 37 D4
Hawthorne Cl CV8 .... 80 A2
Hawthorne Dr B47 .... 69 D3
Hawthorne Terr CV10 .... 28 C3
Hawthorns The B78 .... 15 E4
Hay La Coventry CV1 .... 151 C2
Solihull B90 .... 71 D3
Hay Meadow CV36 .... 149 F3
Hay Pool OX17 .... 133 F5
Hay Wood La B93, CV35 .... 90 A2
Haybarn The B76 .... 22 A4
Haydock Cl Coventry CV6 .... 50 A2
Stratford-u-A CV37 .... 144 C1
Haydon Cl B93 .... 71 F1
Haydon Way B49 .... 118 F8
Haydons Cl GL55 .... 135 B2
Haye La B80 .... 112 A5
Hayes Cl CV21 .... 83 E4
Hayes Green Rd CV12 .... 49 F4
Hayes La CV7 .... 50 A4
Hayes Rd CV10 .... 28 A4
Hayle Ave CV34 .... 104 C1
Hayle Cl CV11 .... 30 A3
Haynes Way CV21 .... 82 C4
Haynestone Rd CV6 .... 60 C3
Hays La LE10 .... 31 D4
Haysum's Cl GL55 .... 135 B1
Hayton Gn CV4 .... 75 F4
Haytor Rise CV2 .... 62 B4
Hayward Cl CV35 .... 114 F3
Hayward's Gn CV6 .... 61 D4
Hayway La CV23 .... 116 B4
Hazel Cl Hartshill CV10 .... 28 A4
Royal Leamington Spa CV32 106 A1
Hazel Croft
Birmingham, Chelmsley Wood
B37 .... 33 D1
Braunston NN11 .... 117 E5
Hazel Dr B47 .... 69 D3
Hazel Gr Bedworth CV12 .... 39 E2
Hockley Heath B94 .... 88 B3
Hazel Rd Coventry CV6 .... 50 A1
Nuneaton CV10 .... 28 B3
Hazelcroft B78 .... 15 E4
Hazelgarth B77 .... 10 A4
Hazelhead St Georges
(Ind Est) CV1 .... 61 F1
Hazell Way CV10 .... 29 D1
Hazeltree Gr B93 .... 71 F2
Hazelwood Cl CV22 .... 99 D2
Hazlemere Cl CV5 .... 60 A2
Headborough Rd CV2 .... 62 A3
Headington Ave CV6 .... 49 D1
Headland Cl CV37 .... 129 A6
Headland Rd CV37 .... 129 A6
Headland Rise CV37 .... 129 A6
Headlands The CV5 .... 60 B2
Healey Cl CV21 .... 83 E4
Health Centre Rd CV8 .... 76 B2
Heanley La CV9 .... 16 B3
Hearsall Com Prim Sch
CV5 .... 60 C1
Hearsall Comm CV5 .... 60 C1
Hearsall Golf Course CV5 .. 76 C4
Hearsall La CV5 .... 60 C1
Heart of England Sch CV7 .. 74 B3
Heart of England Way
CV11 .... 29 F2
Heath Ave CV12 .... 38 C1

Heath Cres CV2 62 A3
Heath End La CV37 121 D7
Heath End Rd CV10 28 C1
Heath Farm La CV35 123 C3
Heath La CV23 64 C1
Heath Rd Bedworth CV12 38 C1
Coventry CV2 62 A2
Hollywood B47 69 D4
Heath Terr CV32 105 F1
Heath The CV22 99 E2
Heath Way CV22 100 B4
Heathcote Ind Est CV34 109 E3
Heathcote La
Royal Leamington Spa CV34 109 E2
Warwick CV34 109 D3
Heathcote Rd CV31 110 A2
Heathcote St CV6 61 D4
Heathcote Way CV34 109 E2
Heather Cl Birmingham B36 33 D4
Nuneaton CV10 28 C2
Rugby CV22 82 C1
Southam CV33 147 D3
Stratford-u-A CV37 144 B2
Heather Dr CV12 38 C1
Heather Rd Binley Woods CV3 79 E4
Coventry CV2 50 B1
Heathfield Cl B93 72 A3
Heathfield Rd Coventry CV5 60 B1
Norton WR11 127 B2
Heathfields Cty Inf Sch B77 9 F3
Heathgreen Cl B37 33 E2
Heathley La B78 8 C3
Hebden B77 10 A4
Hebden Ave CV34 104 C1
Hebden Way CV11 30 A1
Heber Dr CV33 123 E6
Heckley Rd CV7 50 A4
Heddle Gr CV6 62 A4
Hedgerow Wlk CV6 49 D2
Hedgerows The CV10 28 C3
Hedges Cl CV33 124 D6
Hedgetree Croft B37 33 E1
Hedging La B77 9 F3
Hedging Lane Ind Est B77 9 F3
Hedingham Gr B37 33 E1
Hedley Croft B35 22 A2
Heemstede La CV32 106 A1
Heera Cl CV6 61 E4
Hele Rd CV3 77 E3
Helen St CV6 61 F3
Helena Cl CV10 28 C2
Hellidon Cl 4 CV32 106 A1
Hellidon Rd CV23 125 F4
Helmdon Cl CV21 83 E3
Helmsdale Rd CV32 106 A3
Helmswood Dr B37 44 B4
Helston Cl CV11 30 A3
Helvellyn Way CV21 83 E4
Hemdale CV11 30 A2
Heming Rd B98 103 F4
Hemingford Rd CV2 63 D4
Hemlingford Croft B37 44 A4
Hemlingford Rd
Kingsbury B78 15 E2
Sutton Coldfield B76 22 A3
Hemmings Cl CV31 110 C3
Hemmings Mill CV35 122 A7
Hemsby Cl CV4 76 A4
Hemsworth Dr CV12 40 A1
Hen La CV6 49 E2
Henbrook La OX15 137 E2
Hendre Cl CV5 60 B1
Henley Cl CV11 29 F4
Henley Coll CV2 62 B4
Henley Mill La CV2 62 B4
Henley Park Ind Est CV2 62 C4
Henley Rd Claverdon CV35 113 E4
Coventry CV2 62 B4
Lowsonford B95 113 D6
Norton Lindsey CV35 114 D3
Royal Leamington Spa CV31 110 A3
Henley St Alcester B49 143 E2
Stratford-u-A CV37 145 D2
Henley-in-Arden High Sch
B95 113 B4
Henley-in-Arden Prim Sch
B95 113 B4
Henley-in-Arden Sta B95 113 A4
Henrietta St CV6 61 F3
Henry Bellairs CE Mid Sch
CV12 39 E2
Henry Boteler Rd CV4 76 A4
Henry Hinde Fst Sch CV22 82 B1
Henry Hinde Mid Sch CV22 82 A1
Henry St Coventry CV1 151 B3
Kenilworth CV8 93 D3
Nuneaton CV11 29 E1
Rugby CV21 83 D2
Henson Rd CV12 38 C1
Henwood La B91 56 A2
Hepworth Rd CV3 63 D1
Herald Bsns Pk CV3 78 C4
Herald Way Coventry CV3 79 D4
Hinckley LE10 31 E2
Herbert Art Gall & Mus
CV1 151 C2
Herbert Fowler Mid Sch
CV10 26 C1
Herbert St CV10 28 C2
Herbert's La CV8 93 D3
Herdwycke Cl CV33 147 E2
Hereford Rd CV11 40 C3
Hereward Coll of FE CV4 59 F1
Herford Way LE10 31 F3
Heritage Ct CV4 76 B2
Heritage Motor Ctr CV35 123 D1
Hermes Cl CV34 109 F3
Hermes Cres CV2 62 C3
Hermit's Croft CV3 77 E4
Hermitage Dr B76 13 D2
Hermitage La B78 4 C1
Hermitage Rd CV2 62 B2
Hermitage Way CV8 93 D2
Heron Cl Alcester B49 143 D3
Cheswick Green B90 70 B2
Heron La CV37 144 B3
Herrick Rd CV2 62 B2
Hertford Cl CV10 28 C2
Hertford Pl CV1 151 A2
Hertford Rd Alcester B49 143 E3
Stratford-u-A CV37 144 C1
Hertford St CV1 151 B2
Hertford Way B93 72 A2
Hesleden B77 10 A4
Heslop Cl CV3 78 C4
Hetton Cl 8 CV34 104 C1
Hewitt Ave CV6 61 D2
Hexby Cl CV2 63 D3
Hexworthy Ave CV3 77 D3
Heybrook Cl CV2 62 B4
Heycroft CV4 76 B2
Heydons Terr OX17 133 F4
Heyford Gr B91 71 E4
Heyford Leys CV22 99 F3
Heyford Way B35 22 A3
Heyville Croft CV8 93 E2
Heywood Cl CV6 62 A4
Hibberd Ct CV8 92 C2
Hibbert Cl CV22 83 D1
Hickman Rd CV10 27 F3
Hicks Cl CV34 104 C1
Hidcote Ave B76 22 A4
Hidcote Cl Nuneaton CV11 39 F4
28 Royal Leamington Spa
CV31 110 B3
Hidcote Gr B37 44 A4
Hidcote Manor Garden
GL55 135 D5
Hidcote Rd Ebrington GL55 135 D3
Kenilworth CV8 93 E3
High Ash Cl CV7 49 F4
High Beech CV5 60 A3
High Brink Rd B46 33 F4
High Cross La
Claybrooke Magna LE17 43 E3
Lowsonford CV35 113 F6
High La OX15 137 E2
High Mdw OX15 138 D1
High Meadow Fst Sch B46 33 F4
High Park Cl CV5 59 F2
High St Alcester B49 143 D2
Astwood Bank B96 102 C1
Barford CV35 122 B8
Bedworth CV12 39 D1
Bidford-on-A B50 148 C2
Bidford-on-A,Broom B50 148 A4
Bishops Itchington CV33 124 A4
Braunston NN11 117 D5
Charwelton NN11 126 D2
Chipping Campden GL55 135 B2
Coleshill B46 34 A3
Coventry CV1 151 C2
Coventry, Keresley CV6 48 C1
Cropredy OX17 134 C1
Cubbington CV32 106 C3
Fenny Compton CV33 133 D7
Great Rollright OX7 142 A2
Hampton in A B92 57 D4
Harbury CV33 123 F6
Henley-in-A B95 113 B5
Hook Norton OX15 142 D4
Hurley CV9 16 B3
Kenilworth CV8 92 C3
Knowle B93 72 B3
Lower Brailes OX15 137 F2
Marton CV23 115 C7
Mickleton GL55 135 C6
Moreton-in-M GL56 140 A3
Napton CV23 125 C7
Nuneaton CV11 29 D2
Polesworth B78 5 D1
Ratley OX15 133 A2
Royal Leamington Spa CV31 110 A4
Rugby CV21 83 D2
Rugby,Hillmorton CV21 101 D4
Ryton-on-D CV8 79 D1
Shipston-on-S CV36 149 F3
Shutford OX15 139 A3
Southam CV33 147 D2
Stockton CV23 147 F4
Stoke Golding CV13 21 E4
Stratford-u-A CV37 145 D1
Studley B80 103 F2
Tamworth B77 9 E2
Warwick CV34 108 C3
Welford on A CV37 129 A7
High Trees Cl B98 102 C4
High Trees Rd B93 72 A4
High View Dr CV7 49 E4
High View Rd CV32 106 B3
Higham La Nuneaton CV11 29 F4
Stoke Golding CV13 21 E3
Stoke Golding,Wykin LE10 21 F2
Higham Lane Sch CV10 29 E3
Higham on the Hill
CE Prim Sch CV13 21 D2
Higham Way LE10 31 F4
Highbury Gn CV10 28 B4
Highclere Gdns OX16 139 F3
Highcliffe Rd B77 9 E4
Highcroft CV35 113 F3
Highcroft Cres CV32 105 E1
Highdown Cres 3 B90 71 D3
Highdown Rd CV31 110 A3
Highfield CV7 46 B1
Highfield Ave Redditch B97 102 B4
Tamworth B77 4 A3
Highfield Cl Kenilworth CV8 92 C2
Snitterfield CV37 121 B7
Highfield Rd Coventry CV2 61 F2
Nuneaton CV11 29 F1
Redditch B97 102 B4
Stratford-u-A CV37 144 C3
Studley B80 103 E2
Highfield Terr CV32 105 E1
Highgrove Coventry CV4 75 F3
Rugby CV22 99 E4
Highland Rd Coventry CV5 60 C1
Kenilworth CV8 93 E4
Royal Leamington Spa CV32 106 A2
Highland Way B98 103 D4
Highlands OX16 139 F5
Highlands Cl CV34 109 D4
Highlands Rd B90 70 C4
Highview CV9 16 B2
Highwaymans Croft CV4 76 B3
Hiker Gr 3 B37 33 E1
Hilary Bevins Cl CV13 20 C2
Hilary Dr B76 13 D3
Hilary Rd Coventry CV4 76 C3
Nuneaton CV10 28 C3
Hill Cl Northend CV33 133 B7
Royal Leamington Spa CV32 106 A2
Hill Cres CV23 96 C3
Hill Crest CV32 106 C3
Hill Crest Hospl B98 103 E3
Hill Farm Ave CV11 30 A1
Hill Farm Prim Sch CV6 61 D4
Hill Fray Dr CV3 78 A3
Hill La Middleton B75 7 D1
Upper Brailes OX15 137 E3
Upper Quinton CV37 129 D1
Hill Rd Grandborough CV23 116 E6
Keresley CV7 48 C3
Lower Boddington NN11 134 E7
Hill Rise OX7 142 A2
Hill Row NN11 117 E4
Hill Side Coventry CV2 62 A3
Kingsbury B78 15 E2
Hill St Bedworth CV12 39 D3
Coventry CV1 151 B3
Hinckley LE10 31 F4
Nuneaton CV10 28 B2
Royal Leamington Spa CV32 106 A1
Rugby CV21 83 D2
Warwick CV34 109 D4
Hill Top Baddesley Ensor CV9 11 D1
Coventry CV1 151 C3
Hill Top Ave CV9 11 D1
Hill View CV33 124 A4
Hill View Rd B50 148 C3
Hill Wootton Rd CV35 105 E3
Hillary Rd CV22 99 F4
Hillborough La B50 128 E7
Hillcrest Rd Nuneaton CV10 28 C3
Polesworth B78 11 D4
Hillfield Mews 3 B91 71 D4
Hillfield Rd CV22 82 B1
Hillhurst Gr B36 22 B1
Hilliard Cl CV12 39 D2
Hillman Gr B36 22 C1
Hillmorton La
Clifton u D CV23 84 A2
Lilbourne CV23 84 C3
Hillmorton Prim Sch CV21 101 D4
Hillmorton Rd Coventry CV2 50 B1
Knowle B93 72 A3
Rugby CV22 83 E1
Hillrise LE10 31 F4
Hillside Appleby Magna DE12 3 F4
Hartshill CV10 28 A4
Napton CV23 125 C8
Hillside Dr CV10 28 B4
Hillside N CV2 62 A3
Hillside Rd Hinckley LE10 31 E3
Stratford-u-A CV37 144 B2
Hilltop Cl Honiley CV8 90 C4
Southam CV33 147 D3
Hillwood Ave B90 71 D3
Hillyard Rd CV33 147 D3
Hilmore Way B77 9 F4
Hilton Ave CV10 28 A3
Himbleton Croft 1 B90 71 D3
Himley Rd CV12 38 B1
Hinckley Bsns Pk LE10 30 C4
Hinckley CE Jun & Inf Sch
LE10 31 E4
Hinckley & District Hospl
LE10 31 E4
Hinckley La CV13 21 E2
Hinckley Rd Ansty CV2, CV7 51 E1
Aston Flamville LE10 32 B4
Burton Hastings LE10 31 F1
Burton Hastings LE10 41 E4
Coventry CV2 63 D4
Hinckley LE10 32 A3
Nuneaton CV11 29 F3
Stoke Golding CV13 21 F4
Hinckley Sta LE10 31 E4
Hind Cl CV34 104 C1
Hinde Cl CV21 83 E4
Hindlip Cl B98 112 A6
Hintons Coppice B93 71 F3
Hipsley Cl B36 22 B1
Hipsley La CV9 16 C3
Hipswell Highway CV2 62 B2
Hipton Hill WR11 127 B3
Hiron Croft CV3 77 E4
Hiron The CV3 77 E4
Hiron Way CV34 108 A4
Hirst Cl CV23 82 A3
Hitchman Mews CV31 110 A3
Hitchman Rd CV31 110 A3
Hithersand Cl CV35 121 F4
Hoarestone Ave CV11 40 A4
Hob La Balsall Common CV7 74 C2
Burton Green CV8 75 D2
Knowle B92 73 D4
Hob Lane CE Fst Sch CV12 39 E2
Hobbins The CV36 149 F3
Hobley Cl CV22 99 E4
Hockett St CV3 77 E4
Hocking Rd CV2 62 C2
Hockley Cl CV23 116 F5
Hockley Heath Prim Sch
B94 88 B3
Hockley La Coventry CV5 59 E3
Ettington CV37 131 B3
Hockley Rd Shrewley CV35 114 C6
Tamworth B77 9 F3
Hoden La WR11 128 B3
Hodge La B77 4 A3
Hodgett's La Berkswell CV7 74 C4
Coventry CV7 75 D3
Hodgson Rd CV37 144 C3
Hodnell Cl B36 22 B1
Hodnell Dr CV33 147 E2
Hodnet Cl CV8 93 D3
Hogarth Cl CV12 39 D2
Hogarth Rd CV37 144 B1
Hogg End OX17 134 F3
Hoggrills End La B46 25 D2
Holbeche Cres CV7 36 C2
Holbeche Rd Knowle B93 72 A4
Sutton Coldfield B75 13 D3
Holbein Cl CV12 39 D2
Holborn Ave CV6 49 E1
Holbrook Ave CV21 83 D2
Holbrook La CV6 49 E1
Holbrook Park Est CV6 61 E4
Holbrook Prim Sch CV6 49 F1
Holbrook Rd
Long Lawford CV23 82 A3
Stratford-u-A CV37 144 B2
Holbrook Way CV6 49 E1
Holcot Leys CV22 100 A4
Holder Cl B50 148 B3
Hole House La B94 88 C1
Holioak Dr CV34 109 D3
Holland Ave B93 72 A4
Holland Cl B50 148 B2
Holland Rd CV6 61 D3
Hollberry Cl B98 112 A6
Hollick Cres CV7 37 D4
Hollicombe Terr CV2 62 B4
Hollies Inf Sch The CV10 28 C3
Hollies Rd B78 11 D4
Hollies The CV23 67 F1
Hollin Brow Cl B93 72 A2
Hollings Gr B91 71 D4
Hollington Way B90 71 E4
Hollinwell Cl CV11 40 B4
Hollis La CV8 92 C4
Hollis Rd CV3 62 A1
Hollow Cres CV6 61 D3
Hollow Way CV23 125 C8
Holloway Field CV6 61 D3
Holloway Hill OX15 138 A1
Holloway La OX15 138 A1
Holloway The
Mollington OX17 134 A2
Priors Marston CV23 125 E4
Warwick CV34 108 B3
Hollowell Way CV21 83 E4
Holly Bank Est CV9 3 D1
Holly Cl LE10 31 F3
Holly Dr Hollywood B47 69 D4
Hurley CV9 16 B2
Holly Farm Bsns Pk CV8 91 D4
Holly Gr
Church Lawford CV23 81 D3
Coventry CV4 60 A1
Holly La Atherstone CV9 12 B1
Balsall Common CV7 74 A2
Portway B48 85 F3
Wishaw B76 13 E2
Holly Lane Ind Est CV9 12 B1
Holly Lodge CV35 146 B2
Holly St CV32 106 A1
Holly Stitches Rd CV10 28 C3
Holly Tree Wlk LE17 43 F3
Holly Wlk Baginton CV8 77 F1
Nuneaton CV11 29 F1
Royal Leamington Spa CV32 106 A1
Stratford-u-A CV37 144 B2
Hollyberry Ave B91 71 D4
Hollybush La Coventry CV6 50 A2
Priors Marston CV23 125 E4
Hollybush Rd OX15 142 D4
Hollyfast La CV7 48 B2
Hollyfast Prim Sch CV6 60 C4
Hollyfast Rd CV6 60 C3
Hollyhurst B46 23 E1
Hollyland B46 24 C1
Hollywell Rd B93 72 A3
Hollywood La B47 69 D4
Holman Way CV11 29 E2
Holmcroft CV2 62 C4
Holme Cl CV21 83 E3
Holme Way CV23 101 E1
Holmes Dr CV5 59 E3
Holmes Rd CV31 110 A2
Holmewood Cl CV8 93 D3
Holmfield Rd CV2 62 A2
Holmsdale Rd CV6 61 F4
Holsworthy Cl CV11 29 F3
Holt Ave CV33 122 E8
Holt Gdns B80 103 F1
Holt Leys CV33 147 E2
Holt Rd Hinckley LE10 31 F3
Studley B80 103 F1
Holt The Mollington OX17 133 F2
Royal Leamington Spa CV32 106 A2
Holte Rd CV9 18 B4
Holtom St CV37 144 C1
Holwick B77 10 A4
Holy Cross RC Jun &
Inf Sch B76 13 D2
Holy Family RC Prim Sch
CV6 49 D2
Holyhead Rd CV5 60 C3
Holyoak Cl Bedworth CV12 38 C1
Rugby CV22 99 E4
Holywell Cl CV4 59 E1
Holywell Rd CV33 147 D2
Home Cl Bubbenhall CV8 95 E3
Staverton NN11 126 E8
Home Farm CV35 104 C3
Home Farm Cl CV9 19 D4
Home Farm Cres CV31 110 A2
Home Furlong CV35 146 B1
Home Mdw CV35 113 F3
Home Park Rd CV11 29 E2
Homefield La CV22 99 F2
Homefield Sch CV22 99 F2
Homeward Way CV3 63 D1
Honeybourne Cl CV5 60 A2
Honeybourne Rd B50 148 C2
Honeyfield Rd CV1 61 E3
Honeysuckle Cl CV23 83 E4
Honeysuckle Dr CV2 50 A1
Honiley Rd Honiley CV8 91 D3
Meer End CV8 74 A1
Honiley Way CV2 50 B1
Honington Hall CV36 137 A5
Honiton Rd CV2 62 B3
Honiwell Cl CV33 123 E6
Hoo La GL55 135 A2
Hood St CV1 61 F2
Hood's Way CV22 82 B1
Hook Norton CE Sch
OX15 142 D4
Hook Norton Rd OX15 142 D8
Hoopers La B96 102 C1
Hope Cl CV7 49 D4
Hope St CV1 61 D1
Hopedale Cl CV2 62 C2
Hopkins Field CV37 129 B3
Hopkins Prec The B49 143 E2
Hopkins Rd CV6 61 D2
Hopper's La CV35 146 B2
Hopton Cl CV5 60 A2
Hopton Crofts CV32 105 E1
Horley Path Rd OX15 139 D5
Hornbeam B77 4 A2
Hornbeam Dr CV4 59 E1
Hornbeam Gr CV31 110 B3
Hornchurch Cl CV1 151 B1
Horndean Cl CV6 61 F4
Horne Cl CV21 101 D4
Horninghold Cl CV3 78 C4
Hornsey Cl CV2 62 C4
Horse Shoe Rd CV6 50 A2
Horsefair CV36 149 F3
Horsefair The 4 LE10 31 E4
Horsepool LE10 32 A3
Horsewell CV33 147 D2
Horsfall Rd B75 13 D3
Horsford Rd CV3 77 F3
Horsham Cl OX16 139 F5
Horton Cl B49 143 E3
Horton Cres CV22 83 D1
Horton Gr B90 71 D3
Hosiery St CV12 39 E1
Hoskyn Cl CV21 100 C4
Hospital La CV12 38 A1
Hospital of St Cross CV22 83 D1
Hospl Rd (West St) GL56 140 A3
Hotchkiss Cl CV35 146 B1
Hotchkiss Way CV3 79 D4
Hothorpe Cl CV3 62 C1
Houldsworth Cres CV6 49 E2
Houndsfield Cl B47 69 E3
Houndsfield Gr B47 69 D3
Houndsfield La B47 69 E3
Houston Rd CV21 83 E3
Houting B77 9 E3
Hove Ave CV5 59 F2
Hovelands Cl CV2 62 B4
Howard Cl Bidford-on-A B50 148 B2
Coventry CV5 59 F2
Dunchurch CV22 99 E2
Howard Rd Nuneaton CV10 29 D2
Redditch B98 103 E4
Howard St CV1 151 C4
Howard Wlk CV31 109 E4
Howat Rd CV7 48 C4
Howcombe La CV23 125 C7
Howcotte Gn CV4 75 F4
Howe Green La CV7 37 E2
Howells Cl CV12 38 B1
Howes Croft B35 22 A1
Howes La CV3 77 E2
Howes Prim Sch CV3 77 F3
Howkins Rd CV21 83 E3
Howlette Rd CV4 59 F1
Hoylake B77 4 A2
Hoylake Cl CV11 30 A1
Huckson Rd CV33 124 B4
Huddisdon Cl 12 CV34 104 C1
Hudson Ave B46 33 F3
Hudson Rd CV22 82 C1
Hugh Rd CV3 62 A1
Hughes Cl Harvington WR11 127 D4
Warwick CV34 104 B1
Whitnash CV31 110 A1
Hughes Hill CV35 114 B6

Hughes La WR11 127 D4
Hulme Cl CV3 63 D1
Humber Ave Coventry CV1 61 F1
Sutton Coldfield B76 22 A4
Humber Cl NN11 117 F2
Humber Gr B36 22 C1
Humber Rd CV3 78 A4
Humber Wlk OX16 139 F4
Humberstone Rd 3 CV6 61 D3
Humphrey Burton's Rd CV3 77 E4
Humphrey-Davy Rd CV12 49 E4
Humphris St CV34 109 D4
Hungerfield Rd B36 22 B1
Hunningham Gr 6 B91 71 D4
Hunscote La CV35 121 F1
Hunt Cl CV35 114 F3
Hunt End La B97 102 B3
Hunt Hall La CV37 129 A6
Hunt La CV9 19 D4
Hunt Paddocks CV8 92 C1
Hunt Terr CV4 76 A4
Hunter Bvd LE17 55 D3
Hunter St CV21 83 E2
Hunter Terr CV5 76 B4
Hunters Cl CV3 63 D1
Hunters La
Fenny Drayton CV13 20 A3
Rugby CV21 83 D3
Hunters Lane Ind Est CV21 83 D3
Hunters Pk CV9 11 E1
Hunters Wlk CV9 19 D4
Huntingdon Rd CV5 77 D4
Huntingdon Way CV10 28 C2
Hunts Rd CV37 145 E1
Hurdlers La CV37 121 B6
Hurlbutt Rd CV34 109 E2
Hurley Cl CV32 106 A1
Hurley Comm CV9 16 B3
Hurley La B46 25 F3
Hurley Prim Sch CV9 16 B2
Hurn Way CV6 50 A2
Hurst Green Rd
Bentley Heath B93 71 F2
Minworth B76 22 B3
Hurst Rd Bedworth CV12 39 D2
Coventry CV6 50 A2
Hinckley LE10 31 E4
Southam CV33 147 D2
Hurst The B47 69 D3
Husbandmans Cl CV36 149 F3
Hyacinth Way LE10 31 E3
Hyde Pl CV32 109 F4
Hyde Rd Coventry CV2 62 C2
Kenilworth CV8 93 D3
Hydes La LE10 30 C2

Ibex Cl CV3 62 C1
Ibstock Rd CV6 50 A3
Icknield Cl B50 148 C2
Icknield Ct B50 148 C2
Icknield Row B49 143 D2
Icknield St
Bidford-on-A B50 148 C2
Portway B48 85 D3
Icknield Street Dr B98 103 E4
Iden Rd CV1 61 F2
Idlicote Rd CV36 137 B8
Ilam Pk CV8 93 E3
Ilex Ct CV34 109 D4
Ilford Cl CV12 39 D2
Ilford Dr CV3 77 D3
Ilfracombe Gr CV3 77 D3
Illshaw Cl B98 112 A6
Illshaw Heath Rd B94 70 B1
Ilmer Cl CV21 83 F4
Ilmington Cl CV3 77 D3
Ilmington Prim Sch CV36 136 A6
Ilmington Rd
Ilmington CV36 136 D7
Tredington CV36 136 E6
Ilminster Cl LE10 32 A4
Imperial Rise B46 23 F1
Inca Cl CV3 78 C4
Inchbrook Rd CV8 93 E3
Inchford Ave CV34 104 C1
Inchford Cl CV11 29 F1
Ingleton Cl CV11 30 A1
Inglewood Cl CV32 106 A2
Ingon La CV37 121 B5
Ingram Pit La B77 4 A3
Ingram Rd CV5 76 B4
Innace Park Small Ind Units
CV9 12 B1
Innage Cl CV31 110 A4
Innage Terr CV9 18 B4
Innage The B47 69 D3
Innis Rd CV5 76 C4
Innisfree House Sch B47 69 E2
Innsworth Dr B35 22 A2
Instone Rd CV6 49 D1
International Dr B26 44 B2
Inveraray Cl CV8 93 E2
Inverlea Ct GL55 135 B6
Inverness Cl CV5 60 A2
Invicta Rd CV3 78 C4
Ipsley Fst Sch B98 102 C4
Ipswich Wlk B37 33 D1
Irelands La B95 113 D7
Ireton Cl CV4 59 E1
Iris Cl LE10 31 F3
Ironmonger Row CV1 151 B3
Ironstone Hollow OX15 142 E4
Irving Rd CV1 61 F1
Isis Gr B36 33 D4
Islington Cres CV9 10 B1
Ivanhoe Ave CV11 29 F1
Ivor Rd Atherstone CV9 18 C4
Coventry CV6 49 F1
Ivy Cl CV13 21 E4
Ivy Farm La CV4 76 B3
Ivy La Ettington CV37 131 A3
Harbury CV33 123 F6
Mollington OX17 134 A2
Ivy Lodge Cl B37 44 A4
Ivybridge Rd CV3 77 E3
Ivycroft Rd B79 5 F2
Ivyhouse Wlk B77 9 F3
Izod's Cl GL55 135 A1

Jack O'Watton Bsns Pk
B46 23 E2
Jack Thomson Croft WR11 127 F6
Jackdaw Dr B36 33 D4
Jacker's Rd CV2 50 A2
Jacklin Dr CV3 77 E2
Jacknell Rd LE10 30 B4
Jackson Cl
Hampton Magna CV35 114 F3
Keresley CV7 49 D4
Jackson Rd Coventry CV6 49 E1
Rugby CV21 84 A1
Jackson Wlk B35 22 A1
Jacobean La B93 56 A1
Jacox Cres CV8 93 E3
Jade Cl CV1 151 D4
James Dawson Dr CV5 59 D4
James Galloway Cl CV3 78 C4
James Green Rd CV4 59 F1
James Rd B46 33 F4
James St Arley CV7 37 D4
Nuneaton CV11 29 D3
Rugby CV21 83 D2
James Watt Cl NN11 117 F2
Jamescroft CV3 78 C3
Jaques Cl B46 23 D1
Jardine Cres CV4 59 F1
Jasmine Gr Coventry CV3 78 B4
Royal Leamington Spa CV32 106 A1
Jasmine Rd B77 4 A2
Jays Cl B98 112 A6
Jean St CV9 11 E1
Jedburgh Gr CV3 77 D2
Jeff's Cl OX15 137 F2
Jeffrey Cl CV12 49 E4
Jeliff St CV4 59 F1
Jenkins Ave CV5 59 F2
Jenkins Rd CV21 84 A1
Jenner St CV1 151 C4
Jenton Rd CV31 110 A3
Jephcott Cl B49 143 D2
Jersey Croft B36 33 D3
Jervis Rd B77 9 F3
Jesmond Rd CV1 61 F2
Jesson Rd B75 13 D3
Jill La B96 103 D1
Jim Forrest Cl 4 CV3 78 C4
Joan Ward St CV3 77 E4
Joan's Cl 20 CV31 110 B3
Joanna Dr CV3 77 E2
Job's La CV4 60 A1
Jodrell St CV11 29 D3
Joe Williams Cl 7 CV3 78 C4
John Grace St CV3 77 E4
John Gulson Prim Sch CV1 61 E3
John Knight Rd CV12 39 D3
John McGuire Cres CV3 78 C4
John Nash Sq CV8 92 C2
John Nichols St LE10 31 D4
John O'Gaunt Rd CV8 92 C2
John Rous Ave CV4 76 A4
John Shelton Prim Sch
CV6 49 E2
John Simpson Cl CV8 80 A2
John St Bedworth CV12 39 D1
Nuneaton, Coton CV11 29 E1
Nuneaton, Stockingford CV10 28 C2
Royal Leamington Spa CV32 109 F4
Stratford-u-A CV37 145 D2
John Taylor Way CV35 122 E3
John Thwaites Cl CV22 83 D1
John's Cl LE10 31 E3
Johndory B77 9 E3
Johns Cl B80 103 E2
Johnson Ave CV22 82 C1
Johnson Pl B95 113 B5
Johnson Rd Bedworth CV12 39 E2
Coventry CV6 62 A4
Johnson St CV9 10 B1
Jolyffe Park Rd CV37 145 D2
Jon Baker Ct LE10 31 F4
Jonathan Rd CV2 62 C4
Jones Rd CV7 39 D1
Jones Wood Cl B76 22 A4
Jonkel Ave B77 10 A3
Jordan Cl CV8 93 D1
Jordan Well CV1 151 C2
Jordans Cl B97 102 B3
Jordans The CV5 60 B2
Joseph Cash Prim Sch
CV6 61 E4
Joseph Creighton Cl CV3 78 C4
Joseph Luckman Rd CV12 39 D2
Joseph Way CV37 144 C3
Joyce Pool 15 CV34 108 C4
Jubilee Ave
Lower Shuckburgh NN11 116 E1
Redditch B97 102 B4
Jubilee Cl B50 148 C3
Jubilee Cres CV6 61 D4
Jubilee Ct B78 15 E3
Jubilee St CV21 82 C2
Jubilee Terr CV12 39 D2
Judd Cl CV12 38 C2
Judds La CV6 49 F2
Judge Cl CV23 82 A3
Juggins La B94 86 A4
Julian Cl CV2 62 C4
Juliet Cl CV11 30 A1
Juliet Dr CV22 99 E3
Julius Dr B46 23 F1
Junction St CV1 151 A2
Junewood Cl CV21 83 E4
Juniper B77 4 A2
Juniper Dr Coventry CV5 59 F3
Sutton Coldfield B76 22 A4
Jury St CV34 108 C3
Justins Ave CV37 144 C3

Kanzan Rd CV2 50 A2
Kareen Gr CV3 79 E4
Karen Cl CV10 28 C4
Karlingford Cl CV5 76 B4
Kathleen Ave CV12 38 C1
Kay Cl CV21 83 E4
Kaysbrook Dr CV23 97 D3
Keats Cl CV10 28 A2
Keats Rd Coventry CV2 62 B1
Stratford-u-A CV37 145 D1
Keble Rd GL56 140 A2
Kebull Gn CV4 75 F4
Keeling Rd CV8 93 D3
Keenan Dr CV12 38 B1
Keepers Cl B46 34 A2
Keepers Wlk CV12 38 B1
Keetley Cl CV36 149 F2
Kegworth Cl CV6 50 A2
Keir Cl CV32 106 A1
Keith Rd CV32 106 A2
Kele Rd CV4 76 A4
Kelmscote Rd CV6 60 C4
Kelsey Cl CV11 29 F2
Kelsey La CV7 74 B3
Kelsey's Cl CV8 79 F2
Kelsull Croft B37 33 D1
Kelvin Ave CV2 62 B3
Kelvin Rd CV32 106 B3
Kelway CV3 63 D1
Kem St CV11 29 F1
Kemble Dr B35 22 A2
Kemerton Way B90 70 C3
Kemp Cl CV34 109 D4
Kempley Ave CV2 62 B1
Kemps Green Rd
Balsall Common CV7 74 A3
Tanworth-in-A B94 88 A1
Kempsey Cl B98 103 D4
Kempsford Cl B98 102 C3
Kempton Cres CV32 106 B2
Kendal Ave Coleshill B46 33 F4
Royal Leamington Spa CV32 105 E1
Kendal Cl Nuneaton CV11 30 A3
Redditch B98 112 A6
Kendal Rise CV5 60 B2
Kendall Ave CV37 145 D2
Kendon Ave CV6 60 C3
Kendrick Cl CV6 50 A2
Kenhill Rd OX15 138 F5
Kenilworth Castle CV8 92 B3
Kenilworth Cl B97 102 B3
Kenilworth Ct CV3 77 E4
Kenilworth Dr CV11 29 D2
Kenilworth Rd
Balsall Common CV7, CV8 74 B2
Coventry CV3 76 C2
Cubbington CV32 106 B3
Hampton in A B92 57 F3
Kenilworth CV8 93 E4
Knowle B93 72 C3
Lighthorne Heath CV35 123 D2
Meriden CV7 45 E1
Royal Leamington Spa CV32 105 F3
Kenilworth Sch CV8 93 E3
Kenilworth Sch Castle
Sixth Form Ctr CV8 92 C1
Kenilworth St 12 CV32 105 F1
Kenilworth Way OX16 139 F3
Kennan Ave CV31 109 F3
Kennedy Dr CV22 82 B1
Kennedy Sq 11 CV32 106 A1
Kennel La CV9 19 D4
Kennet Cl CV2 62 B4
Kenning Cl CV23 115 C4
Kenpas Highway CV3 77 D3
Kensington Rd CV5 61 D1
Kent Cl CV3 77 F3
Kent Rd CV33 132 F5
Kent The CV21 84 A1
Kenthurst Cl CV5 59 E2
Kentmere Cl CV2 50 C1
Kents La CV37 131 A4
Kenway B47 69 D4
Kenwyn Gdns CV7 50 A4
Keppel Cl CV22 82 B1
Keppel St CV1 61 F3
Keresley Brook Rd CV6 49 D1
Keresley Cl CV6 49 D1
Keresley Grange Prim Sch
CV6 48 C1
Keresley Green Rd CV6 48 C1
Keresley Newland
Comb Sch CV7 48 C4
Keresley Rd CV6 61 D4
Kerns Terr CV37 145 D2
Kerr Way GL56 140 C3
Kerria Ctr B77 4 A2
Kerria Rd B77 4 A2
Kerris Way CV3 63 D1
Kerswell Dr B90 71 D3
Kestrel B77 10 A3
Kestrel Cl Hinckley LE10 31 F3
Stratford-u-A CV37 145 D3
Kestrel Croft 2 CV3 78 C4
Keswick Cl CV11 30 A3
Keswick Dr CV21 83 E4
Keswick Gn CV32 105 E1
Keswick Wlk CV2 62 C2
Kettlebrook Rd B90 71 E3
Kettlewell Cl CV34 104 C1
Keviliok St CV3 77 E3
Kew Cl CV8 93 E3
Kew Rd CV21 83 D2
Keys Dr CV22 82 B1
Keys Hill CV9 11 E1
Keys La CV23 125 F4
Keyte Rd CV36 136 B6
Keyte's La CV35 122 B7
Keytes Acre GL55 135 E3
Kiblers La CV35 131 D2
Kielder Dr CV10 28 C1
Kiftsgate Court Gardens
GL55 135 C6
Kilburn Dr CV5 60 C2
Kilby Gn LE10 31 F3
Kilby Gr CV31 110 B3
Kilbye Cl B77 9 F3
Kildale Cl CV1 151 D3
Kildwick Way 5 CV34 104 C1
Killworth Rd CV21 101 D4
Kiln Cl
Royal Leamington Spa CV32 106 A1
Studley B80 103 E2
Kiln Way Polesworth B78 4 C1
Shilton CV12 51 F4
Kilnsey Gr CV34 104 C1
Kilsby Gr B91 71 E4
Kilsby La CV21 101 E4
Kilsby Rd CV23 101 E1
Kimbell Cl CV33 124 B1
Kimberley B77 9 F4
Kimberley Cl CV5 59 F2
Kimberley Rd Baginton CV8 77 F1
Bedworth CV12 39 E2
Rugby CV21 83 D2
Kimberley Wlk B76 22 B3
Kimble Cl CV5 60 A2
Kinchford Cl B91 71 D4
Kineton CE Jun & Inf Sch
CV35 132 B6
Kineton High Sch CV35 132 C6
Kineton La B94 71 D1
Kineton Rd Coventry CV2 62 B3
Kenilworth CV8 93 E2
Southam CV33 147 D2
Wellesbourne CV35 146 C1
Kineton Road Ind Est
CV33 147 D2
King Edward Rd
Coventry CV1 61 F2
Nuneaton CV11 29 E2
Rugby CV21 83 D2
King Edward VI Coll CV11 29 E2
King Edward VI Gram Sch
CV37 145 D1
King George's Ave
Bedworth CV12 39 D3
Coventry CV6 49 F1
King George's Ct CV23 82 A3
King George's Way LE10 31 D4
King Henry VIII Sch CV1 151 A1
King John's La CV35 132 E2
King John's Rd CV35 132 B6
King Richard St CV2 61 F2
King St Bedworth CV12 39 E1
Royal Leamington Spa CV32 106 A1
Rugby CV21 83 D2
King William St CV1 61 F2
King's Hill La CV8 77 D1
King's La Broom B50 148 A3
Newton Regis B79 2 B2
Norton WR11 127 B2
Snitterfield CV37 121 B6
Stratford-u-A CV37 144 C4
Kingcomb La GL55 135 A2
Kingfield Rd CV1, CV6 61 E4
Kingfisher B77 10 A3
Kingfisher Ave CV10 28 B3
Kingfisher Dr B36 33 D4
Kingfisher Way B49 143 D3
Kingham Cl B98 112 A6
Kingham Hill Sch OX7 150 A1
Kingland Dr CV32 105 E1
Kingley Ave B49 143 E3
Kings Ave CV9 18 C4
Kings Coughton La B49 143 D3
Kings Gdns CV12 39 E1
Kings Gr CV2 62 A2
Kings High Sch for Girls
CV34 108 C4
Kings Newnham La CV23 80 C4
Kings Newnham Rd CV23 81 D3
Kingsbridge Rd CV10 29 E3
Kingsbrook Dr B91 71 D4
Kingsbury Bsns Pk B76 22 C3
Kingsbury Cl B76 22 B3
Kingsbury Fst Sch B78 15 E3
Kingsbury Mid Sch B78 15 E3
Kingsbury Rd Coventry CV6 60 C3
Curdworth B76 23 D4
Minworth B76 22 B3
Sutton Coldfield B35, B76 22 A3
Kingsbury Sch B78 15 E3
Kingsbury Water Park B76 15 D3
Kingscote Gr CV3 77 D2
Kingscote Rd B93 71 F1
Kingsfield Ind Est CV1 61 E3
Kingsford Cl B36 22 B1
Kingshurst CV31 110 C3
Kingshurst Inf Sch B37 33 D3
Kingshurst Jun Sch B37 33 D3
Kingsland Ave CV5 60 C1
Kingsland Dr B93 71 F2
Kingsley Ave CV21 83 F1
Kingsley Cres CV12 40 A2
Kingsley Orch CV21 83 F1
Kingsley Prep Sch B93 72 A2
Kingsley Rd 12 CV33 122 F8
Kingsley Sch The CV32 105 F1
Kingsley Terr CV2 62 C4
Kingsley Wlk CV2 62 C4
Kingston La CV35 113 E3
Kingston Mews CV31 110 B3
Kingston Rd CV5 60 C1
Kingsway Coventry CV2 62 A2
Kingsbury B78 15 E3
Lighthorne Heath CV35 123 D2
Nuneaton CV11 29 D2
Royal Leamington Spa CV31 109 F3
Rugby CV22 83 D1
Kingswood Ave CV7 48 A4
Kingswood Cl Coventry CV6 49 E1
Lapworth B94 89 F3
Kingswood Rd CV10 28 A2
Kington Rise CV35 113 E2
Kinman Way CV21 83 E3
Kinross Cl CV10 28 C1
Kinross Rd CV32 106 A2
Kinsall Gn B77 10 B3
Kinsham Dr B91 71 D4
Kintyre The CV2 63 D4
Kinver Cl CV2 50 C1
Kinver Croft B76 22 A4
Kinwalsey La CV7 46 C3
Kinwarton Dovecote B49 143 F3
Kinwarton Farm Rd B49 143 E3
Kinwarton Rd B49 143 E2
Kinwarton Workshops
B49 143 E3
Kipling Ave CV34 108 B2
Kipling Cl CV10 28 A3
Kipling Rd Coventry CV6 61 D4
Stratford-u-A CV37 130 A8
Kirby Ave CV34 104 C1
Kirby Cl Brandon CV8 79 F3
Coventry CV1 61 E3
Kirby Cnr CV4 76 A3
Kirby Corner Rd CV4 76 A3
Kirby Rd Coventry CV5 60 C1
Rugby CV21 83 F1
Kirigushi Rd CV35 132 E5
Kirkby Cl CV21 83 F3
Kirkdale Ave CV6 49 E2
Kirkland Way B78 8 A4
Kirkstone CV21 83 E4
Kirkstone Rd CV12 39 D1
Kirkstone Wlk CV11 30 A3
Kirkwall CV33 147 D2
Kirtland Cl CV9 3 D1
Kirton Cl Coventry CV6 48 C1
Whitnash CV31 110 A2
Kissing Tree La CV37 121 D3
Kitchener Rd CV6 61 F4
Kitebrook Cl 9 B90 71 D4
Kites Cl CV34 104 C1
Kites Nest La CV35 114 E8
Kittermaster Rd CV7 46 B1
Kitwood Ave B78 10 C3
Kixley La B93 72 B3
Klevedon Cl CV11 30 A1
Knebley Cres CV10 29 E1
Knibbs Sh Ctr The 13
CV34 108 C4
Knight Ave CV1 61 F1
Knightcote Dr
Royal Leamington Spa CV32 109 F4
Solihull B91 71 D4
Knightley Cl CV32 106 C3
Knightlow Ave CV3 78 B3
Knightlow CE Mid Sch
CV23 96 C4
Knightlow Cl CV8 93 E2
Knightlow Way CV33 123 F6
Knights Cl LE10 31 E2
Knights Ct LE10 30 C4
Knights La CV37 145 F2
Knightsbridge Ave CV12 39 E2
Knob Hill CV23 96 C3
Knoll Croft
Cheswick Green B90 70 B2
Coventry CV3 77 E3
Knoll Dr Coventry CV3 77 E3
Warwick CV34 104 C1
Knottesford Cl B80 103 E2
Knowlands Rd B90 71 D4
Knowle CE Jun & Inf Sch
B93 72 B3
Knowle Hill Hurley CV9 16 B2
Kenilworth CV8 93 E3
Knowle Rd B92 56 C1
Knowle Wood Rd B93 72 A2
Knowles Ave CV10 28 B2
Knox Cres CV11 29 F4
Kranji Rd CV33 132 F5
Kurtus B77 9 E3
Kyetts Cnr OX17 134 C1
Kynner Way CV3 79 D4
Kyter La B35 22 A1

Laburnum Ave
Coventry CV6 60 C3
Kenilworth CV8 93 D2
Laburnum Cl
Bedworth CV12 38 C1
Hollywood B47 69 D3
Kingsbury B78 15 E3
Laburnum Dr
Sutton Coldfield B76 13 D2
Whitnash CV31 110 A2

Laburnum Gr
Nuneaton CV10 .... 28 B3
Rugby CV22 .... 99 F4
Warwick CV34 .... 105 D1
Lacell Cl CV34 .... 104 C1
Ladbroke By – Pass CV31 . 124 D5
Ladbroke Pk CV34 .... 104 C1
Ladbroke Rd CV33 .... 124 B4
Ladbrook Cl B98 .... 102 C4
Ladbrook Rd CV5 .... 60 A2
Lady Byron La Knowle B93 .. 71 F4
Knowle,Copt Heath B93 .... 56 A1
Lady Katherine Leveson
CE Prim Sch B93 .... 73 D3
Lady La Coventry CV6 .... 49 F2
Earlswood B90, B94 .... 70 A2
Lady Warwick Ave CV12 ...... 39 E1
Ladycroft CV32 .... 106 C3
Ladyfields Way CV6 .... 49 D2
Ladygrove Cl B98 .... 103 D4
Ladymead Dr CV6 .... 49 D1
Lair The B78 .... 10 C4
Lake View Rd CV5 .... 60 A2
Lakeland Dr B77 .... 10 A4
Lakes Sta The B94 .... 86 C4
Lakeside CV12 .... 39 D1
Lakeside Dr B90 .... 70 C4
Lakin Cl CV34 .... 108 C4
Lakin Dr CV33 .... 124 A4
Lamb St CV1 .... 151 B3
Lambert Cl B50 .... 148 B3
Lambert Cl CV34 .... 145 D3
Lambert Specl Sch CV37 . 145 D3
Lambeth Cl Birmingham B37 . 33 D2
Coventry CV2 .... 62 C4
Lambourn Cres CV31 .... 110 B3
Lambourne Cl CV5 .... 60 A2
Lamerton Cl CV2 .... 62 B3
Lamintone Dr CV32 .... 105 E1
Lammas Croft CV31 .... 110 A2
Lammas Ct CV8 .... 80 A2
Lammas Rd CV6 .... 60 C2
Lammas Wlk CV34 .... 108 B4
Lamorna Cl CV11 .... 29 F2
Lamp La CV7 .... 36 C3
Lampitts Grn OX15 .... 139 D4
Lamprey D7 .... 9 E3
Lancaster Cl Atherstone CV9 . 12 C1
Wellesbourne CV35 .... 146 B1
Lancaster Pl CV8 .... 92 C1
Lancaster Rd Hinckley LE10 . 31 E4
Rugby CV21 .... 83 D2
Lance Cl LE10 .... 31 E3
Lanchester Dr OX16 .... 139 F4
Lanchester Rd CV6 .... 61 D3
Lanchester Way
Birmingham B36 .... 22 C1
Daventry NN11 .... 117 F2
Lancia Cl CV4 .... 50 A2
Lancing Rd CV12 .... 40 B1
Land La B37 .... 44 A4
Landor Rd Knowle B93 .... 72 A3
Redditch B98 .... 103 D4
Warwick CV34 .... 108 B4
Whitnash CV31 .... 110 A2
Landrail Wlk B36 .... 33 D4
Landsdowne Pl CV21 .... 83 E1
Landseer Cl CV21 .... 84 A1
Lane Cl OX15 .... 139 D6
Lane Croft B76 .... 22 A4
Lane The Burmington CV36 . 137 A1
Little Compton CV36 .... 141 A6
Lanes Cl CV3 .... 78 C1
Langbank Ave CV3 .... 78 B4
Langcliffe Ave CV34 .... 104 C1
Langcomb Rd B90 .... 70 A4
Langdale Ave CV6 .... 49 E2
Langdale Cl
Royal Leamington Spa CV32 . 106 B2
Rugby CV21 .... 83 E4
Langdale Dr CV11 .... 30 A3
Langdale Rd LE10 .... 31 D4
Langfield Rd B93 .... 72 A4
Langlands The CV35 .... 121 F4
Langley Croft CV4 .... 60 A1
Langley Dr B35 .... 22 A1
Langley Hall Rd B75 .... 13 D3
Langley Hall Rd B75 .... 13 D3
Langley Heath Dr B76 .... 13 D2
Langley Rd Claverdon CV35 . 113 E3
Whitnash CV31 .... 110 A2
Langley Sch B75 .... 13 D3
Langley Wlk B37 .... 33 D1
Langlodge Rd CV6 .... 49 D1
Langnor Rd CV2 .... 62 B3
Langton Cl CV3 .... 78 C4
Langton Rd CV21 .... 83 F1
Langwood Cl CV4 .... 76 A4
Lankett The CV33 .... 133 D7
Lansbury Cl CV2 .... 62 C4
Lansdowne Cir CV32 .... 106 A1
Lansdowne Cl CV12 .... 39 D2
Lansdowne Cres
Royal Leamington Spa
CV32 .... 106 A1
Studley B80 .... 103 E2
Tamworth B77 .... 9 E4
Lansdowne Rd
Lonbridge Rd CV32 .... 106 C3
Ledbury Rd CV31 .... 110 B3
Ledbury Way B76 .... 22 A4
Lee Cl CV34 .... 104 C1
Lee Rd Hollywood B47 .... 69 D4
Royal Leamington Spa CV31 . 109 F3
Lansdowne Rd
Royal Leamington Spa CV32 . 106 A1
Studley B80 .... 103 E2
Lansdowne St Coventry
CV2 .... 61 F2
Royal Leamington Spa CV31 . 106 A1
Lant Cl CV7 .... 75 D4
Lapwing B77 .... 10 A3
Lapwing Dr B92 .... 57 D4
Lapworth CE Jun & Inf Sch
B94 .... 89 E2
Lapworth Cl B98 .... 102 C4
Lapworth Oaks B94 .... 89 E2
Lapworth Rd CV2 .... 50 B1
Lapworth St B94 .... 89 D1
Lapworth Sta B94 .... 89 E2
Larch Cl Alcester B49 .... 143 D3
Rugby CV22 .... 82 A1
Stratford-u-A CV37 .... 145 D2
Larch Croft B37 .... 33 D1
Larch Gr CV34 .... 105 D1
Larch Tree Ave CV4 .... 60 A1
Larches The Bedworth CV7 . 50 A4
Kingsbury B78 .... 15 E4
Larchfields CV8 .... 80 A2
Larchwood Rd CV7 .... 39 D1
Larkfield Way CV5 .... 60 A3
Larkin Cl CV12 .... 40 A2
Larkspur Rugby CV23 .... 83 E4
Tamworth B77 .... 9 F3
Latham Rd CV5 .... 61 D1
Latimer Cl CV8 .... 92 C1
Latymer Cl B76 .... 22 A4
Lauderdale Ave CV6 .... 49 E2
Lauderdale Cl CV23 .... 82 A2
Launceston Dr CV11 .... 29 F2
Laurel Ave B78 .... 11 D4
Laurel Cl CV2 .... 50 C1
Laurel Dr Hartshill CV10 ..... 28 A4
Rugby CV22 .... 82 A1
Stockton CV23 .... 147 D4
Laurel Gdns CV22 .... 99 F4
Laurels Cres CV7 .... 74 B3
Laurels The Bedworth CV12 . 38 C1
Kingsbury B78 .... 15 E4
Lavender Ave CV6 .... 60 C3
Lavender Cl CV23 .... 83 E4
Lavender Hall La CV7 .... 58 B1
Lavenham Cl CV11 .... 40 B4
Lawford Cl CV3 .... 62 C1
Lawford Heath Ind Est
CV23 .... 98 B4
Lawford Heath La CV23 ...... 98 B3
Lawford La CV22 .... 82 A1
Lawford Rd
Royal Leamington Spa CV31 . 110 A3
Rugby CV21 .... 82 B2
Lawley Cl CV4 .... 60 A1
Lawns The Bedworth CV12 . 38 B1
Hinckley LE10 .... 31 F4
Lawnsdale Cl B46 .... 33 F4
Lawnswood Hinckley LE10 . 31 D4
Sutton Coldfield B76 .... 22 A4
Lawrence Cl B79 .... 2 C1
Lawrence Gdns CV8 .... 93 D3
Lawrence Mackie Gdns
CV5 .... 146 C2
Lawrence Rd Bedworth CV7 . 38 A4
Rugby CV21 .... 83 E2
Lawrence Saunders Rd
CV6 .... 61 D3
Lawrence Sheriff Sch
CV21 .... 83 D2
Lawrence Sherriff St CV22 . 83 D1
Lawson Ave CV37 .... 145 F2
Lawton Cl LE10 .... 30 C4
Lay Gdns CV31 .... 110 C3
Le Hanche Cl CV7 .... 49 D4
Lea Cl Alcester B49 .... 143 E3
Stratford-u-A CV37 .... 144 A2
Lea Cres CV21 .... 82 B3
Lea Croft Rd B97 .... 102 B3
Lea Green La B47 .... 69 E3
Leacrest Rd CV6 .... 49 D1
Leaf La Coventry CV3 .... 77 E5
Coventry CV3 .... 77 F3
Leafield Cl CV2 .... 62 C4
Leagh Cl CV8 .... 93 D4
Leam Cl CV11 .... 29 F1
Leam Gn CV4 .... 76 B3
Leam Rd
Lighthorne Heath CV35 ...... 123 D2
Royal Leamington Spa CV31 . 109 E4
Leam St CV31 .... 110 A4
Leam Terr CV31 .... 110 A4
Leam The NN11 .... 117 F1
Leamington Hastings
CE Inf Sch CV23 .... 116 B6
Leamington Rd Coventry
CV3 .... 77 E3
Kenilworth CV8 .... 93 D1
Long Itchington CV23 .... 115 C4
Princethorpe CV23 .... 96 B1
Ryton-on-D CV23 .... 96 A4
Southam CV33 .... 124 C8
Leamington Spa Sta CV31 . 109 F4
Lear Gr CV34 .... 109 F2
Leas Cl CV12 .... 39 D2
Leasowe's Ave CV3 .... 76 C2
Leasowes Children's
Farm The B94 .... 87 E1
Leather St CV23 .... 115 D4
Leathermill La CV10 .... 19 E2
Leaward Cl CV10 .... 28 C1
Ledbrook Rd CV32 .... 106 C3
Ledbury Rd CV31 .... 110 B3
Ledbury Way B76 .... 22 A4
Lee Cl CV34 .... 104 C1
Lee Rd Hollywood B47 .... 69 D4
Royal Leamington Spa CV31 . 109 F3
Lee The CV5 .... 60 A2
Leeder Cl CV6 .... 49 E1
Leek Wootton CE Fst Sch
CV35 .... 105 D3
Leeming Cl CV4 .... 76 B3
Leicester Cswy CV1 .... 61 E3
Leicester Ct CV12 .... 40 B1
Leicester La Cubbington
CV32 .... 94 C1
Royal Leamington Spa CV32 . 106 B3
Leicester Rd Atherstone
CV9 .... 12 C1
Bedworth CV12 .... 39 D2
Nuneaton CV11 .... 29 E3
Rugby CV21 .... 83 D4
Shilton CV7 .... 51 F3
Leicester Row CV1 .... 151 B4
Leicester St Bedworth CV12 . 39 D2
Bulkington CV12 .... 40 B1
Royal Leamington Spa CV32 . 106 A1
Leigh Ave CV3 .... 77 E2
Leigh CE Prim Sch CV4 .... 75 E4
Leigh Cres CV23 .... 115 D3
Leigh Rd Rugby CV21 .... 82 C4
Sutton Coldfield B75 .... 13 D3
Leigh St 3 CV1 .... 61 F2
Leighton Cl Coventry CV4 ... 76 B1
Royal Leamington Spa CV32 . 106 B2
Leisure Wlk B77 .... 9 F3
Lennon Cl CV21 .... 101 E4
Lennox Cl CV3 .... 78 C3
Lenton's La CV2 .... 50 C2
Leofric St CV6 .... 61 D3
Leopold Rd CV1 .... 61 F3
Lesingham Dr CV4 .... 59 F1
Lestock Cl CV22 .... 82 B1
Letchlade Cl CV2 .... 62 B4
Level The OX15 .... 138 F5
Leven Cl LE10 .... 31 D4
Leven Croft B76 .... 22 A4
Leven Way CV2 .... 63 D4
Lever Rd CV21 .... 84 A1
Leveson Cres CV7 .... 74 A3
Levett Rd B77 .... 4 A3
Levy Cl CV21 .... 82 C2
Lewis Cl CV9 .... 18 C3
Lewis Rd Coventry CV1 .... 61 E3
Radford Semele CV31 .... 110 C3
Leyburn Cl Coventry CV6 .... 49 F1
Nuneaton CV11 .... 30 A1
Leycester Pl CV34 .... 108 C3
Leycester Rd CV8 .... 93 D1
Leyes La CV8 .... 93 E3
Leyes The CV23 .... 84 A1
Leyfields Cres CV34 .... 108 B2
Leyland Rd Bulkington CV12 . 40 A1
Coventry CV5 .... 60 B2
Nuneaton CV11 .... 29 F1
Leyland Specl Sch CV11 ..... 29 F1
Leymere Cl CV7 .... 46 B1
Leys Cl Northend CV33 ..... 133 B7
Wroxton OX15 .... 139 D4
Leys High Sch The B98 .... 103 E3
Leys La CV7 .... 46 B1
Leys Rd Harvington WR11 . 127 B5
Rugby CV21 .... 101 E4
Leys The Bidford-on-A B50 . 148 C3
Halford CV36 .... 137 A8
Salford OX7 .... 150 C3
Upper Boddington NN11 .... 134 E8
Leysbourne GL55 .... 135 B2
Leysfield WR11 .... 127 C4
Leyside CV3 .... 78 C3
Libbards Gate 4 B91 .... 71 E4
Libbards Way B91 .... 71 D4
Liberty Rd B77 .... 9 E3
Liberty Way CV11 .... 29 F2
Library Cl LE10 .... 32 A3
Lichen Gn CV4 .... 76 B3
Lichfield Cl Arley CV7 .... 37 D4
Nuneaton CV11 .... 30 A4
Lichfield Rd Coventry CV3 ... 77 E4
Water Orton B46, B76 .... 23 E2
Wishaw B76 .... 14 A2
Lichfield St B78 .... 9 D4
Liecester Rd LE10 .... 41 F3
Lifford Way CV3 .... 79 D4
Light Hall Sch B90 .... 70 A4
Light La CV1 .... 151 B4
Lighthorne Rd CV35 .... 132 B6
Lightoak Cl B97 .... 102 B3
Lightwood Cl B93 .... 72 A4
Lilac Ave CV6 .... 60 C3
Lilac Cl LE10 .... 31 F3
Lilac Dr CV22 .... 82 A1
Lilac Gr CV35 .... 105 D1
Lilac Rd CV12 .... 39 E3
Lilbourne Rd CV23 .... 84 B3
Lilley Cl CV6 .... 49 E1
Lilley Green Rd B48 .... 85 E3
Lillington Ave CV32 .... 105 F1
Lillington CE Fst Sch
CV32 .... 106 A2
Lillington Cl
Royal Leamington Spa CV32 . 106 A2
Sutton Coldfield B75 .... 13 D2
Lillington Prim Sch CV32 . 106 B2
Lillington Rd Coventry CV2 . 50 B1
Royal Leamington Spa CV32 . 106 B3
Solihull B90 .... 70 A4
Limbrick Ave CV4 .... 60 A1
Limbrick Wood Prim Sch
CV4 .... 59 F1
Lime Ave CV32 .... 106 A2
Lime Cl B47 .... 69 D3
Lime Gr
Birmingham, Chemsley Wood
B37 .... 33 D1
Coventry CV4 .... 60 A1
Hurley CV9 .... 16 B2
Kenilworth CV8 .... 93 D2
Nuneaton CV10 .... 28 C3
Lime Kiln B78 .... 11 D4
Lime Rd CV33 .... 147 D3
Lime Tree Ave Coventry CV4 . 60 A1
Rugby CV22 .... 99 D4
Limekiln La B94 .... 70 B1
Limes Ave CV37 .... 144 B1
Limes Coppice CV10 .... 27 F4
Limes The CV12 .... 38 C1
Limestone Hall La CV23 ..... 81 D2
Linaker Rd CV3 .... 78 B3
Lincoln Ave CV10 .... 28 A4
Lincoln Cl Warwick CV34 ... 104 C1
Wellesbourne CV35 .... 146 B1
Lincoln Gr B37 .... 33 D1
Lincoln St CV1 .... 151 C4
Lincroft Cres CV5 .... 60 C2
Lindale CV21 .... 83 E4
Linden Ave CV35 .... 146 C2
Linden Cl CV34 .... 104 C1
Linden Lea CV12 .... 39 D2
Lindera B77 .... 4 A3
Lindfield The CV3 .... 78 B4
Lindhurst Dr B94 .... 88 B3
Lindisfarne Dr CV8 .... 93 E2
Lindley Rd Bedworth CV12 . 38 B1
Coventry CV3 .... 62 A1
Lindridge Cl B98 .... 112 A6
Lindridge Dr B76 .... 22 B3
Lindridge aun Sch B75 .... 13 D3
Lindridge Rd B75 .... 13 D3
Lindsay Wlk CV33 .... 132 F7
Lindsey Cres CV8 .... 93 D1
Lineholt Cl B98 .... 103 D3
Linen St CV34 .... 108 B3
Linford Wlk CV2 .... 50 C1
Lingard Rd B75 .... 13 D3
Lingwood Dr CV10 .... 28 C2
Links Rd CV6 .... 61 D4
Linkway CV31 .... 109 F3
Linley Rd CV33 .... 147 D3
Linnell Rd CV21 .... 83 F1
Linnet Cl CV3 .... 78 B3
Linstock Way CV6 .... 50 A2
Linthouse Wlk B77 .... 9 F3
Lintly B77 .... 4 A1
Linwood Dr CV2 .... 50 C1
Lion Fields Ave CV5 .... 60 A3
Liskeard Cl CV11 .... 30 A3
Liskeard Rd CV35 .... 132 D3
Lisle Gdns 3 CV35 .... 122 F8
Lister Cres CV9 .... 12 C1
Lister St CV11 .... 29 F2
Little Acre B97 .... 102 B3
Little Brom CV9 .... 11 E1
Little Church St
Coventry CV1 .... 151 C4
Rugby CV21 .... 83 D2
Little Duke St CV11 .... 29 D2
Little Elborow St CV21 ...... 83 D2
Little Farm CV3 .... 78 B3
Little Field CV2 .... 62 B4
Little Forge Rd B98 .... 103 E4
Little Gr CV22 .... 83 E1
Little Heath Ind Est CV6 ..... 61 F4
Little Lawford La CV21 .... 82 A4
Little London La CV23 .... 68 A1
Little Park St 3 CV1 .... 151 C2
Little Pennington St 3
CV21 .... 82 C2
Little Pittern CV35 .... 132 B6
Little Pk CV33 .... 147 D2
Little South St CV1 .... 61 F2
Little Woods B97 .... 102 C3
Littlemead Rd B90 .... 69 F4
Littleshaw Croft B47 .... 69 E2
Littleshaw La B47 .... 69 E2
Littlethorpe CV3 .... 78 B3
Littleton CE Fst Sch WR11 . 127 F1
Littleton Cl Kenilworth CV8 . 93 D4
Sutton Coldfield B75 .... 13 D1
Littlewood Cl 6 B91 .... 71 D4
Littlewood Gn B80 .... 103 E2
Littleworth
Chipping Campden GL55 .... 135 A2
Henley-in-A B95 .... 113 B4
Litton B77 .... 4 B1
Liveridge Cl B93 .... 71 F3
Liveridge Hill B95 .... 113 B7
Livery St CV32 .... 109 F4
Livingstone Ave CV23 .... 81 F2
Livingstone Rd CV6 .... 61 F4
Liza Ct CV21 .... 83 E4
Llewellyn Rd CV31 .... 110 A3
Lloyd Cl
Hampton Magna CV35 ...... 114 F3
Norton WR11 .... 127 C2
Nuneaton CV11 .... 29 E1
Lloyd Cres CV2 .... 62 C3
Lloyd Rd CV21 .... 83 E3
Loach Dr CV7 .... 50 A2
Lobelia Cl LE10 .... 31 F3
Lochmore Cl LE10 .... 31 D4
Lochmore Dr LE10 .... 31 D4
Lochmore Way LE10 .... 31 D4
Lock Cl CV37 .... 145 D2
Lock La CV34 .... 108 B4
Locke Cl CV6 .... 49 D1
Lockhart Cl CV8 .... 93 D2
Lockheed Cl CV31 .... 109 F3
Lockhurst La CV6 .... 61 D4
Locking Croft B35 .... 22 A2
Locks The CV21 .... 84 A1
Loder Cl CV4 .... 59 F2
Lodge Cl Atherstone CV9 .... 19 D3
Hinckley LE10 .... 31 F4
Lodge Cres CV34 .... 108 B2
Lodge Green La CV7 .... 46 C1
Lodge Green La N CV7 .... 46 C2
Lodge Rd Coventry CV3 ...... 62 A1
Knowle B93 .... 72 A3
Rugby CV21 .... 83 D2
Stratford-u-A CV37 .... 144 C2
Logan Rd CV2 .... 62 C4
Lollard Croft CV3 .... 77 E2
Lomita Cres B77 .... 9 E4
Lomond Cl LE10 .... 31 D4
London End NN11 .... 134 EB
London Rd
Coventry, Cheylesmore CV3 .. 77 F4
Coventry, Willenhall CV3 ..... 78 A3
Hinckley LE10 .... 31 F4
Middleton B75, B78 .... 13 E4
Moreton-in-M GL56 .... 140 B3
Ryton-on-D CV8 .... 79 D1
Shipston-on-S CV36 .... 149 F2
Stretton-on-D CV23 .... 96 C4
Sutton Coldfield B75 .... 7 D2
Willoughby CV23 .... 117 C6
Long Brook La CV7 .... 73 F3
Long Close Ave CV5 .... 60 A3
Long Close Wlk B35 .... 22 A2
Long Furlong CV22 .... 100 A4
Long Hyde Rd WR11 .... 127 F1
Long Itchington
CE Prim Sch CV23 .... 115 D4
Long St Atherstone CV9 ...... 18 B4
Bulkington CV12 .... 40 A1
Dordon B78 .... 11 D3
Longborough Cl B97 .... 102 A3
Longcroft Cl B35 .... 22 A1
Longdon Cl B98 .... 103 D4
Longdon Rd B93 .... 72 A3
Longdown La CV37 .... 117 D7
Longfellow Ave CV34 .... 108 B2
Longfellow Cl B97 .... 102 B4
Longfellow Rd CV2 .... 62 B2
Longfield Rd CV31 .... 110 A3
Longford Cl
Bidford-on-A B50 .... 148 C3
Dorridge B93 .... 72 A2
Longford Park Prim Sch
CV6 .... 50 A2
Longford Rd Bedworth CV7 . 50 A2
Coventry CV6 .... 50 A2
Longford Sq CV6 .... 50 A2
Loghope Cl B98 .... 112 A6
Longleat Dr B90 .... 70 C3
Longleat Gr 22 CV31 .... 110 B3
Longley Ave B76 .... 22 B3
Longrood Rd CV22 .... 99 E3
Longstone Cl B90 .... 71 D3
Longwood Cl CV4 .... 75 D3
Lonscale Dr CV3 .... 77 D3
Lonsdale Rd CV32 .... 106 A2
Lord Lytton Ave CV2 .... 62 B3
Lord St CV5 .... 60 C1
Lords La B80 .... 103 F3
Lorenzo Cl CV3 .... 78 B3
Lothersdale B77 .... 10 B4
Loudon Ave CV6 .... 61 D3
Loughshaw B77 .... 4 B1
Louisa Ward Cl CV23 .... 115 C2
Love La LE10 .... 32 A3
Love Lyne B97 .... 102 A3
Loveday Cl Atherstone CV9 . 12 B1
Royal Leamington Spa CV32 . 105 F3
Lovelace Ave B91 .... 71 E4
Lovell Cl CV7 .... 50 A4
Lovell Rd CV12 .... 39 D2
Loverock Cres CV21 .... 83 F3
Lovetts Cl LE10 .... 30 C4
Low Rd WR11 .... 127 A6
Lowbrook La B90 .... 69 E2
Lowdham B77 .... 4 B1
Lowe Rd CV6 .... 49 D1
Lower Ave CV31 .... 109 F4
Lower Cape CV34 .... 108 B4
Lower Cladswell La B49 .... 118 C5
Lower Eastern Green La
CV5 .... 59 F2
Lower End Bubbenhall CV8 . 95 E3
Salford OX7 .... 150 C3
Shutford OX15 .... 139 A3
Lower Farm La OX17 .... 133 F2
Lower Ford St CV1 .... 151 D3
Lower Grinsty La B97 .... 102 A4
Lower High St GL55 .... 135 A2
Lower Hillmorton Rd
CV21 .... 83 E1
Lower Holyhead Rd CV1 .... 151 A3
Lower House La CV9 .... 31 D2
Lower Ladyes Hills CV8 ...... 93 D3
Lower Leam St CV31 .... 110 A4
Lower Prec CV1 .... 151 B3
Lower Rd CV7 .... 51 E3
Lower St Rugby CV21 .... 101 D4
Willoughby CV23 .... 117 B6
Lower Villiers St 3 CV32 . 106 A1
Lowes Ave CV34 .... 104 C1
Lowes La CV35 .... 146 B1
Lowesmater Cl CV11 .... 30 A3
Loweswater Rd CV3 .... 62 C1
Lowforce B77 .... 10 B4
Lowry Cl CV12 .... 38 A4
Lowther St CV1 .... 61 F2
Loxley CE Prim Sch CV35 . 130 F7
Loxley Cl Coventry CV2 .... 50 B1
Wellesbourne CV35 .... 146 B2

Loxley Rd Alveston CV37 ..... 121 D1
Stratford-u-A CV37 ..... 145 E1
Wellesbourne CV35 ..... 146 B1
Loxley Way CV32 ..... 106 A1
Lucas Rd LE10 ..... 31 E3
Luce Cl B35 ..... 22 A2
Lucian Cl CV2 ..... 63 D4
Luddington Rd CV37 ..... 129 E8
Ludford Cl Ansley CV10 ..... 27 D2
Stratford-u-A CV37 ..... 144 B2
Ludford Rd CV10 ..... 28 B3
Ludgate Ct B77 ..... 4 A3
Ludlow Cl B37 ..... 33 E1
Ludlow Rd CV5 ..... 61 D1
Ludlow's La CV35 ..... 114 C7
Luff Cl CV3 ..... 78 A4
Lugtrout La B91 ..... 56 A3
Lulworth Pk CV8 ..... 93 E3
Lumley Gr B37 ..... 33 E1
Lumsden Cl CV2 ..... 62 C4
Lunar Cl CV4 ..... 76 B3
Lundy View B36 ..... 33 D3
Lunn Ave CV8 ..... 92 C2
Lupin Cl LE10 ..... 31 E3
Lupton Ave CV3 ..... 77 E4
Luscombe Rd CV2 ..... 62 C4
Luther Way CV5 ..... 59 F2
Lutterworth Rd
Brinklow CV23 ..... 64 C2
Churchover CV23 ..... 67 E3
Coventry CV2 ..... 62 B3
Hinckley LE10 ..... 32 B2
Nuneaton CV11 ..... 40 B4
Pailton CV23 ..... 54 B1
Shawell LE17 ..... 68 B3
Wolvey LE10 ..... 41 F3
Lutterworth Road Commercial Est LE10 ..... 32 A3
Luxor La CV5 ..... 59 D4
Lychgate Cl LE10 ..... 32 A3
Lychgate La LE10 ..... 32 B3
Lydd Croft B35 ..... 22 A2
Lydford Cl CV2 ..... 62 B4
Lydgate Rd CV6 ..... 61 D3
Lydstep Gr CV31 ..... 110 B4
Lye Green Rd CV35 ..... 113 F4
Lyecroft Ave B37 ..... 33 E1
Lymesy St CV3 ..... 77 E4
Lymington Cl CV6 ..... 61 E4
Lymore Croft CV2 ..... 63 D4
Lynbrook Cl B47 ..... 69 D4
Lynbrook Rd CV5 ..... 76 B4
Lynch The Nuneaton CV11 ..... 29 E1
Polesworth B78 ..... 4 C1
Lynchgate Rd CV4 ..... 76 B3
Lyndale B77 ..... 9 F3
Lyndale Rd CV5 ..... 60 B2
Lyndhurst Cl LE10 ..... 32 A4
Lyndhurst Croft CV5 ..... 59 E2
Lyndhurst Rd CV21 ..... 83 F1
Lyndon Croft B37 ..... 44 A4
Lyneham Gdns B76 ..... 22 A3
Lyng Cl CV5 ..... 60 A2
Lyng Hall Sch CV2 ..... 62 B3
Lynmouth Cl CV11 ..... 29 F3
Lynmouth Rd CV2 ..... 62 C4
Lynton Cl CV34 ..... 104 C1
Lynton Rd CV6 ..... 49 F1
Lynwood Wlk 18 CV31 ..... 110 B3
Lysander Cl CV35 ..... 146 B1
Lysander Ct CV37 ..... 145 D1
Lysander St CV3 ..... 78 B3
Lyster Cl CV34 ..... 108 A4
Lythall Cl CV31 ..... 110 C3
Lythalls La CV6 ..... 49 F1
Lythalls Lane Ind Est CV6 ..... 49 F1
Lytham B77 ..... 4 B3
Lytham Cl B76 ..... 22 A3
Lytham Rd CV22 ..... 82 C1
Lyttelton Rd CV34 ..... 108 C4
Lyttleton Cl CV3 ..... 63 D1

M40 Distribution Pk CV35 146 A1
Macaulay Rd Coventry CV2 ..... 62 B2
Rugby CV22 ..... 99 F4
Macbeth App CV34 ..... 109 E2
Macbeth Cl CV22 ..... 99 F3
Macdonald Rd CV2 ..... 62 B2
Macefield Cl CV2 ..... 50 B1
Mackenzie Cl CV5 ..... 60 A4
Mackley Way CV33 ..... 123 E6
Madam's Hill Rd B90 ..... 70 B4
Madden Pl CV22 ..... 82 B1
Madeira Croft CV5 ..... 60 C1
Madrona B77 ..... 4 A2
Magdalen Cl CV37 ..... 129 D2
Magdalen Rd CV23 ..... 117 C6
Magna Park LE17 ..... 55 E3
Magnet La CV22 ..... 99 E4
Magnolia B77 ..... 4 A2
Magnolia Cl CV3 ..... 77 D3
Magnus B77 ..... 9 F3
Magpie La CV7 ..... 73 F3
Maguire Ind Est CV4 ..... 75 F4
Magyar Cres CV11 ..... 40 A4
Maidavale Cres CV3 ..... 77 E2
Maidenhair Dr CV23 ..... 83 E4
Maidenhead Cl CV37 ..... 145 D2
Maidenhead Rd CV37 ..... 145 D2
Maidwell Dr B90 ..... 70 C4
Main Ave B26 ..... 44 B2
Main Rd Ansty CV7 ..... 51 E2
Austrey CV9 ..... 3 D1
Baxterley CV9 ..... 17 D4
Binton CV37 ..... 120 A1
Broughton OX15 ..... 139 E1
Claybrooke Magna LE17 ..... 43 F3
Kilsby CV23 ..... 101 F2
Main Rd continued
Lower Quinton CV37 ..... 129 E2
Meriden CV7 ..... 58 B4
Newton Regis B79 ..... 2 B2
Main St Aston le W NN11 ..... 134 F5
Badby NN11 ..... 126 F5
Birdingbury CV23 ..... 115 F7
Burmington CV36 ..... 141 A8
Church Lench WR11 ..... 127 A6
Cleeve Prior WR11 ..... 128 A4
Clifton u D CV23 ..... 83 F3
Easenhall CV23 ..... 65 F2
Frankton CV23 ..... 97 E1
Grandborough CV23 ..... 116 F6
Hanwell OX17 ..... 139 F6
Harborough Magna CV23 ..... 66 A2
Higham-on-t-H CV13 ..... 21 D2
Littleton WR11 ..... 127 F1
Long Lawford CV21 ..... 82 A3
Long Lawford,Newbold on A CV21 ..... 82 B4
Mollington OX17 ..... 134 A2
Monks Kirby CV23 ..... 53 F2
Newton LE17 ..... 68 A1
North Newington OX15 ..... 139 D2
Offenham WR11 ..... 127 D1
Orton-on-t-H CV9 ..... 6 B2
Rugby CV22 ..... 99 E4
Shawell LE17 ..... 68 B3
Sibford Gower OX15 ..... 142 D8
Stoke Golding CV13 ..... 21 E4
Stretton u F CV23 ..... 65 D4
Thurlaston CV23 ..... 98 C2
Tiddington CV37 ..... 145 F2
Tysoe CV35 ..... 138 B7
Willey CV23 ..... 54 C3
Willoughby CV23 ..... 117 C6
Withybrook CV7 ..... 52 C3
Wolston CV8 ..... 80 A2
Wroxton OX15 ..... 139 D4
Makepeace Ave CV34 ..... 104 C1
Malam Cl CV4 ..... 60 A1
Maldale B77 ..... 4 B1
Maldens The CV36 ..... 149 F3
Malham Cl CV11 ..... 30 A1
Malham Rd Tamworth B77 ..... 10 B4
Warwick CV34 ..... 104 C1
Malins The CV34 ..... 109 D3
Mallaby Cl B90 ..... 70 A4
Mallard Ave CV10 ..... 28 B3
Mallard Cl CV37 ..... 144 B3
Mallard Rd B80 ..... 103 F2
Mallender Dr B93 ..... 71 F3
Mallerin Croft CV10 ..... 28 A3
Mallory Dr CV34 ..... 108 B4
Mallory Rd
Bishops Tachbrook CV33 ..... 122 F8
Lighthorne Heath CV35 ..... 123 D2
Mallory Way CV6 ..... 49 F2
Mallow Way CV23 ..... 83 E4
Malmesbury Rd CV6 ..... 49 D2
Malt House Cl CV33 ..... 133 B7
Malt House La WR11 ..... 127 A6
Malthouse Cl Ansley CV10 ..... 27 D2
Harvington WR11 ..... 127 D3
Malthouse La Earlswood B94 86 C4
Kenilworth CV8 ..... 92 C3
Long Compton CV36 ..... 141 C3
Shutford OX15 ..... 139 A3
Malthouse Row B37 ..... 44 A4
Maltings The Nuneaton CV11 29 F3
Royal Leamington Spa CV32 . 105 F1
Studley B80 ..... 103 E2
Maltmill La B49 ..... 143 E2
Malvern Ave Nuneaton CV10 . 28 A2
Rugby CV22 ..... 83 E1
Malvern Dr B76 ..... 22 A4
Malvern Rd
Balsall Common CV7 ..... 74 B3
Coventry CV5 ..... 60 C2
Redditch B97 ..... 102 B4
Manby Rd B35 ..... 22 A2
Mancetter Rd Atherstone CV9 ..... 19 D3
Nuneaton CV10 ..... 28 B4
Mander Gr CV34 ..... 108 B2
Manderley Cl CV5 ..... 59 E3
Manfield Ave CV2 ..... 63 D4
Mann's Cl CV8 ..... 96 A4
Manning Wlk CV21 ..... 83 D2
Mannings Cl OX15 ..... 142 D8
Manor Barns CV36 ..... 136 B6
Manor Cl Charwelton NN11 . 126 D2
Hinckley LE10 ..... 31 E3
Manor Court Ave CV11 ..... 29 D3
Manor Court Rd CV11 ..... 29 D3
Manor Ct Cleeve Prior WR11 128 A4
Ettington CV37 ..... 131 A3
Fenny Compton CV33 ..... 133 D7
Manor Cty Prim Sch B78 ..... 8 C3
Manor Dr Stretton on D CV23 . 96 C3
Ullenhall B80 ..... 112 D4
Wilmcote CV37 ..... 120 C4
Manor Est CV8 ..... 79 F2
Manor Farm Cl CV23 ..... 101 E1
Manor Farm Rd CV36 ..... 136 F6
Manor Gn CV37 ..... 145 E1
Manor Ho B96 ..... 102 C2
Manor House Cl
Aston Flamville LE10 ..... 32 C3
Rugby CV21 ..... 82 B4
Manor House Dr CV1 ..... 151 B2
Manor House La B46 ..... 23 D2
Manor La Claverdon CV35 ..... 114 A4
Clifton u D CV23 ..... 84 A3
Ettington CV37 ..... 131 A3
Honiley CV8 ..... 91 D3
Kineton CV35 ..... 132 B5
Manor La continued
Shipston-on-S CV36 ..... 149 F3
Wroxall CV35 ..... 90 C2
Manor Mews B80 ..... 103 F2
Manor Orch Harbury CV33 .. 123 E6
Horley OX15 ..... 139 D6
Manor Park OX17 ..... 134 B4
Manor Park Jun & Inf Sch CV3 ..... 77 E4
Manor Park Rd CV11 ..... 29 D3
Manor Park Sch CV11 ..... 29 D3
Manor Pk WR11 ..... 127 D3
Manor Rd Atherstone CV9 ..... 18 C3
Bishops Itchington CV33 ..... 124 A4
Claybrooke Magna LE17 ..... 43 E3
Coventry CV1 ..... 151 B1
Dorridge B93 ..... 71 F2
Harbury CV33 ..... 123 F6
Kenilworth CV8 ..... 92 C3
Littleton WR11 ..... 127 F1
Loxley CV35 ..... 130 F7
Royal Leamington Spa CV32 106 A2
Rugby CV21 ..... 83 D2
Staverton NN11 ..... 126 D8
Stockton CV23 ..... 147 F4
Stratford-u-A CV37 ..... 145 E1
Studley B80 ..... 103 F2
Wythall B47 ..... 69 D2
Manor Rd Ind Est CV9 ..... 18 C4
Manor Way LE10 ..... 31 E3
Mansard Ct B46 ..... 34 A4
Manse Cl CV7 ..... 39 D1
Mansel St CV6 ..... 61 F4
Mansell Rd B97 ..... 102 B4
Mansell St CV37 ..... 144 C2
Mansion St 1 LE10 ..... 31 E4
Mansions Cl CV33 ..... 124 A4
Mansley Bsns Ctr The CV37 ..... 144 B2
Manson's Bridge Rd B35 ..... 22 A2
Manston Dr CV35 ..... 146 B1
Manta Rd B77 ..... 9 E3
Mantilla Dr CV3 ..... 77 D3
Manton Croft B93 ..... 71 F2
Maple Ave CV7 ..... 39 D1
Maple Cl LE10 ..... 31 F3
Maple Dr B78 ..... 15 E4
Maple Gr Rugby CV21 ..... 83 D2
Stratford-u-A CV37 ..... 144 C3
Warwick CV34 ..... 105 D1
Maple Leaf Dr B37 ..... 44 B4
Maple Rd Nuneaton CV10 ..... 28 C3
Royal Leamington Spa CV31 . 109 F3
Maple Rise B77 ..... 4 A2
Maple Wlk 3 B37 ..... 33 D1
Maplebeck Cl CV5 ..... 61 D2
Maples The CV12 ..... 38 C1
Mapleton Rd CV6 ..... 60 C4
Maplewood B76 ..... 22 A4
Mapperley Cl CV2 ..... 63 D4
Mappleborough Green Jun & Inf Sch B98 ..... 112 A5
Marble Alley B80 ..... 103 D2
March Rd OX17 ..... 133 E2
March Way CV3 ..... 78 B4
Marchant Rd LE10 ..... 31 E4
Marchfont Cl CV11 ..... 30 A1
Marcos Dr B36 ..... 22 C1
Marcroft Pl CV31 ..... 110 B3
Mardol Cl CV2 ..... 62 B4
Marfield Cl B76 ..... 22 A3
Margaret Ave CV12 ..... 39 D2
Margaret Cl CV33 ..... 123 F6
Margaret Rd CV9 ..... 18 C4
Margeson Cl CV2 ..... 62 C1
Margetts Cl CV8 ..... 92 C2
Marie Brock Cl CV4 ..... 60 A1
Marie Cl CV9 ..... 19 D4
Marie Corelli Sch CV37 ..... 144 B2
Marigold Dr LE10 ..... 31 F3
Marina Cl CV4 ..... 75 F4
Marion Rd CV6 ..... 61 E4
Mark Antony Dr CV34 ..... 109 E2
Market End Cl CV12 ..... 38 B1
Market Hill CV33 ..... 147 D2
Market Mall CV21 ..... 83 D2
Market Pl Alcester B49 ..... 143 D2
Hinckley LE10 ..... 31 E4
Nuneaton CV11 ..... 29 E2
Rugby CV21 ..... 83 D2
Shipston-on-S CV36 ..... 149 F3
2 Warwick CV34 ..... 108 C3
Market Sq CV35 ..... 132 B6
Market St Atherstone CV9 ..... 18 B4
Polesworth B78 ..... 5 D1
Rugby CV21 ..... 83 D2
Warwick CV34 ..... 108 B3
Market Way CV1 ..... 151 B2
Markham Dr CV31 ..... 110 A2
Marlborough Cl LE10 ..... 32 A4
Marlborough Dr CV31 ..... 110 B3
Marlborough Rd
Coventry CV2 ..... 62 A2
Nuneaton CV11 ..... 29 D2
Rugby CV22 ..... 99 F4
Marlborough Way B77 ..... 9 F4
Marlcroft CV3 ..... 78 C3
Marleigh Rd B50 ..... 148 B3
Marlene Croft B37 ..... 33 E1
Marler Rd CV4 ..... 75 F4
Marlin B77 ..... 9 E3
Marlissa Dr CV6 ..... 49 F1
Marloes Wlk CV31 ..... 110 B3
Marlow Cl CV5 ..... 60 A2
Marlow Rd CV9 ..... 16 B3
Marlowe Cl Banbury OX16 ... 139 F3
Nuneaton CV10 ..... 27 F3
Marlston Wlk CV5 ..... 60 A2
Marlwood Cl CV6 ..... 49 F2
Marner Cres CV6 ..... 61 D3
Marner Rd Bedworth CV12 ..... 39 D2
Nuneaton CV10 ..... 29 D1
Marnhull Cl CV2 ..... 62 C2
Marrick B77 ..... 4 B1
Marriners La CV5 ..... 60 A3
Marriott Rd Bedworth CV12 ..... 38 B1
Coventry CV6 ..... 61 D2
Marsdale Dr CV10 ..... 28 C2
Marsett B77 ..... 10 B4
Marsh La
Bradnock's Marsh B92 ..... 57 E3
Curdworth B76 ..... 23 E3
Hampton in A B92 ..... 57 D3
Water Orton B46 ..... 23 E2
Marsh Rd CV37 ..... 120 B5
Marshall Ave CV36 ..... 149 F3
Marshall Lake Rd B90 ..... 70 B4
Marshall Rd CV7 ..... 49 F4
Marshalls Cl OX15 ..... 138 F5
Marsham Cl CV34 ..... 109 D4
Marshbrook Cl CV2 ..... 50 C2
Marshdale Ave CV6 ..... 49 F2
Marshfield Dr CV4 ..... 76 B1
Marston Ave CV35 ..... 123 D2
Marston Cl 8 CV32 ..... 106 A1
Marston Dr B37 ..... 33 D3
Marston Green Jun & Inf Sch B37 ..... 44 A4
Marston La Bedworth CV12 ..... 39 E3
Nuneaton CV11 ..... 39 F4
Wishaw B76 ..... 14 C1
Marten Cl CV35 ..... 108 A4
Martin Cl Coventry CV5 ..... 59 F2
Stratford-u-A CV37 ..... 145 D3
Martin La CV22 ..... 99 E4
Martindale Rd CV7 ..... 50 B4
Martins Dr CV9 ..... 12 C1
Martins Rd CV12 ..... 38 C1
Martlesham Sq B35 ..... 22 A2
Martley Cl B98 ..... 103 D4
Martley Croft B91 ..... 71 D4
Marton Rd Birdingbury CV23 115 E7
Long Itchington CV23 ..... 115 D5
Martyrs' Cl The CV3 ..... 77 E4
Mary Arden's House CV37 ..... 120 D5
Mary Herbert St CV3 ..... 77 E4
Mary Slessor St CV3 ..... 78 B4
Marystow Cl CV5 ..... 60 A4
Masefield Ave CV34 ..... 108 B2
Masefield Rd CV37 ..... 145 D1
Maseley Ct CV37 ..... 129 D2
Mason Ave CV32 ..... 106 B2
Mason Cl Bidford-on-A B50 ..... 148 C3
Redditch B97 ..... 102 B4
Mason Croft The Shakespeare Inst (Univ of Birmingham) CV37 ..... 144 C1
Mason Ct LE10 ..... 31 D4
Mason La B94 ..... 69 F1
Mason Rd Coventry CV6 ..... 49 F1
Redditch B97 ..... 102 B4
Masons Rd CV37 ..... 144 B2
Masons Way CV37 ..... 144 B2
Masser Rd CV6 ..... 49 E2
Massey Shan Ave GL56 ..... 140 C3
Master's Yd CV23 ..... 115 F7
Masters Rd CV31 ..... 110 A2
Mathe Croft CV31 ..... 110 B3
Matlock Cl CV21 ..... 83 E4
Matlock Rd CV1 ..... 61 E3
Matterson Rd CV6 ..... 61 D3
Matthews Cl CV37 ..... 145 D2
Maud Rd B46 ..... 23 E2
Maudslay Rd CV5 ..... 60 C1
Maureen Cl CV4 ..... 59 E1
Mavor Dr CV12 ..... 38 B1
Mawby's La DE12 ..... 3 F4
Mawnan Cl CV7 ..... 50 A4
Max Rd CV6 ..... 60 C3
Maxstoke Cl Meriden CV7 ..... 46 A1
Tamworth B77 ..... 9 E2
Maxstoke Croft B90 ..... 70 B4
Maxstoke La Coleshill B46 ..... 34 A3
Meriden CV7 ..... 46 A1
May Farm Cl B47 ..... 69 D3
May La Ebrington GL55 ..... 135 E2
Hollywood B47 ..... 69 D4
Rugby CV22 ..... 82 B1
May St CV6 ..... 61 F4
May's Hill B95 ..... 113 A4
Mayama Rd B78 ..... 8 C4
Maybird Ctr CV37 ..... 144 C2
Maybridge Dr B91 ..... 71 D4
Maybrook Ind Est CV37 ..... 144 C2
Maybrook Rd
Stratford-u-A CV37 ..... 144 C2
Sutton Coldfield B76 ..... 22 A3
Maycock Rd CV6 ..... 61 E4
Mayfair Dr CV10 ..... 27 F2
Mayfield B77 ..... 10 B4
Mayfield Ave CV37 ..... 145 D2
Mayfield Cl Bedworth CV12 ..... 39 D2
17 Royal Leamington Spa CV31 ..... 110 B3
Mayfield Ct CV37 ..... 145 D2
Mayfield Dr Henley-in-A B95 113 A5
Kenilworth CV8 ..... 93 E2
Mayfield Rd Coventry CV5 ..... 61 D1
Nuneaton CV11 ..... 29 F1
Southam CV33 ..... 147 D3
Mayflower Dr CV2 ..... 62 C1
Mayhurst Cl B47 ..... 69 E3
Mayhurst Rd B47 ..... 69 D3
Maynard Ave Bedworth CV12 49 E4
Warwick CV34 ..... 109 D4
Mayne Cl CV35 ..... 114 F3
Mayo Rd CV36 ..... 149 F4
Mayor's Croft CV4 ..... 76 A4
Maypole La CV9 ..... 11 E1
Maypole Rd B79 ..... 5 F2
Mayswood Rd B95 ..... 113 A3
Maythorn Ave B76 ..... 22 A3
Maythorn Gr 4 B91 ..... 71 D4
Maytree Cl B37 ..... 33 D1
Mc Kinnell Cres CV21 ..... 83 F2
McDonnell Dr CV6 ..... 49 F3
McMahon Rd CV12 ..... 49 F4
Mead The OX17 ..... 133 F2
Meadfoot Rd CV3 ..... 78 C3
Meadow Cl Ansty CV7 ..... 51 E2
Hockley Heath B94 ..... 88 B3
Kingsbury B78 ..... 15 E3
Royal Leamington Spa CV32 . 106 B2
Stratford-u-A CV37 ..... 144 B2
Stretton on D CV23 ..... 97 D3
Wolvey LE10 ..... 41 E2
Meadow Croft Arley CV7 ..... 26 C1
Wythall B47 ..... 69 D2
Meadow Crofts CV33 ..... 124 B5
Meadow Ct CV11 ..... 29 D2
Meadow Dr Hampton in A B92 ..... 57 D4
Hinckley LE10 ..... 32 A4
Meadow Gdns CV9 ..... 17 E4
Meadow Green Prim Sch B47 ..... 69 D2
Meadow La B94 ..... 89 E2
Meadow Rd Alcester B49 ..... 143 D3
Coventry CV6 ..... 49 D2
Hartshill CV10 ..... 28 A4
Henley-in-A B95 ..... 113 B4
Hurley CV9 ..... 16 B3
Rugby CV21 ..... 82 C3
Southam CV33 ..... 147 D3
Warwick CV34 ..... 109 D4
Wolston CV8 ..... 80 A2
Wythall B47 ..... 69 D2
Meadow Rise B95 ..... 112 E6
Meadow St Atherstone CV9 ..... 18 B4
Coventry CV1 ..... 151 A2
Nuneaton CV11 ..... 29 D3
Meadow Sweet Rd CV37 ..... 144 C3
Meadow Way
Fenny Compton CV33 ..... 133 E7
Harborough Magna CV23 ..... 66 A2
Meadows Sch CV4 ..... 59 F2
Meadows The
Bidford-on-A B50 ..... 148 B3
Hinckley LE10 ..... 32 A4
Leek Wootton CV35 ..... 105 D4
Meadowside CV11 ..... 40 A4
Meadowsweet CV23 ..... 83 E4
Meadway CV2 ..... 62 A3
Meadway N CV2 ..... 62 A3
Meadway The Hinckley LE10 . 31 F4
Redditch B97 ..... 102 B4
Mearse La WR7 ..... 118 B5
Medhurst Cl CV22 ..... 99 E2
Medina Rd CV6 ..... 49 F1
Medland Ave CV3 ..... 76 C3
Meer End Rd CV8 ..... 74 B1
Meer St CV37 ..... 145 D2
Meerhill Ave B90 ..... 71 D3
Meeting House La CV7 ..... 74 B3
Meeting La B49 ..... 143 E2
Meir Rd B98 ..... 103 E4
Melbourne Cl CV11 ..... 39 F4
Melbourne Rd CV5 ..... 61 D1
Meldrum Ct CV33 ..... 132 F7
Meldrum Rd CV10 ..... 28 B2
Melfort Cl CV3 ..... 62 C1
Melksham Sq B35 ..... 22 A2
Mellish Ct CV22 ..... 82 C1
Mellish Rd CV22 ..... 82 C1
Mellor Rd CV21 ..... 101 D4
Mellowdew Rd CV2 ..... 62 B2
Mellowship Rd CV5 ..... 59 E3
Mellwaters B77 ..... 10 B4
Melmerby B77 ..... 10 B4
Melrose Ave CV12 ..... 49 E4
Melrose Cl LE10 ..... 31 D4
Melton Rd CV32 ..... 106 A2
Melville Cl Bedworth CV7 ..... 50 A4
Rugby CV22 ..... 82 C1
Melville Rd CV1 ..... 61 D2
Memorial Rd CV33 ..... 133 D7
Menai Wlk B37 ..... 33 D2
Mendip Dr CV10 ..... 28 A2
Mendip Way B77 ..... 4 B1
Meon Cl CV37 ..... 129 D1
Meon Rd GL55 ..... 135 C7
Mercer Ave Coventry CV2 ..... 62 A3
Water Orton B46 ..... 23 D2
Mercia Ave CV8 ..... 92 C2
Mercia Bsns Village CV4 ..... 75 F3
Mercia Way CV34 ..... 109 D4
Mercian Pk B77 ..... 4 A2
Mercian Way B77 ..... 4 A2
Mercot Cl B98 ..... 103 D3
Mercury Ct B77 ..... 4 A2
Mere Ave B35 ..... 22 A2
Mere La LE10 ..... 42 B2
Meredith Rd CV2 ..... 62 B1
Merevale Ave Hinckley LE10 .. 31 E4
Nuneaton CV11 ..... 29 D2
Merevale Cl Hinckley LE10 ..... 31 E4
Redditch B98 ..... 103 E4
Merevale La CV9 ..... 17 F4
Merevale Rd CV9 ..... 12 B1
Merevale View CV9 ..... 18 B4

Merganser B77 10 A3
Meriden CE Prim Sch CV7 46 B1
Meriden Cl B98 112 A6
Meriden Dr B37 33 D3
Meriden Hill CV7 58 C4
Meriden Rd Berkswell CV7 58 B2
Fillongley CV7 36 B1
Hampton in A B92 57 D4
Meriden St CV1 61 D2
Merlin Ave CV10 28 A3
Merlin Cl B77 10 A3
Merrifield Gdns LE10 31 F3
Merrington Cl 5 B91 71 E4
Merrivale Rd CV5 60 C2
Merryfields Way CV2 50 C1
Mersey Rd CV12 40 A2
Merstone Sch B37 33 D1
Merttens Dr CV22 82 C1
Meryton Ave CV4 76 C3
Meschines St CV3 77 E3
Metalloys Ind Est B76 22 A3
Metcalfe Cl OX15 139 E4
Metchley Croft B90 70 C3
Mews Rd CV32 109 E4
Mews The Atherstone CV9 18 B4
Bedworth CV12 39 D1
Kenilworth CV8 92 C2
Rugby CV21 84 A1
Mica Cl B77 4 A1
Michael Blanning Gdns B93 71 F2
Michael Drayton Mid Sch CV10 28 A4
Michaelmas Rd CV3 151 B1
Michell Cl CV3 78 A4
Mickle Mdw B46 23 D2
Micklehill Dr B90 70 A4
Mickleton Cl B98 102 C4
Mickleton Cty Prim Sch GL55 135 B6
Mickleton Dr CV35 114 F5
Mickleton Rd Coventry CV5 77 D4
Ilmington CV36 136 A7
Middelburg Cl CV11 30 A1
Middle Bickenhill La B92 45 D2
Middle Hill OX15 142 D4
Middle La
Nether Whitacre B46 24 C3
Shotteswell OX17 139 E8
Wroxton OX15 139 B4
Middle Lock La CV35 114 E5
Middle Rd CV33 123 D7
Middle Ride CV3 78 C3
Middle St Ilmington CV36 136 B6
Tredington CV37 136 F7
Middleborough Rd CV1 151 A4
Middlecotes CV4 60 A1
Middlefield Ave B93 72 A2
Middlefield Dr CV3 63 D1
Middlefield La CV37 130 E1
Middlefleld Dr CV3 63 D1
Middlemarch Bsns Pk CV3 78 B1
Middlemarch Mid Sch CV10 29 D1
Middlemarch Rd
Coventry CV6 61 E4
Nuneaton CV10 29 E1
Middlemore Cl B80 103 E2
Middlesmoor B77 10 B4
Middleton Cl CV35 138 B6
Middleton Hall B78 8 C1
Middleton La B78 13 F3
Middletown
Moreton Morrell CV35 122 F3
Studley B80 103 E1
Middletown La B96 103 E1
Midland Air Mus CV3 78 A2
Midland Oak Trad Est CV6 49 F1
Midland Rd Coventry CV6 61 F3
Nuneaton CV11 29 D3
Midland Trad Est CV21 83 D3
Midpoint Park Ind Est B76 22 B3
Milburn B77 10 B4
Milburn Hill Rd CV4 76 A3
Milby Dr CV11 30 A4
Milby Fst & Mid Sch CV11 29 F4
Milcote Cl B98 103 D4
Milcote Rd CV37 129 C6
Mildmay Cl CV37 144 C1
Mile La CV1 151 C1
Mile Tree La CV2 50 C4
Milebush Ave B36 22 B1
Miles Mdw CV6 50 A1
Milestone Dr CV22 99 F4
Milestone Rd CV37 130 B8
Milford Cl Allesley CV5 60 A3
Redditch B97 102 B3
Milford Gr B90 71 E4
Milford St CV10 29 D1
Mill Bank B46 25 E2
Mill Bank Mews CV8 93 D3
Mill Cl Braunston NN11 117 D5
Broom B50 148 A4
Coventry CV2 50 A2
Hollywood B47 69 D4
Norton Lindsey CV35 114 C2
Nuneaton CV11 29 F1
Southam CV33 147 D3
Mill Cres Kineton CV35 132 B6
Kingsbury B78 15 E2
Southam CV33 147 D3
Mill Ct CV36 149 F3
Mill End CV8 93 D3
Mill Farm Cl CV22 99 E2
Mill Hill CV8 77 E2
Mill House Cl CV32 109 E4
Mill House Dr CV32 109 E4
Mill House Terr CV32 109 E4
Mill La Alcester B49 143 D1
Aston Cantlow B95 119 F6
Barford CV35 122 A7
Bentley Heath B93 71 F2
Bramcote CV11 40 C4
Broom B50 148 A4
Bulkington CV12 40 A2
Chipping Warden OX17 134 F3
Cleeve Prior WR11 128 A4
Clifton u D CV23 83 F3
Coventry CV3 62 C1
Cubbington CV32 106 C3
Drayton OX15 139 E4
Earlswood B94 86 A4
Fazeley B78 9 D4
Fenny Compton CV33 133 D7
Fillongley CV7 36 B3
Halford CV36 136 F8
Harbury CV33 123 F7
Kineton CV35 132 B6
Lapworth B94 89 E2
Lowsonford,Finwood CV35 113 E7
Lowsonford,Turner's Green CV35 113 F8
Mickleton GL55 135 B6
Newbold-on-S CV37 130 F1
Shrewley CV35 114 C6
Stratford-u-A CV37 145 D1
Tredington CV36 136 F6
Welford on A CV37 129 A7
Witherley CV9 19 D3
Wolvey LE10 41 F3
Wythall B47 69 D1
Mill Pleck B80 103 F2
Mill Pool La B93 89 D4
Mill Race La CV6 50 A2
Mill Race View CV9 12 B1
Mill Rd
Royal Leamington Spa CV31 110 A4
Rugby CV21 83 E3
Southam CV33 147 D3
Mill Row LE10 41 F3
Mill St Bedworth CV12 39 D2
Coventry CV1 151 A3
Harbury CV33 123 E7
Kineton CV35 132 B6
Nuneaton CV11 29 E2
Royal Leamington Spa CV31 110 A4
Shipston-on-S CV36 149 F3
Warwick CV34 108 C3
Mill Terr CV12 39 D3
Mill Wlk CV11 29 E2
Millais Cl CV12 39 D2
Millbank CV34 105 D1
Millbeck CV21 83 E4
Miller's Bank B50 148 A4
Millers Cl Dunchurch CV22 99 D2
Lower Boddington NN11 134 E6
Welford on A CV37 129 B6
Millers Dale Cl CV21 83 E4
Millers Gn LE10 31 F3
Millers La Hornton OX15 139 B8
Monks Kirby CV23 53 E2
Millers Rd CV34 108 C4
Millfield Prim Sch B78 9 D4
Millfields Ave CV21 100 C4
Millholme Cl CV33 147 E2
Millhouse Ct CV6 61 F4
Milliners Ct CV9 18 B4
Millison Gr B90 71 D4
Mills La OX15 139 D4
Millway Dr 1 CV33 122 F8
Milner Cl CV12 40 B1
Milner Cres CV2 50 C1
Milner Dr B79 4 C4
Milrose Way CV4 75 F4
Milton Ave CV34 108 B3
Milton Cl Bedworth CV12 39 E1
Bentley Heath B93 71 F2
Redditch B97 102 B4
Milton Rd B93 71 F2
Milton St CV2 62 A2
Milverton Comb Sch CV32 105 F1
Milverton Cres 1 CV32 105 F1
Milverton Cres W 2 CV32 105 F1
Milverton Hill CV32 109 F4
Milverton House Prep Sch CV11 29 E2
Milverton Rd Coventry CV2 50 B1
Knowle B93 72 B3
Milverton Terr CV32 109 F4
Miners Wlk B78 4 C1
Minions Cl CV9 18 B4
Miniva Dr B76 13 D1
Minster Cl
Hampton Magna CV35 114 F3
Knowle B93 72 A4
Minster Rd CV1 61 D2
Minton Rd CV2 50 C1
Minworth Ind Pk B76 22 A3
Minworth Jun & Inf Sch B76 22 B3
Minworth Rd B46 23 D2
Mira Dr CV10 20 B2
Miranda Cl CV3 78 B4
Mistral Cl LE10 31 F4
Mitcheldean Cl B98 102 C4
Mitchell Ave CV4 76 A4
Mitchell Rd CV12 39 E1
Mitchison Cl CV23 117 E8
Moat Ave CV3 76 C3
Moat Cl Bubbenhall CV8 95 E3
Thurlaston CV23 98 C1
Moat Croft Birmingham B37 33 D1
Sutton Coldfield B76 22 A4
Moat Dr B78 8 C3
Moat Farm Dr
Bedworth CV12 49 E4
Rugby CV21 101 D4
Moat Farm La B95 112 E6
Moat Gn CV35 108 A1
Moat House Ct B80 103 F4
Moat House La Coventry CV4 76 B4
Shustoke B46 25 D1
Moat La LE10 41 F3
Mobbs La OX15 142 D4
Mockley Wood Rd B93 72 A4
Modbury Cl CV3 77 E3
Model Village The CV23 115 D3
Molesworth Ave CV3 62 A1
Mollington La OX17 133 D2
Mollington Prim Sch OX17 133 F2
Mollington Rd CV31 110 A2
Momus Bvd CV2 62 B1
Moncrieff Dr CV31 110 B3
Monk's Croft The CV3 77 E4
Monks Dr B80 103 E2
Monks Kirby La CV23 53 F3
Monks Rd Binley Woods CV3 79 E4
Coventry CV1 61 F1
Monks Way CV34 108 B3
Monkspath B90 71 D3
Monkspath Bsns Pk B90 70 C4
Monkspath Cl B90 70 B4
Monkspath Hall Rd B90 71 D4
Monkspath Jun & Inf Sch B90 71 D3
Monkswood Cres CV2 62 B4
Monmouth Cl Coventry CV5 60 A2
Kenilworth CV8 92 C3
Monmouth Gdns CV10 28 C2
Montague Rd Rugby CV22 99 E3
Warwick CV34 109 D4
Montague's Cnr CV37 129 A6
Montalt Rd CV3 77 F4
Montana Wlk CV10 28 C2
Montfort Rd B46 33 F3
Montgomery Ave CV35 114 F3
Montgomery Cl Coventry CV3 78 B2
Stratford-u-A CV37 144 C1
Montgomery Dr CV22 82 B1
Montilo La CV23 66 B3
Montjoy Cl CV3 78 B4
Montley B77 10 B4
Montpellier Cl CV3 77 E3
Montrose Ave CV32 106 A3
Montrose Dr Birmingham B35 22 A2
Nuneaton CV10 28 C2
Montrose Rd CV22 83 D1
Montsford Cl B93 71 F3
Monument Way CV37 145 D3
Monwode Lea La B46 26 A2
Moor Burgess Activity Ctr B77 4 A1
Moor Farm Cl CV23 96 C3
Moor Fields B49 143 E2
Moor La
Tamworth, Amington B77 4 A3
Willoughby CV23 117 B6
Moor Rd CV10 28 A4
Moor St CV5 60 C1
Moor The B76 22 A4
Moor Wood Farm CV10 18 C1
Moorcroft Cl Nuneaton CV11 30 A1
Redditch B97 102 A3
Moore Cl Appleby Magna DE12 3 F4
Warwick CV34 104 C1
Moore Wlk CV34 109 E4
Moorend Ave B37 33 D1
Moorfield Ave B93 71 F3
Moorfield Rd B49 143 D2
Moorfield The CV3 78 A4
Moorhill Rd CV31 110 A2
Moorhills Croft B90 70 A4
Moorlands Ave CV8 92 C2
Moorpark Cl CV11 40 B4
Moorwood Cres CV10 28 A4
Moorwood La Hartshill CV10 28 A4
Nuneaton CV10 27 F4
Morar Cl B35 22 B2
Moray Cl LE10 31 D4
Mordaunt Rd CV35 146 C2
Moreall Mdws CV4 76 B2
Moreland Croft B76 22 A3
Moreton Cl CV37 145 E1
Moreton Hall Ag Coll CV35 122 E2
Moreton Morrell La CV35 123 B2
Moreton-in-Marsh District Hospl GL56 140 A3
Moreton-in-Marsh Sta GL56 140 A3
Morgan Cl Arley CV7 36 C4
Banbury OX16 139 F4
Norton Lindsey CV35 114 C2
Studley B80 103 F1
Morgan Gr B36 22 C1
Morgans Rd CV5 59 E2
Morgrove Ave B93 71 F3
Morland Cl CV12 40 B1
Morland Rd CV6 49 E1
Morningside CV5 77 D4
Mornington Ct B46 34 A4
Morpeth B77 9 E4
Morrell St CV32 105 F1
Morris Ave CV2 62 B2
Morris Cl CV21 82 C3
Morris Croft B36 22 C1
Morris Dr Banbury OX16 139 F4
Nuneaton CV11 29 E1
Whitnash CV31 110 A1
Morris Hill B78 11 D4
Morris Rd NN11 117 F2
Morse Rd CV31 110 A2
Morson Cres CV21 83 F1
Morston B77 9 E2
Mortimer Rd CV8 92 C1
Morton Cl CV6 49 D1
Morton Gdns CV21 83 E1
Morton La B97 102 A4
Morton Morrell CE Prim Sch CV35 122 F2
Morton St CV32 105 F1
Morville Cl B93 71 E2
Mosedale
Moreton-in-M GL56 140 B3
Rugby CV21 83 E4
Moseley Ave CV6 61 D2
Moseley Prim Sch CV6 61 D2
Moseley Rd CV8 93 D2
Moss Cl CV22 82 C1
Moss La Beoley B98 112 A8
Newbold-on-S CV37 130 E1
Moss St 8 CV31 110 A4
Mossdale B77 10 B4
Mossdale Cl CV6 61 D3
Mossdale Cres CV10 28 C1
Mosspaul Cl CV32 105 E1
Mottistone Cl CV3 77 E3
Moultrie Rd CV22 83 D1
Mount Cres CV37 144 B2
Mount Dr CV12 39 D2
Mount Nod Prim Sch CV5 60 A2
Mount Nod Way CV5 60 A2
Mount Pleasant
Bishops Itchington CV33 124 A4
Stockton CV23 147 F4
Stratford-u-A CV37 144 B2
Tamworth B77 9 E4
Mount Pleasant Cl CV23 147 F4
Mount Pleasant La B95 112 E6
Mount Pleasant Rd CV12 39 D2
Mount Pleasant Terr CV10 28 C3
Mount Rd Henley-In-A B95 113 B4
Hinckley LE10 31 E4
Mount St Coventry CV5 60 C1
Nuneaton CV11 29 D2
Mount Street Pas CV11 29 D2
Mount The Coventry CV3 77 F4
Curdworth B76 23 E3
Mountbatten Ave CV8 93 E2
Mountbatten Cl CV37 144 B1
Mountford Cl CV35 146 C2
Mountford Rise CV35 123 B2
Mowbray St CV2 61 F2
Mowe Croft B37 44 A4
Mows Hill Rd B94 113 A8
Moxhull Rd B37 33 D3
Moyeady Ave CV22 100 C4
Moyle Cres CV5 59 E2
Much Park St CV1 151 C2
Muirfield B77 4 A3
Muirfield Cl CV11 40 B4
Mulberry Cl CV32 106 A1
Mulberry Ctr The CV37 145 D2
Mulberry Dr 5 CV34 108 C4
Mulberry Rd Coventry CV6 62 A4
Rugby CV22 82 A1
Mulberry St CV37 145 D2
Mull Croft B36 33 D4
Mullard Dr CV31 110 A2
Mullensgrove Rd B37 33 D3
Mulliner St CV6 61 F3
Mulliners Cl 2 B37 33 E1
Muntz Cres B94 88 B3
Murcott Rd CV31 110 A2
Murcott Rd E CV31 110 A2
Murray Rd Coventry CV6 61 D4
Rugby CV21 83 D2
Murrayian Cl CV21 83 D2
Murton B77 10 B4
Musborough Cl B36 22 B1
Myatt Rd WR11 127 D1
Myatt's Field WR11 127 D4
Myers Rd CV21 101 E4
Mylgrove CV3 77 E2
Mynors Cres B47 69 D3
Myrtle Gr CV5 60 C1
Mythe La CV9 19 D4
Mythe View CV9 12 C1
Myton Cres CV34 109 E3
Myton Crofts CV31 109 E4
Myton Gdns CV34 109 D3
Myton La CV34 109 E3
Myton Rd CV31, CV34 109 D3
Myton Sch CV34 109 D3
Mytton Rd B46 22 C2

Nailcote Ave CV4 75 E4
Nailcote La CV7 75 D4
Nailsworth Rd B93 71 E1
Nairn Cl CV10 29 D1
Napier St CV1 61 F2
Naples Rd CV35 132 F5
Napton Dr CV32 106 A1
Napton Gn CV5 60 A2
Napton Rd CV23 147 F4
Napton Rise CV33 147 E2
Narberth Way CV2 62 C4
Nares Cl CV22 82 C1
Narrow La B95 113 F6
Narrows The LE10 31 F4
Naseby Cl CV3 78 C4
Naseby Rd CV22 83 E1
Nash's La GL55 135 E3
Nashes The CV37 129 F7
Nathaniel Newton Fst Sch CV10 28 A4
National Ag Ctr CV8 94 A2
National Ex Ctr B40 44 C2
National Motorcycle Mus The B92 45 D1
Navigation Way CV6 62 A4
Neal Ct CV2 63 D4
Neale Ave CV5 60 A3
Neale Cl CV12 40 B1
Neale's Cl CV33 123 F7
Nebsworth La CV36 135 F5
Needhill Cl B93 71 F3
Needle Cl B80 103 F2
Needlers End La CV7 74 A4
Neilston St CV31 110 A4
Nellands Cl CV36 136 B6
Nelson Ave CV34 109 D4
Nelson Cl CV37 131 A4
Nelson La CV34 109 D4
Nelson St 5 CV1 61 F2
Nelson Way CV22 82 B1
Nemesia B77 4 A2
Nene Cl CV3 78 B4
Nene Side Cl NN11 126 F6
Nene Wlk NN11 117 F1
Nesfield Gr B92 57 D4
Nesscliffe Rd CV33 132 F5
Netherfield B98 103 D4
Nethermill Rd 1 CV6 61 D3
Nethersole Sch The B78 5 D1
Nethersole St B78 5 D1
Netherwood La B93 90 A4
Netting St OX15 142 D4
Nevada Way B37 33 E1
Nevill Cl CV31 109 F3
Neville Gr CV34 104 C1
Neville Rd
Birmingham, Castle Bromwich B36 22 C1
Hollywood B90 69 F4
Neville Wlk B35 22 A1
New Ash Dr CV5 59 F3
New Bldgs CV1 151 C3
New Broad St CV37 144 C1
New Brook St 2 CV32 109 F4
New Century Pk CV3 62 B1
New Century Way CV11 29 D2
New Cl CV35 114 F3
New End Rd B46 35 D2
New Inn La WR11 127 D5
New Leasow B76 22 A4
New Mill La B78 9 D4
New Park Cotts OX15 137 F2
New Rd Alderminster CV37 130 D3
Appleby Magna DE12 3 F4
Ash Green CV7 49 D3
Astwood Bank B96 118 C8
Bedworth CV12 38 A2
Coventry CV6 48 C1
Ebrington GL55 135 E3
Henley-in-A B95 113 A4
Hinckley LE10 32 A3
Hollywood B47 69 D4
Kineton CV33 132 F6
Lowsonford CV35 113 E6
Norton Lindsey CV35 114 C2
Pebworth CV37 128 F1
Ratley OX15 133 A2
Shotteswell OX17 139 E8
Shuttington B79 1 B1
Studley B80 103 F2
Tamworth B77 9 F4
Temple Grafton B49 119 E1
Temple Herdewyke CV33 133 A6
Water Orton B46 23 D2
New Row B78 8 C3
New St Baddesley Ensor CV9 11 E1
Bedworth CV12 39 E1
Birchmoor B78 10 C4
Bulkington CV12 40 B1
Cubbington CV32 106 C3
Dordon CV9 11 D3
Fazeley B78 9 D4
Kenilworth CV8 92 C3
Napton CV23 125 C7
Royal Leamington Spa CV31 110 A4
Rugby CV22 82 C2
Shipston-on-S CV36 149 F3
Stratford-u-A CV37 144 C1
Tiddington CV37 145 F2
Warwick CV34 108 C3
New Union St CV1 151 B2
Newall Cl CV23 83 F3
Newbold Avon Mid Sch CV21 82 C3
Newbold Cl
Bentley Heath B93 71 F3
Coventry CV3 62 C1
Newbold Comyn Pk CV32 110 B4
Newbold Pl
Royal Leamington Spa CV32 110 A4
Wellesbourne CV35 146 C2
Newbold Rd Rugby CV21 82 C3
Wellesbourne CV35 146 C3
Newbold St CV32 110 A4
Newbold Terr CV32 110 A4
Newbold Terr E CV32 110 A4
Newbold & Tredington CE Prim Sch Newbold-on-S CV37 130 E1
Tredington CV36 136 F6
Newborough Cl CV9 3 D1

Newburgh Cres CV34 108 C4
Newburgh Prim Sch CV34 108 B2
Newbury Cl 12 CV31 110 B3
Newby Cl CV3 77 F3
Newby Gr B37 33 D2
Newcastle Croft B35 22 B2
Newcombe Cl CV22 99 E2
Newcombe Rd CV5 61 D1
Newcomen Cl CV12 49 E4
Newcomen Rd CV12 38 B1
Newdegate Pl CV11 29 E2
Newdegate Rd CV12 39 D2
Newdegate St CV11 29 E2
Newdigate CV31 110 B3
Newdigate Cty Fst & Mid Sch CV12 38 B1
Newdigate Rd Coventry CV6 61 F3
Sutton Coldfield B75 13 D3
Newent Cl B98 112 A6
Newey Ave CV12 49 E4
Newey Rd CV2 62 B2
Newfield Ave CV8 93 D2
Newfield Rd CV1 61 E3
Newgale Wlk CV31 110 B4
Newhall Rd CV2 62 B4
Newham Gn CV10 28 B4
Newhaven Cl CV6 60 C3
Newhouse Croft CV7 74 A3
Newington Cl CV6 60 B3
Newington Rd B37 44 A4
Newland Cl B98 103 D4
Newland La CV7 49 D4
Newland Rd Coventry CV1 61 E3
Royal Leamington Spa CV32 106 B2
Newland St CV22 82 C2
Newlands La B37 44 A3
Newlands Rd
Baddesley Ensor CV9 11 E1
Bentley Heath B93 71 F2
Newlands The B80 103 E2
Newlyn Cl CV11 29 F2
Newman Cl CV12 39 D2
Newmarket Cl CV6 50 A2
Newmarsh Rd B76 22 A3
Newnham La B95 120 C7
Newnham Rd Coventry CV1 61 F3
Royal Leamington Spa CV32 106 A2
Newport Cl B97 102 A3
Newport Dr B49 143 D2
Newport Rd CV6 49 E1
Newquay Cl CV11 29 F3
Newscut La OX17 134 C1
Newsholme Cl 1 CV34 104 C1
Newstead Ave LE10 31 E2
Newstead Cl CV11 29 F1
Newstead Dr CV33 147 D2
Newstead Way CV3 63 D1
Newton Cl Coventry CV2 62 C4
Hartshill CV10 19 D1
Redditch B98 103 D3
Newton La Newton CV23 68 A2
Newton Regis B79 2 A2
Newton Regis B79 2 C1
Newton Manor La CV21 83 F4
Newton Rd Hinckley LE10 30 C4
Knowle B93 72 A4
Newton CV23 84 A4
Newton Regis CE Prim Sch B79 2 B2
Newtown Rd Bedworth CV12 39 D1
Nuneaton CV11 29 E3
Nibbits La NN11 117 E5
Nicholas Chamberlaine Comp Sch CV12 39 E2
Nicholls St CV2 61 F2
Nicholson Cl CV34 104 C1
Nickson Rd CV4 59 F1
Nightingale B77 10 A3
Nightingale Ave B36 33 D4
Nightingale Cl
Atherstone CV9 12 C1
Great Alne B49 119 D6
Nightingale La
Cleeve Prior WR11 128 A4
Coventry CV5 76 C4
Nimbus B77 9 E2
Nine Days La B98 103 D3
Nineacres Dr B37 33 D2
Ninefoot La B77 9 F4
Ninian Pk B77 9 E3
Ninian Way B77 9 F3
Niton Rd CV10 29 E3
Niven Cl CV5 60 A3
No Man's Heath La CV9 3 D2
Noble Cl CV34 108 B3
Nod Rise CV5 60 A2
Node Hill Cl B80 103 E2
Nolans Cl CV6 49 E2
Nook The CV11 29 F1
Norcombe Gr B90 71 D3
Nordic Drift CV2 63 D3
Norfolk Cl LE10 31 E2
Norfolk Cres CV10 28 C2
Norfolk St Coventry CV1 61 D2
Royal Leamington Spa CV32 106 A1
Norfolk Terr CV4 76 A4
Norluck Ct CV36 149 F3
Norman Ashman Coppice CV3 79 E4
Norman Ave Coventry CV2 50 C1
Nuneaton CV11 29 D2
Norman Place Rd CV6 60 C4
Norman Rd CV21 82 C3
Normanby Mdws CV31 110 A1
Normandy Cl CV35 108 A4
North Ave Bedworth CV12 39 E1
Birmingham B40 44 C3
Coventry CV2 62 A2
North Brook Rd CV5 60 B4
North Cl Braunston NN11 117 E5
Cubbington CV32 106 C3
Hinckley LE10 31 F3
North Leamington Sch CV32 105 F2
North Leamington Sch (Binswood Hall) CV32 105 F1
North Rd CV23 83 F3
North St Atherstone CV9 18 C4
Coventry CV2 62 A3
Kilsby CV23 101 F2
Marton CV23 115 C7
Nuneaton CV10 28 C2
Rugby CV21 83 D2
North View CV7 51 D1
North Villiers St CV32 106 A1
North Warwickshire & Hinkley Coll Hinckley LE10 31 F4
Nuneaton CV11 29 F3
Northampton La CV22 99 E2
Northcote Rd CV21 82 C1
Northcote St 12 CV31 110 A4
Northcote Wlk CV9 12 B1
Northend Rd CV33 133 C7
Northey Rd CV6 61 E4
Northfield Rd Coventry CV1 61 F1
Hinckley LE10 31 E4
Southam CV33 147 D2
Northgate St CV34 108 C4
Northlands Cty Prim Sch CV21 83 D2
Northolt Dr B35 22 A2
Northside Cl B98 102 C4
Northumberland Ave CV10 28 C2
Northumberland Rd
Coventry CV1 61 D2
Royal Leamington Spa CV32 105 F1
Northvale Cl CV8 93 D3
Northway Birmingham B40 44 C3
Royal Leamington Spa CV31 110 A3
Rugby CV21 83 D2
Norton Curlieu La CV35 114 C3
Norton Dr CV34 104 C1
Norton Green La B93 72 B1
Norton Hill CV9 3 E1
Norton Hill Dr CV2 62 C3
Norton La B47, B94 69 F2
Norton Lea CV35 114 C2
Norton Leys CV22 99 F3
Norton Rd B46 33 F4
Norton View GL55 135 B6
Nortons Cl CV33 133 B7
Norwich Cl CV11 30 A4
Norwich Dr CV3 77 D3
Norwood Gr CV2 50 C1
Nova Croft CV5 59 E2
Novotel Way B26 44 B2
Nuffield Rd Coventry CV6 62 A4
Hinckley LE10 30 C4
Nugent Gr B90 70 B2
Nuneaton La CV13 20 C1
Nuneaton Rd Bedworth CV12 39 D2
Bulkington CV12 40 A2
Fillongley CV7 36 C2
Furnace End B46,CV10 26 B3
Hartshill CV10 19 D1
Nuneaton Trent Valley Sta CV11 29 E3
Nunts La CV6 49 D2
Nunts Park Ave CV6 49 D2
Nunwood La CV23 96 A1
Nursery Cl Mickleton GL55 135 C7
Moreton-in-M GL56 140 A4
Nursery Hill Fst Sch CV10 27 F4
Nursery La CV31 110 A3
Nursery Rd Ansley CV10 27 F4
Atherstone CV9 18 C4
Nutbrook Ave CV4 59 F1
Nuthurst B75 13 D2
Nuthurst Cres CV10 27 E2
Nuthurst Gr B93 72 A2
Nuthurst Grange Rd B94 88 B2
Nuthurst La CV10 27 E1
Nuthurst Rd B94 113 B8
Nutt's La LE10 31 D4
Nymet B77 9 F4

Oak Avenue Woodside CV7 26 C1
Oak Cl Baginton CV8 77 F1
Bedworth CV12 39 E2
Hinckley LE10 31 F3
Oak Ct CV34 109 F1
Oak Farm Cl B76 22 A4
Oak La Allesley CV5 47 F1
Barston B92 57 D1
Oak Leigh CV35 123 D2
Oak Rd CV37 145 F2
Oak Rise B46 33 F3
Oak St CV22 83 D1
Oak Tree Ave CV3 77 D3
Oak Tree Cl
Bentley Heath B93 71 F2
Royal Leamington Spa CV32 106 A1
Oak Tree La Cookhill B49 118 D5
Hollywood B47 69 D3
Sambourne B96 103 D1
Oak Tree Rd Coventry CV3 79 D4
Harvington WR11 127 C4
Oak Way CV4 59 E1
Oakdale Rd CV3 79 E4
Oakdene Cl CV35 113 F3
Oakdene Cres Hatton CV35 114 C5
Nuneaton CV10 29 E4
Oakenhayes Cres B76 22 B3
Oakey Cl CV6 49 F2
Oakfield Gdns CV9 18 C4
Oakfield Jun Sch CV9 18 C4
Oakfield Rd Coventry CV6 60 C3
Rugby CV22 82 C1
Oakfields Way B91 56 A3
Oakford Dr CV5 59 F3
Oakhall Dr B93 71 F2
Oakham Cl B98 103 D3
Oakham Cres CV12 40 B1
Oakham La NN11 126 D8
Oakham Rd GL56 141 A1
Oaklands B76 23 D3
Oaklands Croft B76 22 A4
Oaklands The
Birmingham B37 44 A4
Coventry CV4 60 A1
Oakleigh Rd CV37 144 C3
Oakley CV8 73 F1
Oakley Wood Rd CV33 122 F7
Oakmoor Rd CV6 50 A2
Oakridge Rd CV32 106 B2
Oakroyd Cres CV10 28 B4
Oaks Pl CV6 50 A2
Oaks Rd CV8 92 C1
Oaks The CV12 38 C1
Oakthorpe Dr B37 33 D3
Oaktree Cl Bearley CV37 120 D7
Kingsbury B78 15 E3
Moreton Morrell CV35 122 E3
Oaktree Farm Mobile Homes Pk B94 86 A4
Oakwood Cl CV9 11 E1
Oakwood Gr CV34 105 D1
Oakwood Rd B47 69 D3
Oakworth Cl CV2 62 C4
Oaston Rd CV11 29 E2
Oban Dr CV10 29 D1
Oban Rd Coventry CV6 49 F3
Hinckley LE10 31 D4
Oberon Cl Nuneaton CV11 30 A1
Royal Leamington Spa CV34 109 F2
Rugby CV22 99 E3
Occupation Rd CV2 62 B2
Oddicombe Croft CV3 77 E3
Odingsel Dr CV23 115 C4
Odstone Dr LE10 30 C4
Offa Dr CV8 93 D2
Offa Rd CV31 110 A3
Offchurch La CV31 110 C3
Offchurch Rd CV32 106 C2
Offenham CE Fst Sch WR11 127 D1
Ogley Dr B75 13 D3
Okehampton Rd CV3 77 F3
Okement Gr CV23 82 A3
Oken Rd CV34 108 B4
Olaf Pl CV2 63 D4
Old Brewery Cl CV36 137 A4
Old Budbrooke Rd
Hampton Magna CV35 114 F4
Warwick CV35 108 A4
Old Church Rd Coventry CV6 50 A1
Water Orton B46 23 D2
Old Crown Mews CV2 50 B3
Old Damson La B92 44 A1
Old Farm La B46 25 D3
Old Farm Rd CV9 18 C3
Old Ford Ave CV33 147 D3
Old Forge Dr B98 103 E4
Old Forge Rd
Fenny Drayton CV13 20 A3
Great Rollright OX7 142 A2
Old Green La CV8 73 E1
Old Hedging La B77 9 E3
Old Hinckley Rd CV10 29 E3
Old House La CV7 48 A4
Old Kingsbury Rd B76 22 B3
Old La B48 85 E2
Old Leicester Rd CV21 83 D4
Old Manor Cl B78 8 C3
Old Meeting Yd CV12 39 D2
Old Mill Ave CV4 76 B3
Old Mill Rd B46 33 F4
Old Milverton La CV32 105 F3
Old Milverton Rd CV32 105 E1
Old Orchard The GL55 135 E3
Old Rd
Bishops Itchington CV33 124 B4
Braunston NN11 117 E4
Meriden CV7 46 C1
Ratley OX15 132 F2
Shipston-on-S CV36 149 F3
Southam CV33 147 D2
Old Rectory Cl CV23 67 E3
Old Rectory Gdn B49 143 D2
Old Red Lion Ct CV37 145 D1
Old School Cl WR11 127 D1
Old School End OX15 142 D4
Old School La
Hampton Magna CV35 114 F3
Lighthorne CV35 123 C2
Wilmcote CV37 120 C4
Old School Mews CV32 106 A2
Old Snitterfield Rd CV37 120 E7
Old Sq 1 CV34 108 C3
Old Station Rd B92 57 D4
Old Town CV37 145 D1
Old Town Mews CV37 144 C1
Old Tramway Wlk CV37 145 D1
Old Tree La CV35 138 B6
Old Warwick Rd
Lapworth B94, CV35 89 E2
Rowington CV35 114 A7
Royal Leamington Spa CV31 109 F4
Old Winnings Rd CV7 48 C3
Oldany Way CV10 28 C1
Oldberrow Cl 4 B90 71 D3
Oldbury Rd CV10 18 C1
Oldbury View CV10 19 D1
Oldbutt Rd CV36 149 F3
Oldfield Rd CV5 60 C2
Oldham Ave CV2 62 C2
Oldham Way CV23 82 A2
Oldington Gr B91 71 D4
Oldwich La E Honiley CV8 90 C4
Knowle CV8 73 E1
Oldwich La W B93 90 B4
Olive Ave CV2 62 B3
Oliver St Coventry CV6 61 F3
Rugby CV21 82 C2
Olivier Way CV2 63 D4
Olney Rd CV35 132 D3
Olton Ave CV5 59 F2
Olton Cl CV11 41 D4
Olton Pl CV11 28 C2
Olympus Ave CV34 109 E3
Olympus Cl CV5 59 D4
Omar Rd CV2 62 B1
Ombersley Cl B98 103 E4
Omega Pl CV21 83 D2
Onley La CV22 100 B3
Onley Terr CV4 76 B4
Onslow Croft CV32 105 F1
Openfield Croft B46 23 E1
Oratory Dr CV3 78 B3
Orchard Cl Austrey CV9 3 D1
Badby NN11 126 F6
Bidford-on-A B50 148 B2
Bishops Itchington CV33 124 B4
Bubbenhall CV8 95 E3
Coleshill B46 33 F4
Curdworth B76 23 D4
Hartshill CV10 28 A4
Hinckley LE10 32 A3
Hurley CV9 16 B2
Lower Brailes OX15 137 F2
Mickleton GL55 135 C7
Polesworth B78 5 D2
Salford OX7 150 C2
Shipston-on-S CV36 149 F3
Tamworth B77 9 E3
Welford on A CV37 129 B6
Witherley CV9 19 D4
Wolvey LE10 41 E2
Orchard Cres CV3 77 E4
Orchard Ct Atherstone CV9 18 B4
Coventry CV3 63 D1
Orchard Dr Alcester B49 143 D2
Coventry CV5 59 E2
Orchard Gr
Astwood Bank B96 118 C8
Stockton CV23 147 F4
Orchard Meadow Wlk B35 22 A2
Orchard Piece OX17 134 A2
Orchard Pl
Harvington WR11 127 D4
Redditch B80 103 F4
Orchard Rd
Hockley Heath B94 88 B3
Hook Norton OX15 142 D4
Orchard Rise CV9 11 E1
Orchard St Bedworth CV12 39 D2
Hinckley LE10 31 F4
Nuneaton CV11 29 E2
Orchard The Baxterley CV9 17 E4
Lower Quinton CV37 129 D2
Marton CV23 115 C7
Staverton NN11 126 D8
Whatcote CV36 137 E7
Orchard View OX17 134 C1
Orchard Way Hollywood B47 69 D4
Long Itchington CV23 115 C4
Nuneaton CV10 28 B3
Rugby CV22 99 E4
Southam CV33 147 D3
Stratford-u-A CV37 144 C1
Stretton on D CV23 96 C3
Studley B80 103 F1
Orchards The
Cheswick Green B90 70 B2
Hollywood B47 69 D4
Newton CV23 68 A1
Orchid Way CV23 83 E4
Ordnance Rd CV6 61 F3
Orford Cl CV35 146 C2
Orford Rise CV10 27 F2
Oriel Gr GL56 140 A2
Orion Cres CV2 50 C1
Orkney Cl CV10 29 D1
Orkney Croft B36 33 D4
Orlando Cl CV22 99 E3
Orlescote Rd CV4 76 C3
Orpington Dr CV6 49 E2
Orrian Cl CV37 144 C3
Orson Leys CV22 99 F4
Orton Ave B76 22 A3
Orton Cl B46 23 D2
Orton Hill CV9 6 C4
Orton La Austrey CV9 6 B3
Orton-on-t-H CV9 6 C1
Twycross CV9 3 F1
Orton Rd Coventry CV6 49 E2
Warton B79 5 F2
Orton Way B35 22 A1
Orwell Cl Clifton u D CV23 84 A3
Nuneaton CV10 28 A3
Orwell Rd CV1 61 F1
Osbaston Cl CV5 59 F2
Osborne Ct CV31 110 A2
Osborne Rd CV5 77 D4
Osbourne Croft B90 70 B3
Oslo Gdns CV2 63 D4
Osney Cl OX15 142 D4
Osprey B77 10 A3
Osprey Cl Coventry CV2 63 D3
Nuneaton CV11 40 A4
Ossetts Hole La CV35 113 E4
Oswald Rd CV32 109 E4
Oswald Way CV22 82 B2
Oswestry Cl B97 102 B4
Oswin Gr CV2 62 B2
Othello Cl CV22 99 E3
Ottery B77 10 A3
Our Lady of the Angels RC Fst Sch CV11 29 E2
Our Lady of the Assumption RC Prim Sch CV4 59 F1
Our Lady Of the Wayside RC Prim Sch B90 70 B4
Our Lady & St Teresa's RC Comb Sch CV32 106 B3
Our Lady's RC Prim Sch
Alcester B49 143 D3
Princethorpe CV23 96 B1
Ousterne La CV7 36 B2
Outermarch Rd CV6 61 E4
Outwood Cl B98 102 C4
Outwoods Cl CV9 18 B4
Oval Rd CV22 100 B4
Over St CV6 62 A4
Overbare Cl B94 87 D1
Overberry Cl CV2 50 B1
Overberry Orch 5 CV33 122 E8
Overdale B96 102 C1
Overdale Rd CV5 60 B2
Overell Gr CV32 105 E1
Overslade Cres CV6 60 C4
Overslade Manor Dr CV22 99 F4
Oversley Rd B76 22 A3
Overstone Rd CV7 52 C3
Overton Dr B46 23 E2
Overtons Cl CV31 110 C3
Overwoods Rd B77 10 A2
Owen Sq CV9 18 B4
Owen St CV9 18 B4
Owenford Rd CV6 61 E4
Owl End La NN11 134 E7
Owl End Way NN11 134 E7
Ox Cl CV2 62 A3
Ox Leys Rd B75, B76 13 E2
Oxendon Way CV3 78 C4
Oxford Cl CV11 29 F4
Oxford Rd Marton CV23 115 C8
Marton CV23 115 D7
Princethorpe CV8,CV23 96 B2
Oxford Row 11 CV32 105 F1
Oxford St Coventry CV1 61 F2
Moreton-in-M GL56 140 A3
Royal Leamington Spa CV32 105 F1
Rugby CV21 83 E2
Southam CV33 147 D2
Oxford Way CV35 146 A1
Oxhayes Cl CV7 74 B3
Oxhey Hill OX17 134 B2
Oxhill Bridle Rd CV35 131 E3
Oxhill Rd CV35 138 B6
Oxley Dr CV3 77 E2
Oxstall Cl B76 22 B3
Oxway Cl CV36 149 F3

Packington Ave CV5 60 A3
Packington La Coleshill B46 34 A1
Little Packington CV7 45 E3
Maxstoke B46 35 D1
White Stitch CV7 46 A2
Packington Pl 4 CV31 110 A4
Packmore St CV34 108 C4
Packsaddle Hill CV37 145 F4
Packwood Ave CV21 101 E4
Packwood Cl
Bentley Heath B93 71 F2
26 Royal Leamington Spa CV31 110 B3
Packwood Cotts B93 71 F1
Packwood Gn CV5 60 A2
Packwood House B94 89 D3
Packwood La B94 89 D2
Packwood Rd B94 89 D4
Paddiford Pl CV10 28 B2
Paddock Cl CV23 125 C8
Paddock Dr B93 72 A1
Paddock La Redditch B98 102 C4
Stratford-u-A CV37 144 C1
Paddock The
Lower Boddington NN11 134 E7
Newton CV23 68 A1
Paddocks Cl Polesworth B78 4 C1
Wolston CV8 80 A2
Paddocks The
Bulkington CV12 40 A2
Mollington OX17 133 F2
Norton WR11 127 B2
Stretton on D CV23 96 C3
Warwick CV34 108 C4
Paddox Cl CV22 100 C4
Paddox Mid Sch CV22 100 B4
Paddox Prim Sch CV22 100 C4
Padgate Cl B35 22 A2
Padmore Ct CV31 110 A3
Padstow Cl CV11 29 F3
Padstow Rd CV4 75 F4
Page Rd CV4 75 F4
Pages La OX15 139 B7
Paget Ct CV2 50 A2
Paget's La CV8 95 E3
Pailton Cl CV2 50 B1
Pailton Rd CV23 66 A2
Painswick Cl B98 102 C3
Pake's Croft 2 CV6 61 D3
Palefield Rd B90 70 C3
Palermo Ave CV3 77 F3

Pallett Dr CV11 29 F4
Palm Tree Ave CV2 50 B1
Palmer La CV1 151 B3
Palmer Rd CV31 110 A2
Palmer's Cl CV21 101 D4
Palmerston Rd CV5 76 C4
Pampas Cl CV37 144 C3
Pancras Cl CV2 50 C1
Pandora Rd CV2 62 C4
Pangbourne Cl CV11 29 F4
Pangbourne Rd CV2 62 B4
Pangfield Pk CV5 60 B2
Pantolf Pl CV21 82 C4
Papenham Gn CV4 76 A4
Parade CV32 109 F4
Parade The Birmingham B37 33 D3
Nuneaton CV11 29 E2
Paradise St Coventry CV1 151 C1
Rugby CV21 83 E2
Warwick CV34 108 C4
Paradise Way CV7 51 D1
Paragon Way CV7 50 A4
Parbrook Cl CV4 75 F4
Parbury B77 9 E3
Park Ave Coleshill B46 33 F3
Coventry CV6 49 E2
Nuneaton CV11 29 F2
Polesworth B78 11 D4
Studley B80 103 F2
Park Cl Avon Dassett CV33 133 C4
Claverdon CV35 113 F3
Hanwell OX17 139 F6
Hook Norton OX15 142 D3
Kenilworth CV8 93 D3
Park Croft B47 69 D3
Park Ct CV37 144 C2
Park Dr Claverdon CV35 113 F3
Royal Leamington Spa CV31 109 F4
Park Farm Ind Est B98 103 E4
Park Gr B46 23 E1
Park Hall WR11 127 E6
Park Hall Cres B36 22 B1
Park Hall Mews WR11 127 E6
Park Hall Sch B36 22 C1
Park Hill Hook Norton OX15 142 D4
Kenilworth CV8 93 D3
Lower Shuckburgh NN11 116 F1
Park Hill Cty Mid Sch CV8 93 E3
Park Hill La Allesley CV5 60 A3
Coventry CV5 60 A3
Park Hill Prim Sch CV5 60 A2
Park La Astley CV10 37 E3
Berkswell CV7 58 A1
Birmingham B26 44 B2
Birmingham, Castle Vale B35 22 B2
Great Alne B49 119 D6
Harbury CV33 123 F6
Ilmington CV36 135 F7
Lower Shuckburgh NN11 116 F1
North Newington OX15 139 E2
Nuneaton CV10 27 F2
Snitterfield CV37 121 C6
Southam CV33 147 D2
Swalcliffe OX15 142 F8
Park Paling The CV3 77 F4
Park Piece CV35 132 B6
Park Rd Baddesley Ensor B78 11 D1
Bedworth CV12 39 D1
Chipping Campden GL55 135 A1
Coleshill B46 33 F3
Coventry CV1 151 B1
Hinckley LE10 31 F4
Hook Norton OX15 142 D4
Kenilworth CV8 93 D3
Polesworth B78 11 D4
Royal Leamington Spa CV32 106 A2
Rugby CV21 83 D2
Stratford-u-A CV37 144 C2
Tamworth B77 9 E3
Park Sq B37 44 B4
Park St Coventry CV6 61 F4
Nuneaton CV11 29 E2
Royal Leamington Spa CV32 105 F1
Park Street Ind Est CV6 61 E4
Park The OX15 137 F3
Park View Cookhill B96 118 F3
Hockley Heath B94 88 B3
Park View Cl CV7 50 A4
Park Wood La CV4 75 E4
Parkend CV21 83 E4
Parkers La GL56 140 A3
Parkes St CV34 108 B4
Parkfield Cl B77 9 E4
Parkfield Cres B77 9 E4
Parkfield Dr Birmingham B36 22 B1
Kenilworth CV8 93 D3
Parkfield Prim Sch B77 9 E4
Parkfield Rd Coleshill B46 33 F3
Keresley CV7 49 D3
Rugby CV21 82 C3
Parkfields CV33 147 D2
Parkgate Prim Sch CV6 49 D2
Parkgate Rd CV6 49 E2
Parkhill Dr CV5 60 A3
Parkinson Dr CV9 12 C1
Parkland Cl CV6 49 E2
Parklands Ave CV32 106 B2
Parkside CV1 151 C2
Parkstone Rd CV6 49 F1
Parkville Cl CV6 49 D2
Parkville Highway CV6 49 D2
Parkway CV2 63 D4
Parmington Cl B97 102 A3
Parnell Cl CV21 82 C2
Parr Cl CV34 109 E3
Parrotts Gr CV2 50 B3
Parry Rd CV2 62 B4
Parson St B77 9 F4
Parson's La LE10 31 F4
Parson's Nook CV2 62 A3
Parsonage Cl 13 CV33 122 F8
Parsons Cl CV36 149 F3
Partridge Cl B37 33 E2
Partridge Croft CV6 50 A1
Partridge La B97 102 A4
Partridge Rd CV37 144 B2
Patch La B98 102 C3
Patrcia Cl CV4 59 E1
Pattens Rd CV34 105 D1
Patterdale CV21 83 E4
Patterton Dr B76 22 A4
Pattison Coll CV3 62 A1
Pauline Ave CV6 50 A1
Pavilion Way CV5 60 C2
Paxmead Cl CV6 49 D1
Paxton Rd CV6 61 D2
Paybody Hospl CV5 60 B3
Payne Cl CV32 106 A1
Payne's La CV1 61 F2
Paynell Cl CV6 49 D1
Paynes La CV21 82 B2
Payton St CV37 145 D2
Peace Wlk B37 33 D1
Peacock Ave CV2 50 C1
Peacock Ct CV35 146 B2
Peacock La CV35 138 C7
Peacocks The CV34 108 A1
Peake Ave CV11 29 F4
Pear Tree Ave Kingsbury B78 15 E3
Nuneaton CV10 28 C3
Pear Tree Cl
Chipping Campden GL55 135 B1
Shuttington B79 4 C4
Pear Tree Way CV22 82 A1
Pearl Hyde Prim Sch CV2 63 D3
Pearmans Croft B47 69 D3
Pears Cl CV8 92 C3
Pearson Ave CV6 50 A1
Peat Cl CV22 82 C1
Pebble Cl B77 4 A2
Pebworth Ave B90 71 D3
Pebworth Cl CV5 60 A2
Pebworth Cty Fst Sch CV37 128 F1
Peddimore La B76 22 B4
Pedmore Cl B98 103 D4
Peel Cl Coventry CV6 61 F3
Drayton Bassett B78 8 C3
Hampton in A B92 57 D3
Peel La CV6 61 F3
Peel Rd CV34 108 C4
Peel St CV6 61 F3
Pegasus Jun & Inf Sch B35 22 A2
Pegmill Cl CV3 77 F4
Pelham La B49 119 D5
Pembridge Rd B93 71 F2
Pembroke Cl Bedworth CV12 38 B1
1 Warwick CV34 108 C4
Pembroke Gdns CV35 146 B1
Pembroke Way CV11 29 E2
Pembrook Rd CV6 49 E1
Pembury Ave CV6 50 A2
Penarth Gr CV3 78 C4
Pencraig Cl CV8 93 E3
Pendenis Cl CV6 62 A4
Pendicke St CV33 147 D2
Pendigo Way B40 44 C2
Pendred Rd CV22 82 C2
Pendrell Cl B37 33 D2
Penelope Cl CV33 123 F6
Penfold Cl 3 CV33 122 F8
Penmire Cl CV9 11 E2
Penn La Tanworth-in-A B94 86 B2
Wibtoft LE17 43 E1
Pennant Rd LE10 31 E3
Pennine Way Nuneaton CV10 28 A2
Tamworth B77 10 A4
Pennington Mews 4 CV21 82 C2
Pennington St 1 CV21 82 C2
Pennington Way CV6 61 F4
Penns Cl CV32 106 C3
Penns La B46 33 F4
Penny Park La CV6 49 D2
Pennyford La B95 113 B1
Pennymoor Rd B77 10 A4
Pennystone Cl CV31 110 B3
Penrhyn Cl OX16 139 F4
Penrith Cl Coventry CV6 49 E1
Royal Leamington Spa CV32 105 E1
Penrith Gr B37 33 E1
Penrose Cl CV4 76 A4
Penryhn Cl CV8 93 E3
Penryn Cl CV11 30 A2
Pensham Croft B90 71 D3
Penshurst Way CV11 39 F4
Pensilva Way 2 CV1 61 F2
Pentire Cl CV11 29 F3
Penzance Way CV11 30 A3
Pepper La CV1 151 B2
Pepys Cnr CV4 59 F2
Perch Ave B37 33 D2
Percival Dr CV33 123 F6
Percival Rd CV22 100 B4
Percy Cres CV8 92 C1
Percy Rd Kenilworth CV8 92 C1
Warwick CV34 108 C4
Percy St Coventry CV1 151 A3
Stratford-u-A CV37 145 D2
Percy Terr 7 CV32 105 E1
Peregrine Dr CV5 60 A3
Perimeter Rd
Birmingham B40 44 B2
Birmingham B40 44 C2
Perkins Cl Hornton OX15 139 B8
Salford Priors WR11 127 E6
Perkins Gr CV21 83 F1
Permian Cl CV21 83 E3
Perry Mill La B95 112 E6
Perryfields Cl B98 102 C3
Perryford Dr B91 71 E4
Perryman Dr B78 15 F4
Perrymill La B96 103 D1
Pershore Pl CV4 76 C3
Perth Rise CV5 60 A2
Peter Hall La
Brinklow CV7,CV23 64 A3
Coventry CV7 63 F3
Peterbrook Cl B98 102 C4
Peterbrook Rd B90 69 F4
Peterlee Wlk 6 CV2 63 D4
Petitor Cres CV2 50 B1
Pettiford La B95 113 C3
Pettiver Cres CV21 83 F1
Pettyfields Cl B93 72 A3
Peveril Dr CV3 77 D3
Peyto Cl CV6 49 E1
Pheasant Cl Bedworth CV12 38 B1
Stratford-u-A CV37 144 B2
Pheasant Ct B36 33 D4
Pheasant La B98 102 C4
Phillippes Rd 13 CV34 104 C1
Phipps Ave CV21 83 F1
Phoenix Bsns Pk LE10 30 C4
Phoenix Way CV6 49 F2
Piccadilly B78 9 F1
Piccadilly Cl B37 33 E1
Piccadilly Cres B78 9 F1
Pickard Cl CV21 83 F4
Pickard St CV34 109 D4
Pickford Cl CV11 30 A1
Pickford Grange La CV5 59 E4
Pickford Green La CV5 59 E4
Pickford Way CV5 60 A3
Picton Croft 4 B37 33 E1
Piers Cl CV34 108 C4
Pike Cl LE10 31 E3
Pike Dr B37 33 E2
Pikehorne Croft B36 22 B1
Pikers La CV7 48 A2
Pilgrims Gate LE10 32 A3
Pilgrims La CV23 67 F1
Pilkington Rd CV5 76 B4
Pill La GL56 140 F1
Pilling Cl CV2 62 C4
Pimlico La CV37 121 D2
Pinbury Croft B37 33 D1
Pinchester Cl GL56 141 A1
Pinders La CV21 83 D2
Pine Cl Stoke Golding CV13 21 F4
Stratford-u-A CV37 144 B1
Pine Ct CV32 106 A2
Pine Gr CV21 84 A1
Pine Sq B37 33 D1
Pine Tree Ave CV4 60 A1
Pine Tree Rd CV12 39 E2
Pine Trees Cres CV33 147 E3
Pineham Ave CV33 123 F6
Pinehurst CV32 106 C3
Pines The Bedworth CV12 38 C1
Cheswick Green B90 70 B3
Coventry CV4 75 E4
Pinewood Ave CV9 10 B1
Pinewood Dr CV3 79 E4
Pinewood Gr CV5 77 D4
Pinfold Gn NN11 126 F6
Pinfold St CV21 82 C2
Pingle Ct CV11 29 E1
Pink Green La B98 112 A8
Pinley Fields CV3 78 A4
Pinner's Croft CV2 62 A3
Pinnock Pl CV4 59 F1
Pinwall La CV9 12 C2
Pioneer Units CV11 29 F2
Pipe La CV9 6 B2
Piper's End LE10 41 E2
Piper's La CV8 93 D3
Pipers La CV10 27 E4
Pipers Rd B98 103 E4
Pipewell Cl CV22 82 B1
Pirie Cl CV33 123 F6
Pit Hill CV8 95 E3
Pitt La B92 44 B1
Pittons La CV23 101 E1
Pittway Ave CV36 149 F3
Pixhall Wlk B35 22 A2
Plain Rd The OX15 139 A3
Plane Gr B37 33 D1
Plank La B46 23 D1
Plantagenet Dr CV22 99 F3
Plantation The OX17 134 C1
Plants Brook Rd B76 22 A4
Plants Hill Cres CV4 59 F1
Pleasant Way CV32 106 A1
Pleck The B50 148 B2
Plexfield Rd CV22 82 B1
Pleydell Cl CV3 78 B3
Plomer Cl CV22 99 E4
Plot Rd OX15 139 A3
Plott La CV23 96 C3
Plough Hill Rd CV10 28 A3
Plough La CV33 124 A4
Ploughmans Holt CV33 147 D3
Plover Cl Alcester B49 143 D3
Stratford-u-A CV37 144 B3
Plowden Cl NN11 134 F5
Plowman St CV21 82 C2
Plymouth Cl CV2 62 B4
Plymouth Pl CV31 110 A4
Poitiers Rd CV3 77 E3
Polesworth High Sch B78 10 C4
Polesworth Sta B78 5 D2
Polperro Dr CV5 60 A3
Pomeroy Cl CV4 75 E4
Pondthorpe CV3 78 C3
Pontrilas Rd CV35 132 D4
Pontypool Ave CV3 78 C3
Pool Bank St CV11 29 D2
Pool Cl Little Compton GL56 140 F1
Rugby CV22 99 E4
Welford on A CV37 129 B6
Pool Close Cotts GL56 140 F1
Pool End Cl B93 71 F3
Pool Mdw B76 22 A4
Pool Rd Nuneaton CV10 28 C3
Studley B80 103 F2
Poole Rd CV6 61 D3
Pooley La B78 4 C1
Pooley Veiw B78 5 D1
Poolgate CV35 138 B6
Poolhead La Earlswood B94 86 B4
Tanworth-in-A B94 86 C3
Poolside Gdns CV3 77 D3
Pope St CV22 82 C2
Popes La B96 102 C1
Poplar Ave Bedworth CV12 39 E1
Birmingham, Coleshill Heath B37 44 B4
Poplar Cl Alcester B49 143 E2
Knightcote CV33 124 B1
Poplar Gr CV21 83 D2
Poplar Rd
Bishops Itchington CV33 124 B4
Coventry CV5 60 C1
Dorridge B93 71 F2
Napton CV23 125 C8
Poplars Cl GL55 135 A1
Poplars La B96 102 A1
Poplars The CV10 28 B2
Poplars Trad Est B80 103 E3
Poppy Dr CV23 83 F4
Poppyfield Ct CV4 76 B2
Porchester Cl CV3 63 D1
Porlock Cl CV3 77 F3
Porter Cl CV4 75 F4
Portia Cl CV11 30 A1
Portland Dr CV10 28 B2
Portland Pl
6 Royal Leamington Spa CV32 109 F4
Rugby CV21 83 E1
Portland Pl E 5 CV32 109 F4
Portland Pl W 4 CV32 109 F4
Portland Rd CV21 83 E1
Portland St CV32 109 F4
Portleys La B78 8 B2
Portree Ave CV3 62 C1
Portsea Cl CV3 77 E3
Portway Cl Coventry CV4 75 F4
Royal Leamington Spa CV31 110 B3
Portwrinkle Ave CV6 62 A3
Post House Gdns CV23 66 A4
Post Office La
Lighthorne CV35 123 B2
Stockton CV23 147 F4
Witherley CV9 19 D4
Post Office Rd CV9 11 E1
Post Office Wlk B96 102 C1
Post Office Yd CV23 64 C2
Postbridge Rd CV3 77 E3
Postle Cl CV23 101 F1
Potters Cl CV23 64 C2
Potters Green Prim Sch CV2 50 C1
Potters Green Rd CV2 50 C1
Potters La Darlingscott CV36 136 D5
Polesworth B78 11 D4
Potters Rd CV12 38 C1
Potton Cl CV3 78 C3
Potts Cl CV8 93 E2
Poultney Rd CV6 61 D3
Pound Cl Berkswell CV7 58 B2
Lapworth B94 89 D2
Shipston-on-S CV36 149 F3
Pound House La
Tanworth-in-A B94 87 F2
Tanworth-in-A B94 88 A2
Pound La Badby NN11 126 F6
Coleshill B46 34 A2
Furnace End B46 25 E2
Mickleton GL55 135 B6
Royal Leamington Spa CV32 106 A2
Sibford Gower OX15 138 D1
Pound The OX15 139 D2
Powell Rd CV2 62 A2
Powell Way CV11 29 E2
Powis Gr CV8 93 E3
Powys Gr OX16 139 F4
Poyser Rd CV10 39 E4
Pratts La B80 112 A4
Prebend The CV33 133 B7
Precinct The CV1 151 B3
Precision Way B49 143 E3
Prescelly Cl CV10 28 A2
Prescott Ave OX16 139 F3
President Kennedy Sch & Com Coll CV6 49 D2
Prestbury Cl B98 112 A6
Preston Cl CV4 75 F4
Preston Fields La B95 113 D6
Preston La CV37 130 A4
Prestwick Rd B35 22 A2
Pretorian Way CV21 83 D4
Price Rd CV32 106 C3
Pridmore Rd CV6 61 E4
Priest Meadow Cl B96 102 B1
Priestfield Rd B97 102 C3
Priesthills Rd LE10 31 E4
Primley Ave B77 9 F3
Primrose Cl CV23 83 F4
Primrose Ct GL56 140 A3
Primrose Dr LE10 31 F3
Primrose Hill CV34 104 C1
Primrose Hill St CV1 151 C4
Primrose La B49 143 E1
Primsland Cl B90 71 E4
Prince Harry Rd B95 113 B4
Prince Of Wales Rd CV5 60 C2
Prince William Cl CV6 60 C3
Prince's Ave CV11 29 D2
Prince's Dr CV31 109 E4
Prince's Rd B78 5 D1
Prince's St Nuneaton CV11 29 E2
Royal Leamington Spa CV32 106 A1
Princes Cl CV3 78 A4
Princes Dr CV8 93 D4
Princes Rd CV9 16 B3
Princes St CV21 83 D2
Princess Rd Atherstone CV9 18 C4
Hinckley LE10 31 F4
Princess St CV6 61 F4
Princethorpe Coll CV23 96 B2
Princethorpe Way CV3 78 C4
Prior Deram Wlk CV4 76 B4
Priors Cl CV7 74 A3
Priors Field Comb Sch CV8 92 B4
Priors Harnall CV1 151 D4
Priors Mdw CV33 147 E2
Priors The CV12 39 E1
Priorsfield Rd
4 Coventry CV6 61 D2
Kenilworth CV8 92 B3
Priorsfield Rd N 3 CV6 61 D2
Priorsfield Rd S CV6 61 D2
Priory Cl Coleshill B46 34 A3
Lapworth B94 89 E3
Priory Croft CV8 93 D2
Priory Ct B80 103 F3
Priory La CV35 131 D2
Priory Mews CV34 108 C4
Priory Rd Alcester B49 143 D2
Kenilworth CV8 93 D2
Warwick CV34 108 C4
Wolston CV8 80 A2
Priory Row CV1 151 C3
Priory St Coventry CV1 151 C3
Nuneaton CV10 28 B2
Royal Leamington Spa CV31 109 F3
Priory Terr CV31 110 A4
Priory Wlk CV9 18 C3
Privet Rd CV2 50 A1
Proffitt Ave CV6 50 A1
Progress Cl CV3 79 D4
Progress Way CV3 79 D4
Prospect Rd CV31 110 A3
Prospect Way
Daventry NN11 117 F2
Rugby CV21 83 E3
Prossers Wlk B46 33 F4
Providence St CV5 76 C4
Provost Williams CE Prim Sch CV8 79 D1
Provost Williams CE Prim Sch (annexe) CV8 95 E3
Ptarmigan Pl CV11 29 F2
Puckering's La 3 CV34 108 C3
Pudding Bag La CV23 98 C1
Pudlicott La GL55 135 E1
Pughe's Cl LE10 32 A3
Pullman Cl B77 4 A1
Pump La CV7 36 B2
Purbrook B77 9 F4
Purcell Ave CV11 40 A4
Purcell Cl CV32 110 A4
Purcell Rd CV6 62 A4
Purefoy Rd CV3 77 E4
Purley Chace La CV9 18 B2
Purley Way CV9 18 C3
Purlieu La CV8 92 B3
Purnells Way B93 72 A3
Purser Dr CV34 108 A2
Purton Cl B49 143 E3
Purton Mews CV31 110 B3
Putney Wlk B37 33 D2
Pyeharps Rd LE10 31 F3
Pyt Pk CV5 60 B2
Pytchley Rd CV22 83 E1
Pytman Dr B76 22 A4

Quadrant The Coventry CV1 151 B2
Nuneaton CV11 29 F2
Quail La CV37 144 B2
Quaker Cl CV13 20 A3
Quantock Dr CV10 28 A2
Quarry Cl
Leek Wootton CV35 104 C4
Rugby CV21 82 C3
Quarry Fields CV35 104 C4
Quarry La Atherstone CV9 19 D3
Chadwick End CV35 90 B1
Cleeve Prior WR11 128 A4
Nuneaton CV11 29 F1
Quarry Rd CV8 92 C3
Quarry St CV32 109 E4
Quarry Yd CV10 28 B2
Quarryfield La CV1 151 C1
Quarrywood Gr CV2 62 A2
Queen Eleanors Dr B93 72 A4
Queen Elizabeth Rd CV10 28 B3
Queen Elizabeth Sch CV9 18 C4
Queen Isabel's Ave CV3 77 E4
Queen Margaret's Rd CV4 76 B4

Queen Mary's Rd
Bedworth CV12 39 E3
Coventry CV6 61 F4
Queen Philippa St CV3 77 E3
Queen St Astwood Bank B96 102 C1
Bedworth CV12 39 E1
Coventry CV1 151 C4
Cubbington CV32 106 C3
Hook Norton OX15 142 D4
Royal Leamington Spa CV32 106 A1
Rugby CV21 83 D2
Queen Victoria Rd CV1 151 B2
Queen Victoria St CV21 83 E2
Queen's Cl CV8 92 C2
Queen's Cres OX15 139 E4
Queen's Dr CV35 114 A8
Queen's Rd Atherstone CV9 18 C4
Coventry CV1 151 A2
Hinckley LE10 31 F4
Kenilworth CV8 92 C2
Nuneaton CV11 29 D2
Queen's Sq CV34 108 B3
Queens Arc CV11 29 E2
Queens Ave CV36 149 F3
Queens CE Mid Sch CV11 29 D2
Queens Cl Harbury CV33 123 F6
Shipston-on-S CV36 149 F3
Queens Rd Bretford CV23 80 C4
Tredington CV36 136 F6
Queens St CV36 136 F8
Queens Way Dordon B78 10 C3
Hurley CV9 16 B2
Queensferry Cl CV22 99 E4
Queensland Ave CV5 60 C1
Queenspark CV31 109 F3
Queensway
Bidford-on-A B50 148 B3
Nuneaton CV10 29 E3
Royal Leamington Spa CV31 109 F3
Queensway Trad Est CV31 109 F3
Quilletts Cl CV6 50 A1
Quince B77 4 A2
Quince Tree Specl Sch
B77 4 A2
Quiney's Leys CV37 129 A7
Quiney's Rd CV37 144 B1
Quinn Cl CV3 78 A4
Quinney's Ct B50 148 B2
Quinney's La B50 148 C3
Quinneys La B98 103 D3
Quinton Par CV3 77 E4
Quinton Pk CV3 77 E4
Quinton Prim Sch CV37 129 D2
Quinton Rd CV1 151 C1
Quorn Way CV3 78 C4

Race Leys Fst Sch CV12 39 D2
Race Leys Mid Sch CV12 39 D2
Racemeadow Prim Sch
CV9 12 C1
Racemeadow Rd CV9 12 C1
Radbourn La CV33 124 E5
Radbourne Cl CV33 147 E2
Radbrook Way CV31 110 B3
Radcliffe Rd CV5 76 C4
Radford Circ 5 CV6 61 D2
Radford Cl CV9 12 C1
Radford Prim Sch CV6 61 D3
Radford Rd Coventry CV1 61 D3
Royal Leamington Spa CV31 110 B4
Radford Semele
CE Prim Sch CV31 110 C3
Radley Dr CV10 29 D1
Radnor Dr CV10 28 C1
Radnor Wlk CV2 62 C4
Radway Rd B90 70 C4
Raglan Cl CV11 29 E2
Raglan Gr CV8 93 D3
Raglan St CV1 151 D3
Raglan Way B37 33 E1
Ragley Cl B93 72 A4
Ragley Hall B96 118 F2
Ragley Mill La B49 143 D2
Ragley Rd WR11 127 D4
Ragley Way CV11 29 F1
Railway St CV23 82 A2
Railway Terr Atherstone CV9 18 B4
Rugby CV21 83 D2
Rainsbrook Ave CV22 100 C4
Rainsbrook Cl CV33 147 E2
Rainsbrook Dr
Nuneaton CV11 30 A1
Solihull B90 70 C3
Rainsbrook Valley Rly
CV22 100 B3
Rainscar B77 10 A4
Rainsford Cl CV37 129 F7
Raison Ave CV11 29 F4
Raleigh Rd CV2 62 A1
Ralph Cres B78 15 E3
Ralph Rd CV6 60 C3
Ramp Rd B26 44 B3
Ramsay Cres CV5 60 A4
Ramsden Ave CV10 28 B3
Ramsden Rd CV9 19 D4
Ramsey Rd CV31 110 A4
Ramshill La B94 112 E7
Ran-tan The B97 102 C3
Ranby Rd CV2 61 F2
Rance Way B78 15 E3
Randall Rd CV8 92 C2
Randle Rd CV10 28 B2
Randle St CV6 61 D3
Randolph Cl CV31 110 B3
Ranelagh St CV31 110 A3
Ranelagh Terr CV31 109 F3
Range Meadow Cl CV32 105 E2
Rangemoor CV3 78 B3
Rangeworthy Cl B97 102 B4
Rankine Cl CV21 82 B4
Rannoch Cl LE10 31 D4
Rannock Cl CV3 62 C1
Ransom Rd CV6 61 F4
Ransome Rd CV7 37 D4
Ranulf Croft CV3 77 E4
Ranulf St CV3 77 E4
Raphael Cl CV5 60 B2
Ratcliffe La CV9 12 C2
Ratcliffe Rd Atherstone CV9 12 C1
Hinckley LE10 31 F3
Ratcliffe St CV9 18 B4
Rathbone Cl Keresley CV7 49 D3
Rugby CV21 101 D4
Rathlin Croft B36 33 D3
Ratliffe Rd CV22 99 F4
Rattlecombe Rd OX15 138 E5
Raveloe Dr CV11 29 E1
Raven Cragg Rd CV5 76 C4
Raven Way CV11 29 F1
Ravenglass CV21 83 E4
Ravensdale Ave CV32 105 E1
Ravensdale Prim Sch CV2 62 B2
Ravensdale Rd CV2 62 B2
Ravenshaw La B91 56 A2
Ravenshaw Way B91 56 A2
Ravensthorpe Cl CV3 78 C4
Ravenstone B77 10 A4
Ravenswood Hill B46 33 F4
Rawlins Croft B35 22 B2
Rawlinson Rd CV32 106 A1
Rawn View CV9 18 C3
Rawnsley Dr CV8 93 E3
Raygill B77 10 A4
Raymond Cl CV6 49 F3
Raynor Cres CV12 38 B1
Raynsford Wlk CV34 104 B1
Raywoods The CV10 28 C2
Read St CV1 61 F2
Reading Ave CV11 29 F4
Reading Cl CV2 50 A2
Readings The CV33 133 E7
Reardon Ct CV34 104 C1
Recreation Rd CV6 50 A2
Rectory Cl Allesley CV5 60 B3
Barby CV23 101 E1
Bedworth CV7 39 D1
Drayton Bassett B78 8 C3
Harvington WR11 127 D3
Stockton CV23 147 F4
Warmington OX17 133 D2
Whitnash CV31 110 A2
Rectory Dr CV7 39 D1
Rectory Gdns OX15 139 E4
Rectory La Allesley CV5 60 B3
Barby CV23 101 E1
Lower Brailes OX15 137 F2
Rectory Rd Arley CV7 26 C1
Hook Norton OX15 142 D4
Sutton Coldfield B75 13 D3
Red Deeps CV11 39 E4
Red Deeps Specl Sch CV10 39 D4
Red Hill CV35 131 B8
Red Hill Cl B80 103 F3
Red La Astley CV10 37 F4
Burton Green CV8 75 E1
Coventry CV6 61 F3
Kenilworth CV8 92 B4
Red Lion Cl CV33 147 D3
Red Lion St OX17 134 C1
Red Lodge Dr CV22 99 F4
Red Rd CV35 132 B5
Red Wing Wlk B36 33 D4
Redcap Croft CV6 49 E2
Redcar Cl CV32 106 B2
Redcar Rd CV1 61 F3
Reddicap Heath Rd B75 13 D2
Reddings La B46 25 D3
Reddings The B47 69 D3
Redditch Rd B80 103 E3
Redditch Wlk 4 CV2 63 D4
Redesdale Ave CV6 60 C3
Redesdale Pl GL56 140 A2
Redfern Ave CV8 93 D3
Redhill Bank CV37 130 B3
Redhill Cl CV35 146 B1
Redhouse Cl B93 71 F2
Redlake B77 9 F4
Redland Cl CV2 50 C1
Redland Rd CV31 110 A3
Redlands Cres CV37 144 B2
Redliff Ave B36 22 B1
Redmoor Way B76 22 B3
Redruth Cl Coventry CV6 62 A4
Nuneaton CV11 30 A2
Redwing B77 10 A3
Redwing Cl CV37 144 B3
Redwood Croft CV10 29 D1
Redwood Dr B78 15 E4
Reed Sq B35 22 A2
Reeds Pk CV33 111 F1
Rees Dr CV3 77 E2
Reeve Dr CV8 93 D2
Reeves Rd LE10 31 F3
Regal Ct CV9 18 C4
Regal Rd CV37 144 C2
Regal Road Trad Est
CV37 144 C2
Regency Cl Henley-in-A
B95 113 B4
Nuneaton CV10 29 E3
Regency Ct CV5 76 C4
Regency Dr Alcester B49 143 D3
Coventry CV3 76 C3
Kenilworth CV8 92 C2
Regency Ho CV32 110 A4
Regent Gr CV32 109 F4
Regent Pl
2 Royal Leamington Spa
CV31 110 A4
Rugby CV21 83 D2
Regent St Bedworth CV12 39 E2
Coventry CV1 151 A2
Hinckley LE10 31 E4
Nuneaton CV11 29 E3
Royal Leamington Spa
CV32 109 F4
Rugby CV21 83 D2
Regina Cres CV2 63 D4
Regis Wlk CV2 62 C4
Reindeer Rd B78 8 C4
Relay Dr B77 10 B4
Relton Mews CV6 61 F3
Rembrandt Cl CV5 60 B2
Remburn Gdns CV34 108 C4
Remembrance Rd CV3 78 B3
Renfrew Sq B35 22 A2
Renfrew Wlk CV4 76 A4
Renison Rd CV12 38 C1
Repington Ave CV9 12 B1
Repington Rd N B77 4 A3
Repington Rd S B77 4 A3
Repington Way B75 13 D3
Repton Dr CV6 50 A1
Reservoir Dr B46 24 C1
Reservoir Rd CV21 83 E3
Retreat St B96 102 C1
Revel CE Prim Sch The
CV23 53 F1
Rex Cl CV4 75 E4
Reynolds Cl CV21 84 A1
Reynolds Rd CV12 39 D2
Rhoose Croft B35 22 A2
Rhyl Rd CV11 40 C3
Ribble Cl CV12 40 A1
Ribble Rd CV3 61 F1
Ribblesdale B77 10 A4
Ribbonfields CV11 29 E2
Rich Cl CV34 109 D4
Richard Joy Cl CV6 49 E1
Richard Lee Prim Sch CV2 62 C2
Richards Cl CV8 92 C3
Richardson Cl CV34 104 C1
Richman Gdns OX16 139 F4
Richmond Rd Atherstone
CV9 18 B4
Hollywood B47 69 E4
Nuneaton CV11 29 D2
Rugby CV21 83 E1
Richmond St CV2 62 A2
Richmond Way 2 B37 33 E2
Rickard Cl B93 71 F3
Riddell Cl B49 143 E2
Riddings Gdns B78 11 D4
Riddings La CV9 11 E2
Riddings The Coventry CV5 76 C4
Grendon CV9 11 E1
Sutton Coldfield B76 22 A4
Riddon Dr LE10 31 D4
Ridge Ct CV5 60 A3
Ridge La CV10 18 A1
Ridgeley Cl CV34 104 C1
Ridgethorpe CV3 78 C3
Ridgeway Ave CV3 77 E3
Ridgeway Cl B80 103 F1
Ridgeway Mid Sch B96 118 C8
Ridgeway Specl Sch CV34 105 D1
Ridgeway The
Astwood Bank B96 118 D6
Barby CV23 117 F8
Hinckley LE10 31 E3
Warwick CV34 105 D1
Ridgewood Cl CV32 105 E1
Ridgewood Rise B77 4 A3
Ridgley Rd CV4 75 F4
Ridgway The CV37 120 C3
Ridley La B46 25 D3
Ridsdale Cl WR11 127 F6
Rigby Cl CV34 109 E2
Rigdale Cl CV2 62 C1
Riley Cl Daventry NN11 117 F2
Kenilworth CV8 93 E2
Riley Dr Banbury OX16 139 F4
Birmingham B36 23 D1
Riley Sq CV2 50 A1
Rimell Cl CV37 130 E1
Ringway Hill Cross CV1 151 A3
Ringway Queens CV1 151 A2
Ringway Rudge CV1 151 A2
Ringway St Johns CV1 151 C2
Ringway St Nicholas CV1 151 B3
Ringway St Patricks CV1 151 B1
Ringway Swanswell CV1 151 C3
Ringway Whitefriars CV1 151 C3
Ringwood Highway CV2 50 C1
Rinhill Gr 8 CV31 110 B3
Riplingham 13 CV32 105 F1
Ripon Cl CV5 60 A4
Risborough Cl CV5 60 B2
Risdale Cl CV32 105 E1
Rise The B37 44 A4
Rising La Chadwick End B93 90 A3
Lapworth B94 89 F3
Rising Rd B94 89 E3
River Cl Bedworth CV12 38 C1
Royal Leamington Spa CV32 109 E4
River Dr CV9 12 B1
River House Specl Sch
B95 113 B4
River Way CV36 137 A3
River Wlk CV2 50 B1
Riverford Croft CV4 76 B2
Rivermead CV11 29 D2
Rivermead Dr CV37 145 F2
Riversdale Rd CV9 19 D4
Riverside Alcester B49 143 E2
Studley B80 103 F2
Witherley CV9 19 D4
Riverside Cl CV3 78 A4
Riverside Ct 1 B46 33 F4
Riverside Gdns B95 113 B4
Riverside Ind Est B78 9 D4
Riversleigh Rd CV32 105 E1
Riversley Rd CV11 29 E2
Ro-Oak Rd CV6 60 C3
Roach B77 9 E3
Roach Cl B37 33 E2
Roanne Ringway CV11 29 D2
Robert Cl CV3 78 B2
Robert Cramb Ave CV4 75 F4
Robert Hill Cl CV21 84 A1
Robert Rd CV7 49 F4
Roberts Cl CV23 96 C3
Roberts La WR11 127 F1
Robertson Cl CV23 84 A3
Robey's La B78 4 B2
Robin Cl B36 33 D4
Robin Hood Rd CV3 78 B3
Robinia Cl CV32 106 A1
Robins Cl OX7 142 A2
Robins Gr CV34 108 B2
Robins Way CV10 28 A2
Robinson Rd CV12 49 E4
Robinson Way LE10 31 F2
Robinson's End Mid Sch
CV10 28 A2
Robinson's Way B76 22 B3
Robotham Cl CV21 82 C3
Rocheberie Way CV22 99 F4
Rochester Cl CV11 29 D2
Rochester Rd CV5 76 C4
Rochford Cl B76 22 A4
Rochford Ct B90 71 D3
Rock Cl Coventry CV6 50 A1
Nuneaton CV10 27 F2
Rock La CV7 48 B4
Rock Mill La CV32 109 E4
Rocken End CV6 61 E4
Rockford Cl B98 102 C3
Rockingham Cl B93 71 E1
Rocky La CV8 93 E1
Rodborough Rd B93 71 F2
Rodhouse Cl CV4 59 E1
Rodney Cl CV22 82 B1
Rodway Dr CV5 59 E2
Roe Cl CV34 108 C4
Roebuck Pk B49 143 D3
Rogers La CV37 131 A3
Rogers Way CV34 108 A2
Rokeby County Inf Sch
CV22 100 A4
Rokeby Ct CV22 99 F4
Rokeby Jun Sch CV22 100 A4
Rokeby St CV21 83 E2
Rolan Dr B90 69 F4
Roland Ave CV6 49 E2
Roland Mount CV6 49 E2
Rollason Cl CV6 61 E4
Rollason Rd CV6 61 D4
Rolling Stones GL55 135 B2
Rollright Stones OX7 141 D1
Roman Cl LE17 43 F3
Roman Ct B77 9 F4
Roman Rd CV2 62 A2
Roman Row CV36 141 F5
Roman Way Alcester B49 143 D2
Coleshill B46 23 F1
Coventry CV3 77 E2
Dordon B78 11 D3
Halford CV36 136 F8
Rugby CV21 83 D4
Southam CV33 147 E2
Romford Rd CV6 49 D1
Romilly Cl B76 13 D2
Romney B77 9 F4
Romney Rd OX16 139 F5
Romsey Ave CV10 29 E4
Ronald Gr B36 22 B1
Rookery Cl CV13 20 A4
Rookery La Coventry CV6 49 D2
Ettington CV37 131 A3
Newbold-on-S CV37 130 E1
Preston Bagot B95 113 E5
Rookery The
Birchley Heath CV10 17 F1
Nuneaton CV10 27 F3
Rooks Nest CV23 64 C2
Roosevelt Dr CV4 59 F1
Rope Way OX15 142 D3
Roper Cl CV21 101 D4
Ropewalk B49 143 D2
Rosaville Cres CV5 60 A3
Rose Ave Coventry CV6 60 C3
Henley-in-A B95 113 B5
Rose Croft CV8 92 C3
Rose Hill CV9 18 C4
Rose La Napton CV23 125 C7
Nuneaton CV11 29 E2
Rose Rd B46 33 F4
Roseberry Ave CV2 50 B1
Rosebery Rd B77 9 E2
Rosefield Pl 10 CV32 109 F4
Rosefield St CV32 110 A4
Rosefield Wlk 9 CV32 109 F4
Rosegreen Cl CV3 77 F3
Rosehall Cl B98 102 C3
Rosehip Dr CV2 62 A3
Roseland Rd CV8 92 C2
Roselands Ave CV2 62 B4
Rosemary Cl CV4 59 F2
Rosemary Hill CV8 92 C3
Rosemary Way LE10 31 D4
Rosemount Cl CV2 62 C4
Rosemullion Cl CV7 50 A4
Roses La OX7 150 C3
Roseway CV13 21 E4
Rosewood CV11 29 F1
Rosewood Ave CV22 100 A4
Rosewood Cl LE10 31 F3
Rosewood Cres CV32 106 A1
Ross Cl CV5 60 A3
Ross Way CV11 40 A4
Rossendale Way CV10 28 C1
Rosslyn Ave CV6 60 C3
Roston Dr LE10 31 D4
Rothay B77 9 F4
Rother Rd OX16 139 F5
Rother St CV37 144 C1
Rotherby Gr B37 44 A4
Rotherfield Cl CV31 110 A4
Rotherham Rd CV6 49 E1
Rotherhams Oak La B94 87 F4
Rothermans Hill CV9 17 E4
Rothesay Ave CV4 60 A1
Rothesay Cl CV10 29 D1
Rothley Dr CV21 83 F4
Rothwell Rd CV34 104 B1
Rough Coppice Wlk B35 22 A1
Rough Hill Dr B98 102 C3
Rough The B97 102 B4
Roughknowles Rd CV4 75 E3
Rouncil La CV8 104 B4
Round Ave CV23 82 A3
Round Close Rd OX15 142 D4
Round House Rd CV3 78 A4
Round Moor Wlk B35 22 A2
Round Oak Specl Sch
CV32 106 A2
Round St 2 CV21 82 C2
Roundhill Rd OX17 134 A2
Rounds Gdns CV21 82 C2
Rounds Hill CV8 92 C1
Rouse La CV35 137 F8
Rover Dr B36 22 C1
Rover Rd CV1 151 B2
Row The CV7 51 E2
Rowan Cl Binley Woods CV3 79 E4
Hollywood B47 69 D3
Kingsbury B78 15 E3
Stratford-u-A CV37 144 C3
Rowan Dr Rugby CV22 82 A1
6 Warwick CV34 108 C4
Rowan Gr CV2 50 C1
Rowan Rd CV10 28 B3
Rowan Way B37 33 E1
Rowans The Bedworth CV12 38 C1
Harvington WR11 127 D4
Rowborough Cl CV35 114 F5
Rowbrook Cl B90 69 F4
Rowcroft Rd CV2 63 D3
Rowington Cl CV6 60 B3
Rowington Gn CV35 114 B8
Rowland Ave Polesworth B78 5 D2
Studley B80 103 F2
Rowland Ct CV7 26 C1
Rowland St CV21 82 C2
Rowland Way CV9 12 B1
Rowley Cres CV37 145 D2
Rowley Dr CV3 78 A2
Rowley La CV3 78 B2
Rowley Rd Coventry CV3, CV8 78 A2
Whitnash CV31 110 A1
Rowley's Green La CV6 49 F2
Rowleys Green Lane
Ind Est CV6 49 F2
Rowse Cl CV21 83 E4
Rowthorn Dr B90 71 D3
Roxburgh Croft CV32 106 B3
Roxburgh Rd CV11 29 F1
Royal Cres CV3 78 B3
Royal Ct LE10 31 E4
Royal Leamington Spa
Rehabilitation Hospl
CV34 109 F2
Royal Oak Ind Est NN11 117 F2
Royal Oak La CV12 49 E4
Royal Oak Way N NN11 117 F2
Royal Oak Way S NN11 117 F2
Royal Oak Yd CV12 39 D2
Royal Shakespeare
Theatre CV37 145 D1
Royston Cl CV3 63 D2
Rubens Cl CV5 60 B2
Rudge Rd CV1 151 A2
Rufford Cl Alcester B49 143 E3
Hinckley LE10 31 E2
Rugby Coll CV21 83 E1
Rugby High Sch CV22 99 E3
Rugby La CV23 97 D3
Rugby Midland Sta CV21 83 E2
Rugby Rd Barby CV23 101 E1
Binley Woods CV3 79 E4
Brandon CV8 80 A3
Brinklow CV23 64 C2
Bulkington CV12 40 B1
Church Lawford CV23 81 E3
Clifton u D CV23 83 F3
Dunchurch CV22 99 E2
Easenhall CV23 65 F2
Harborough Magna CV23 66 A1
Hinckley LE10 31 E3
Kilsby CV21,CV23 101 F3
Lilbourne CV23 84 C3
Long Lawford CV23 82 A2
Pailton CV23 66 A4
Princethorpe CV23 96 C1
Royal Leamington Spa CV32 105 E1
Shawell LE17 68 A4

Rugby Sch CV22 83 D1
Ruislip Cl B35 22 A2
Rumbush La B94 69 F2
Rumer Cl CV37 129 B4
Runcorn Cl Birmingham B37 33 E2
Redditch B98 102 C4
Runcorn Wlk 10 CV2 63 D4
Runnymede Gdns CV10 28 C2
Runnymede Dr CV7 74 B3
Rupert Brooke Rd CV22 99 F4
Rupert Kettle Dr CV33 124 B4
Rupert Rd CV6 61 D4
Rush La B77 9 D4
Rushbrook La B94 86 B2
Rushbrook Rd CV37 145 E1
Rushford Cl B90 71 D4
Rushleigh Rd B90 69 F4
Rushmoor Dr CV5 60 C2
Rushmore St CV31 110 A4
Rushmore Terr 13 CV31 110 A4
Rushock Cl B98 103 E4
Rushton Cl CV7 74 B4
Rushwick Gr B90 71 D3
Ruskin Cl Coventry CV6 60 B3
Nuneaton CV10 28 A3
Rugby CV22 99 F3
Russell Ave CV22 99 E2
Russell Cl CV23 115 D4
Russell St Coventry CV1 151 C4
Royal Leamington Spa CV32 105 F1
Russell St N CV1 151 C4
Russell Terr CV31 110 A4
Russelsheim Way CV22 83 D1
Rutherford Glen CV11 29 F1
Rutherglen Ave CV3 78 A3
Rutland Ave Hinckley LE10 31 E4
Nuneaton CV10 28 C2
Rutland Croft 3 CV3 78 C4
Rydal B77 10 A4
Rydal Ave CV11 30 A3
Rydal Cl Allesley CV5 60 A4
Hinckley LE10 30 C4
Rugby CV21 83 E3
Ryde Ave CV10 29 E4
Ryder Cl CV35 114 F3
Ryder Row CV7 37 D4
Ryders Hill Cres CV10 28 B4
Rye Cl Banbury OX16 139 F5
Stratford-u-A CV37 144 C3
Rye Croft B47 69 D3
Rye Fields 1 CV33 122 E8
Rye Grass Wlk B35 22 A2
Rye Hill CV5 60 A3
Rye Piece Ringway CV12 39 E2
Ryeclose Croft B37 33 E2
Ryefield La B76 14 A1
Ryegrass La B97 102 B3
Ryelands The CV23 98 B4
Ryhope Cl CV12 38 B1
Ryknild St B49 143 D3
Ryland Cl CV31 110 B3
Ryland Rd CV35 122 B8
Ryland St CV37 144 C1
Rylston Ave CV6 49 D1
Rylstone Way 4 CV34 104 C1
Ryon Hill CV37 145 F4
Ryton B77 9 F4
Ryton Cl CV4 76 A4
Ryton Gardens CV8 79 F1

Sabin Cl CV23 115 C4
Sabin Dr CV33 107 E4
Sackville Cl Hanwell OX17 139 F6
Stratford-u-A CV37 144 B2
Sacred Heart RC Prim Sch CV2 62 A2
Saddington Rd CV3 78 C4
Saddlebow La CV35 114 B2
Saddlers Cl LE10 31 F3
Saddleton St CV35 138 C7
Sadler Cl CV37 144 C3
Sadler Rd CV6 61 D4
Sadlers Ave CV36 149 F3
Sadlers Cl CV36 149 F3
Sadlerswell La B94 88 A3
Saffron B77 4 A2
Saffron Cl CV23 83 F4
Saffron Mdw CV37 144 C1
Saffron Wlk CV37 144 C1
Saintbury Cl CV37 145 E1
Saintbury Dr B91 71 E4
Saints Way CV10 29 E3
SS Peter & Paul RC Prim Sch CV2 62 C4
St Agatha's Rd CV2 62 A2
St Agnes Cl B80 103 E2
St Agnes La CV1 151 B3
St Agnes Way CV11 29 F2
St Albans Cl CV32 105 E1
St Andrew's CE Inf Sch CV5 59 E3
St Andrew's Cres CV37 144 C1
St Andrew's Rd Coventry CV5 76 C4
Royal Leamington Spa CV32 106 A3
St Andrews B77 4 A2
St Andrews Benn CE Fst Sch CV21 83 E2
St Andrews Benn CE Prim Sch CV21 83 E2
St Andrews Cres CV22 100 A4
St Andrews Dr CV11 30 A1
St Ann's Cl CV31 110 B4
St Ann's Rd CV2 62 A2
St Anne's RC Prim Sch
Birmingham B37 33 D1
Coventry CV3 78 B3
Nuneaton CV10 28 B4
St Anne's Rd CV22 82 C1
St Annes Gr B93 72 A3
St Anthony's RC Comb Sch CV31 110 B4
St Antony's RC Prim Sch B37 33 D3
St Asaphs Ave B80 103 E2
St Athan Croft B35 22 A2
St Augustine's RC Comb Sch CV8 92 C4
St Augustine's RC Prim Sch CV6 61 D4
St Augustine's RC Sch B97 102 B3
St Augustine's Wlk CV6 61 D4
St Austell Cl CV11 30 A3
St Austell Rd CV2 62 C2
St Bartholemews Cl CV3 63 D1
St Bartholomew's CE Prim Sch CV3 78 C4
St Benedict's RC High Sch B49 143 E2
St Benedict's RC Prim Sch
Atherstone CV9 18 C4
Coventry CV1 61 F2
St Benedicts Cl CV9 18 B4
St Bernards Wlk CV3 78 B3
St Blaise Ave B46 23 E1
St Bride's Cl 8 CV31 110 B3
St Catherine's LE10 31 F4
St Catherine's Cl CV3 78 A4
St Catherine's Cres CV31 109 F2
St Catherine's RC Prim Sch GL55 135 A2
St Chads Rd
3 Bishops Tachbrook CV33 122 E8
Studley B80 103 E2
St Christian's Croft CV3 77 F4
St Christian's Rd CV3 77 F4
St Christopher Prim Sch CV5 60 B2
St Christopher's Cl CV34 108 B4
St Columba's Cl CV1 151 B4
St David's Cl CV31 110 B4
St David's Prim Sch GL56 140 A3
St Davids Orch CV3 78 C4
St Davids Way CV10 39 D3
St Edith's Cl CV23 53 F2
St Edith's Gn 1 CV34 109 D4
St Editha's Ct B78 5 D1
St Edithas Rd B78 11 D4
St Edmonds Rd CV9 16 B3
St Edward's RC Prim Sch B46 34 A3
St Edwin's Cl WR11 127 B2
St Elizabeth's RC Prim Sch CV6 61 F4
St Elizabeth's Rd CV6 61 F4
St Faith's CE Jun Sch B49 143 E2
St Faith's Rd B49 143 E3
St Francis RC Comb Sch CV12 39 E2
St George & St Teresa RC Sch B93 72 A2
St George's Cl
Moreton-in-M GL56 140 A3
Stratford-u-A CV37 144 B2
St George's Rd
Atherstone CV9 12 C1
Coventry CV1 61 F1
Royal Leamington Spa CV31 109 F3
Solihull B90 70 B4
St Georges Ave CV22 99 F4
St Georges Way CV10 39 D4
St Gerard's (Warwickshire) Orthopaedic Hospl B46 34 A3
St Gerards RC Jun & Inf Sch B35 22 A2
St Giles Cty Mid Sch CV7 49 F4
St Giles Rd Coventry CV7 49 E3
Gaydon CV35 132 E8
St Govan's Cl 4 CV31 110 B3
St Gregory's RC Prim Sch
Coventry CV2 62 C2
Stratford-u-A CV37 145 E3
St Gregory's Rd CV37 145 D2
St Helen's Rd CV31 110 A3
St Helen's Way CV5 60 A4
St Helena Rd B78 11 D4
St Ives Rd CV2 62 C2
St Ives Way CV11 29 F3
St James' Ave CV35 146 C2
St James CE Fst Sch CV33 147 D3
St James CE Mid Sch CV12 40 B1
St James Cl WR11 127 D3
St James Cres CV33 147 D3
St James Ct GL56 140 A2
St James Gdns CV12 40 B1
St James' La CV3 78 B3
St James Meadow Rd CV32 105 E1
St James Rd CV33 147 D3
St James's Cl LE10 31 E3
St John Fisher RC Prim Sch CV2 62 B3
St John St CV21 83 D2
St John the Baptist CE Fst Sch CV31 109 F4
St John the Baptist RC Prim Sch B36 33 D4
St John the Divine CE Prim Sch CV3 78 B3
St John Vianney RC Prim Sch CV5 60 A2
St John's Ave CV8 93 D2
St John's CE Prim Sch CV5 60 B2
St John's Cl
Cherington CV36 141 D7
Henley-in-A B95 113 A4
St John's Ct 9 CV34 108 C4
St John's La CV23 82 A3
St John's Rd
Cherington CV36 141 D7
Royal Leamington Spa CV31 110 A3
St John's St Coventry CV1 151 C2
Kenilworth CV8 93 D2
St Johns CV34 108 C4
St Johns Ave CV22 100 C4
St Johns Cl Knowle B93 72 A3
Stratford-u-A CV37 144 C1
St Johns Mid Sch CV8 92 C1
St Johns Rd CV10 27 F4
St Joseph's RC Comb Sch CV31 110 A2
St Joseph's RC Mid Sch CV11 29 E2
St Joseph's RC Prim Sch OX16 139 F3
St Joseph's RC Sch CV23 53 F2
St Joseph's Sch CV8 93 D4
St Jude's Cres CV3 78 B4
St Judes Ave B80 103 E2
St Laurence Ave CV34 108 B3
St Laurence Cl CV35 114 A8
St Lawrence CE Prim Sch CV23 125 C7
St Lawrence Cl Knowle B93 72 A3
Napton CV23 125 C8
St Lawrence Rd CV10 27 D2
St Lawrence's Rd CV6 49 F1
St Leonard's Wlk CV8 79 D1
St Leonards Cl
Birmingham B37 44 A4
Dordon B78 11 D3
St Leonards View B78 10 C4
St Luke's Rd CV6 49 E2
St Margaret Rd Coventry CV1 61 F1
Stoke Golding CV13 21 F4
St Margaret's CE Mid Sch CV31 110 A2
St Margaret's CE Prim Sch CV8 80 A2
St Margaret's Rd CV31 110 A3
St Margaret's Specl Sch CV12 39 D2
St Margarets CE Prim Sch CV13 21 E4
St Marie's RC Inf Sch CV22 83 D1
St Marie's RC Mid Sch CV22 82 C1
St Mark's Annexe (Coventry & Warwickshire Hospl) CV1 151 C4
St Mark's Ave CV22 99 E4
St Mark's Cl Gaydon CV35 132 E8
Ullenhall B95 112 E6
St Mark's Mews CV32 105 F1
St Mark's Rd CV32 105 E1
St Martin's LE10 31 F3
St Martin's Catholic High Sch CV13 21 F4
St Martin's Cl CV37 144 C1
St Martin's Rd CV8 77 E1
St Martins Ave B80 103 E2
St Mary St CV1 151 C2
St Mary's CE Jun Sch B80 103 F2
St Mary's Cl
Priors Hardwick CV23 125 D3
Southam CV33 147 E3
Ullenhall B95 112 E6
Warwick CV34 108 B4
St Mary's Cres CV31 110 A4
St Mary's La OX7 142 F2
St Mary's RC Comb Sch CV33 147 E2
St Mary's RC Jun & Inf Sch B80 103 F2
St Mary's RC Prim Sch
Aston le W NN11 134 F5
Coventry CV1 61 F2
St Mary's Rd Alcester B49 143 E2
Atherstone CV9 18 C4
Fillongley CV7 36 C2
Hinckley LE10 31 E4
Nuneaton CV11 29 D3
Royal Leamington Spa CV31 110 A4
Stratford-u-A CV37 145 D2
St Mary's Terr CV31 110 A4
St Marys Acre CV37 120 E7
St Marys Gr B79 2 B2
St Matthews Cl WR11 127 E6
St Matthews St CV21 83 D2
St Mawgen Cl B35 22 B2
St Michael's Cl Arley CV7 37 D4
Bishops Itchington CV33 124 A4
Claverdon CV35 113 F3
Weston u W CV33 107 E4
Wood End CV9 10 B1
St Michael's Cres CV23 147 F4
St Michael's Dr DE12 3 F4
St Michael's Hospl CV34 108 C4
St Michael's Rd
Claverdon CV35 113 F3
Coventry CV2 62 A2
Warwick CV34 108 B4
St Michael's Way CV10 28 B2
St Michaels Cl CV9 12 C1
St Michales Cl CV33 111 F1
St Milburgh Cl WR11 127 D1
St Nicholas Ave CV8 92 C2
St Nicholas CE Comb Sch CV8 92 C3
St Nicholas Church St CV34 108 C4
St Nicholas Cl Alcester B49 143 E2
Austrey CV9 3 D1
Coventry CV1 61 E3
St Nicholas Est CV9 11 E1
St Nicholas Rd
Henley-in-A B95 113 B4
Radford Semele CV31 110 C3
St Nicholas St CV1 151 B4
St Nicholas Wlk B76 23 D3
St Nicolas CE Fst Sch CV11 29 F3
St Nicolas Park Dr CV11 29 F4
St Nicolas Rd CV11 29 E3
St Osburg's RC Prim Sch CV1 151 A3
St Osburg's Rd CV2 62 A2
St Oswalds CE First Sch CV21 82 B2
St Patrick's CE Prim Sch B94 70 B1
St Patrick's RC Prim Sch
Birmingham B37 33 E1
Coventry CV2 50 B1
St Patrick's Rd CV1 151 B1
St Patricks RC Comb Sch CV31 109 F3
St Paul's CE Comb Sch CV32 106 A1
St Paul's CE Comb Sch (Annexe) CV32 106 A1
St Paul's CE Fst Sch CV10 28 B2
St Paul's Cl CV34 108 B3
St Paul's Cres 3 B46 33 F4
St Paul's Ct B77 9 E2
St Paul's Rd Coventry CV6 61 F3
Nuneaton CV10 28 B2
St Paul's Sq 12 CV32 106 A1
St Paul's Terr CV34 108 B3
St Peter's Ave CV9 19 D4
St Peter's CE Prim Sch CV35 122 B7
St Peter's Cl Redditch B97 102 C3
Water Orton B46 23 D1
Witherley CV9 19 D4
St Peter's Ct CV1 151 D4
St Peter's Dr CV10 27 F2
St Peter's Rd
7 Royal Leamington Spa CV32 109 F4
Rugby CV21 83 E2
Wellesbourne CV35 146 B2
St Peters La B92 44 B1
St Peters Rd Atherstone CV9 19 D4
Kineton CV35 132 B6
St Swithin's Dr CV37 129 D2
St Thomas More RC Fst Sch B98 103 D4
St Thomas More RC Prim Sch CV3 77 E3
St Thomas More Sch CV10 29 D2
St Thomas' Rd CV6 50 A2
St Thomas's Ct CV1 61 D1
St Wulstan Way CV33 147 E3
Salcombe Cl Coventry CV3 78 B3
Nuneaton CV11 29 F3
Salem Rd LE10 31 F3
Salford Cl Coventry CV2 62 A3
Redditch B98 103 D3
Salford Priors CE Prim Sch WR11 127 F6
Salford Rd B50 148 B2
Salisbury Ave CV3 77 E3
Salisbury Dr Nuneaton CV10 28 A4
Water Orton B46 23 E2
Salisbury Rd LE10 32 A4
Salt La CV1 151 B2
Salt Way B96 118 B7
Salt Way La OX15 137 F2
Salter St B94 70 B1
Salters La B95 120 C7
Saltisford CV34 108 B4
Saltisford Gdns CV34 108 B4
Salts La B78 8 C2
Sam Gault Cl CV3 78 C4
Sambourne La
Astwood Bank B96 102 C1
Coughton B49 118 E7
Sambourne B96 103 D1
Sambourne Park La B96 118 D8
Sammons Way CV4 59 E1
Sampson Cl CV2 62 B4
Sanby Cl CV12 39 D2
Sanctus Dr CV37 144 C1
Sanctus Rd CV37 144 C1
Sanctus St CV37 144 C1
Sand Barn La CV37 121 D6
Sanda Croft B36 33 D3
Sandbarn Cl B90 70 C3
Sandel Cl CV37 144 C2
Sanders Cl Atherstone CV9 12 C1
Braunston NN11 117 D5
Sanders Rd Bedworth CV6 50 A3
Salford Priors WR11 127 F6
Sandfield Cl B90 70 A4
Sandfield Rd CV37 144 C1
Sandfine Rd OX15 139 D1
Sandford Cl CV2 50 C2
Sandford Gn OX16 139 F4
Sandford Way CV22 99 E2
Sandgate Cres CV2 62 C1
Sandhills Cres B91 71 D4
Sandhurst Gr CV6 61 D3
Sandilands Cl CV2 62 C2
Sandon Rd CV11 29 D3
Sandown Ave CV6 49 F1
Sandown Cl CV32 106 B2
Sandown Rd CV21 83 E2
Sandpiper B77 10 A3
Sandpiper Cl CV37 144 B3
Sandpiper Rd CV2 50 A2
Sandpits Cl Curdworth B76 23 D3
Tysoe CV35 138 B6
Sandpits La CV6 48 C1
Sandpits Rd CV35 138 B7
Sandpits The CV12 40 B1
Sandwick Cl CV3 78 C4
Sandy La Blackdown CV32 105 F3
Coventry CV1 61 E3
Furnace End B46 25 F2
Marton CV23 115 D7
Monks Kirby CV23 53 F2
Newton Regis B79 2 B3
Royal Leamington Spa CV32 105 E2
Rugby CV21 82 C2
Sandy Lane Bsns Pk CV1 61 E3
Sandy Way Barford CV35 122 B7
Tamworth B77 4 A2
Sandy Way La B78 11 E4
Sandythorpe CV3 78 C3
Sankey Gr GL56 140 A2
Santos Cl CV3 78 C4
Sapcote Rd LE10 32 A4
Saplings The B76 22 A4
Sapphire Dr CV31 109 F3
Sapphire Gate CV2 62 B1
Saracen Dr CV7 73 F3
Sargeaunt St CV31 109 F4
Sark Dr B36 33 D3
Satchwell Wlk 8 CV32 109 F4
Saumur Way CV34 109 E3
Saunders Ave CV12 39 D1
Saunton Cl CV5 60 A4
Saunton Rd CV22 82 C1
Savages Cl CV33 122 F8
Savernake Rd CV35 132 C4
Saville Gr CV8 93 E3
Sawbridge Rd CV23 116 F5
Saxon Cl Binley Woods CV3 79 E4
Polesworth B78 4 C1
Stratford-u-A CV37 145 E1
Studley B80 103 F3
Tamworth B77 9 F3
Saxon Mdws CV32 105 E1
Saxon Rd CV2 62 A2
Saxon Wood Rd B90 70 B3
Saxonfields B50 148 B2
Scafell CV21 83 E4
Scafell Cl CV5 60 A2
Scammerton B77 10 A4
Scar Bank CV34 104 C1
Scarborough Way CV4 75 F4
Schofield Rd B37 33 D3
Scholars La CV37 144 C1
Scholfield Rd CV7 49 D3
School Ave WR11 127 F6
School Cl Birmingham B37 33 D3
Braunston NN11 117 E5
Coventry CV3 61 F1
Great Alne B49 119 D6
Hinckley LE10 32 A3
Long Compton CV36 141 C3
School Dr B47 69 D2
School Gdns CV21 84 A1
School Hill Hartshill CV10 28 A4
Mollington OX17 133 F2
Napton CV23 125 C8
Offchurch CV33 111 D4
School House La CV2 63 D3
School La Badby NN11 126 F6
Bearley CV37 120 E7
Bedworth CV7 49 F4
Kenilworth CV8 92 C3
Ladbroke CV33 124 D5
Lea Marston B76 24 A4
Littleton WR11 127 F1
Lower Brailes OX15 137 F2
North Newington OX15 139 E2
Nuneaton CV10 27 F3
Priors Marston CV23 125 E4
Radford Semele CV31 110 C3
Shuttington B79 4 C4
Stretton on D CV23 96 C3
Tamworth B77 9 E3
Tiddington CV37 145 F2
Warmington OX17 133 D2
Wolvey LE10 41 F2
Wroxall CV35 90 C2
School Rd Alcester B49 143 D2
Bulkington CV12 40 B1
Great Alne B49 119 D6
Henley-in-A B95 113 B4
Hockley Heath B94 88 A4
Pebworth CV37 128 F1
Salford Priors WR11 127 F6
Snitterfield CV37 121 B6
Wellesbourne CV35 146 C2
School St
Church Lawford CV23 81 D3
Churchover CV23 67 E3
Dunchurch CV22 99 E2
Long Lawford CV23 82 A2
Rugby CV21 84 A1
Southam CV33 147 E2
Stockton CV23 147 F4
Wolston CV8 80 A2
School Wlk CV11 29 F1
Scotchill The CV6 49 D1
Scotland End OX15 142 D4
Scots Cl CV22 99 E4
Scots La CV6 60 C3
Scott Ave CV10 29 E4

Scott Cl B50 ... 148 B3
Scott Rd Kenilworth CV8 ... 92 C1
Redditch B97 ... 102 B4
Royal Leamington Spa CV31 110 A3
Seabroke Ave CV22 ... 82 C2
Seafield La B48 ... 85 F2
Seaford Cl CV6 ... 50 A2
Seagrave Rd CV1 ... 151 D1
Sealand Dr CV12 ... 39 D2
Sear Hills Cl CV7 ... 74 A3
Seathwaite CV21 ... 83 E4
Seaton B77 ... 9 F4
Seaton Cl Hinckley LE10 ... 32 A4
Nuneaton CV11 ... 29 F3
Sebastian Cl CV3 ... 78 A3
Seckington La B79 ... 2 B2
Second Ave CV3 ... 62 B1
Second Exhibition Ave B40 44 B2
Sedgemere Gr CV7 ... 74 B3
Sedgemoor Rd CV3 ... 78 A3
Sedlescombe Pk CV22 ... 99 F4
Seed Field Croft CV3 ... 77 F4
Seekings The CV31 ... 110 A2
Seeney La B76 ... 15 D1
Seeswood Cl CV10 ... 28 B1
Sefton Rd Coventry CV4 ... 76 C3
Tamworth B77 ... 9 E2
Seggs La B49 ... 143 D2
Segrave Cl CV35 ... 132 B6
Selborne Rd CV22 ... 99 E4
Selby Way CV10 ... 28 A3
Selsdon Cl B47 ... 69 E3
Selsey Cl CV3 ... 78 B2
Selside CV21 ... 83 E4
Selworthy Rd CV6 ... 49 F2
Semele Cl CV31 ... 110 C3
Seneschal Rd CV3 ... 77 F4
Sennen Cl CV11 ... 30 A3
Seven Acre Cl 4 CV33 ... 122 E8
Seven Meadows Rd CV37 . 144 C1
Severn Ave LE10 ... 31 D4
Severn Cl CV32 ... 106 B2
Severn Rd Bulkington CV12 ... 40 A2
Coventry CV1 ... 61 F1
Severn Stars Ind Est CV3 ... 78 A4
Sevincott Cl CV37 ... 144 B2
Sevington Cl B91 ... 71 E4
Sewall Highway CV2 ... 62 A3
Seymour Cl Coventry CV3 ... 78 B3
Hampton Magna CV35 ... 114 F3
Seymour Gate GL55 ... 135 B2
Seymour Gr CV34 ... 109 E3
Seymour Rd Alcester B49 ... 143 E3
Nuneaton CV11 ... 29 E2
Rugby CV21 ... 83 E3
Stratford-u-A CV37 ... 144 B1
Shackleton Way LE17 ... 55 E3
Shadow Brook La B92 ... 56 C4
Shadowbrook Rd CV6 ... 61 D3
Shaft La CV7 ... 47 D2
Shaftesbury Ave CV7 ... 49 D4
Shaftesbury Rd CV5 ... 76 C4
Shakers La CV23 ... 115 C5
Shakesfield Cl CV36 ... 136 F6
Shakespeare Ave
Bedworth CV12 ... 39 E1
Warwick CV34 ... 108 B2
Shakespeare Ctr Mus The
CV37 ... 145 D2
Shakespeare Dr CV11 ... 30 A1
Shakespeare Gdns CV22 ... 99 F4
Shakespeare La WR11 ... 127 D3
Shakespeare Rd B90 ... 70 B4
Shakespeare St
Coventry CV2 ... 62 A2
Stratford-u-A CV37 ... 145 D2
Shakespeares Birthplace
Mus CV37 ... 145 D2
Shakleton Rd CV5 ... 61 D1
Shanes Castle Rd CV35 ... 132 D3
Shanklin Dr CV10 ... 29 E3
Shanklin Rd CV3 ... 78 A2
Shannon B77 ... 9 F4
Shap Fell CV21 ... 83 E4
Sharnford Rd LE10 ... 32 C3
Sharp Cl CV6 ... 49 E1
Sharpe Cl CV34 ... 108 C4
Sharpe St B77 ... 4 A3
Sharpless Rd LE10 ... 31 F4
Sharpley Ct CV2 ... 63 D4
Sharratt Rd CV12 ... 39 D1
Shaw's La CV35 ... 114 C8
Shawberry Ave B35 ... 22 A2
Shawbury La B46 ... 35 E4
Shawbury Village B46 ... 35 F3
Shawe Ave CV10 ... 29 E4
Shawell Rd LE17 ... 68 B4
Shawfield B47 ... 69 D3
Shawhurst Croft B47 ... 69 D4
Shawhurst La B47 ... 69 D3
Shearings The OX15 ... 142 D4
Sheep Dip La CV23 ... 96 C1
Sheep St
Chipping Campden GL55 ... 135 A1
Rugby CV21 ... 83 D2
Shipston-on-S CV36 ... 149 F3
Stratford-u-A CV37 ... 145 D1
Sheepclose Dr B37 ... 33 D2
Sheepcote Cl CV32 ... 106 A1
Sheepy La CV9 ... 6 C2
Sheepy Rd Atherstone CV9 ... 12 B1
Sheepy Magna CV9 ... 12 C3
Shefford Rd CV35 ... 132 D3
Shelbourne Rd CV37 ... 144 A2
Sheldon Gr 6 CV34 ... 104 C1
Sheldon Rd B98 ... 103 D4
Shelfield Cl CV5 ... 60 A2
Shelley Ave CV34 ... 108 B2
Shelley Cl Bedworth CV12 ... 39 E1
Redditch B97 ... 102 B4
Shelley Rd Coventry CV2 ... 62 B2
Stratford-u-A CV37 ... 145 D1
Shellon Cl CV3 ... 78 C4
Shelly Cres B90 ... 71 D3
Shelly La B90 ... 71 D3
Shelton Sq CV1 ... 151 B2
Shelton St B77 ... 9 F4
Shelwick Gr B93 ... 71 F2
Shenington CE Prim Sch
OX15 ... 138 F5
Shenstone Ave CV22 ... 83 F1
Shenstone Dr CV7 ... 74 A3
Shenton Cl CV13 ... 21 F4
Sheperds Hill CV33 ... 147 E2
Shepherd Cl CV4 ... 59 F2
Shepherd Pl CV35 ... 132 B5
Shepherd St CV23 ... 115 C7
Shepherds Cl CV23 ... 115 D3
Shepperton Bsns Pk CV11 ... 29 E1
Shepperton St CV11 ... 29 E1
Sheppey Dr B36 ... 33 D3
Sherard Croft B36 ... 33 D3
Sherborne Cl B46 ... 34 A2
Sherborne Rd LE10 ... 32 A4
Sherbourne Ave CV10 ... 28 A2
Sherbourne Cres CV5 ... 60 C2
Sherbourne Fields Sch CV6 60 B3
Sherbourne St CV1 ... 61 D1
Sherbrooke Ave B77 ... 9 F3
Sherdmore Croft B90 ... 70 C3
Sheridan Cl CV22 ... 99 F4
Sheridan Dr CV10 ... 27 F3
Sheridan Wlk B35 ... 22 A2
Sheriff Ave CV4 ... 76 A4
Sheriff Rd CV21 ... 83 E2
Sheriffs Orch CV1 ... 151 B2
Sheringham Cl CV11 ... 29 F1
Sherington Ave CV5 ... 60 B2
Sherlock Rd CV5 ... 60 B2
Sherwell Dr B49 ... 143 D2
Sherwood Cl CV9 ... 10 B1
Sherwood Jones Cl CV6 ... 61 D3
Sherwood Rd CV13 ... 21 F4
Sherwood Wlk CV32 ... 106 B2
Shetland Cl CV5 ... 60 A2
Shetland Dr CV10 ... 29 D1
Shetland Wlk B36 ... 33 D3
Shevlock Way CV6 ... 62 A3
Shillingstone Cl CV2 ... 63 D2
Shilton & Ansty Fst Sch
CV7 ... 51 F3
Shilton Cl B90 ... 70 C3
Shilton Ind Est CV7 ... 51 F4
Shilton La Barnacle CV2, CV7 . 51 D2
Bulkington CV12 ... 40 B1
Coventry CV2 ... 50 C2
Shilton CV7, CV12 ... 51 E4
Shinehill La WR11 ... 128 A1
Shipston Rd
Alderminster CV37 ... 130 B5
Coventry CV2 ... 62 B3
Long Compton CV36 ... 141 C4
Upper Tysoe CV35 ... 138 B6
Shipton-on-Stour
Prim Sch CV36 ... 149 F3
Shire Cl CV6 ... 50 A1
Shirebrook Cl CV2 ... 50 B1
Shires Gate Ret Pk CV31 ... 109 F3
Shires Ret Pk CV34 ... 109 E3
Shires The CV23 ... 81 D3
Shirlett Cl CV2 ... 50 A2
Shirley La CV7 ... 59 D3
Shirley Rd CV2 ... 63 D4
Shirrall Dr B78 ... 7 F2
Shopping Ctr The CV31 ... 110 A3
Shopping Prec The CV34 . 105 D1
Shorncliffe Rd CV6 ... 60 C3
Short Acres CV35 ... 132 C6
Short La CV23 ... 115 C4
Short St Coventry CV1 ... 151 C2
Nuneaton CV10 ... 28 B2
Shortland Cl B93 ... 72 A4
Shortlands CV7 ... 49 E3
Shortley Rd CV3 ... 77 F4
Shortwoods The B78 ... 11 D3
Shottery CV37 ... 144 B1
Shottery CE Prim Sch
CV37 ... 144 B1
Shottery Cl CV5 ... 60 A2
Shottery Rd CV37 ... 144 C1
Shotteswell Rd B90 ... 70 A4
Shoulderway La CV36 ... 149 F1
Showell La CV7 ... 47 D1
Shrewley Comm CV35 ... 114 B6
Shrubberies The CV4 ... 76 C2
Shrubland St CV31 ... 110 A3
Shrubland Street
Com Prim Sch CV31 ... 110 A3
Shuckburgh Cres
Bourton on D CV23 ... 97 F1
Rugby CV22 ... 100 B4
Shuckburgh Gr 3 CV32 ... 106 A1
Shuckburgh Rd
Napton CV23 ... 125 C8
Priors Marston CV23 ... 125 E4
Shulman's Wlk CV2 ... 62 B4
Shultern La CV4 ... 76 B3
Shuna Croft CV2 ... 63 D4
Shustoke CE Prim Sch
B46 ... 25 D1
Shutford Rd
North Newington OX15 ... 139 D2
Shutford OX15 ... 139 B1
Shutt La B94 ... 70 A1
Shuttington Rd B79 ... 4 A3
Shuttle St CV6 ... 62 A4
Shuttleworth Rd CV23 ... 83 F3
Sibford Gower Rrim Sch
OX15 ... 142 D8
Sibford Rd
Hook Norton OX15 ... 142 D4
Shutford OX15 ... 138 F2
Sibford Sch OX15 ... 142 D8
Sibree Rd CV3 ... 78 A2
Sibton Cl CV2 ... 50 B1
Sidbury Gr B93 ... 71 F2
Siddeley Ave Coventry CV3 ... 62 A1
Kenilworth CV8 ... 92 C2
Siddeley Way NN11 ... 117 F2
Sidelands Rd CV37 ... 144 B2
Sidenhill Cl B90 ... 70 A4
Sidmouth Cl Coventry CV2 ... 62 B4
Nuneaton CV11 ... 29 F3
Sidney Rd CV22 ... 100 B4
Sidney Stringer
Com Tech Coll CV1 ... 151 C3
Signal Hayes Rd B76 ... 13 D1
Signal Wlk B77 ... 4 A1
Silica Rd B77 ... 4 A1
Silksby St CV3 ... 77 E4
Silver Birch Ave CV12 ... 38 C1
Silver Birch Dr B47 ... 69 D3
Silver Birch Gr CV31 ... 109 F3
Silver Link Rd B77 ... 4 A1
Silver St Coventry CV1 ... 151 B3
Newton CV23 ... 68 A1
Wroxton OX15 ... 139 D4
Silver Trees Dr CV12 ... 40 A2
Silver Wlk CV10 ... 28 C2
Silverbirch Cl CV10 ... 28 A4
Silverdale Cl CV2 ... 50 A2
Silverstone Dr CV6 ... 49 F3
Silverton Rd CV6 ... 61 F4
Simmonds Way CV9 ... 12 B1
Simmons Cl B78 ... 8 A1
Simmons Ct CV35 ... 146 B2
Simms La B47 ... 69 D3
Simon Cl CV11 ... 29 E1
Simon Rd B47 ... 69 D4
Simon Stone St CV6 ... 61 F4
Simpkins Cl CV33 ... 107 E4
Simpson Rd CV36 ... 149 F3
Sinclair Ave OX16 ... 139 F4
Singer Cl CV6 ... 62 A4
Singer Croft B36 ... 22 C1
Sir Henry Parkes Prim Sch
CV4 ... 76 B4
Sir Henry Parkes Rd CV5 ... 76 B4
Sir John Moore CE Sch
DE12 ... 3 F4
Sir Thomas White's Rd
CV5 ... 60 C1
Sir William Lyons Rd CV4 ... 76 B3
Sir Winston Churchill Pl
CV3 ... 79 E4
Siskin Dr CV3 ... 78 B2
Siskin Parkway E CV3 ... 78 B1
Siskin Parkway W CV3 ... 78 B1
Sitwell Ave CV23 ... 115 D3
Sixteen Acres La B50 ... 148 C1
Skelwith Rise CV11 ... 30 A3
Sketchley Hall Gdns LE10 ... 31 E3
Sketchley Hill Cty Prim Sch
LE10 ... 31 F3
Sketchley La LE10 ... 31 E3
Sketchley La Ind Est LE10 ... 31 D3
Sketchley Manor La LE10 ... 31 E3
Sketchley Mdws LE10 ... 31 E3
Sketchley Meadows
Bsns Pk LE10 ... 31 E2
Sketchley Old Village LE10 . 31 E3
Sketchley Rd LE10 ... 31 F3
Skiddaw CV21 ... 83 E4
Skidmore Ave B77 ... 9 E3
Skilts Sch B98 ... 112 B6
Skipton Gdns CV2 ... 62 A3
Skipwith Cl CV23 ... 64 B2
Skipworth Rd CV3 ... 63 D1
Sky Blue Way CV1 ... 61 F2
Skye Cl Birmingham B36 ... 33 D3
Nuneaton CV10 ... 28 C1
Slack's Ave CV9 ... 18 B4
Slade Cl CV11 ... 40 B4
Slade Gr B93 ... 71 F3
Slade Hill CV35 ... 114 F4
Slade La Sutton Coldfield
B75 ... 7 D2
Tamworth B77 ... 9 E2
Slade Mdw CV31 ... 110 C3
Slade Rd CV21 ... 83 E1
Slade The CV33 ... 133 E6
Slateley Cres B90 ... 70 C3
Slater Rd B93 ... 71 F2
Sleath's Yd CV12 ... 39 D2
Sledmere Cl CV2 ... 50 A2
Sleets Yd CV12 ... 39 D1
Slimbridge Cl Redditch
B97 ... 102 C3
2 Solihull B90 ... 71 D3
Slingates Rd CV37 ... 145 D2
Slingsby B77 ... 9 E4
Slingsby Cl CV11 ... 29 F1
Slough The B97 ... 103 D2
Slowley Hill CV7 ... 26 A1
Small Brook Bsns Ctr
B50 ... 148 C3
Small Ho OX15 ... 142 D8
Small La B94 ... 86 C3
Smalley Pl CV8 ... 92 C2
Smarts La CV35 ... 138 B6
Smarts Rd CV12 ... 38 C1
Smeaton La CV23 ... 64 C3
Smercote Cl CV12 ... 38 B1
Smite Cl CV23 ... 53 F2
Smith St Bedworth CV12 ... 38 C1
Coventry CV6 ... 61 F3
13 Royal Leamington Spa
CV31 ... 109 F4
Warwick CV34 ... 108 C4
Wood End CV9 ... 10 B1
Smith's La CV37 ... 121 B6
Smith's Way B49 ... 143 E3
Smithford Way CV1 ... 151 B3
Smiths La B93 ... 71 F4
Smiths Way B46 ... 23 D2
Smiths Wood Sch B36 ... 33 D3
Smithy La Aston Flamville LE9 32 B4
Church Lawford CV23 ... 81 E3
Tamworth B77 ... 9 F4
Smithy Rd CV9 ... 17 E3
Smockington La LE10 ... 42 A4
Smorrall La CV12 ... 38 B1
Smythe Gr CV34 ... 104 C1
Snape Rd CV2 ... 62 C3
Snarestone Rd DE12 ... 3 F4
Sniterfield La CV37 ... 121 C7
Snitterfield La CV37 ... 114 C1
Snitterfield Prim Sch
CV37 ... 121 B6
Snitterfield Rd CV37 ... 120 E7
Snitterfield St CV35 ... 121 F4
Snowdon Cl CV10 ... 28 A2
Snowford Hill CV33 ... 115 A5
Snows Drive Hill B90 ... 70 B3
Snowshill Cl CV11 ... 39 F4
Snuff La OX17 ... 139 E8
Soar Way LE10 ... 31 D4
Soden Cl CV3 ... 78 B3
Soden's Ave CV8 ... 79 D1
Solent Dr CV2 ... 50 C1
Solihull Coll
Chelmsley Campus B37 ... 33 E2
Solihull Parkway B37 ... 44 C4
Solihull Rd B92 ... 56 C3
Solway Cl CV31 ... 110 B3
Somerby Dr B91 ... 71 D4
Somerly Cl CV3 ... 78 C4
Somers Pl 3 CV32 ... 109 F4
Somers Rd Keresley CV7 ... 49 D3
Meriden CV7 ... 45 F1
Rugby CV22 ... 82 B2
Somerset Dr CV10 ... 28 C2
Somerset Rd CV1 ... 61 E3
Somerton Dr B37 ... 44 A4
Sommerville Rd CV2 ... 62 B2
Soot La OX17 ... 133 D2
Sopwith Croft B35 ... 22 A1
Sorbus B77 ... 4 A2
Sorrel B77 ... 4 A3
Sorrel Cl CV4 ... 75 F4
Sorrel Dr Kingsbury B78 ... 15 E4
Rugby CV23 ... 83 E4
Sorrell Rd CV10 ... 39 E4
South Ave CV2 ... 62 A1
South Car Park Rd B40 ... 44 C2
South Cl NN11 ... 117 E5
South Dr B46 ... 33 F3
South End OX7 ... 142 A2
South Green Dr CV37 ... 144 B2
South Par CV33 ... 123 F6
South Rd CV23 ... 84 A3
South Ridge CV5 ... 60 A2
South St Atherstone CV9 ... 18 B4
Coventry CV1 ... 61 F2
Rugby CV21 ... 83 E2
South Terr CV31 ... 110 A2
South View B78 ... 15 E2
South View Rd
Long Lawford CV23 ... 81 F2
Royal Leamington Spa CV32 . 106 B3
South Way B40 ... 44 C2
Southam Cl CV4 ... 75 F4
Southam Cres CV35 ... 123 D2
Southam Dr CV33 ... 147 D1
Southam Prim Sch CV33 .. 147 D3
Southam Rd Cropredy OX17 134 A2
Dunchurch CV22 ... 99 D1
Kineton CV35 ... 132 B6
Ladbroke CV33 ... 124 D6
Long Itchington CV23 ... 115 D3
Mollington OX17 ... 134 A2
Priors Marston CV23 ... 125 E4
Southam CV33 ... 124 B8
Ufton CV33 ... 111 E2
Ufton CV33 ... 115 A1
Southam Sch CV33 ... 147 D3
Southam St CV35 ... 132 B6
Southbank Rd Coventry CV6 . 60 C3
Kenilworth CV8 ... 92 C2
Southbrook Rd CV22 ... 83 D1
Southcott Way CV2 ... 50 C1
Southern La CV37 ... 145 D1
Southey Cl B91 ... 71 D4
Southey Rd CV22 ... 99 F4
Southfield Cl CV10 ... 29 E3
Southfield Dr CV8 ... 93 D3
Southfield Rd Hinckley LE10 ... 31 F4
Rugby CV22 ... 83 E1
Southam CV33 ... 147 D1
Southfields Cl B46 ... 34 A2
Southlands Atherstone CV9 ... 18 C4
11 Royal Leamington Spa
CV31 ... 110 A4
Southlea Ave CV31 ... 109 F3
Southlea Cl CV31 ... 109 F3
Southleigh Ave CV5 ... 76 C4
Southlynn Gdns CV36 ... 149 F3
Southmead Gdns B80 ... 103 F2
Southport Cl CV3 ... 78 A3
Southrop Rd OX15 ... 142 D3
Southway CV31 ... 110 A3
Sovereign Cl CV8 ... 92 C1
Sovereign Rd CV5 ... 61 D1
Sovereign Row CV1 ... 61 D1
Sowe Valley Prim Sch CV3 . 78 B4
Spa View CV31 ... 110 A2
Sparkbrook St CV1 ... 61 F2
Sparrow Cock La B93 ... 73 E1
Sparrowdale Specl Sch
CV9 ... 11 E2
Sparta Cl CV21 ... 83 D3
Spartan Cl CV34 ... 109 F2
Speedway La CV8 ... 79 F4
Speedwell Dr CV7 ... 74 A3
Speedwell La CV9 ... 11 D1
Speedwll Cl CV23 ... 83 F4
Spencer Ave CV5 ... 61 D1
Spencer Rd CV5 ... 151 A1
Spencer St CV31 ... 109 F4
Spencer Yd CV31 ... 109 F4
Spencer's La CV7 ... 58 C1
Spernal Ash B49 ... 103 F1
Spernal La Great Alne B80 .. 119 C7
Studley B80 ... 112 A1
Spetchley Cl B97 ... 102 B3
Sphinx Dr CV3 ... 62 A1
Spicer Pl CV22 ... 82 B1
Spiers Cl B93 ... 72 A3
Spilsbury Cl CV32 ... 105 F1
Spilsbury Croft B91 ... 71 D4
Spindle St CV1 ... 61 E3
Spindles The LE10 ... 31 F3
Spinney Cl Arley CV7 ... 36 C4
Binley Woods CV3 ... 79 F4
Birchmoor B78 ... 10 C4
Spinney Dr B90 ... 70 B2
Spinney Hill
Braunston NN11 ... 117 E5
Warwick CV34 ... 105 D1
Spinney La CV10 ... 28 B2
Spinney Rd LE10 ... 31 E3
Spinney The Atherstone CV9 . 19 D4
Bishops Itchington CV33 ... 124 B4
Coventry CV4 ... 76 B2
Long Lawford CV23 ... 82 A3
Royal Leamington Spa CV32 . 105 E1
Wythall B47 ... 69 D2
Spire Bank CV33 ... 147 D2
Spires The CV10 ... 28 B2
Spon End CV1, CV5 ... 61 D2
Spon Gate Prim Sch CV1 ... 61 D2
Spon La CV9 ... 11 F3
Spon St CV1 ... 151 A3
Spring Cl 10 Coventry CV1 ... 61 F2
Ettington CV37 ... 131 A3
Spring Coppice Dr B93 ... 72 A2
Spring Ct CV8 ... 95 E3
Spring Hill Arley CV7 ... 36 C4
Bubbenhall CV8 ... 95 E3
Combrook CV35 ... 131 F7
Spring Hill Rd CV10 ... 28 B3
Spring La Combrook CV35 ... 131 E6
Lapworth B94 ... 88 B2
Radford Semele CV31 ... 110 C3
Tanworth-in-A B94 ... 88 A3
Spring Pool CV34 ... 108 C4
Spring Rd Barnacle CV7 ... 51 D3
Coventry CV6 ... 49 F1
Spring St CV21 ... 83 D2
Springbrook Cl B36 ... 22 B1
Springbrook La B94 ... 87 D4
Springfield OX17 ... 139 F6
Springfield Cl CV36 ... 149 F3
Springfield Cres
Bedworth CV12 ... 39 D1
Sutton Coldfield B76 ... 13 D2
Springfield Gr CV33 ... 147 D3
Springfield House
Specl Sch B93 ... 73 D3
Springfield Pl CV1 ... 151 C4
Springfield Rd
Coventry CV1 ... 151 C4
Hinckley LE10 ... 31 E4
Nuneaton CV11 ... 29 F1
Shipston-on-S CV36 ... 149 F2
Sutton Coldfield B76 ... 13 D2
Tamworth B77 ... 9 E4
Springfields B46 ... 33 F3
Springfields Rd B49 ... 143 D3
Springhill CV10 ... 28 A4
Springs Cres CV33 ... 147 D3
Springside B98 ... 103 E4
Springwell Rd 6 CV31 ... 110 B3
Spruce B77 ... 4 A2
Spruce Gr CV31 ... 109 F3
Squadron Cl B35 ... 22 B2
Square La CV7 ... 37 D1
Square The Dunchurch CV22 . 99 E2
Ettington CV37 ... 131 A3
Fazeley B78 ... 9 D4
Kenilworth CV8 ... 92 C2
Nuneaton CV11 ... 29 F1
Stockton CV33 ... 147 F4
Swalcliffe OX15 ... 142 F8
Tysoe CV35 ... 138 B7
Wolvey LE10 ... 41 E2
Wootton Wawen B95 ... 113 A3
Squire Pl CV33 ... 133 D7
Squires Croft Coventry CV2 ... 50 C1
Sutton Coldfield B76 ... 13 D1
Squires Gate Wlk B35 ... 22 A2
Squires Gn LE10 ... 31 F3
Squires Rd CV23 ... 96 C3
Squires Way CV4 ... 76 B3
Squirrel Hollow B76 ... 13 D1
Spring La CV8 ... 93 D3
Stable Wlk CV11 ... 29 F1

Stableford Cl B97 ... 102 B4
Stacey Ct CV22 ... 99 E3
Stadium Cl CV6 ... 49 E1
Stafford Cl CV12 ... 40 B1
Stafford St CV9 ... 18 C4
Staines Cl CV11 ... 29 F4
Stainforth Cl CV11 ... 30 A1
Stainsby Croft B90 ... 71 D3
Staircase La CV5 ... 60 B4
Stamford Ave CV3 ... 77 E3
Stamford Gdns CV32 ... 105 F1
Stanbrook Rd B90 ... 71 D3
Stand St CV34 ... 108 B3
Standard Ave CV4 ... 60 A1
Standedge B77 ... 10 A4
Standish Cl CV2 ... 62 C1
Standlake Mews 23 CV31 ... 110 B3
Stanford Cl B97 ... 102 A3
Stanier Ave CV1 ... 61 D2
Stanley Ct CV31 ... 110 B4
Stanley Rd Atherstone CV9 ... 18 B4
Coventry CV5 ... 76 C4
Nuneaton CV11 ... 29 D3
Rugby CV21 ... 83 F1
Stannells Cl CV37 ... 129 E8
Stansfield Gr CV8 ... 93 E2
Stanton Bridge Prim Sch CV6 ... 61 F3
Stanton Rd 13 CV31 ... 110 B3
Stanton Wlk CV34 ... 104 B1
Stanway Rd CV5 ... 77 D4
Stapenhall Rd B90 ... 71 D3
Stapledon Gn CV33 ... 132 F7
Staples Cl CV12 ... 40 B2
Stapleton Cl Studley B80 ... 103 E2
Sutton Coldfield B76 ... 22 A3
Stapleton Dr B37 ... 33 D2
Stapleton La CV13 ... 21 F4
Stapleton Rd B80 ... 103 E2
Star Cnr CV23 ... 101 E1
Star Ind Pk CV2 ... 62 C3
Star La CV35 ... 114 A4
Starbold Cres B93 ... 72 A3
Starbold Rd CV33 ... 124 A4
Starcross Cl CV2 ... 62 B4
Stare Gn CV4 ... 76 B3
Stareton Cl CV4 ... 76 C3
Starkey Croft B37 ... 33 E1
Starley Pk CV7 ... 50 A4
Starley Rd CV1 ... 151 A2
Starley Way B37 ... 44 B3
Starmer Pl CV35 ... 114 D6
Startin Cl CV7 ... 49 F4
Station App Dorridge B93 ... 71 F1
Royal Leamington Spa CV31 . 109 F4
Station Ave Coventry CV4 ... 75 E4
Warwick CV34 ... 108 C4
Station Dr B94 ... 69 E1
Station La B94 ... 89 E2
Station Rd Alcester B49 ... 143 D2
Arley CV7 ... 36 B4
Balsall Common CV7 ... 74 A4
Birmingham B37 ... 44 A4
Bishops Itchington CV33 ... 124 A4
Chipping Campden GL55 ... 135 C2
Claverdon CV35 ... 114 A3
Clifton u D CV23 ... 83 F3
Coleshill B46 ... 23 F1
Cropredy OX17 ... 134 C1
Fenny Compton CV33 ... 133 E7
Hampton in A B92 ... 57 D4
Harvington WR11 ... 127 D3
Hatton CV35 ... 114 C5
Henley-in-A B95 ... 113 A5
Higham-on-t-H CV13 ... 20 C2
Hinckley LE10 ... 31 E4
Hook Norton OX15 ... 142 E4
Kenilworth CV8 ... 92 C2
Knowle B93 ... 72 A2
Lapworth B94 ... 89 E2
Long Marston CV37 ... 129 C2
Moreton-in-M GL56 ... 140 A3
Polesworth B78 ... 5 D1
Salford Priors WR11 ... 127 F6
Shipston-on-S CV36 ... 149 F3
Shustoke B46 ... 24 B2
Stockton CV23 ... 116 A3
Stoke Golding CV13 ... 21 E4
Stratford-u-A CV37 ... 144 C2
Studley B80 ... 103 E2
Warwick CV34 ... 108 C4
Wilmcote CV37 ... 120 C5
Wythall B47 ... 69 D2
Station Sq CV1 ... 151 B1
Station St CV9 ... 18 B4
Station St E CV6 ... 61 F4
Station St W CV6 ... 61 F4
Station Way B26 ... 44 B2
Staunton Rd CV31 ... 110 A3
Staveley Way CV21 ... 83 E3
Staverton CE Prim Sch NN11 ... 126 E8
Staverton Cl CV5 ... 60 A2
Staverton Leys CV22 ... 100 A4
Staverton Rd NN11 ... 126 F8
Staverton Sports Ctr NN11 117 F1
Steele St CV22 ... 82 C2
Steels La CV36 ... 141 D7
Steeping Rd CV23 ... 82 A3
Steeplefield Rd CV6 ... 61 D3
Steeples The CV23 ... 116 F5
Stefen Way NN11 ... 126 F8
Stella Croft B37 ... 33 E1
Stennels Cl CV6 ... 60 C4
Stephen St CV21 ... 82 C2
Stephens Rd B76 ... 13 D2
Stephenson Cl
Daventry NN11 ... 117 F2
Royal Leamington Spa CV32 . 105 E1
Tamworth B77 ... 4 A1
Stephenson Dr B37 ... 33 D1
Stephenson Rd
Bedworth CV7 ... 50 B4
Hinckley LE10 ... 30 C4
Stepney Rd CV2 ... 62 A2
Steppes Piece B50 ... 148 B3
Stepping Stones Rd CV5 ... 60 C2
Sterling Way CV11 ... 39 F4
Stevenage Wlk 2 CV2 ... 63 D4
Stevenson Rd CV6 ... 61 D4
Stewart Cl CV4 ... 60 B1
Stewart St CV11 ... 29 E2
Stidfall Gr CV31 ... 110 B3
Stileman Cl CV37 ... 129 D2
Stiper's Hill B78 ... 5 D1
Stirling Ave CV32 ... 106 A3
Stirling Cl CV3 ... 78 C4
Stirling Ct OX16 ... 139 F3
Stirling Rd B90 ... 70 C4
Stivichall Croft CV3 ... 77 D3
Stivichall Prim Sch CV3 ... 77 D3
Stocking La OX15 ... 138 E5
Stocking Mdw CV23 ... 53 F2
Stockingford Fst & Mid Sch CV10 ... 28 B2
Stocks La CV23 ... 98 C2
Stockton Cl Birmingham B76 . 22 B3
Knowle B93 ... 72 A2
Stockton Gr 1 CV32 ... 106 A1
Stockton Prim Sch CV23 ... 147 F4
Stockton Rd Coventry CV1 .. 151 D4
Long Itchington CV23 ... 115 E3
Stockwells GL56 ... 140 A3
Stoke Gn CV3 ... 62 A1
Stoke Heath Prim Sch CV2 ... 62 A3
Stoke La LE10 ... 21 F4
Stoke Park Sch & Com Coll CV2 ... 62 A2
Stoke Prim Sch CV2 ... 62 A2
Stoke Rd Fenny Drayton CV13 ... 20 C4
Stoke Golding CV13 ... 21 F3
Stoke Row CV2 ... 62 A2
Stokesay Cl CV11 ... 29 D2
Stone Ave B75 ... 13 D3
Stone Bridge GL56 ... 140 D7
Stone Cross B46 ... 23 D2
Stone Ct OX7 ... 142 A2
Stone Pits Mdw CV37 ... 120 C5
Stonebow Ave B91 ... 71 D4
Stonebridge Highway CV3 .. 77 F2
Stonebridge Rd Coleshill B46 ... 33 F3
Lighthorne Heath CV35 ... 123 C3
Little Packington B46 ... 45 D4
Long Itchington CV23 ... 115 B4
Stonebridge Trad Est CV3 .. 78 A2
Stonebrook Way CV6 ... 49 F2
Stonebury Ave CV5 ... 59 F2
Stonefield Cl CV2 ... 63 D4
Stonehaven Dr CV3 ... 77 E2
Stonehill Croft B90 ... 70 C3
Stonehill Wlk B77 ... 9 F3
Stonehills CV21 ... 83 E4
Stonehouse Cl CV32 ... 106 B3
Stonehouse La CV3 ... 78 B2
Stoneleigh Ave CV8 ... 93 D3
Stoneleigh Cl Hartshill CV10 . 19 D1
Redditch B98 ... 102 C3
Stoneleigh CV8 ... 94 B3
Stoneleigh Rd
Blackdown CV32 ... 106 A4
Coventry CV4 ... 76 C1
Kenilworth CV8 ... 93 D3
Stoneleigh CV8 ... 94 A2
Stonely Rd CV13 ... 21 E3
Stonepits La B97 ... 102 B2
Stoneton Cl CV33 ... 147 E2
Stoneton Cres CV7 ... 74 A3
Stoneway NN11 ... 126 F5
Stoneway Gr 11 CV31 ... 110 B3
Stonewell Cres CV11 ... 40 A4
Stoney Ct CV3 ... 79 D4
Stoney La CV35 ... 114 C6
Stoney Rd Coventry CV1 ... 151 B1
Nuneaton CV10, CV11 ... 29 D3
Stoney Stanton Rd CV1, CV6 ... 61 F3
Stoneydelph Inf Sch B77 ... 4 A1
Stoneydelph Jun Sch B77 ... 4 A1
Stoneymoor Dr B36 ... 22 B1
Stoneywood Rd CV2 ... 62 C4
Stonleigh Ave CV5 ... 76 C4
Stonydelph La B77 ... 10 A4
Stornoway Rd B35 ... 22 A2
Storrage La B48 ... 85 D2
Stour B77 ... 10 A3
Stour Ct CV36 ... 149 F3
Stour Valley Com Sch CV36 ... 149 F3
Stour View CV36 ... 137 A8
Stourton Cl B93 ... 72 A4
Stow Rd GL56 ... 140 A3
Stowe Dr CV33 ... 147 D2
Stowe Pl CV4 ... 59 E1
Strachey Ave CV32 ... 105 F1
Straight Mile CV23 ... 98 A2
Stratford Ave CV9 ... 18 B4
Stratford Cty Prim Sch CV37 ... 144 C1
Stratford Rd Alcester B49 ... 143 E2
Bidford-on-A B50 ... 128 D7
Stratford Rd continued
Dorridge B94 ... 71 D2
Drayton OX15 ... 139 F4
Hampton Lucy CV35 ... 121 E4
Hampton Lucy CV35 ... 121 F2
Henley-in-A B95 ... 113 A3
Hockley Heath B94 ... 88 B3
Ilmington CV36 ... 136 B7
Lighthorne Heath CV35 ... 123 D2
Loxley CV35 ... 130 F8
Mickleton GL55 ... 135 B7
Newbold-on-S CV37 ... 130 E1
Shenington OX15 ... 138 F7
Shipston-on-S CV36 ... 149 F3
Solihull B90 ... 70 B4
Temple Grafton B49 ... 119 E3
Warwick CV34 ... 108 B2
Wellesbourne CV35 ... 146 A2
Wroxton OX15 ... 139 C4
Stratford St Coventry CV2 ... 62 A2
Nuneaton CV11 ... 29 E2
Stratford-upon-Avon Coll CV37 ... 144 C2
Stratford-upon-Avon Gram Sch For Girls CV37 144 B1
Stratford-upon-Avon High Sch CV37 ... 144 C2
Stratford-upon-Avon Hospl CV37 ... 144 C2
Stratford-upon-Avon Racecourse CV37 ... 129 E8
Stratford-upon-Avon Sta CV37 ... 144 C2
Strathearn Rd CV32 ... 105 F1
Strathmore Ave CV1 ... 61 F1
Strathmore Rd LE10 ... 31 D4
Strawberry Fields CV7 ... 46 A1
Strawberry Wlk CV2 ... 50 B1
Streamside Cl CV5 ... 60 A4
Stretton Ave CV3 ... 78 B3
Stretton Cl LE10 ... 31 E3
Stretton Cres CV31 ... 110 A3
Stretton Ct Hinckley LE10 ... 31 E2
Rugby CV21 ... 83 E4
Stretton Rd Nuneaton CV10 ... 29 D2
Solihull B90 ... 70 A4
Wolston CV8 ... 80 A1
Stroma Way CV10 ... 28 C1
Strutt Rd LE10 ... 32 A3
Stuart Cl CV34 ... 108 B3
Stuart Ct CV6 ... 62 A4
Stuart Gdns CV33 ... 132 F7
Stubbs Cl CV12 ... 39 D2
Stubbs Gr CV2 ... 62 A3
Studland Ave CV21 ... 83 F1
Studland Gn CV2 ... 63 D2
Studley Cty Inf Sch B80 ... 103 F2
Studley High Sch B80 ... 103 F2
Studley Rd B98 ... 103 D4
Sturley Cl CV8 ... 93 D3
Sturminster Cl CV2 ... 63 D2
Styles Cl CV31 ... 110 A4
Styvechale Ave CV5 ... 77 D4
Sudbury Cl CV32 ... 106 B2
Sudeley B77 ... 9 E4
Sudeley Cl B36 ... 22 A1
Sudeley Rd CV10 ... 39 E4
Suffolk Cl Bedworth CV12 ... 39 D2
Coventry CV5 ... 60 A2
Nuneaton CV10 ... 28 C2
Suffolk St CV32 ... 106 A1
Sugarswell La OX15 ... 138 D7
Sulgrave Cl CV2 ... 62 C4
Sullivan Rd CV6 ... 62 A4
Sumburgh Croft B35 ... 22 A2
Summer La B76 ... 22 B3
Summerhouse Cl B97 ... 102 A3
Summerton Rd CV31 ... 110 A2
Sumner Cl CV35 ... 114 F3
Sumner Rd B46 ... 34 A3
Sun Rising Hill OX15 ... 132 D1
Sun St CV21 ... 83 E2
Sunbeam Cl B36 ... 22 C1
Sunbury Rd CV3 ... 78 B3
Suncliffe Dr CV8 ... 93 D1
Sunderland Pl CV35 ... 146 B1
Sundew St CV2 ... 50 B1
Sundorne Cl CV5 ... 60 A2
Sunningdale B77 ... 4 B3
Sunningdale Ave
Coventry CV6 ... 49 E1
Kenilworth CV8 ... 93 D2
Sunningdale Cl CV11 ... 30 A1
Sunnybank Ave CV3 ... 78 A3
Sunnydale Cres LE10 ... 31 D4
Sunnydale Rd LE10 ... 30 C4
Sunnyhill LE10 ... 31 F4
Sunnyhill S LE10 ... 31 F3
Sunnyside B95 ... 119 F7
Sunnyside Cl
Balsall Common CV7 ... 74 B4
Coventry CV5 ... 60 C2
Sunnyside La CV7 ... 74 B4
Sunset Cl B78 ... 11 D4
Sunshine Cl CV8 ... 93 D1
Sunway Gr CV3 ... 77 D3
Surrey Cl Hinckley LE10 ... 31 F2
Nuneaton CV10 ... 28 C2
Sussex Cl CV10 ... 28 C2
Sussex Rd CV5 ... 60 C2
Sutcliffe Ave CV37 ... 130 D3
Sutcliffe Dr CV33 ... 123 E6
Sutherland Ave CV5 ... 60 A2
Sutherland Cl CV34 ... 104 C1
Sutherland Dr CV12 ... 39 D2
Sutton Ave CV5 ... 59 E2
Sutton Cl NN11 ... 134 F6
Sutton La OX15 ... 137 E1
Sutton Rd B78 ... 8 A4
Sutton Sq B76 ... 22 C3
Sutton Stop CV6 ... 50 A3
Swadling St CV31 ... 109 F3
Swain Crofts CV31 ... 110 A3
Swains Gn LE10 ... 31 F3
Swalcliffe Sch OX15 ... 142 F8
Swale Rd B76 ... 13 D1
Swallow Ave B36 ... 33 D4
Swallow Cl CV37 ... 145 D3
Swallow Rd CV6 ... 49 E1
Swallowdean Rd CV6 ... 60 C4
Swallows' Mdw B90 ... 70 B4
Swan Cl GL56 ... 140 A3
Swan Ct CV37 ... 145 D1
Swan La CV2 ... 61 F2
Swan St Alcester B49 ... 143 D2
Royal Leamington Spa CV32 106 A1
Warwick CV34 ... 108 C3
Swan's Nest CV37 ... 145 D1
Swanage Gn CV2 ... 63 D2
Swancroft B95 ... 113 A5
Swancroft Rd CV2 ... 62 A3
Swanfold CV37 ... 120 C5
Swans Cl CV37 ... 120 C5
Swanswell St CV1 ... 151 C4
Swanswood Gr 3 B37 ... 33 E2
Swerford Rd OX15 ... 142 D3
Swift Cl B36 ... 33 D4
Swift Rd CV37 ... 145 D3
Swift Valley Ind Est CV21 ... 82 C4
Swift's Cnr CV3 ... 77 F4
Swillington Rd CV6 ... 61 D3
Swinburne Ave CV2 ... 62 B1
Swinburne Cl CV10 ... 28 A3
Swinburne Rd B97 ... 102 B4
Swindale B77 ... 10 A4
Swindale Croft CV3 ... 78 C4
Swinford Gr B93 ... 71 F2
Swinford Rd
Lutterworth LE17 ... 68 C4
Shawell LE17 ... 68 B3
Swinnerton Mid Sch CV11 .. 29 E1
Swiss Lodge Dr B78 ... 8 C4
Sycamore B77 ... 9 F4
Sycamore Ave B78 ... 11 D4
Sycamore Cl Hinckley LE10 ... 31 F3
Sibford Gower OX15 ... 142 D8
Stockton CV23 ... 147 F4
Stratford-u-A CV37 ... 144 C3
Wellesbourne CV35 ... 146 C2
Sycamore Cres Arley CV7 ... 37 D4
Birmingham B37 ... 44 A4
Sycamore Dr B47 ... 69 D3
Sycamore Gr Rugby CV21 ... 83 D2
Southam CV33 ... 147 D3
Warwick CV34 ... 105 D1
Sycamore Rd Coventry CV2 ... 50 A1
Kingsbury B78 ... 15 E3
Nuneaton CV10 ... 28 B3
Sycamores The CV12 ... 38 C1
Sydenham Dr CV31 ... 110 A3
Sydenham Ind Est CV31 ... 110 A3
Sydenham Prim Sch CV31 ... 110 B3
Sydnall Fields CV6 ... 49 F2
Sydnall Rd CV6 ... 49 F2
Sykesmoor B77 ... 10 A4
Sylvan Dr CV3 ... 76 C3
Synkere Cl CV7 ... 49 D3
Sywell Leys CV22 ... 99 F3

Table Oak La CV8 ... 74 A1
Tachbrook Cl CV2 ... 50 B1
Tachbrook Park Dr CV34 ... 109 F3
Tachbrook Rd CV31 ... 109 F2
Tachbrook St CV31 ... 110 A3
Tackford Cl B36 ... 22 B1
Tackford Rd CV6 ... 62 A4
Tackley Cl B90 ... 70 A4
Tailor's La CV37 ... 129 D1
Tainters Hill CV8 ... 93 D3
Talbot Cl OX16 ... 139 F4
Talbot Rd CV37 ... 145 D2
Talisman Cl CV8 ... 92 C2
Talisman Sq CV8 ... 92 C2
Talland Ave CV6 ... 62 A3
Tallants Cl CV6 ... 62 A4
Tallants Rd CV6 ... 62 A4
Talton Cl B90 ... 71 D3
Tamar Cl CV23 ... 82 A3
Tamar Dr B76 ... 22 A4
Tamar Rd Bulkington CV12 ... 40 A1
Tamworth B77 ... 10 A3
Tame Bank B78 ... 15 E3
Tame Valley Bsns Ctr B77 ... 9 F3
Tame Valley Ind Est B77 ... 9 F4
Tame Way LE10 ... 31 D4
Tameside Dr B35 ... 22 A1
Tamworth Bsns Ctr B77 ... 4 A2
Tamworth Bsns Pk B77 ... 4 A2
Tamworth Rd Cliff B78 ... 9 E1
Corley CV7 ... 37 D1
Fillongley CV7 ... 36 B3
Keresley CV6, CV7 ... 48 B3
Kingsbury B78 ... 15 E4
Polesworth B78 ... 4 C1
Sutton Coldfield B75 ... 7 D1
Tamworth B77 ... 9 E4
Tamworth Rd (Dosthill) B77 ... 9 E3
Tangmere Dr B35 ... 22 A2
Tanhill B77 ... 10 A4
Tankards Hill GL56 ... 136 B1
Tanners Green La B47 ... 69 D1
Tanners' La CV4, CV7 ... 59 D1
Tannery Cl CV9 ... 18 C4
Tansley Cl B93 ... 71 F2
Tanwood Cl Redditch B97 ... 102 A3
Solihull B91 ... 71 D4
Tanworth La
Henley-in-A B95 ... 113 A7
Redditch B98 ... 112 B8
Solihull B90 ... 70 B3
Tanworth-in-Arden CE Sch B94 ... 87 D1
Tanyard Cl CV4 ... 59 E1
Tapcon Way CV2 ... 62 C3
Tappinger Gr CV8 ... 93 E3
Tapster La B94 ... 88 C1
Tarlington Rd CV6 ... 60 C3
Tarn Cl CV12 ... 39 D1
Tarquin Cl CV3 ... 78 B4
Tarragon Cl CV2 ... 50 B1
Tarrant B77 ... 9 F4
Tarrant Wlk CV2 ... 63 D3
Tatnall Gr CV34 ... 108 C4
Tattle Bank CV33 ... 147 D2
Taunton Way CV6 ... 49 D1
Tavern La CV37 ... 144 B1
Taverners La CV9 ... 18 B4
Tavistock St CV32 ... 105 F1
Tavistock Way CV11 ... 29 F3
Tavistock Wlk CV2 ... 62 B4
Tay Croft B37 ... 33 E2
Tay Rd CV6 ... 61 D3
Taylor Ave CV32 ... 106 A1
Taylor Cl CV8 ... 93 D3
Tea Gdn The CV12 ... 49 F4
Teachers Cl CV6 ... 61 D3
Teal Bsns Ctr LE10 ... 30 B4
Teal Cl CV37 ... 144 B3
Teal Rd B80 ... 103 F2
Teasel Cl CV23 ... 83 E4
Ted Pitts La CV5 ... 48 A1
Teign B77 ... 10 A3
Telegraph St CV36 ... 149 F3
Telephone Rd CV3 ... 62 B1
Telfer Rd CV6 ... 61 D4
Telford Ave CV32 ... 106 A3
Telford Cty Fst & Mid Sch CV32 ... 106 B3
Telford Rd CV7 ... 50 B4
Templar Ave CV4 ... 60 A1
Templars' Fields CV4 ... 76 A4
Templars Prim Sch CV4 ... 60 A1
Templars The CV34 ... 108 C3
Temple Ave CV7 ... 73 F3
Temple End CV33 ... 123 E6
Temple Gr CV34 ... 108 B3
Temple Grafton CE Prim Sch B49 ... 119 E1
Temple Hill LE10 ... 41 F3
Temple La B93 ... 73 D2
Temple Rd B93 ... 72 A2
Temple St CV21 ... 83 E1
Temple Way B46 ... 23 F1
Templeton Cl B93 ... 72 A2
Ten Acres B49 ... 143 E2
Tenby Cl CV12 ... 38 B1
Teneriffe Rd CV6 ... 49 F1
Tenlons Rd CV10 ... 28 C1
Tennant St CV11 ... 29 F2
Tennyson Ave Rugby CV22 ... 99 F4
Warwick CV34 ... 108 B2
Tennyson Cl CV8 ... 93 E2
Tennyson Rd Coventry CV2 ... 62 B2
Redditch B97 ... 102 B4
Stratford-u-A CV37 ... 130 A8
Terrace Rd CV9 ... 18 B4
Terrett Ct CV37 ... 145 D1
Terry Ave CV32 ... 105 E1
Terry Rd CV1 ... 61 F1
Tewkesbury Dr CV12 ... 39 E2
Thackeray Cl
Lower Quinton CV37 ... 129 D2
Nuneaton CV10 ... 28 A2
Rugby CV22 ... 99 F4
Thackhall St CV2 ... 61 F2
Thames Cl CV12 ... 40 A2
Thames Rd NN11 ... 117 F1
Thamley Rd CV6 ... 61 D2
Thatchers Cl OX15 ... 138 D3
Theatre St CV34 ... 108 B4
Thebes Cl CV5 ... 59 D4
Theddingworth Cl CV3 ... 78 C4
Thickthorn Cl CV8 ... 93 D1
Thickthorn Orchs CV8 ... 93 D1
Thimble End Rd B76 ... 13 D1
Thimbler Rd CV4 ... 76 B4
Third Exhibition Ave B40 ... 44 B2
Thirlestane Cl CV8 ... 93 E3
Thirlmere CV21 ... 83 E4
Thirlmere Ave CV11 ... 29 F3
Thirlmere Cl CV4 ... 59 F2
Thirlmere Rd Bedworth CV12 ... 39 D1
Hinckley LE10 ... 31 D4
Thirsk Rd CV3 ... 77 E3
Thistle Way CV23 ... 83 E4
Thistlewood Gr B93 ... 90 A3
Thistley Field E CV6 ... 61 D4
Thistley Field N CV6 ... 61 D4
Thistley Field S CV6 ... 60 C3
Thistley Field W CV6 ... 60 C4
Thomas Jolyffe Cty Prim Sch CV37 ... 145 D3
Thomas Landsdail St CV3 ... 77 E4
Thomas Lane St CV6 ... 50 A1
Thomas Naul Croft CV4 ... 59 F2
Thomas Sharp St CV4 ... 76 A4
Thomas St Bedworth CV12 ... 39 D1
Royal Leamington Spa CV32 106 A1
Thomas Way CV23 ... 82 A3
Thomas Wlk B35 ... 22 A2
Thompson's Rd CV7 ... 48 C3

Thomson Cl CV21 .... 83 D3
Thorn Cl CV21 .... 83 E3
Thorn Stile Cl CV32 .... 106 C3
Thorn Way CV23 .... 115 D4
Thornby Ave Kenilworth CV8 .... 93 D2
Tamworth B77 .... 9 F4
Thorncliffe Cl B97 .... 102 A3
Thorncliffe Way CV10 .... 27 F4
Thorney Rd CV2 .... 62 A3
Thornfield Ave CV13 .... 21 F4
Thornfield Way LE10 .... 31 F4
Thorngrove Ave 7 B91 .... 71 E4
Thornhill Dr CV11 .... 40 B4
Thornhill Rd CV1 .... 61 E3
Thornley Cl CV31 .... 110 C3
Thornley Gr B76 .... 22 B3
Thorns Cty Fst Sch CV8 .... 93 D2
Thornton Cl Coventry CV5 .... 59 E2
Warwick CV34 .... 104 C1
Thornton Rd B90 .... 70 C3
Thorntons La CV23 .... 125 C7
Thorntons Way CV10 .... 28 A2
Thornycroft Rd LE10 .... 31 F4
Thorpe Rd OX17 .... 134 F1
Threadneedle St CV1 .... 61 E3
Three Cocks La WR11 .... 127 D1
Three Corner Cl B90 .... 69 F4
Three Cornered Cl CV32 .... 106 C3
Three Oaks Rd B47 .... 69 D2
Three Pots Rd LE10 .... 31 F2
Three Shires Jct CV6 .... 49 F1
Three Spires Ave CV6 .... 61 D3
Three Spires Ind Est CV6 .... 50 A3
Three Spires Sch CV5 .... 60 B3
Throckmorton Rd
Alcester B49 .... 143 E2
Redditch B98 .... 103 D4
Thurlestone Rd CV6 .... 60 C4
Thurlow Cl CV9 .... 12 B1
Thurne B77 .... 9 F4
Thurnmill Rd CV23 .... 82 B2
Thursfield Rd CV32 .... 106 A2
Tibberton Cl B91 .... 71 D4
Tibbetts Cl B49 .... 143 E2
Tiber Cl CV5 .... 59 F2
Tiber Way CV21 .... 82 C4
Tiberius Cl B46 .... 23 F1
Tidbury Cl B97 .... 102 B3
Tidbury Green Jun & Inf Sch B90 .... 69 F2
Tiddington Cl B36 .... 22 A1
Tiddington Rd CV37 .... 145 E2
Tideswell Cl CV3 .... 63 D1
Tidmarsh Cl CV7 .... 74 A3
Tidmarsh Rd CV35 .... 105 D4
Tidmington Cl CV35 .... 114 F5
Tile Gr B37 .... 33 D3
Tile Hill Coll of FE CV4 .... 59 F1
Tile Hill La
Coventry, Allesley CV4, CV5 .... 60 B1
Coventry, Tile Hill CV4 .... 60 A1
Tile Hill Sta CV4 .... 75 E4
Tile Hill Wood Sch CV4 .... 59 E1
Tile Hurst Dr CV4 .... 59 E1
Tilehouse Green La B93 .... 71 F3
Tilehouse La B90 .... 69 F3
Tilemans La CV36 .... 149 F4
Tilesford Cl B90 .... 71 D3
Tilewood Ave CV5 .... 59 F2
Tilia Rd B77 .... 4 A3
Tilton Rd LE10 .... 31 F3
Timberlake Cl 10 B90 .... 71 D3
Timothy Gr CV4 .... 60 A1
Timothy's Bridge Rd CV37 .... 144 B2
Timsa Rd CV35 .... 132 E5
Tink-A-Tank CV34 .... 108 C4
Tinkers Green Rd B77 .... 9 F3
Tinkers La Earlswood B94 .... 87 F4
Lapworth B94 .... 88 C1
Mollington OX17 .... 133 F2
Tintagel Cl CV3 .... 78 B3
Tintagel Gr CV8 .... 93 D2
Tintagel Way CV11 .... 30 A3
Tintern Way CV12 .... 39 E2
Tipper's Hill La CV7 .... 36 C3
Tippett Cl CV11 .... 40 A4
Tipping's Hill B97 .... 102 B3
Tisdale Rise CV8 .... 93 D3
Tite La OX15 .... 142 D4
Tithe Barn Cl CV35 .... 114 F4
Tithe Barn La B94 .... 87 E3
Tithe Cl CV13 .... 21 E3
Tithe Ct WR11 .... 127 F2
Titheway WR11 .... 127 F2
Tithings The OX15 .... 142 F8
Tiverton Dr CV11 .... 29 F3
Tiverton Gr CV2 .... 62 B3
Tiverton Rd CV2 .... 62 B3
Tiverton Sch CV6 .... 60 B3
Tiveycourt Rd CV6 .... 50 A2
Tocil Croft CV4 .... 76 B2
Toft Hill CV23 .... 99 D1
Tokchong Rd CV35 .... 132 E5
Toler Rd CV11 .... 29 D3
Toll Gate Cl CV37 .... 144 A2
Toll Gate Rd CV33 .... 147 D3
Tollard Cl CV2 .... 62 C3
Tolson Ave B78 .... 9 D4
Tolson Cl B77 .... 9 E3
Tom Brown St CV21 .... 83 E2
Tom Henderson Cl CV3 .... 78 C4
Tom Hill B94 .... 87 D2
Tom Ward Cl CV3 .... 78 C4
Tomkinson Rd CV10 .... 28 C2
Tomlinson Rd B36 .... 22 B1
Tommy's Turn La OX15 .... 137 E1
Tompson Cl NN11 .... 117 E5
Toms Town La B80 .... 103 F2
Tomson Ave CV6 .... 61 D2
Tomwell Cl CV33 .... 147 D3
Tonbridge Rd CV3 .... 78 A3
Top Rd CV7 .... 51 D4
Top St DE12 .... 3 F4
Topcliffe Jun & Inf Sch B35 .... 22 A2
Topp's Dr CV12 .... 38 C1
Topp's Heath CV12 .... 38 C1
Torbay Rd CV5 .... 60 B2
Torcastle Cl CV6 .... 61 F4
Torcross Ave CV2 .... 62 B3
Torpoint Cl CV2 .... 62 B4
Torrance Rd CV21 .... 82 C2
Torridge B77 .... 10 A3
Torrington Ave CV4 .... 75 F4
Torside B77 .... 10 A4
Torwood Cl CV4 .... 75 F3
Totnes Cl CV2 .... 62 B4
Tove Ct CV23 .... 82 A3
Towbury Cl B98 .... 102 C3
Tower Cl Bidford-on-A B50 .... 148 C3
Stratford-u-A CV37 .... 145 D3
Tower Croft
Bidford-on-A B50 .... 148 C3
Birmingham B37 .... 33 D2
Tower Hill B50 .... 148 C3
Tower Rd Bedworth CV12 .... 39 D1
Rugby CV22 .... 83 E1
Tower St Coventry CV1 .... 151 B3
5 Royal Leamington Spa CV31 .... 110 A4
Tower View Cres CV10 .... 28 A2
Towers Cl CV8 .... 92 C1
Town Feilds Cl CV5 .... 60 A4
Town Ground CV35 .... 131 F5
Town Yd CV23 .... 64 C2
Townesend Cl CV34 .... 104 C1
Townhill OX15 .... 133 A2
Townsend Cl B79 .... 2 B2
Townsend Croft CV3 .... 77 E4
Townsend Dr CV11 .... 29 F2
Townsend La
Long Lawford CV23 .... 82 A2
Upper Boddington NN11 .... 134 E8
Townsend Rd Coventry CV3 .... 77 E4
Rugby CV21 .... 83 E2
Tiddington CV37 .... 145 F2
Townsends Cl CV11 .... 31 D1
Trafalgar Ct B50 .... 148 B2
Trafford Cl CV9 .... 12 B1
Trafford Dr CV10 .... 28 B3
Traitor's Ford La OX15 .... 142 B6
Trajan Hill B46 .... 23 F1
Travellers Way B37 .... 33 E2
Tredington Cl B98 .... 103 D4
Tredington Rd CV5 .... 59 F2
Treedale Cl CV4 .... 75 E4
Trefoil B77 .... 4 A3
Treforest Rd CV3 .... 78 B4
Tregorrick Rd CV7 .... 50 A4
Tregullan Rd CV7 .... 50 A4
Trehern Cl B93 .... 72 A3
Treherne Rd CV6 .... 61 D4
Trelawney Rd CV7 .... 50 A4
Tremelline Way CV7 .... 36 C4
Trenance Rd CV7 .... 50 A4
Trench La B49 .... 143 F2
Treneere Rd CV7 .... 50 A4
Trensale Ave CV6 .... 60 C2
Trent Rd Bulkington CV12 .... 40 A1
Hinckley LE10 .... 31 D4
Nuneaton CV11 .... 29 E3
Trent Wlk NN11 .... 117 F1
Trentham Cl CV11 .... 39 F4
Trentham Gdns CV8 .... 93 E3
Trentham Rd Coventry CV1 .... 61 F2
Hartshill CV10 .... 19 D1
Tresillian Rd CV7 .... 50 A4
Trevelyan Cl Claverdon CV35 .... 113 F3
Stratford-u-A CV37 .... 144 B2
Trevelyan Cres CV37 .... 144 B2
Treviscoe Cl CV7 .... 50 A4
Trevor Cl CV4 .... 75 E4
Trevor White Dr CV22 .... 83 D1
Trevose Ave CV7 .... 50 A4
Trewint Cl CV7 .... 50 A4
Triangle The CV5 .... 60 A2
Tribune Trad Est CV21 .... 83 D3
Trident Bsns Pk CV11 .... 29 E2
Trimpley Cl B93 .... 71 F2
Trinity Cl Banbury OX16 .... 139 F4
Stratford-u-A CV37 .... 145 D1
Warton B79 .... 5 F2
Trinity La CV1 .... 151 B3
Trinity RC Sch The
Royal Leamington Spa CV32 .... 105 E1
Warwick CV34 .... 109 E3
Trinity Rd Kingsbury B78 .... 15 F4
Wood End B78 .... 10 A2
Trinity St Coventry CV1 .... 151 B3
Royal Leamington Spa CV32 .... 105 F1
Stratford-u-A CV37 .... 145 D1
Trinity Vicarage Rd LE10 .... 31 E4
Trinity Wlk CV11 .... 29 F2
Triton Pk CV21 .... 82 C4
Triumph Cl CV2 .... 62 C2
Triumph Wlk B36 .... 23 D1
Trojan Bsns Ctr CV34 .... 109 F2
Troon B77 .... 4 B2
Trossachs Rd CV5 .... 59 F2
Troubridge Wlk CV22 .... 82 B1
Troughton Cres CV6 .... 61 D3
Troutbeck Ave CV32 .... 105 E1
Troutbeck Rd CV5 .... 59 F2
Troy Ind Est B96 .... 103 D2
Troyes Cl CV3 .... 77 F4
Trueman Cl CV34 .... 108 C4
Truemans Heath La B47 .... 69 E4
Truggist La CV7 .... 74 C4
Truro Cl CV11 .... 29 F3
Truro Wlk B37 .... 33 D1
Trust Cotts B49 .... 118 D8
Tryan Rd CV10 .... 28 C2
Tuckwell Cl CV23 .... 147 F4
Tudman Cl B76 .... 22 A4
Tudor Ave CV5 .... 59 F2
Tudor Cl CV7 .... 74 A3
Tudor Cres CV9 .... 12 B1
Tudor Ct Coventry CV7 .... 49 F4
Warwick CV34 .... 108 B3
Tudor La CV33 .... 147 D2
Tudor Rd CV10 .... 28 B3
Tuer The WR11 .... 127 A6
Tulip Tree Ave CV8 .... 93 D3
Tulip Wlk B37 .... 44 B4
Tulliver Cl CV12 .... 39 D2
Tulliver Rd CV10 .... 29 E1
Tulliver St CV6 .... 61 D3
Tunnel Rd CV10 .... 27 E2
Turchill Dr B76 .... 22 A4
Turlands Cl CV2 .... 63 D4
Turnberry B77 .... 4 B3
Turnberry Dr CV11 .... 40 B4
Turner Cl Bedworth CV12 .... 39 D2
Rugby CV21 .... 101 D4
Warwick CV34 .... 108 A2
Turner Rd CV5 .... 60 B2
Turnhouse Rd B35 .... 22 A2
Turnpike Dr B46 .... 23 E1
Turpin Ct CV31 .... 109 F3
Turton Way CV8 .... 93 E2
Tutbury B77 .... 9 E4
Tutbury Ave CV4 .... 76 C3
Tutehill B77 .... 10 A4
Tuttle Hill CV10 .... 28 C3
Tuttle Hill Ind Est CV10 .... 28 C4
Twenty One Oaks CV9 .... 17 F3
Twycross La CV9 .... 6 C3
Twycross Rd LE10 .... 31 F3
Twycross Wlk CV34 .... 104 B1
Twycross Zoo CV9 .... 3 F1
Twyford Ctry Ctr WR11 .... 127 C1
Tybalt Cl Coventry CV3 .... 78 B3
Royal Leamington Spa CV34 .... 109 E2
Tyler St CV37 .... 145 D2
Tylers Gr B90 .... 70 C3
Tylney Cl CV3 .... 63 D1
Tyne Cl B37 .... 33 E2
Tyne Rd NN11 .... 126 F8
Tynemouth Cl CV2 .... 50 B3
Tyntesfield Specl Sch CV22 .... 99 F4
Tynward Cl CV3 .... 77 D3
Tysoe CE Prim Sch CV35 .... 138 C7
Tysoe Cl B94 .... 88 B3
Tysoe Croft CV3 .... 78 C4
Tysoe Rd CV35 .... 132 B4
Tythebarn La B90 .... 69 F3
Tything Rd B49 .... 143 E3

Ufton Croft CV5 .... 60 A2
Ufton Fields CV33 .... 123 F8
Ufton Hill CV33 .... 111 F1
Ullapool Cl B97 .... 102 B3
Ullenhall La B95 .... 112 D6
Ullenhall Rd Knowle B93 .... 72 A3
Ullenhall B95 .... 112 E6
Ullenhall St B95 .... 112 E6
Ullswater B77 .... 10 A4
Ullswater Ave Nuneaton CV11 .... 29 F3
Royal Leamington Spa CV32 .... 105 E1
Ullswater Rd Bedworth CV12 .... 39 D1
Coventry CV3 .... 62 C1
Ulverscroft Rd CV3 .... 77 E4
Ulverston CV21 .... 83 E4
Umberslade Rd
Earlswood B94 .... 87 E4
Tanworth-in-A B94 .... 87 F2
Underhill Cl Coventry CV3 .... 77 E2
Redditch B98 .... 102 C3
Underpass The B40 .... 44 C2
Underwood Cl B97 .... 102 A4
Unicorn Ave CV5 .... 59 F2
Unicorn La CV5 .... 59 F2
Union Pl CV6 .... 49 F2
Union Rd CV32 .... 105 F1
Union St Rugby CV22 .... 83 D1
Stratford-u-A CV37 .... 145 D2
Univ of Warwick CV5 .... 76 B2
Univ of Warwick Science Pk CV4 .... 76 A3
Univ of Warwick (Westwood) CV4 .... 76 A3
Upavon Cl B35 .... 22 A2
Uplands CV2 .... 62 A3
Upleadon Cl B97 .... 102 A3
Upper Abbey St CV11 .... 29 D3
Upper Crossgate Rd B98 .... 103 E4
Upper Eastern Green La CV5 .... 59 F3
Upper Grove St 3 CV32 .... 105 F1
Upper Hill St CV1 .... 151 A3
Upper Holly Wlk CV32 .... 106 A1
Upper Pk CV3 .... 78 B3
Upper Ride CV3 .... 78 B3
Upper Rosemary Hill CV8 .... 92 C3
Upper Spon St CV1 .... 61 D2
Upper Spring La CV8 .... 92 C4
Upper Well St CV1 .... 151 B3
Upper York St CV1 .... 61 D1
Upperfield Way CV3 .... 63 D1
Upton House OX15 .... 138 E8
Upton La CV13 .... 21 D4
Upton Rd CV22 .... 82 B2
Utrillo Cl CV5 .... 60 B2
Uxbridge Ave CV3 .... 62 B1

Valanders La CV36 .... 136 B6
Vale Cl CV21 .... 101 D4
Vale The CV3 .... 78 B4
Vale View CV10 .... 28 C2
Valencia Croft B35 .... 22 A2
Valentine Cl CV37 .... 129 F8
Vallet Ave B49 .... 143 D3
Valletta Way CV35 .... 146 B1
Valley Cl B97 .... 102 A3
Valley La Lapworth B94 .... 89 F4
Tamworth B77 .... 9 F4
Valley Rd Coventry CV2 .... 62 A3
Earlswood B94 .... 70 A1
Nuneaton CV10 .... 27 F2
Radford Semele CV31 .... 110 C2
Royal Leamington Spa CV32 .... 106 B2
Valley The CV31 .... 110 C2
Van Dyke Cl CV5 .... 60 B2
Vanguard B77 .... 9 E3
Vardon Dr CV3 .... 77 E2
Vauxhall Cl 8 CV1 .... 61 F2
Vauxhall Cres B36 .... 22 C1
Vauxhall St CV1 .... 61 F2
Vaynor Dr B97 .... 102 B4
Vaynor Fst Sch The B97 .... 102 B4
Veasey Cl CV11 .... 29 F2
Vecqueray St CV1 .... 61 F1
Ventnor Cl CV2 .... 62 C2
Ventnor St CV10 .... 29 E3
Venture Ct LE10 .... 30 C4
Verden Ave CV34 .... 108 A2
Verdon Cl CV35 .... 122 B8
Verdun Cl CV31 .... 110 A1
Vere Rd CV21 .... 83 F1
Vermont Gr CV31 .... 110 B3
Verney Cl
Butlers Marston CV35 .... 131 F4
Lighthorne CV35 .... 123 B2
Verney Dr CV37 .... 144 C3
Verney Gdns CV37 .... 144 C3
Verney Rd CV35 .... 123 C3
Vernon Ave CV22 .... 100 C4
Vernon Cl 9 Coventry CV1 .... 61 F2
Royal Leamington Spa CV32 .... 105 F2
Vernons La CV10, CV11 .... 28 C2
Verona Cl CV11 .... 30 A1
Vesey Cl B46 .... 23 D1
Vicarage Cl Atherstone CV9 .... 18 C4
Dordon B78 .... 10 C3
Vicarage Field CV34 .... 109 D4
Vicarage Gdns OX17 .... 134 C1
Vicarage Hill Badby NN11 .... 126 F5
Clifton u D CV23 .... 83 F3
Middleton B78 .... 14 A4
Tanworth-in-A B94 .... 86 C2
Vicarage La Coventry CV7 .... 49 E4
Dunchurch CV22 .... 99 E2
Harbury CV33 .... 123 F6
Long Compton CV36 .... 141 C3
Priors Marston CV23 .... 125 F4
Warwick CV35 .... 108 A1
Water Orton B46 .... 23 D1
Vicarage Rd
Cheswick Green B94 .... 70 B2
Dorridge B94 .... 88 C4
Flecknoe CV23 .... 117 B2
Napton CV23 .... 125 C8
Royal Leamington Spa CV32 .... 106 A2
Rugby CV22 .... 82 C2
Stoneleigh CV8 .... 94 A3
Vicarage Rise 8 CV33 .... 122 F8
Vicarage St CV11 .... 29 E2
Victoria Ave CV21 .... 82 C2
Victoria Bsns Ctr 10 CV31 .... 110 A4
Victoria Dr B78 .... 9 D4
Victoria Mews CV34 .... 108 B4
Victoria Rd Atherstone CV9 .... 18 C3
Bidford-on-A B50 .... 148 B3
Hartshill CV10 .... 28 A4
Hinckley LE10 .... 31 F3
Royal Leamington Spa CV31 .... 109 F4
Victoria St Coventry CV1 .... 151 D4
Nuneaton CV11 .... 29 E2
Royal Leamington Spa CV31 .... 109 F4
Rugby CV21 .... 82 C2
Warwick CV34 .... 108 B4
Victoria Terr 11 CV31 .... 109 F4
Victoria Way B50 .... 148 B3
Victory Rd CV6 .... 49 F1
Vilia Cl LE10 .... 31 F2
Villa Cl CV12 .... 40 B1
Villa Cres CV12 .... 40 B1
Villa Rd CV6 .... 61 D3
Village Hall Yd CV23 .... 115 D4
Village Mews CV22 .... 99 E4
Village St WR11 .... 127 D4
Villiers Rd CV8 .... 93 D3
Villiers St Coventry CV2 .... 62 A2
Nuneaton CV11 .... 29 D2
Royal Leamington Spa CV32 .... 106 A1
Vincent Ave CV37 .... 145 D2
Vincent St Coventry CV1 .... 61 D1
Royal Leamington Spa CV32 .... 106 A1
Vine La CV34 .... 108 C4
Vine St CV1 .... 151 C3
Vinecote Rd CV6 .... 49 F2
Vineyard The LE17 .... 43 F3
Violet Cl Coventry CV2 .... 50 B2
Rugby CV23 .... 83 F4
Virginia Pl CV10 .... 28 C2
Virginia Rd CV1 .... 61 F2
Viscount Cl Birmingham B35 .... 22 A1
Royal Leamington Spa CV31 .... 109 F3
Vittle Dr CV34 .... 108 B4
Vogue Cl CV1 .... 151 D3
Vulcan Way LE17 .... 55 E4

Wackrill Dr CV32 .... 106 B2
Wade Ave CV3 .... 77 D3
Wade Gr CV34 .... 104 C1
Wade La CV35 .... 123 D2
Wadebridge Dr CV11 .... 29 F3
Waggoner's La B78 .... 7 F4
Waggoners Cl CV8 .... 95 E3
Wagstaffe Cl CV33 .... 123 E6
Wain Cl B49 .... 143 E3
Wainbody Ave N CV3 .... 77 D3
Wainbody Ave S CV3 .... 76 C3
Wainbody Wood Sch CV5 .... 76 B1
Wainrigg B77 .... 10 A4
Wake Gr CV34 .... 108 A3
Wakefield Cl Coventry CV3 .... 78 C4
Hurley CV9 .... 16 B2
Wakefield Gr B46 .... 23 D2
Wakeford Rd CV10 .... 18 A2
Wakehurst Cl CV11 .... 39 F4
Wakelin Rd B90 .... 70 A4
Walcot Gn B93 .... 72 A1
Walcote Cl LE10 .... 30 C4
Walford Gr CV34 .... 104 C1
Walford Pl CV22 .... 100 C4
Walkers Orch CV8 .... 94 A3
Walkers Rd CV37 .... 145 D3
Walkers Way Bedworth CV12 .... 38 C1
Coleshill B46 .... 34 A3
Walkwood CE Mid Sch B97 .... 102 B4
Walkwood Cres B97 .... 102 B3
Walkwood Rd B97 .... 102 B3
Wall Ave B46 .... 33 F3
Wall Hill Rd CV5, CV7 .... 48 A2
Wallace Rd CV6 .... 61 D4
Waller Cl CV35 .... 104 C4
Waller St CV32 .... 106 A1
Wallingford Ave CV11 .... 29 F4
Wallsgrove Cl CV32 .... 106 A2
Walmer Way B37 .... 33 E2
Walmley Ash La B76 .... 22 B3
Walmley Ash Rd B76 .... 22 A4
Walmley Jun & Inf Schs B76 .... 22 A4
Walnut Cl Birmingham B37 .... 33 D1
Braunston NN11 .... 117 E5
Hartshill CV10 .... 28 A4
Harvington WR11 .... 127 D3
Nuneaton CV10 .... 28 C3
Walnut Croft CV9 .... 17 E4
Walnut Dr CV32 .... 106 A2
Walnut Paddocks CV35 .... 138 B6
Walnut St CV2 .... 50 A1
Walnut Tree Cl CV8 .... 93 D2
Walnut Way CV22 .... 82 A1
Walsal End La B92 .... 56 C2
Walsall St CV4 .... 76 A4
Walsgrave CE Prim Sch CV3 .... 63 D3
Walsgrave Gdns 5 CV2 .... 63 D4
Walsgrave Rd CV2 .... 62 A2
Walsh La CV7 .... 46 C1
Walsingham Dr CV10 .... 39 D4
Walter Scott Rd CV12 .... 39 E1
Waltham Cres CV10 .... 28 A3
Walton Cl Coventry CV3 .... 78 C4
Nuneaton CV11 .... 40 A4
Walton Rd
Hampton Lucy CV35 .... 121 F4
Wellesbourne CV35 .... 146 C1
Walton W ay CV35 .... 146 B1
Wandsbeck B77 .... 9 F4
Wanley Rd CV3 .... 77 E3
Wansfell Cl CV4 .... 76 A4
Wantage Rd B46 .... 23 F1
Wappenbury Cl CV2 .... 50 B1
Wappenbury Rd CV2 .... 50 B1
Wapping La B98 .... 112 A7
Ward Gr CV34 .... 109 E4
Warden Rd CV6 .... 61 D3
Wardens Ave The CV5 .... 60 A3
Wardens The CV8 .... 93 E3
Wardour Dr B37 .... 33 E1
Ware Orch CV23 .... 101 E1
Ware Rd CV23 .... 101 E1
Wareham Gn CV2 .... 63 D3
Waring Way CV22 .... 99 E2
Warings Green Rd B94 .... 70 B1
Warkworth Cl OX16 .... 139 F4
Warmington Cl CV3 .... 78 C4
Warmington Gr CV34 .... 108 A4
Warmington Rd B47 .... 69 D3
Warmwell Cl CV2 .... 62 C2
Warneford Pl GL56 .... 140 A3
Warner Cl CV34 .... 104 B1
Warner Row CV6 .... 61 F4
Warren Cl CV32 .... 106 A2
Warren Dr B93 .... 72 A2
Warren Field CV8 .... 79 D1
Warren Gn CV4 .... 75 F4
Warren Rd CV22 .... 83 E1
Warrington Cl B76 .... 13 D1
Warton Cl CV8 .... 93 E2

Warton La Austrey CV9 .... 3 D1
Orton-on-t-H CV9 .... 6 B2
Warton B79 .... 5 F4
Warton Nethersole CE Fst Sch B79 .... 5 F2
Warwick Ave CV5 .... 77 D4
Warwick By-Pass
Warwick, Hampton Magna CV35 .... 108 A3
Warwick, Heathcote CV34 .... 109 D1
Warwick Castle CV34 .... 108 C3
Warwick Cl B80 .... 103 E2
Warwick Cres CV37 .... 145 D2
Warwick Ct CV37 .... 145 D2
Warwick Dr CV9 .... 12 B1
Warwick Gdns CV10 .... 28 C2
Warwick Gn CV12 .... 40 B1
Warwick Highway
Redditch B98 .... 102 C4
Redditch B80 .... 112 A5
Warwick Hospl CV34 .... 108 C4
Warwick La CV1 .... 151 B2
Warwick Mus CV34 .... 108 C4
Warwick New Rd CV32 .... 109 E4
Warwick Pl
Royal Leamington Spa CV32 . 105 F1
Shipston-on-S CV36 .... 149 F3
Southam CV33 .... 147 D2
Warwick Rd
Chadwick End B93 .... 90 A4
Coventry CV3 .... 151 B1
Ettington CV37 .... 131 A4
Hanwell OX17 .... 139 F5
Henley-in-A B95 .... 113 C4
Kenilworth CV8 .... 93 D1
Kineton CV35 .... 132 B6
Knowle B93 .... 72 B2
Leek Wootton CV35 .... 104 C4
Norton Lindsey CV35 .... 114 C2
Sherbourne CV35 .... 121 E7
Snitterfield CV37 .... 121 C5
Southam CV33 .... 147 D2
Stratford-u-A CV37 .... 145 E3
Upper Boddington NN11 .... 134 E8
Wellesbourne CV35 .... 146 B2
Wolston CV8 .... 80 A2
Warwick Row CV1 .... 151 B2
Warwick Sch CV34 .... 109 D3
Warwick St Coventry CV5 .... 60 C1
Royal Leamington Spa CV32 . 105 F1
Southam CV33 .... 147 D2
Warwick St Mary's RC Prim Sch CV34 .... 108 C4
Warwick Sta CV34 .... 108 C4
Warwick Tech Pk CV34 .... 109 D3
Warwick Terr CV32 .... 105 F1
Warwicks The CV35 .... 114 F3
Warwickshire Coll CV32 .... 109 E4
Warwickshire Coll of Ag CV11 .... 29 F3
Warwickshire Mus CV34 .... 108 C3
Warwickshire Nuffield Hospl The CV32 .... 105 F3
Wasdale Cl CV32 .... 105 E1
Washbourne Rd CV31 .... 110 A1
Washbrook La CV5 .... 48 A1
Washbrook Pl CV36 .... 136 B6
Washford Dr B98 .... 103 E4
Washford Ind Est B98 .... 103 F4
Washford La B98 .... 103 E4
Wasperton Cl 6 CV3 .... 78 C4
Wasperton La CV35 .... 122 C7
Waste La Baddesley Ensor CV9 .... 11 F1
Balsall Common CV7 .... 74 C3
Coventry CV6 .... 48 C1
Watch Cl CV1 .... 151 A3
Watchbury Cl B36 .... 22 B1
Watchmaker Ct CV1 .... 151 A2
Watcombe Rd CV2 .... 62 C4
Water La CV35 .... 131 E3
Water Orton La B76 .... 22 C2
Water Orton Prim Sch B46 . 23 D1
Water Orton Rd B36 .... 22 C1
Water Orton Sta B46 .... 23 D2
Water Tower La CV8 .... 92 C3
Watercall Ave CV3 .... 77 E3
Waterdale B90 .... 70 B3
Waterfall Cl CV7 .... 46 B1
Waterfield Gdns CV31 .... 110 B4
Waterfield Way LE10 .... 31 E3
Watergall Cl CV33 .... 147 E2
Waterloo Ave B37 .... 33 D2
Waterloo Cl
Stratford-u-A CV37 .... 130 B8
Wellesbourne CV35 .... 146 B1
Waterloo Cres B50 .... 148 C3
Waterloo Ct CV34 .... 109 D4
Waterloo Dr CV37 .... 145 E1
Waterloo Ind Est
Bidford-on-A B50 .... 148 C3
Birmingham B37 .... 33 D3
Waterloo Pk B50 .... 148 C3
Waterloo Pl 5 CV32 .... 105 F1
Waterloo Rd
Bidford-on-A B50 .... 148 C3
Hinckley LE10 .... 31 E4
Waterloo St 6 Coventry CV1 .... 61 F2
Royal Leamington Spa CV31 110 A4
Waterman Rd CV6 .... 61 F3
Watersbridge Gdns CV10 .... 29 E1
Waterside Polesworth B78 .... 5 D1
Stratford-u-A CV37 .... 145 D1
Waterside Cl B24 .... 22 A3
Waterside Ct CV31 .... 110 A3
Watersmeet Gr CV2 .... 62 A3
Watersmeet Rd CV2 .... 62 A3
Waterson Croft B37 .... 33 E2
Watery La
Cheswick Green B90 .... 70 B2
Corley CV7 .... 47 E3
Coventry CV6 .... 49 D2
Hook Norton OX15 .... 142 D4
Keresley CV7 .... 48 C2
Knowle B93 .... 72 C2
Portway B48 .... 85 E4
Shipston-on-S CV36 .... 149 F3
Shustoke B46 .... 24 B1
Ullenhall B95 .... 112 E6
Warwick CV35 .... 108 A1
Wathen Rd
Royal Leamington Spa CV32 106 A1
Warwick CV34 .... 108 C4
Watling Cl LE10 .... 31 E2
Watling Cres CV23 .... 68 B1
Watling Ct CV11 .... 29 F2
Watling Dr LE10 .... 31 E2
Watling Rd CV8 .... 93 D3
Watling St Atherstone CV9 .... 19 D4
Dordon B78 .... 10 B3
Hinckley CV11, LE10 .... 30 B4
Tamworth B77 .... 9 E4
Watson Cl 3 CV34 .... 104 C1
Watson Rd CV5 .... 60 B1
Wattisham Sq B35 .... 22 A2
Watton Gn B35 .... 22 A2
Watton La B46 .... 23 E1
Watts La CV21 .... 101 D4
Watts Rd B80 .... 103 F1
Waugh Cl B37 .... 33 D1
Wavebeck Ct CV23 .... 82 A3
Waveley Rd CV1 .... 61 D2
Wavendon Cl CV2 .... 50 C1
Waveney B77 .... 9 F4
Waveney Cl LE10 .... 31 D4
Waverley Ave CV11 .... 29 F1
Waverley Rd Kenilworth CV8 .... 93 D2
Royal Leamington Spa CV31 .... 110 A3
Rugby CV21 .... 84 A1
Waverley Sq CV11 .... 29 F1
Waverton Ave B79 .... 5 F2
Waverton Mews 24 CV31 .... 110 B3
Wavytree Cl CV34 .... 108 B4
Wawensmere Rd B95 .... 113 A2
Wayside B37 .... 44 A4
Weale Gr 7 CV34 .... 104 C1
Weatheroak Rd B49 .... 143 E2
Weaver Ave B76 .... 13 D1
Weaver Dr CV21 .... 82 B2
Weavers Cl CV36 .... 149 F3
Weavers Hill B97 .... 102 B2
Weavers Row OX15 .... 139 A3
Weavers Wlk CV6 .... 62 A4
Webb Dr CV21 .... 83 E4
Webb Ellis Rd CV22 .... 82 C1
Webb St CV10 .... 28 B2
Webster Ave CV8 .... 93 D3
Webster Steet CV6 .... 61 F4
Webster Way B76 .... 22 A4
Weddington Fst Sch CV10 .... 29 E4
Weddington La CV10 .... 20 A2
Weddington Rd CV10 .... 29 E4
Weddington Terr CV10 .... 29 E3
Wedgnock Gn CV34 .... 108 B4
Wedgnock Ind Est CV34 .... 104 B1
Wedgnock La CV34 .... 104 B1
Wedon Cl CV4 .... 75 F4
Weford Aviation Mus GL56 .... 140 A3
Weigh Bridge Ct GL55 .... 135 B2
Welbeck Ave LE10 .... 31 E2
Welchman Pl CV35 .... 138 B6
Welcombe Hills Ctry Pk CV37 .... 145 D4
Welcombe Rd CV37 .... 145 D2
Welcome St CV9 .... 18 C4
Welford Cl B98 .... 102 C3
Welford Pl CV6 .... 61 E4
Welford Rd
Bidford-on-A B50 .... 128 D6
Long Marston CV37 .... 129 B4
Rugby CV21 .... 83 E2
Tamworth B77 .... 9 E3
Welford-on-Avon Cty Prim Sch CV37 .... 129 A6
Welgarth Ave CV6 .... 60 C3
Welham Croft B90 .... 71 D3
Well Bank OX15 .... 142 D4
Well Cl B97 .... 102 C3
Well La Shenington OX15 .... 138 F5
Staverton NN11 .... 126 D8
Tanworth-in-A B94 .... 87 D1
Well Spring Cl CV9 .... 18 C4
Well St CV1 .... 151 B3
Welland Cl
Long Lawford CV23 .... 82 B3
Water Orton B46 .... 23 D1
Welland Rd CV1 .... 61 F1
Welland Way B76 .... 22 A4
Wellesbourne CE Prim Sch CV35 .... 146 C2
Wellesbourne Gr CV37 .... 144 C1
Wellesbourne Rd
Alveston CV37 .... 121 D3
Barford CV35 .... 122 B7
Coventry CV5 .... 60 A2
Lighthorne CV35 .... 123 B2
Loxley CV35 .... 130 F8
Wellington Cl CV35 .... 146 B1
Wellington Parkway LE17 .... 55 E3
Wellington Rd
Moreton-in-M GL56 .... 140 B3
Royal Leamington Spa CV32 . 106 B1
Wellington St CV1 .... 151 D4
Wells Cl CV10 .... 27 F2
Wells St CV21 .... 83 D2
Wells Wlk B37 .... 33 D1
Welsh Cl CV34 .... 104 C1
Welsh Rd Aston le W NN11 .... 134 F6
Bascote CV33 .... 115 B2
Coventry CV2 .... 62 A2
Lower Boddington NN11 .... 134 E7
Napton CV33 .... 125 C5
Offchurch CV33 .... 107 D1
Offchurch CV33 .... 111 F4
Welsh Rd E CV33 .... 147 E1
Welsh Rd W CV33 .... 147 D3
Welton Cl B76 .... 13 D1
Welton Pl CV22 .... 100 B4
Welton Rd Braunston NN11 .... 117 E5
Warwick CV34 .... 104 B1
Wembrook Cl CV11 .... 29 E2
Wendiburgh St CV4 .... 76 A4
Wendover Rise CV5 .... 60 B2
Wenlock Way CV10 .... 28 A2
Wensum Cl LE10 .... 31 D4
Wentworth Dr CV11 .... 30 A1
Wentworth Rd
10 Royal Leamington Spa CV31 .... 110 B3
Rugby CV22 .... 82 C1
Wesley Rd CV21 .... 101 D4
Wessenden B77 .... 10 A4
Wessex Cl CV12 .... 39 D2
Wessons Rd B50 .... 148 C3
West Ave Bedworth CV12 .... 39 E1
Coventry CV2 .... 62 A1
West Cl LE10 .... 31 E4
West End Cleeve Prior WR11 .... 128 A4
Hornton OX15 .... 139 B7
West Green Dr CV37 .... 144 A2
West Leyes CV21 .... 83 D2
West of St Laurence CV35 .... 114 A8
West Orchards Sh Ctr CV1 .... 151 B3
West Ridge CV5 .... 60 A3
West Rock CV34 .... 108 B4
West Side WR11 .... 128 A2
West Side Bsns Ctr CV4 .... 75 F4
West St Coventry CV1 .... 61 F2
Long Lawford CV23 .... 82 A2
Royal Leamington Spa CV31 .... 110 A4
Shipston-on-S CV36 .... 149 F3
Shutford OX15 .... 139 A3
Stratford-u-A CV37 .... 144 C1
Warwick CV34 .... 108 B3
West View Rd
Royal Leamington Spa CV32 . 106 B3
Rugby CV22 .... 82 C1
Westbourne Gr CV22 .... 82 C1
Westbury Rd Coventry CV5 .... 60 B3
Nuneaton CV10 .... 28 B2
Westcliff Dr CV34 .... 104 C1
Westcliffe Dr CV3 .... 77 D3
Westcotes CV4 .... 60 A1
Westerham Cl B93 .... 71 F3
Western Dr LE17 .... 43 F3
Western Hill Cl B96 .... 102 C1
Western Rd CV37 .... 144 C2
Western Road Ind Est CV37 .... 144 C2
Westfield Cl Dorridge B93 .... 71 F1
Nuneaton CV10 .... 29 E3
Stratford-u-A CV37 .... 144 C3
Westfield Cres CV35 .... 146 B2
Westfield Cty Fst Sch CV22 .... 82 C1
Westfield Cty Jun & Inf Schs LE10 .... 31 D4
Westfield Rd Hinckley LE10 .... 31 D4
Rugby CV22 .... 82 C1
Southam CV33 .... 147 D2
Westgate Cl CV34 .... 108 B3
Westgate Cty Prim Sch CV34 .... 108 B3
Westgate Rd CV21 .... 83 F1
Westgrove Ave 6 B90 .... 71 D3
Westham La CV35 .... 122 A7
Westhill Rd Blackdown CV32 .... 106 A3
Coventry CV6 .... 60 C3
Westholme Rd B50 .... 148 B3
Westlea Rd CV31 .... 109 F3
Westleigh Ave CV5 .... 76 C4
Westmead Ave B80 .... 103 F2
Westminster Dr
Hinckley LE10 .... 31 F2
Nuneaton CV10 .... 28 A4
Westminster Rd CV1 .... 151 A1
Westmorland Ave CV10 .... 28 C2
Westmorland Rd CV2 .... 62 C2
Weston Cl Dorridge B93 .... 72 A1
Dunchurch CV22 .... 99 E2
Royal Leamington Spa CV31 .... 110 B3
Warwick CV34 .... 108 C4
Weston Ct CV36 .... 141 D3
Weston La Bubbenhall CV8 .... 95 D2
Bulkington CV12 .... 40 A2
Weston St CV1 .... 151 C4
Westonbirt Cl CV8 .... 93 E3
Westway CV21 .... 83 D2
Westwood Bsns Pk CV4 .... 75 F3
Westwood Cres CV9 .... 18 B4
Westwood Heath Rd CV4 .... 75 F3
Westwood Rd
Atherstone CV9 .... 18 B4
Coventry CV5 .... 61 D1
Rugby CV22 .... 100 C4
Westwood Way CV4 .... 76 A3
Wetherell Way CV21 .... 83 E4
Wexford Rd CV2 .... 50 B1
Weymouth Cl CV3 .... 78 B3
Whaley's Croft CV6 .... 61 D4
Wharf Ind Est The CV23 .... 65 D4
Wharf La B94 .... 88 B2
Wharf Rd Coventry CV6 .... 61 F3
Stratford-u-A CV37 .... 144 C2
Wharf St CV34 .... 109 D4
Wharf The CV37 .... 120 C5
Wharrage Rd B49 .... 143 E2
Wharrington Cl B98 .... 103 D4
Wharrington Hill B98 .... 103 D4
Whatcote Rd CV35 .... 137 F8
Whateley Hall Cl B93 .... 72 B4
Whateley Hall Rd B93 .... 72 A4
Whateley La B78 .... 9 F2
Whateley's Dr CV8 .... 93 D3
Wheat St CV11 .... 29 E2
Wheatcroft Dr B37 .... 33 E1
Wheate Croft CV4 .... 59 F1
Wheaten Cl B37 .... 33 E2
Wheatfield Cl B36 .... 33 D4
Wheatfield Ct GL55 .... 135 B6
Wheatfield Rd CV22 .... 82 B1
Wheathill Cl CV32 .... 105 F1
Wheatley Grange B46 .... 33 F3
Wheatsheaf La B94 .... 113 C8
Wheelbarrow La CV35 .... 114 A3
Wheeler Cl B93 .... 90 A4
Wheeley Moor Rd B37 .... 33 D3
Wheelwright La CV6 .... 49 E2
Wheelwright Lane Comb Sch CV7 .... 49 E3
Wheler Rd CV3 .... 78 A4
Whernside CV21 .... 83 E4
Whetstone Dr CV21 .... 83 F4
Whichcote Ave CV7 .... 46 B1
Whiley Cl CV23 .... 83 F3
Whitacre Rd Knowle B93 .... 72 A4
Nuneaton CV11 .... 29 F2
2 Royal Leamington Spa CV32 .... 106 A1
Whitacre Rd Ind Est CV11 .... 29 F2
Whitaker Rd CV5 .... 60 B2
Whitburn Rd CV12 .... 38 B1
Whitchurch Cl B98 .... 102 C3
Whitchurch Way CV4 .... 75 F4
White Beam Rd B37 .... 44 B4
White Friars La CV1 .... 151 C2
White Friars St CV1 .... 151 C2
White Hart La CV33 .... 111 F1
White Horse Hill CV37 .... 121 B6
White House Hill B95 .... 120 B7
White St CV1 .... 151 C3
Whitebeam Cl CV4 .... 59 E1
Whitefield Cl CV4 .... 75 E3
Whitehall Cl CV10 .... 19 D1
Whitehall Rd CV22 .... 83 D1
Whitehead Dr Kenilworth CV8 .... 93 E4
Minworth B76 .... 22 B3
Whitehorn Dr CV32 .... 106 A1
Whitehorse Cl CV6 .... 50 A3
Whitehouse Cres CV10 .... 28 B2
Whitehouse Rd B78 .... 11 D3
Whitelaw Cres CV5 .... 60 B3
Whitemoor Dr B90 .... 71 D4
Whitemoor Hill Rd B96 .... 118 D8
Whitemoor Rd CV8 .... 93 D3
Whitemoors Cl CV13 .... 21 F4
Whitemoors Rd CV13 .... 21 F4
Whitepits La B48 .... 85 F2
Whitepump La B95 .... 112 E7
Whites Row CV8 .... 93 D2
Whiteside Cl CV3 .... 78 C4
Whiteslade Cl B93 .... 72 A4
Whitestitch La CV7 .... 46 B2
Whitestone Fst Sch CV11 .... 40 A4
Whitestone Rd CV11 .... 40 A4
Whiteway OX17 .... 133 F2
Whitfield Cl CV37 .... 145 F2
Whitford Dr B90 .... 71 E4
Whiting B77 .... 9 E4
Whitley Abbey Comp Sch CV3 .... 77 F3
Whitley Abbey Prim Sch CV3 .... 78 A3
Whitley Ct CV3 .... 77 F4
Whitley Rd B95 .... 113 B4
Whitley Village CV3 .... 77 F4
Whitlock's End Halt B90 .... 69 F4
Whitmore Park Prim Sch CV6 .... 49 D1
Whitmore Park Rd CV6 .... 49 E2
Whitmore Rd CV31 .... 110 A2
Whitnash Cl CV7 .... 74 A3
Whitnash Cty Comb Sch CV31 .... 110 A2
Whitnash Gr CV2 .... 62 B3
Whitnash Rd CV31 .... 110 A2
Whittington Cl CV34 .... 109 D4
Whittington La CV9 .... 12 A1
Whittle Cl Coventry CV3 .... 78 C4
Daventry NN11 .... 117 F3
Rugby CV22 .... 99 E4
Whittle Rd LE10 .... 30 C4
Whittleford Gr B36 .... 22 B1
Whittleford Rd CV10 .... 28 B2
Whittons Cl OX15 .... 142 D4
Whitwell Dr B90 .... 71 D3
Whitworth Ave CV3 .... 62 A1
Whitworth Cl CV35 .... 146 B1
Whoberley Ave CV5 .... 60 B1
Whoberley Hall Prim Sch CV5 .... 60 B2
Wickham Cl CV6 .... 48 C1
Wickham Rd B80 .... 103 F2
Wiclif Way CV10 .... 28 A2
Widdecombe Cl CV2 .... 62 B4
Widdrington Rd CV1 .... 61 E3
Widney Cl B93 .... 71 F3
Widney La B91 .... 71 D4
Widney Manor Rd B91 .... 71 E4
Widney Manor Sta B91 .... 71 E4
Widney Rd B93 .... 71 F3
Wigford Rd B77 .... 9 E3
Wiggins Hill Rd B76 .... 22 C4
Wight Croft B36 .... 33 D3
Wigston Hill CV9 .... 17 E3
Wigston Rd Coventry CV2 .... 50 C1
Rugby CV21 .... 84 A1
Wike La B96 .... 118 E8
Wilcox Cl CV33 .... 124 A4
Wild Goose La B98 .... 103 E4
Wildcroft Rd CV5 .... 60 B2
Wildey Rd CV12 .... 38 B1
Wildmoor Cl CV2 .... 50 A2
Wilford Gr B76 .... 22 A3
Wilkes Way B50 .... 148 B3
Wilkins Cl CV35 .... 122 A7
Wilkinson Way B46 .... 25 D1
Willday Dr CV9 .... 12 B1
Willenhall La CV3 .... 78 C4
Willenhall Wood Prim Sch CV3 .... 78 B3
Willes Rd CV31, CV32 .... 110 A4
Willes Terr CV31 .... 110 A4
Willett Gdns CV35 .... 146 B2
William Arnold Cl CV2 .... 62 A2
William Beesley Cres CV11 .... 40 C3
William Bree Rd CV5 .... 59 E3
William Bristow Rd CV3 .... 77 F4
William Cl OX16 .... 139 F4
William Groubb Cl CV3 .... 78 B4
William Iliffe St LE10 .... 31 D4
William McKee Cl CV3 .... 78 C4
William Morris Cty Prim Sch OX16 .... 139 F4
William St Bedworth CV12 .... 39 E1
Nuneaton CV11 .... 29 F2
Royal Leamington Spa CV32 110 A4
Rugby CV21 .... 83 D2
William Tarver Cl CV34 .... 109 D4
Williams Rd CV31 .... 110 C2
Willington St CV11 .... 29 D3
Willis Gr CV12 .... 39 E2
Willoughby Ave CV8 .... 92 C2
Willoughby Cl Alcester B49 143 D3
Coventry CV3 .... 78 C4
Willoughby Pl CV22 .... 100 B4
Willow Bank CV37 .... 129 A7
Willow Bank Rd B93 .... 71 F3
Willow Brook Rd CV8 .... 80 A2
Willow Cl Alcester B49 .... 143 D1
Bedworth CV12 .... 39 D3
Hinckley LE10 .... 31 F3
Kingsbury B78 .... 15 E4
Nuneaton CV10 .... 28 A4
Willow Ctyd CV2 .... 62 B4
Willow Dr
Cheswick Green B90 .... 70 B2
Wellesbourne CV35 .... 146 C2
Willow End GL56 .... 141 A1
Willow Gr CV4 .... 60 A1
Willow Meer CV8 .... 93 D3
Willow Park Ind Est CV13 .... 21 E4
Willow Rd CV10 .... 28 C3
Willow Sheets Mdw CV32 106 C3
Willow Tree Gdns CV21 .... 101 D4
Willow Way B37 .... 33 D1
Willowbank Rd LE10 .... 31 E4
Willowdale LE10 .... 31 D4
Willowfields Rd CV11 .... 30 A1
Willowherb Cl 5 CV3 .... 78 C4
Willows CE Prim Sch The CV37 .... 144 C1
Willows Dr N CV37 .... 144 C2
Willows The Atherstone CV9 .... 12 C1
Bedworth CV12 .... 38 C1
Hollywood B47 .... 69 D3
Stratford-u-A CV37 .... 144 C1
Wilmcote CE Prim Sch CV37 .... 120 C4
Wilmcote Gn CV5 .... 60 A2
Wilmcote La B95 .... 120 A5
Wilmot Ave B46 .... 33 F3
Wilnecote Gr CV31 .... 110 A3
Wilnecote High Sch B77 .... 9 F3
Wilnecote Jun Sch B77 .... 9 F4
Wilnecote Sta B77 .... 9 E4
Wilson Cl CV22 .... 82 B1
Wilson Dr B75 .... 13 D3
Wilson Gn CV3 .... 62 C1
Wilson Gr CV8 .... 93 E2
Wilson's La CV6 .... 49 F3
Wilsons La CV7 .... 50 A3
Wilsons Rd B93 .... 72 B3
Wilton Rd CV7 .... 74 A3
Wiltshire Cl Bedworth CV12 .... 39 D2
Coventry CV5 .... 60 A2
Wimborne Dr CV2 .... 63 D2
Wimbourne Cl CV10 .... 28 A3
Wimbourne Rd B76 .... 13 D2
Wimpstone La CV37 .... 130 B4
Winceby Pl CV4 .... 59 E1
Winchat Cl CV3 .... 62 C1
Winchcombe Rd B49 .... 143 E2
Winchelsea Cl OX16 .... 139 F5

Winchester Ave CV10 29 E4
Winchester Dr
Birmingham B37 33 D1
Hinckley LE10 32 A4
Winchester St CV1 61 F2
Wincott Cl CV37 145 E1
Windermere B77 10 A4
Windermere Ave
Coventry, Binley CV3 62 C1
Coventry, Upper Eastern Green CV5 59 F2
Nuneaton CV11 29 F3
Windermere Cl CV21 83 E4
Windermere Dr CV32 105 E1
Windmill Ave 2 B46 33 F4
Windmill Cl Kenilworth CV8 93 D3
Warton B79 5 F2
Windmill Dr B97 102 B3
Windmill Gdns NN11 126 E8
Windmill Hill
Bidford-on-A B50 128 E8
Royal Leamington Spa CV32 106 B3
Windmill Hill The CV5 60 A4
Windmill Ind Est CV5 59 F4
Windmill La Astley CV10 37 F3
Austrey CV9 3 D1
Balsall Common CV7 74 B2
Baxterley CV9 17 E3
Corley CV7 47 E3
Dorridge B94 89 D4
Dunchurch CV22 99 D2
Ladbroke CV33 124 E5
Staverton NN11 126 E8
Windmill Rd Atherstone CV9 12 B1
Bedworth CV7 50 A4
Coventry CV6 50 A2
Nuneaton CV10 28 B4
Royal Leamington Spa CV31 109 F3
Windmill Way
Southam CV33 147 D3
Tysoe CV35 138 B6
Windridge Cl CV3 78 B3
Windrush Cl B97 102 B3
Windrush Dr LE10 31 D4
Windrush Rd B47 69 D4
Windrush Way CV23 82 A3
Windsor Ct LE10 32 A3
Windsor Pl 7 CV32 105 F1
Windsor Rd B78 5 D2
Windsor St Coventry CV1 61 D1
Hinckley LE10 32 A3
Nuneaton CV11 29 D2
Royal Leamington Spa CV32 109 F4
Rugby CV21 83 E2
Stratford-u-A CV37 144 C2
Windward Way B36 33 D3
Windy Arbor Prim Sch B37 33 E1
Windy Arbour CV8 93 D2
Windyridge Rd B76 22 A3
Winfield Rd CV11 29 D3
Winfield St CV21 83 E2
Wingfield Rd B46 33 F3
Wingfield Way CV6 49 D1
Wingrave Cl CV5 60 A3
Winifred Ave CV5 61 D1
Winnallthorpe CV3 78 C3
Winsford Ave CV5 60 A2
Winsford Cl CV7 74 A3
Winsham Wlk CV3 77 E2
Winslow Cl Coventry CV5 60 A2
4 Royal Leamington Spa CV32 105 E1
Winspear Cl CV7 46 A1
Winster Ave B93 71 F2
Winster Cl CV7 49 D4
Winston Ave CV2 62 B4
Winston Cl Coventry CV2 62 B4
Stratford-u-A CV37 144 B1
Winterton Rd CV12 40 B1
Winthorpe Dr B91 71 E4
Winton Gr B76 22 A3
Winwick Pl CV22 99 E4
Winyates Rd CV35 123 D2
Wise Gr Rugby CV21 83 F1
Warwick CV34 104 C1
Wise St CV31 109 F4
Wise Terr CV31 109 F4
Wishaw Cl B98 103 D4
Wishaw La Curdworth B76 23 D4
Middleton B78 14 B3
Minworth B76 22 C4
Wisley Gr CV8 93 E3
Wistaria Cl CV2 50 A1
Witham The NN11 117 F1
Witherley CE Prim Sch CV9 19 D4
Witherley Rd Atherstone CV9 18 C4
Witherley CV9 19 D3
Withington Gr B93 71 F2
Withum Cl B76 13 D1
Withy Hill Rd B75 13 D4
Withybrook La CV7 51 F3
Withybrook Rd
Bulkington CV12 40 B1
Solihull B90 70 A4
Withycombe Dr OX16 139 F3
Woburn Cl CV31 110 B3
Woburn Dr CV10 29 D1
Wolds End Cl GL55 135 B2
Wolds La LE10 41 F2
Wolfe Rd CV4 75 F4
Wolford Rd GL56 140 D6
Wolfstan Dr CV23 115 D4
Wolseley Cl B36 23 D1
Wolsey Rd CV22 99 E3
Wolsey St CV3 78 B3
Wolston Bsns Pk CV8 80 A2
Wolston La CV8 79 F1
Wolverton Prim Sch CV35 114 B2
Wolverton Rd
Birmingham, Marston Green B37 44 A4
Coventry CV5 60 A2
Norton Lindsey CV35 114 C2
Snitterfield CV37 121 B7
Wolvey CE Prim Sch LE10 41 E2
Wolvey Rd Bulkington CV12 40 C1
Hinckley LE10 31 F2
Wood Cl B46 33 F4
Wood Croft B47 69 D3
Wood End Fst Sch CV9 10 B1
Wood End Jun Sch CV2 50 B1
Wood End La Fillongley CV7 37 D2
Tanworth-in-A B94 86 C3
Wood End Sta B94 86 C2
Wood Hill Rise CV6 49 E1
Wood La Arley CV7 26 B1
Aston Cantlow B95 119 F5
Astwood Bank B96 118 C6
Birmingham, Marston Green B37 44 A4
Cherington CV36 141 D7
Earlswood B94 69 F1
Hampton in A B92 56 C1
Hartshill CV10 28 A4
Higham-on-t-H CV13 20 C2
Shilton CV7 51 E3
Wood St Bedworth CV12 39 D3
Nuneaton CV10 28 C2
Royal Leamington Spa CV32 110 A4
Rugby CV21 83 D2
Southam CV33 147 D2
Stratford-u-A CV37 145 D1
Wood End CV9 10 B1
Wood Terr B96 118 D8
Woodbank LE10 32 A4
Woodberrow La B97 102 B3
Woodberry Dr B76 13 D1
Woodbine St 1 CV32 109 F4
Woodbine Wlk B37 33 E1
Woodburn Cl CV5 60 A2
Woodbury Cl B97 102 A3
Woodby La LE17 55 F4
Woodchester Rd B93 71 F1
Woodclose Ave CV6 60 C3
Woodclose Rd B37 33 D2
Woodcock Cl B94 86 C2
Woodcot Park Dr CV37 120 B5
Woodcote Ave
Kenilworth CV8 92 B3
Nuneaton CV11 29 F4
Woodcote Dr Dorridge B93 72 A1
Leek Wootton CV35 104 C4
Woodcote La CV35 104 C4
Woodcote Rd
Royal Leamington Spa CV32 105 F2
Warwick CV34 108 C4
Woodcraft Cl CV4 60 A1
Woodend Croft CV4 75 F4
Woodfield Rd Coventry CV5 76 C4
Hinckley LE10 31 E3
Woodford Cl Ash Green CV7 49 E3
Nuneaton CV10 28 B2
Woodford La CV10 19 E2
Woodgate Rd LE10 32 A4
Woodgreen Cl B97 102 A4
Woodhall Cl CV11 30 A1
Woodhams Rd CV3 78 B2
Woodhouse Cl CV3 78 C4
Woodhouse High Sch B77 4 A2
Woodhouse La B77 4 A3
Woodhouse St CV34 108 B3
Woodington Fst Sch B75 13 D3
Woodington Rd B75 13 D3
Woodland Ave
Claybrooke Magna LE17 43 F3
Coventry CV5 76 C4
Hinckley LE10 32 A4
Woodland Rd Kenilworth CV8 93 D4
Tamworth B77 4 A2
Woodland Way B78 10 C4
Woodlands Ave B46 23 D1
Woodlands Cl B78 11 D3
Woodlands Inf Sch B90 70 A4
Woodlands Jun & Inf Sch B36 33 D3
Woodlands La
Bedworth CV12 38 C2
Solihull B90 70 A4
Woodlands Rd
Bedworth CV12 38 C2
Binley Woods CV3 79 E4
Stratford-u-A CV37 144 C3
Woodlands Sch The CV4 59 E2
Woodlands The
Hartshill CV10 28 A4
Staverton NN11 126 D8
Wood End CV9 10 B1
Woodlands Way B37 33 E2
Woodloes Ave N CV34 104 C1
Woodloes Ave S CV34 104 C1
Woodloes Fst Sch CV34 104 C1
Woodloes La CV34 104 C1
Woodloes Mid Sch CV34 104 C1
Woodloes Rd B90 70 A4
Woodman Ct CV37 144 C2
Woodpecker Gr B36 33 D4
Woodridge Ave CV5 60 A3
Woodrow Cres B93 72 A3
Woodrow Ctr B98 103 D4
Woodrow Dr B98 103 D3
Woodrow Fst Sch B98 103 D4
Woodrow N B98 103 D4
Woodrow S B98 103 D4
Woodrow Wlk B98 103 D4
Woodrush Dr B47 69 D3
Woodrush High Sch The B47 69 D3
Woodshires Rd CV6 49 F3
Woodsia Cl CV23 83 E4
Woodside Arley CV7 26 B1
Grendon CV9 11 E1
Woodside Ave N CV3 76 C3
Woodside Ave S CV3 76 C3
Woodside Bsns Pk CV21 83 D2
Woodside Cl CV9 10 B1
Woodside Cres B93 72 A2
Woodside Pk CV21 83 D3
Woodstock Cl LE10 32 A3
Woodstock Cres B93 71 F2
Woodstock Rd Coventry CV3 77 E4
Nuneaton CV11 29 F1
Woodston Gr B91 71 E4
Woodville Rd CV34 108 C4
Woodward Cl CV31 110 A1
Woodward Ct CV37 121 B6
Woodway CV35 114 F3
Woodway Ave CV35 114 F3
Woodway Cl CV2 62 C4
Woodway La
Claybrooke Parva LE17 43 E2
Coventry CV2 50 C1
Woodway Park Sch & Com Coll CV2 50 C1
Woodway Rd OX15 142 D8
Woodway Wlk CV2 62 C4
Woolaston Rd B98 103 E4
Woolgrove St CV6 50 A2
Wooll St CV21 83 D2
Woolpack Way CV9 18 B4
Woolwich Rd CV11 40 C3
Wootton Cl CV37 145 E1
Wootton Ct CV2 62 B4
Wootton Green La CV7 74 A4
Wootton La B92 57 F1
Wootton St CV12 39 E2
Wootton Wawen Jun & Inf Sch B95 113 A2
Wootton Wawen Sta B95 113 A2
Worcester Cl CV5 60 A4
Worcester Pl CV36 149 F3
Worcester Rd CV8 93 D2
Worcester St CV21 83 D2
Worcester Wlk B37 33 D1
Wordsworth Ave
Redditch B97 102 B4
Warwick CV34 108 B3
Wordsworth Dr CV8 93 E2
Wordsworth Rd
Bedworth CV12 39 E1
Coventry CV2 62 B2
Rugby CV22 99 F3
Workhouse La LE10 32 A2
Works Rd B26 44 A2
Worsdell Cl CV1 61 D2
Worsfold Cl CV5 60 A4
Worthy Down Wlk B35 22 A2
Wren Cl DE12 3 F4
Wren St CV2 61 F2
Wrenbury Dr CV6 50 A2
Wright Cl B78 15 E3
Wright St CV1 61 F2
Wrigsham St CV3 77 E4
Wroxall Abbey (Sch) CV35 90 C1
Wroxall CE Jun & Inf Sch CV35 90 C2
Wroxall Dr CV3 78 B3
Wroxton CE Prim Sch OX15 139 D4
Wroxton Coll OX15 139 D4
Wroxton Ct OX15 139 D4
Wyatt Rd B75 13 D3
Wyatts Ct CV12 39 D2
Wych Elm Dr CV31 109 F3
Wych-Elm Cl CV22 82 A1
Wychbold Cl B97 102 A3
Wychbury B76 13 D1
Wychwood Ave Coventry CV3 77 E2
Knowle B93 72 A4
Wychwood Cl 14 CV33 122 F8
Wychwood Dr B97 102 B3
Wycliffe Gr CV2 62 A3
Wycliffe Rd W CV2 62 B3
Wye Cl Bulkington CV12 40 A1
Hinckley LE10 31 D4
Royal Leamington Spa CV32 106 B2
Sutton Coldfield B76 22 A4
Wyke Rd CV2 62 B2
Wykeley Rd CV2 62 B2
Wyken Ave CV2 62 B3
Wyken Cl B93 71 F1
Wyken Croft CV2 62 B3
Wyken Croft Prim Sch CV2 62 C3
Wyken Grange Rd CV2 62 B3
Wyken Way CV2 62 A3
Wykham La OX15 139 F1
Wyld Ct CV5 60 A3
Wyley Rd CV6 61 D3
Wynbrook Gr B90 71 D3
Wyncote Cl CV8 93 D2
Wyndshiels B46 34 A3
Wynter Rd CV22 82 B2
Wyre La CV37 129 B3
Wythall Sta B47 69 E2
Wythburn Way CV21 83 E4
Wythwood Gr B47 69 E3
Wythwood Rd B47 69 E3
Wyver Cres CV2 62 B2
Wyvern Cl CV35 146 B1

Yardley Chase Rd CV35 132 D4
Yardley Cl CV34 104 C1
Yardley St CV1 61 F2
Yarmouth Gn CV4 75 F4
Yarn Cl B47 69 D3
Yarningale Cl B98 102 C3
Yarningale La CV35 113 E5
Yarningale Rd CV3 78 B3
Yarranton Cl CV37 144 C3
Yarrow Cl CV23 83 E4
Yates Ave CV21 82 C3
Yatesbury Ave B35 22 A2
Yelverton Rd CV6 61 E4
Yeomanry Cl 10 CV34 108 C4
Yew Cl CV3 62 B1
Yew Tree Cl B94 89 E2
Yew Tree Ct CV9 3 D1
Yew Tree Gdns B95 113 A4
Yew Tree Hill CV23 64 C2
Yew Tree La B94 113 D8
Yew Trees The B95 113 B4
Yew Wlk B37 33 D1
Yewdale Cres CV2 50 C1
Yews The CV12 38 C1
York Ave Atherstone CV9 12 C1
Bedworth CV12 39 E1
York Cl Coventry CV3 78 B3
Studley B80 103 E2
York Rd CV31 109 F4
York St Coventry CV1 61 D1
Nuneaton CV11 29 D2
Rugby CV21 82 C2
Yorkminster Dr B37 33 E2
Yorksand Rd B78 8 C4
Young Cl CV34 108 A3
Yule Rd CV2 62 B3
Yvonne Rd B97 102 B4

Zorrina Cl CV10 28 A3

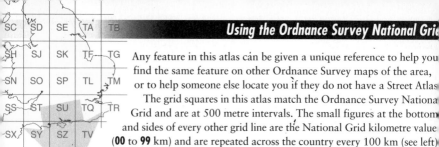

Any feature in this atlas can be given a unique reference to help you find the same feature on other Ordnance Survey maps of the area, or to help someone else locate you if they do not have a Street Atlas.

The grid squares in this atlas match the Ordnance Survey National Grid and are at 500 metre intervals. The small figures at the bottom and sides of every other grid line are the National Grid kilometre values (**00** to **99** km) and are repeated across the country every 100 km (see left).

To give a unique National Grid reference you need to locate where in the country you are. The country is divided into 100 km squares with each square given a unique two-letter reference. The atlas in this example falls across the junction of four such squares. Start by working out on which two-letter square the page falls. The Key map and Administrative map are useful for this.

The bold letters and numbers between each grid line (**A** to **F**, **1** to **8**) are for use within a specific Street Atlas only, and when used with the page number, are a convenient way of referencing these grid squares.

Example The railway bridge over DARLEY GREEN RD in grid square B1 on page 128

Step 1: Identify the two-letter reference, in this case page 128 is in **SP**

Step 2: Identify the 1 km square in which the railway bridge falls. Use the figures in the southwest corner of this square: Eastings **17**, Northings **74**. This gives a unique reference: **SP 17 74**, accurate to 1 km.

Step 3: To give a more precise reference accurate to 100 m you need to estimate how many tenths along and how many tenths up this 1 km square the feature is (to help with this the 1 km square is divided into four 500 m squares). This makes the bridge about **8** tenths along and about **1** tenth up from the southwest corner.

This gives a unique reference: **SP 178 741**, accurate to 100 m.

Eastings (read from left to right along the bottom) come before Northings (read from bottom to top). If you have trouble remembering say to yourself "Along the hall, THEN up the stairs"!

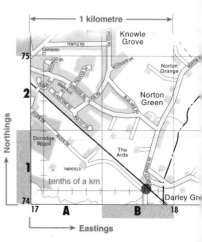

Name and Address	Telephone	Page	Grid Reference

Addresses

Name and Address	Telephone	Page	Grid Reference

The Street Atlases are available from all good bookshops or by mail order direct from th publisher. Orders can be made in the following ways. **By phone** Ring our special Credit Card Hotline on **01933 443863** during office hours (9am to 5pm) or leave a message on the answering machine, quoting your full credit card number plus expiry date and yo full name and address. **By post or fax** Fill out the order form below (you may photoco it) and post it to: **Philip's Direct, 27 Sanders Road, Wellingborough, Northants NN8 4NL** or fax it to: **01933 443849**. Before placing an order by post, by fax or or the answering machine, please telephone to check availability and prices.

STREET ATLASES ORDER FORM

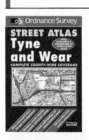

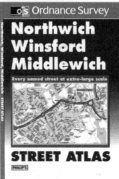

PHILIP'S

COLOUR LOCAL ATLASES

	PAPERBACK	
	Quantity @ £3.50 each	£ Total
CANNOCK, LICHFIELD, RUGELEY	☐ 0 540 07625 2	➤
DERBY AND BELPER	☐ 0 540 07608 2	➤
NORTHWICH, WINSFORD, MIDDLEWICH	☐ 0 540 07589 2	➤
PEAK DISTRICT TOWNS	☐ 0 540 07609 0	➤
STAFFORD, STONE, UTTOXETER	☐ 0 540 07626 0	➤
WARRINGTON, WIDNES, RUNCORN	☐ 0 540 07588 4	➤

COLOUR REGIONAL ATLASES

	HARDBACK	SPIRAL	POCKET	
	Quantity @ £10.99 each	Quantity @ £8.99 each	Quantity @ £5.99 each	£ Total
BERKSHIRE	☐ 0 540 06170 0	☐ 0 540 06172 7	☐ 0 540 06173 5	➤
	Quantity @ £10.99 each	Quantity @ £8.99 each	Quantity @ £4.99 each	£ Total
MERSEYSIDE	☐ 0 540 06480 7	☐ 0 540 06481 5	☐ 0 540 06482 3	➤
	Quantity @ £12.99 each	Quantity @ £9.99 each	Quantity @ £4.99 each	£ Total
DURHAM	☐ 0 540 06365 7	☐ 0 540 06366 5	☐ 0 540 06367 3	➤
HERTFORDSHIRE	☐ 0 540 06174 3	☐ 0 540 06175 1	☐ 0 540 06176 X	➤
EAST KENT	☐ 0 540 07483 7	☐ 0 540 07276 1	☐ 0 540 07287 7	➤
WEST KENT	☐ 0 540 07366 0	☐ 0 540 07367 9	☐ 0 540 07369 5	➤
EAST SUSSEX	☐ 0 540 07306 7	☐ 0 540 07307 5	☐ 0 540 07312 1	➤
WEST SUSSEX	☐ 0 540 07319 9	☐ 0 540 07323 7	☐ 0 540 07327 X	➤
SOUTH YORKSHIRE	☐ 0 540 06330 4	☐ 0 540 06331 2	☐ 0 540 06332 0	➤
SURREY	☐ 0 540 06435 1	☐ 0 540 06436 X	☐ 0 540 06438 6	➤
	Quantity @ £12.99 each	Quantity @ £9.99 each	Quantity @ £5.50 each	£ Total
GREATER MANCHESTER	☐ 0 540 06485 8	☐ 0 540 06486 6	☐ 0 540 06487 4	➤
TYNE AND WEAR	☐ 0 540 06370 3	☐ 0 540 06371 1	☐ 0 540 06372 X	➤
	Quantity @ £12.99 each	Quantity @ £9.99 each	Quantity @ £5.99 each	£ Total
BIRMINGHAM & WEST MIDLANDS	☐ 0 540 07603 1	☐ 0 540 07604 X	☐ 0 540 07605 8	➤
BUCKINGHAMSHIRE	☐ 0 540 07466 7	☐ 0 540 07467 5	☐ 0 540 07468 3	➤